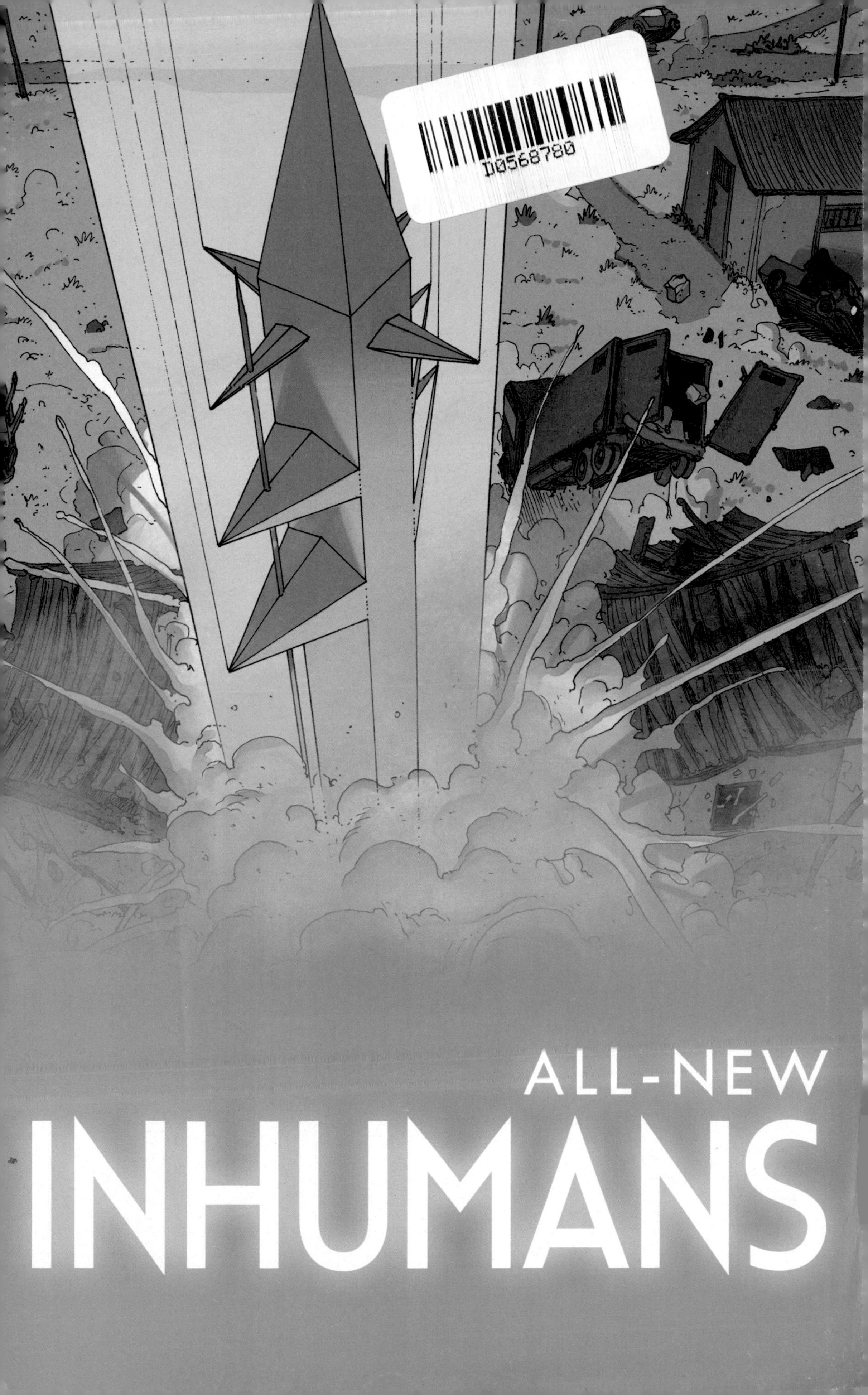

ALL-NEW INHUMANS

ALL-NEW
INHUMANS
SKYSPEARS

JAMES ASMUS
WRITER

ANDRÉ LIMA ARAÚJO (#5-6), STEFANO CASELLI (#7-10) & RHOALD MARCELLIUS (#11)
ARTISTS

ANDRES MOSSA
COLOR ARTIST

VC's CLAYTON COWLES
LETTERER

JAMAL CAMPBELL (#5-8) AND STEFANO CASELLI & ANDRES MOSSA (#9-11)
COVER ART

CHARLES BEACHAM
ASSISTANT EDITOR

DARREN SHAN
EDITOR

NICK LOWE
EXECUTIVE EDITOR

INHUMANS CREATED BY
STAN LEE & JACK KIRBY

ALL-NEW INHUMANS VOL. 2: SKYSPEARS. Contains material originally published in magazine form as ALL-NEW INHUMANS #5-11. First printing 2016. ISBN# 978-0-7851-9639-6. Published by MARVEL WORLDWIDE, INC., a subsidiary of MARVEL ENTERTAINMENT, LLC. OFFICE OF PUBLICATION: 135 West 50th Street, New York, NY 10020. Copyright © 2016 MARVEL No similarity between any of the names, characters, persons, and/or institutions in this magazine with those of any living or dead person or institution is intended, and any such similarity which may exist is purely coincidental. Printed in Canada. ALAN FINE, President, Marvel Entertainment; DAN BUCKLEY, President, TV, Publishing & Brand Management; JOE QUESADA, Chief Creative Officer; TOM BREVOORT, SVP of Publishing; DAVID BOGART, SVP of Business Affairs & Operations, Publishing & Partnership; C.B. CEBULSKI, VP of Brand Management & Development, Asia; DAVID GABRIEL, SVP of Sales & Marketing, Publishing; JEFF YOUNGQUIST, VP of Production & Special Projects; DAN CARR, Executive Director of Publishing Technology; ALEX MORALES, Director of Publishing Operations; SUSAN CRESPI, Production Manager; STAN LEE, Chairman Emeritus. For information regarding advertising in Marvel Comics or on Marvel.com, please contact Vit DeBellis, Integrated Sales Manager, at vdebellis@marvel.com. For Marvel subscription inquiries, please call 888-511-5480. Manufactured between 8/26/2016 and 10/3/2016 by SOLISCO PRINTERS, SCOTT, QC, CANADA.

10 9 8 7 6 5 4 3 2 1

SARAH BRUNSTAD
COLLECTION EDITOR

KATERI WOODY
ASSOCIATE MANAGING EDITOR

JENNIFER GRÜNWALD
SENIOR EDITOR, SPECIAL PROJECTS

MARK D. BEAZLEY
EDITOR, SPECIAL PROJECTS

JEFF YOUNGQUIST
VP PRODUCTION & SPECIAL PROJECTS

DAVID GABRIEL
SVP PRINT, SALES & MARKETING

ADAM DEL RE
BOOK DESIGNER

AXEL ALONSO
EDITOR IN CHIEF

JOE QUESADA
CHIEF CREATIVE OFFICER

DAN BUCKLEY
PUBLISHER

ALAN FINE
EXECUTIVE PRODUCER

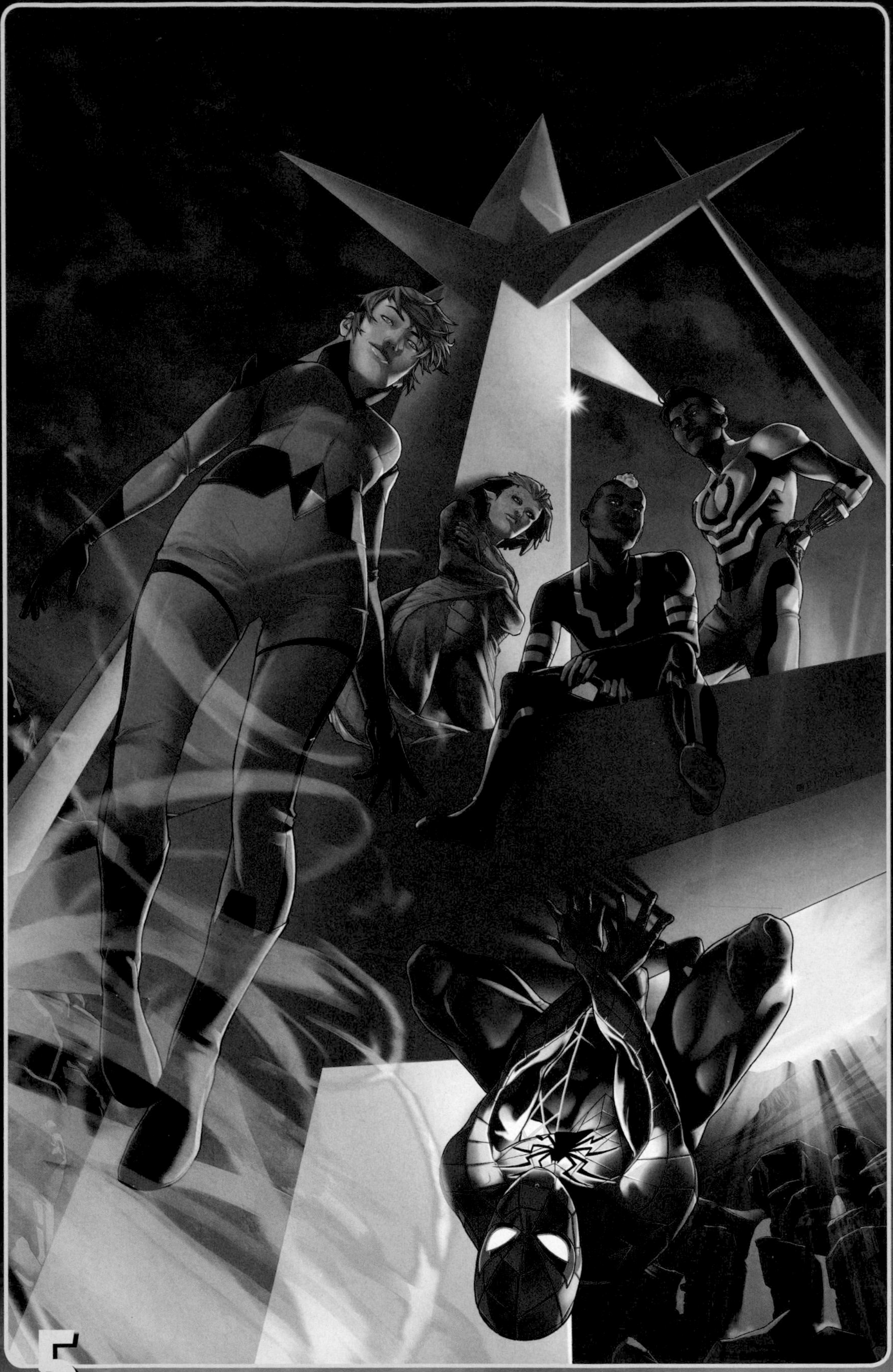

5

In a battle to protect the planet, Black Bolt — the Inhuman King — released colossal clouds of Terrigen Mist into Earth's atmosphere. These strange clouds now traverse the globe awakening superhuman abilities in anyone with traces of Inhuman DNA. They are...

ALL-NEW INHUMANS

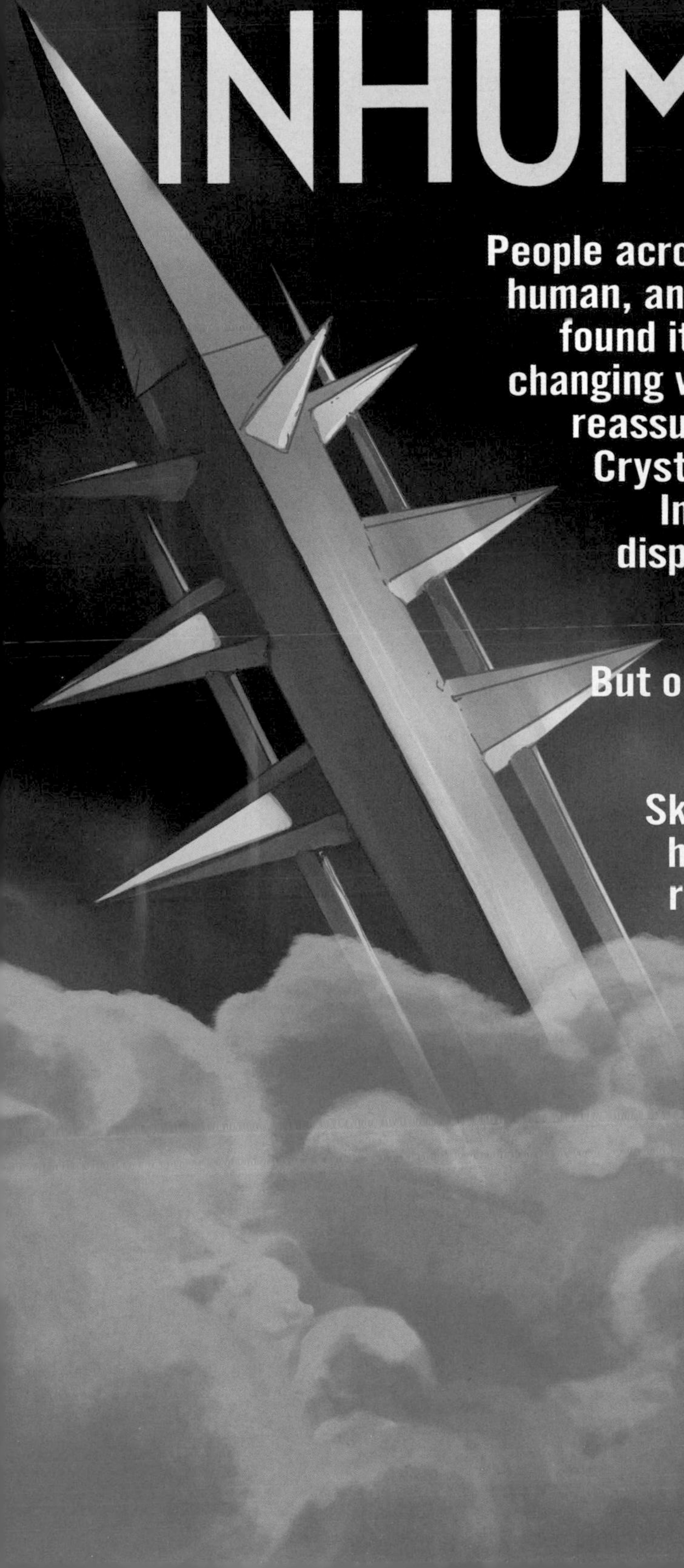

People across the globe — mutant, human, and Inhuman alike — have found it hard to cope with their changing world. So, in an effort to reassure the citizens of Earth, Crystal, sister of Medusa the Inhuman Queen, has been dispatched as New Attilan's Inhuman ambassador.

But one mission that persists involves the strange structures known as Skyspears. These obelisks have landed in seemingly random spots around the world. What purpose they serve and how they are connected to the Inhumans is unknown, but Crystal and her team are determined to find out.

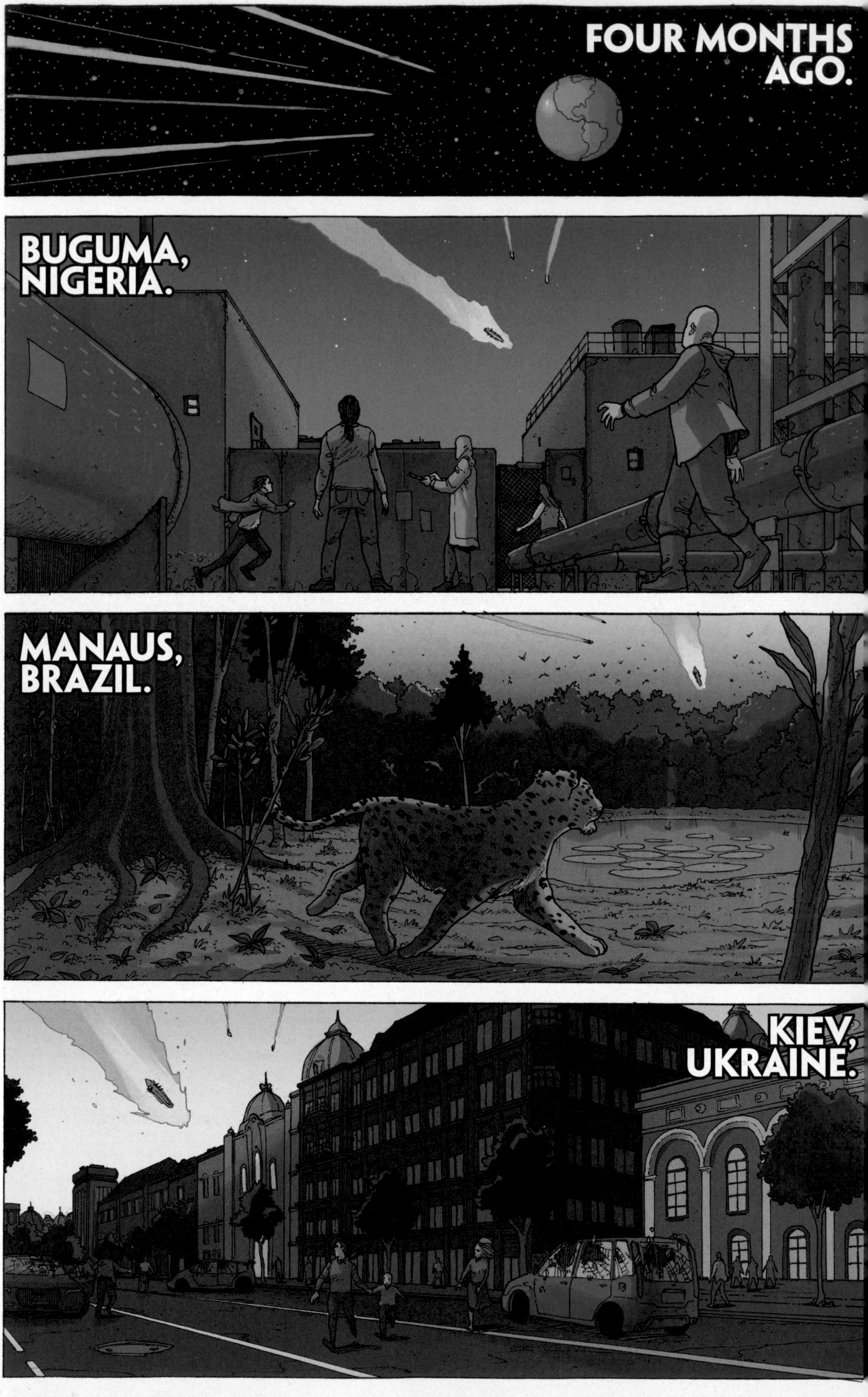
FOUR MONTHS AGO.
BUGUMA, NIGERIA.
MANAUS, BRAZIL.
KIEV, UKRAINE.

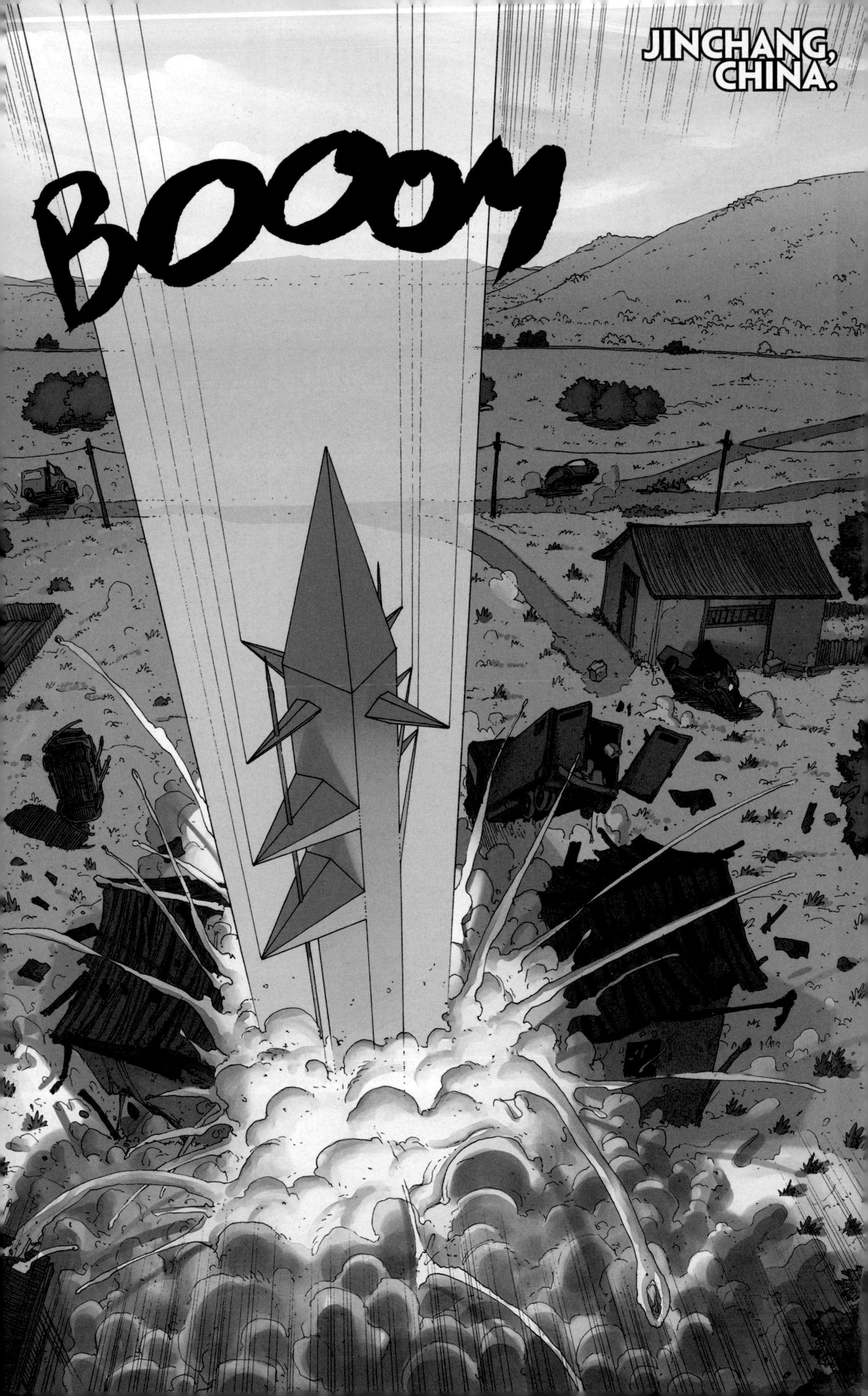
JINCHANG, CHINA.
BOOOM

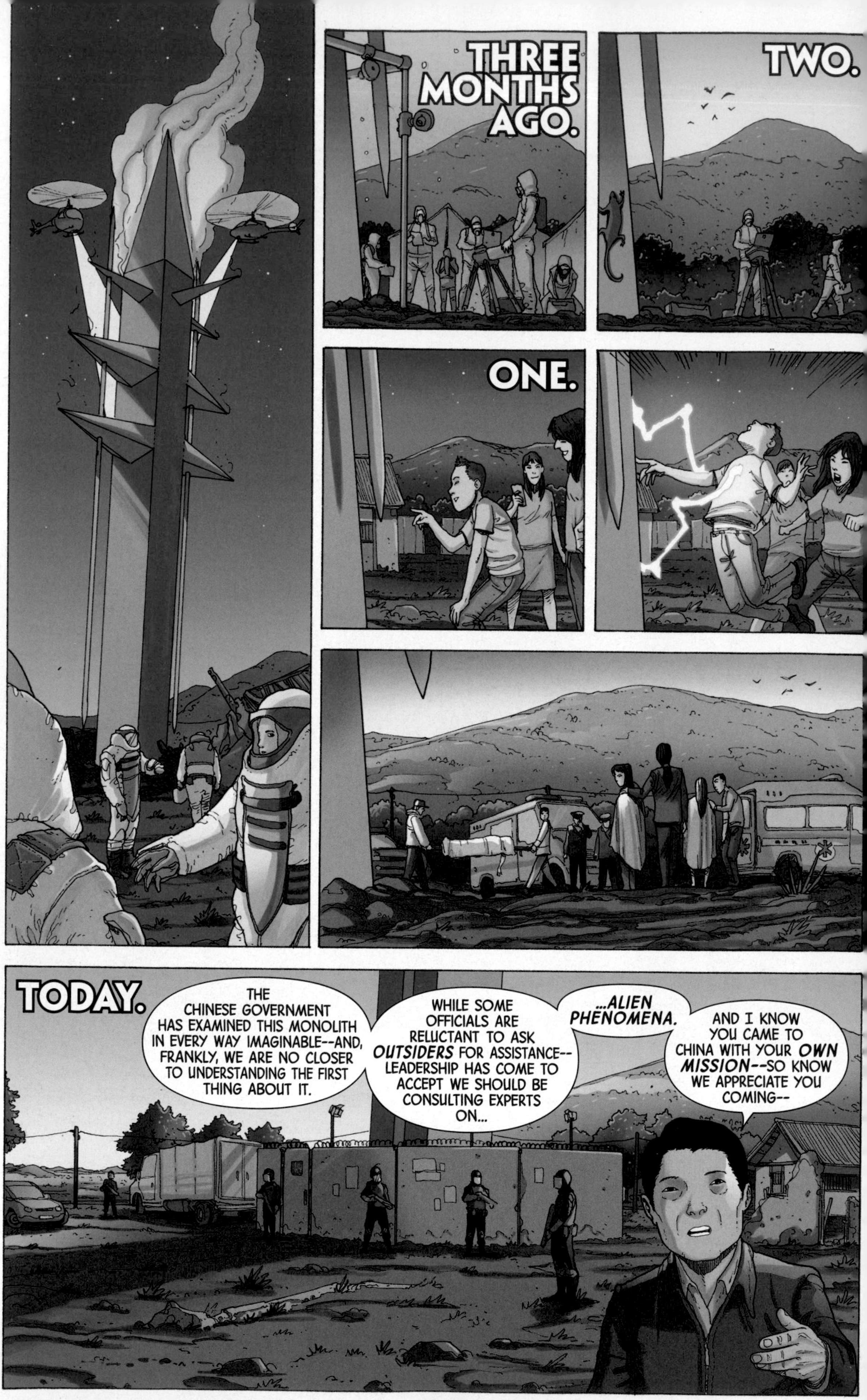
THREE MONTHS AGO.
TWO.
ONE.
TODAY.
THE CHINESE GOVERNMENT HAS EXAMINED THIS MONOLITH IN EVERY WAY IMAGINABLE--AND, FRANKLY, WE ARE NO CLOSER TO UNDERSTANDING THE FIRST THING ABOUT IT.
WHILE SOME OFFICIALS ARE RELUCTANT TO ASK OUTSIDERS FOR ASSISTANCE--LEADERSHIP HAS COME TO ACCEPT WE SHOULD BE CONSULTING EXPERTS ON...
...ALIEN PHENOMENA.
AND I KNOW YOU CAME TO CHINA WITH YOUR OWN MISSION--SO KNOW WE APPRECIATE YOU COMING--

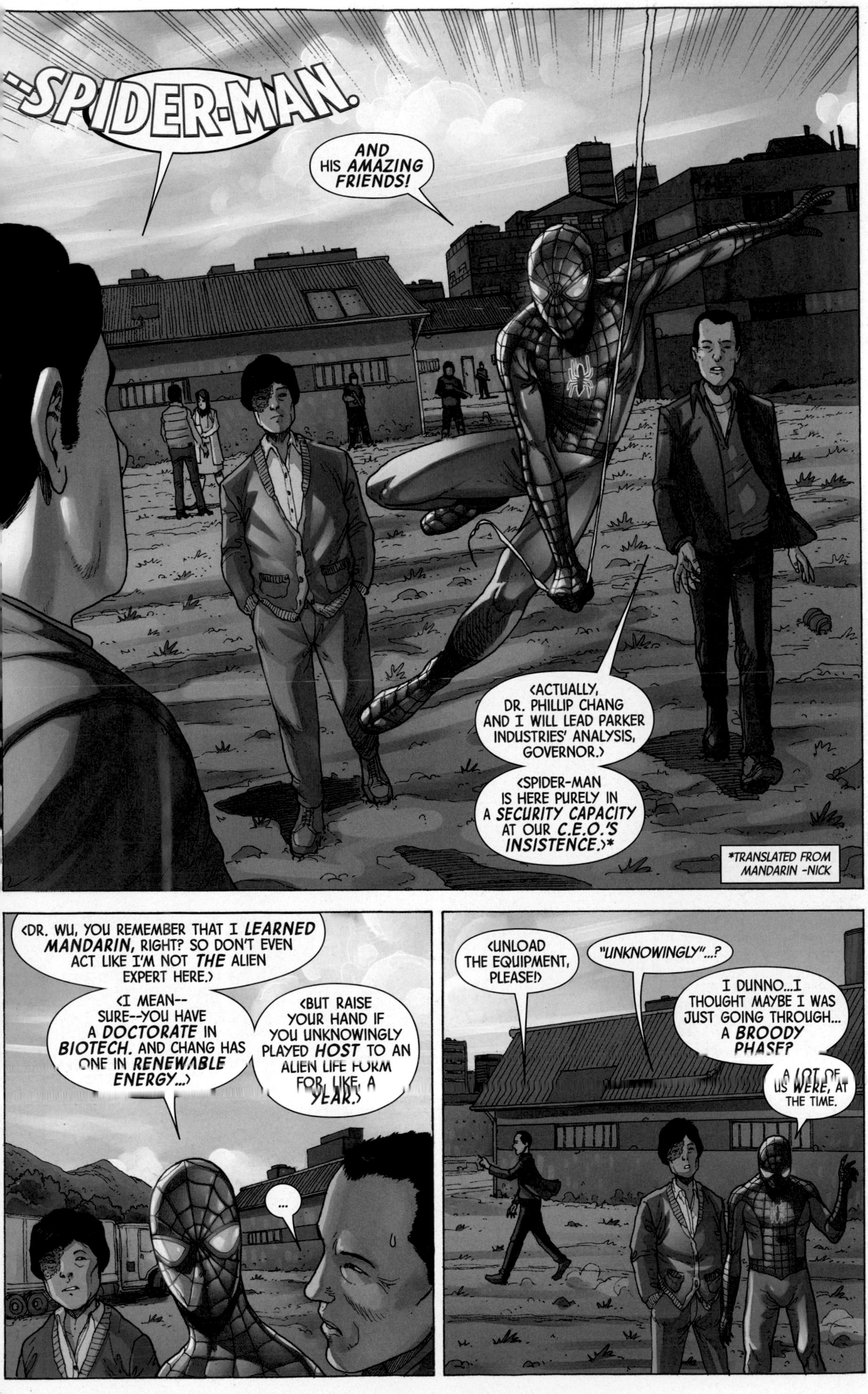
-SPIDER-MAN.
AND HIS AMAZING FRIENDS!
<ACTUALLY, DR. PHILLIP CHANG AND I WILL LEAD PARKER INDUSTRIES' ANALYSIS, GOVERNOR.>
<SPIDER-MAN IS HERE PURELY IN A SECURITY CAPACITY AT OUR C.E.O.'S INSISTENCE.>*
*TRANSLATED FROM MANDARIN -NICK
<DR. WU, YOU REMEMBER THAT I LEARNED MANDARIN, RIGHT? SO DON'T EVEN ACT LIKE I'M NOT THE ALIEN EXPERT HERE.>
<I MEAN-- SURE--YOU HAVE A DOCTORATE IN BIOTECH. AND CHANG HAS ONE IN RENEWABLE ENERGY...>
<BUT RAISE YOUR HAND IF YOU UNKNOWINGLY PLAYED HOST TO AN ALIEN LIFE FORM FOR LIKE, A YEAR.>
...
<UNLOAD THE EQUIPMENT, PLEASE!>
"UNKNOWINGLY"...?
I DUNNO...I THOUGHT MAYBE I WAS JUST GOING THROUGH... A BROODY PHASE?
A LOT OF US WERE, AT THE TIME.

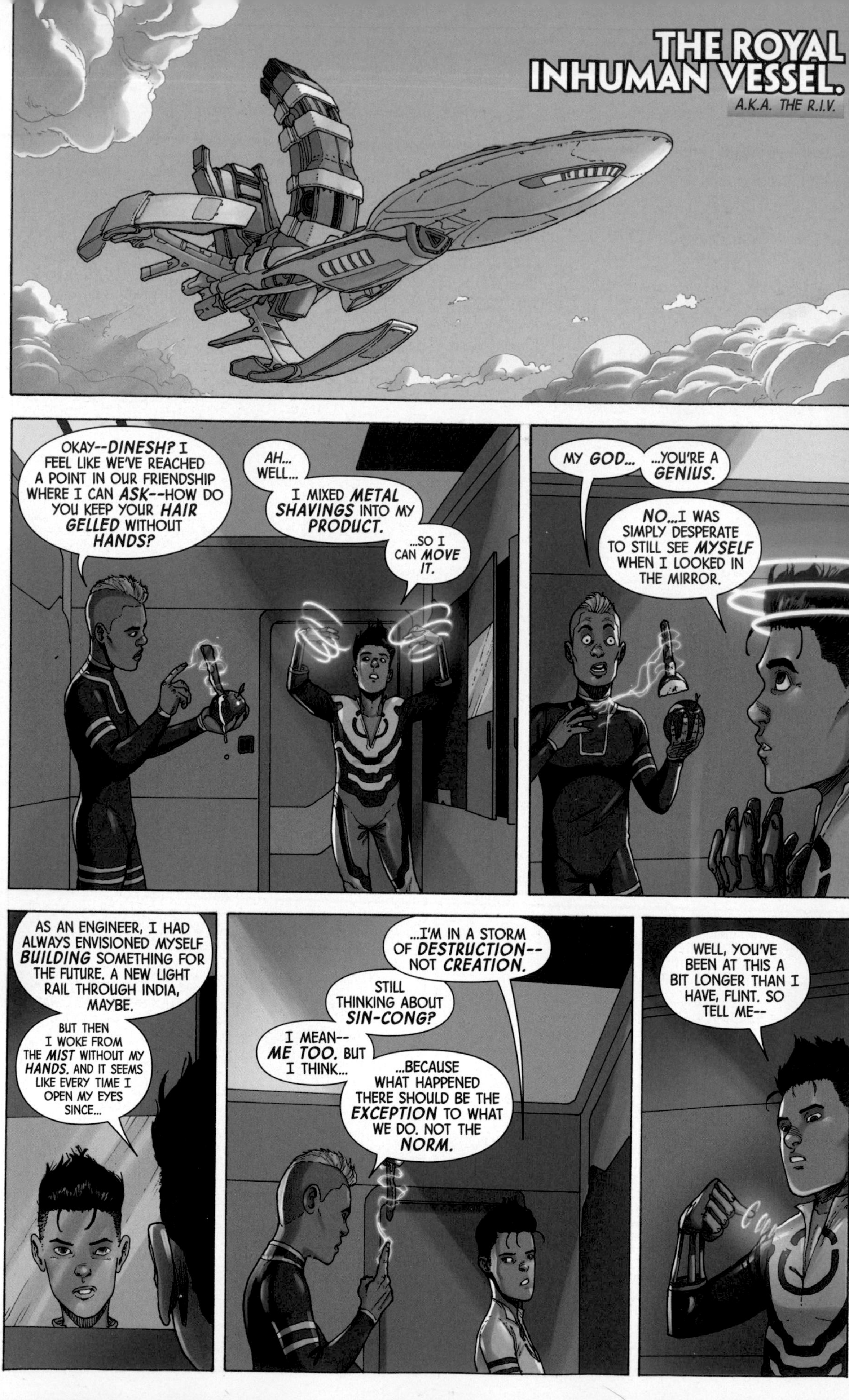
THE ROYAL INHUMAN VESSEL.
A.K.A. THE R.I.V.
OKAY--DINESH? I FEEL LIKE WE'VE REACHED A POINT IN OUR FRIENDSHIP WHERE I CAN ASK--HOW DO YOU KEEP YOUR HAIR GELLED WITHOUT HANDS?
AH... WELL...
I MIXED METAL SHAVINGS INTO MY PRODUCT.
...SO I CAN MOVE IT.
MY GOD...
...YOU'RE A GENIUS.
NO...I WAS SIMPLY DESPERATE TO STILL SEE MYSELF WHEN I LOOKED IN THE MIRROR.
AS AN ENGINEER, I HAD ALWAYS ENVISIONED MYSELF BUILDING SOMETHING FOR THE FUTURE. A NEW LIGHT RAIL THROUGH INDIA, MAYBE.
BUT THEN I WOKE FROM THE MIST WITHOUT MY HANDS. AND IT SEEMS LIKE EVERY TIME I OPEN MY EYES SINCE...
...I'M IN A STORM OF DESTRUCTION-- NOT CREATION.
STILL THINKING ABOUT SIN-CONG?
I MEAN-- ME TOO. BUT I THINK...
...BECAUSE WHAT HAPPENED THERE SHOULD BE THE EXCEPTION TO WHAT WE DO. NOT THE NORM.
WELL, YOU'VE BEEN AT THIS A BIT LONGER THAN I HAVE, FLINT. SO TELL ME--

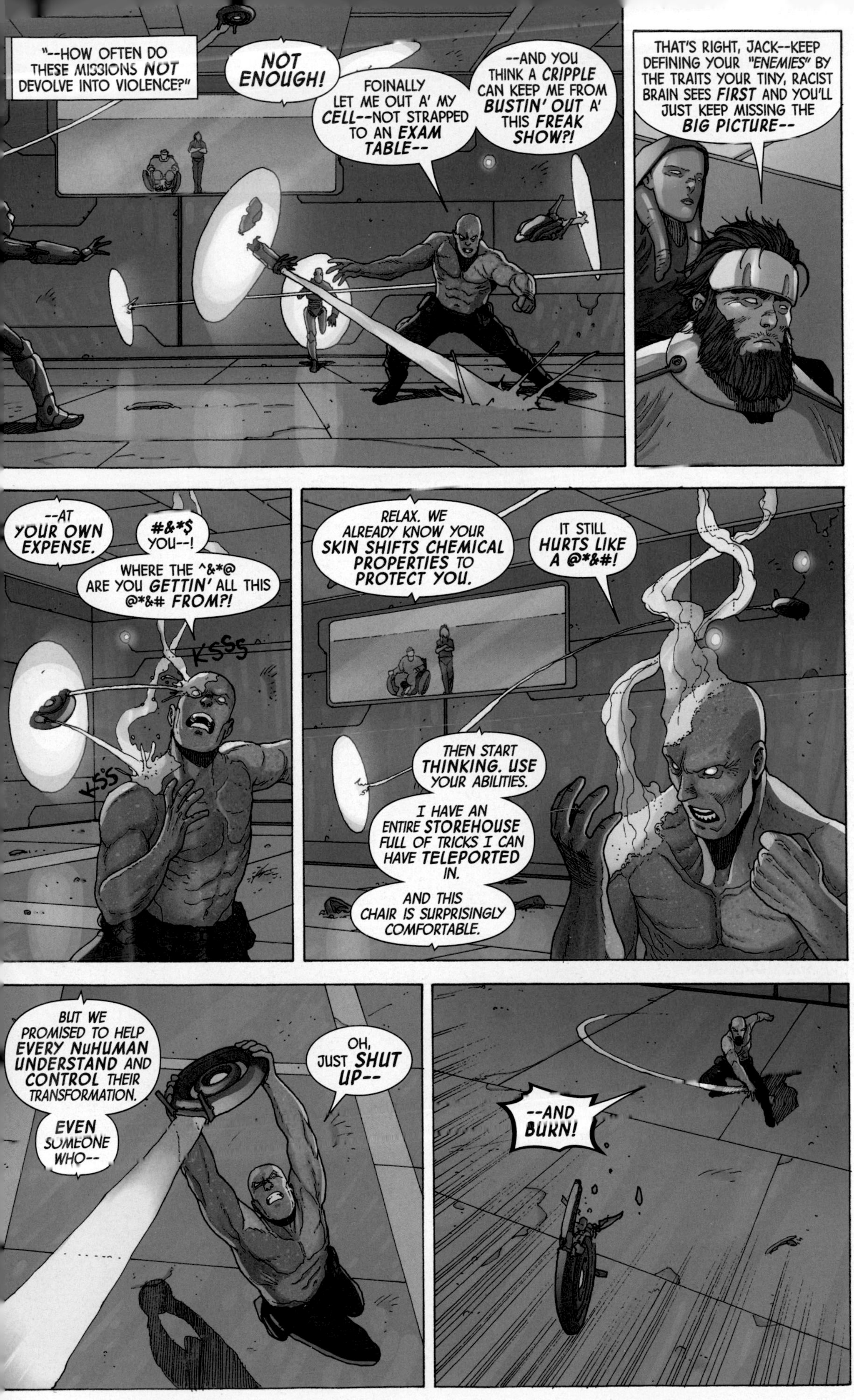
"--HOW OFTEN DO THESE MISSIONS NOT DEVOLVE INTO VIOLENCE?"
NOT ENOUGH!
FOINALLY LET ME OUT A' MY CELL--NOT STRAPPED TO AN EXAM TABLE--
--AND YOU THINK A CRIPPLE CAN KEEP ME FROM BUSTIN' OUT A' THIS FREAK SHOW?!
THAT'S RIGHT, JACK--KEEP DEFINING YOUR "ENEMIES" BY THE TRAITS YOUR TINY, RACIST BRAIN SEES FIRST AND YOU'LL JUST KEEP MISSING THE BIG PICTURE--
--AT YOUR OWN EXPENSE.
#&*$ YOU--!
WHERE THE ^&*@ ARE YOU GETTIN' ALL THIS @*&# FROM?!
KSSS
KSS
RELAX. WE ALREADY KNOW YOUR SKIN SHIFTS CHEMICAL PROPERTIES TO PROTECT YOU.
IT STILL HURTS LIKE A @*&#!
THEN START THINKING. USE YOUR ABILITIES.
I HAVE AN ENTIRE STOREHOUSE FULL OF TRICKS I CAN HAVE TELEPORTED IN.
AND THIS CHAIR IS SURPRISINGLY COMFORTABLE.
BUT WE PROMISED TO HELP EVERY NuHUMAN UNDERSTAND AND CONTROL THEIR TRANSFORMATION.
EVEN SOMEONE WHO--
OH, JUST SHUT UP--
--AND BURN!

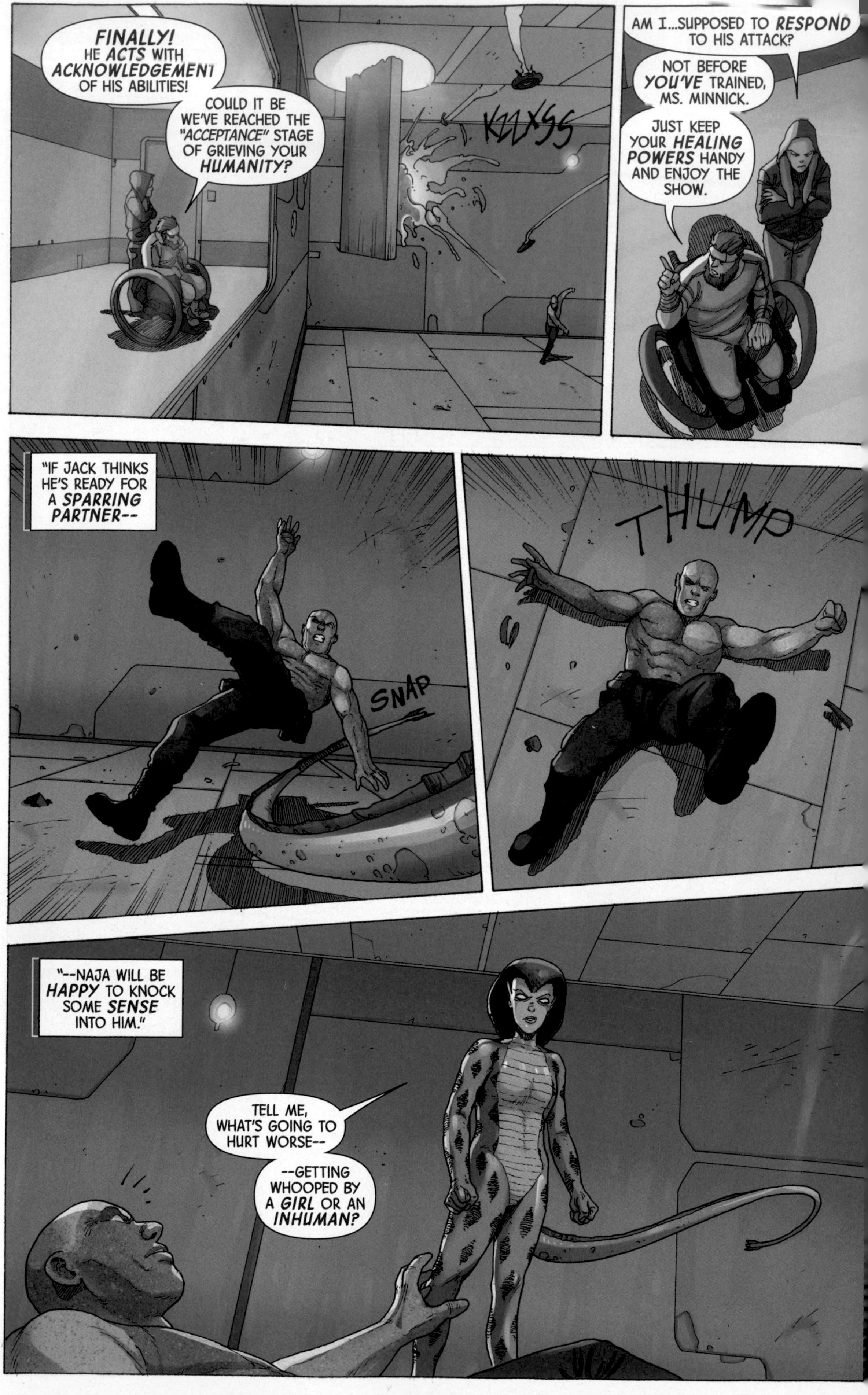
FINALLY! HE ACTS WITH ACKNOWLEDGEMENT OF HIS ABILITIES!
COULD IT BE WE'VE REACHED THE "ACCEPTANCE" STAGE OF GRIEVING YOUR HUMANITY?
KZZXSS
AM I...SUPPOSED TO RESPOND TO HIS ATTACK?
NOT BEFORE YOU'VE TRAINED, MS. MINNICK.
JUST KEEP YOUR HEALING POWERS HANDY AND ENJOY THE SHOW.
"IF JACK THINKS HE'S READY FOR A SPARRING PARTNER--
SNAP
THUMP
"--NAJA WILL BE HAPPY TO KNOCK SOME SENSE INTO HIM."
TELL ME, WHAT'S GOING TO HURT WORSE--
--GETTING WHOOPED BY A GIRL OR AN INHUMAN?

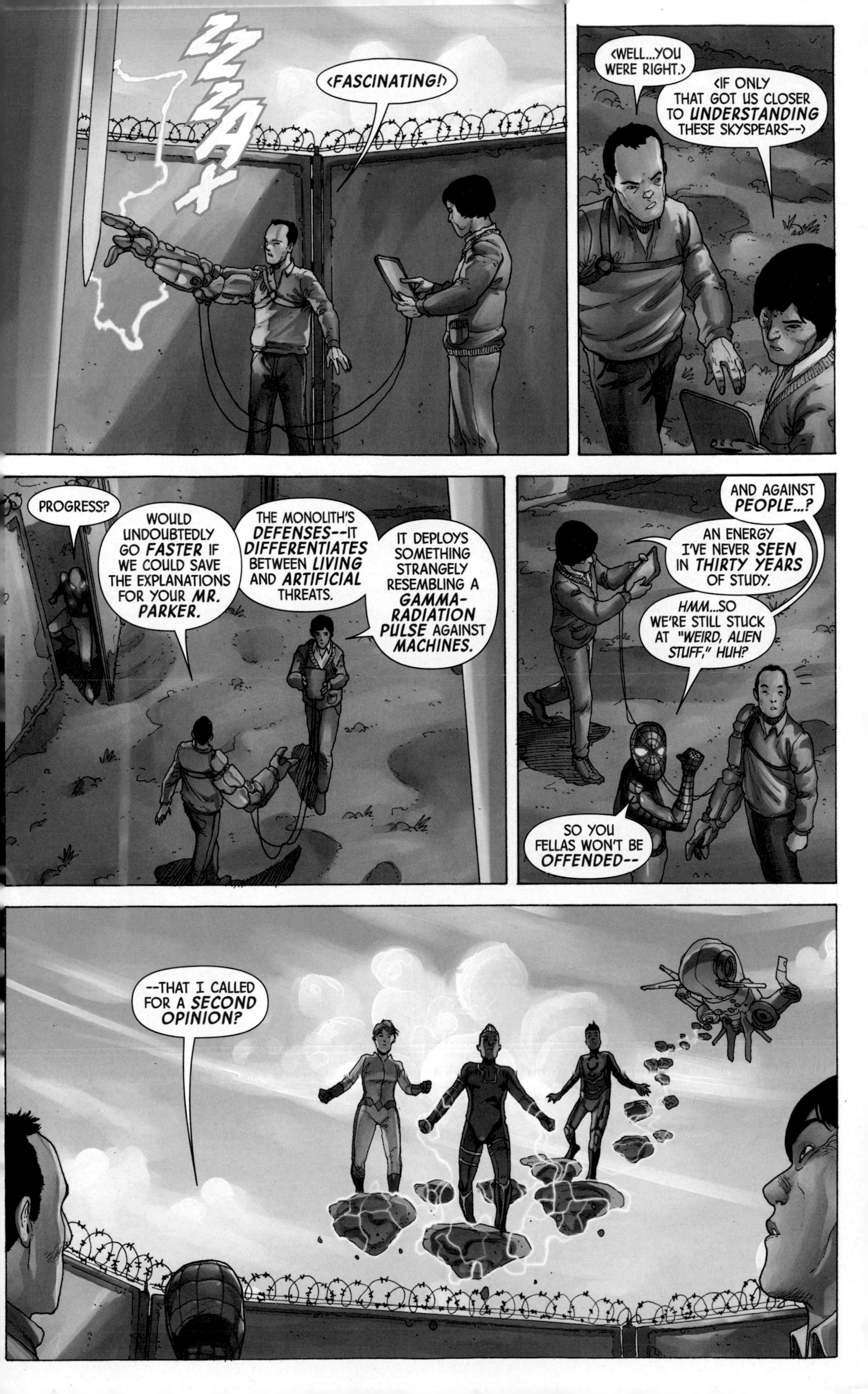
ZZZAX
‹FASCINATING!›
‹WELL...YOU WERE RIGHT.›
‹IF ONLY THAT GOT US CLOSER TO UNDERSTANDING THESE SKYSPEARS--›
PROGRESS?
WOULD UNDOUBTEDLY GO FASTER IF WE COULD SAVE THE EXPLANATIONS FOR YOUR MR. PARKER.
THE MONOLITH'S DEFENSES--IT DIFFERENTIATES BETWEEN LIVING AND ARTIFICIAL THREATS.
IT DEPLOYS SOMETHING STRANGELY RESEMBLING A GAMMA-RADIATION PULSE AGAINST MACHINES.
AND AGAINST PEOPLE...?
AN ENERGY I'VE NEVER SEEN IN THIRTY YEARS OF STUDY.
HMM...SO WE'RE STILL STUCK AT "WEIRD, ALIEN STUFF," HUH?
SO YOU FELLAS WON'T BE OFFENDED--
--THAT I CALLED FOR A SECOND OPINION?

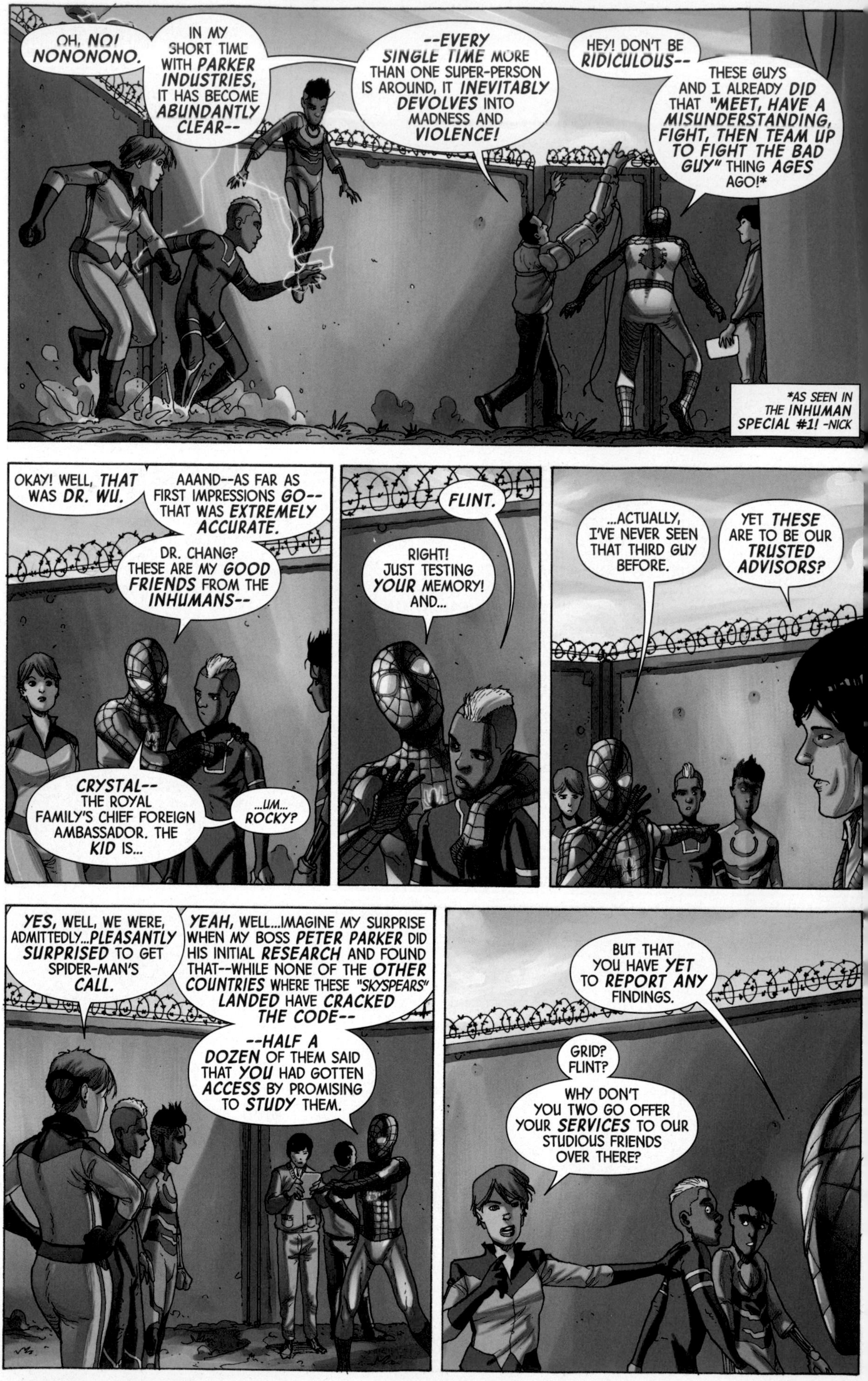
OH, NO! NONONONO.
IN MY SHORT TIME WITH PARKER INDUSTRIES, IT HAS BECOME ABUNDANTLY CLEAR--
--EVERY SINGLE TIME MORE THAN ONE SUPER-PERSON IS AROUND, IT INEVITABLY DEVOLVES INTO MADNESS AND VIOLENCE!
HEY! DON'T BE RIDICULOUS--
THESE GUYS AND I ALREADY DID THAT "MEET, HAVE A MISUNDERSTANDING, FIGHT, THEN TEAM UP TO FIGHT THE BAD GUY" THING AGES AGO!*
*AS SEEN IN THE INHUMAN SPECIAL #1! -NICK
OKAY! WELL, THAT WAS DR. WU.
AAAND--AS FAR AS FIRST IMPRESSIONS GO--THAT WAS EXTREMELY ACCURATE.
DR. CHANG? THESE ARE MY GOOD FRIENDS FROM THE INHUMANS--
CRYSTAL--THE ROYAL FAMILY'S CHIEF FOREIGN AMBASSADOR. THE KID IS...
...UM... ROCKY?
FLINT.
RIGHT! JUST TESTING YOUR MEMORY! AND...
...ACTUALLY, I'VE NEVER SEEN THAT THIRD GUY BEFORE.
YET THESE ARE TO BE OUR TRUSTED ADVISORS?
YES, WELL, WE WERE, ADMITTEDLY...PLEASANTLY SURPRISED TO GET SPIDER-MAN'S CALL.
YEAH, WELL...IMAGINE MY SURPRISE WHEN MY BOSS PETER PARKER DID HIS INITIAL RESEARCH AND FOUND THAT--WHILE NONE OF THE OTHER COUNTRIES WHERE THESE "SKYSPEARS" LANDED HAVE CRACKED THE CODE--
--HALF A DOZEN OF THEM SAID THAT YOU HAD GOTTEN ACCESS BY PROMISING TO STUDY THEM.
BUT THAT YOU HAVE YET TO REPORT ANY FINDINGS.
GRID? FLINT?
WHY DON'T YOU TWO GO OFFER YOUR SERVICES TO OUR STUDIOUS FRIENDS OVER THERE?

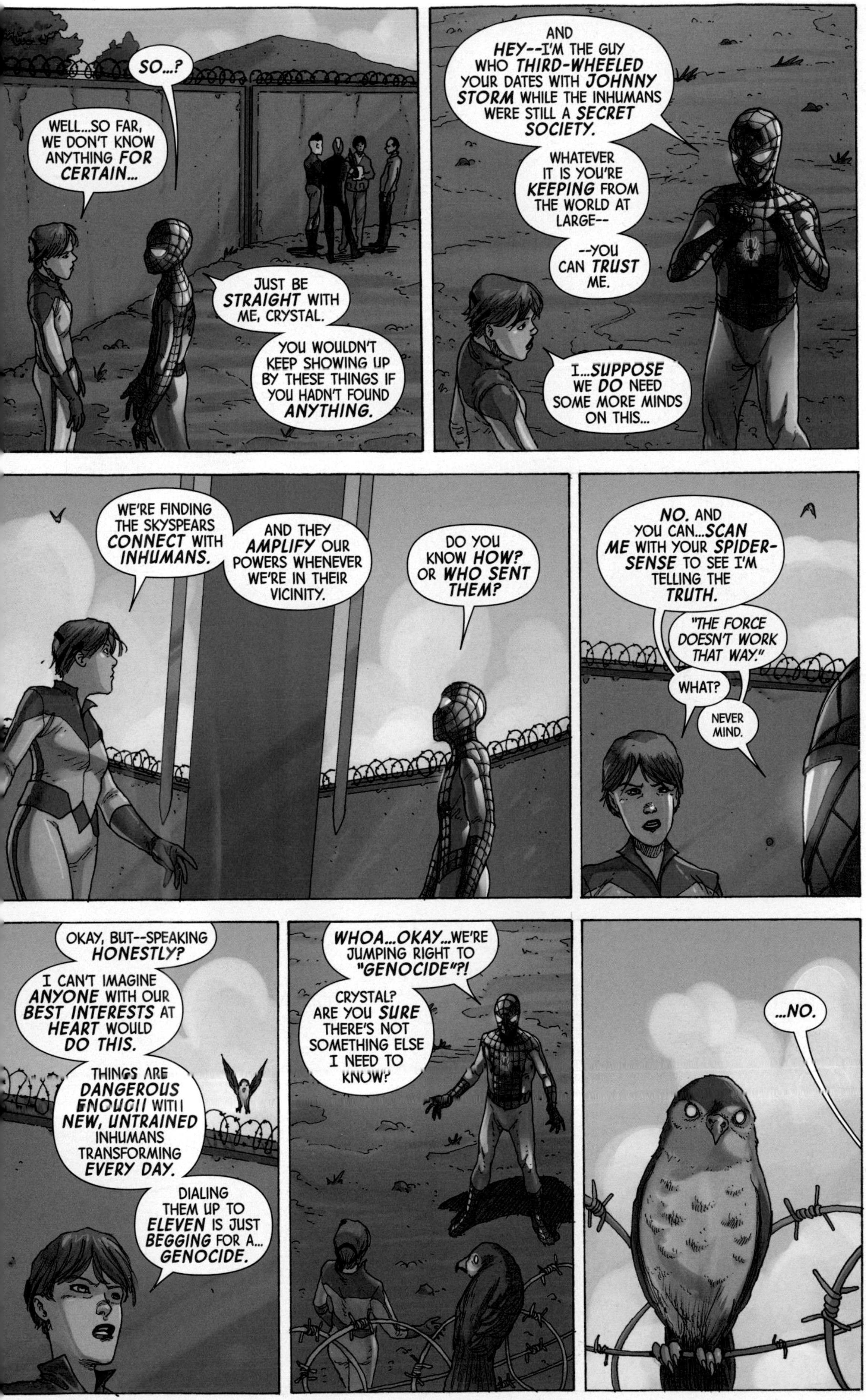
SO...?
WELL...SO FAR, WE DON'T KNOW ANYTHING FOR CERTAIN...
JUST BE STRAIGHT WITH ME, CRYSTAL.
YOU WOULDN'T KEEP SHOWING UP BY THESE THINGS IF YOU HADN'T FOUND ANYTHING.
AND HEY--I'M THE GUY WHO THIRD-WHEELED YOUR DATES WITH JOHNNY STORM WHILE THE INHUMANS WERE STILL A SECRET SOCIETY.
WHATEVER IT IS YOU'RE KEEPING FROM THE WORLD AT LARGE--
--YOU CAN TRUST ME.
I...SUPPOSE WE DO NEED SOME MORE MINDS ON THIS...
WE'RE FINDING THE SKYSPEARS CONNECT WITH INHUMANS.
AND THEY AMPLIFY OUR POWERS WHENEVER WE'RE IN THEIR VICINITY.
DO YOU KNOW HOW? OR WHO SENT THEM?
NO. AND YOU CAN...SCAN ME WITH YOUR SPIDER-SENSE TO SEE I'M TELLING THE TRUTH.
"THE FORCE DOESN'T WORK THAT WAY."
WHAT?
NEVER MIND.
OKAY, BUT--SPEAKING HONESTLY?
I CAN'T IMAGINE ANYONE WITH OUR BEST INTERESTS AT HEART WOULD DO THIS.
THINGS ARE DANGEROUS ENOUGH WITH NEW, UNTRAINED INHUMANS TRANSFORMING EVERY DAY.
DIALING THEM UP TO ELEVEN IS JUST BEGGING FOR A... GENOCIDE.
WHOA...OKAY...WE'RE JUMPING RIGHT TO "GENOCIDE"?!
CRYSTAL? ARE YOU SURE THERE'S NOT SOMETHING ELSE I NEED TO KNOW?
...NO.

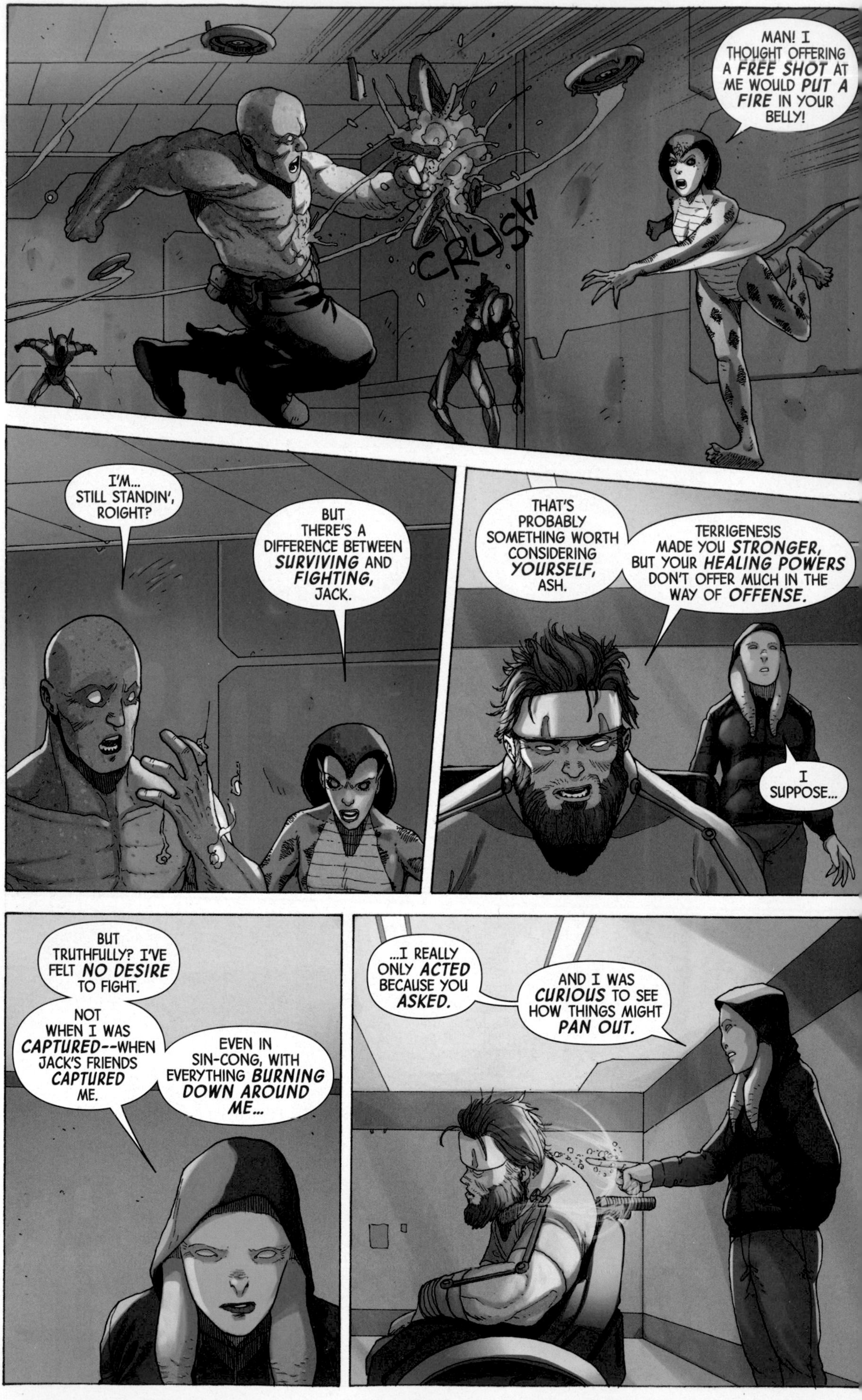
MAN! I THOUGHT OFFERING A FREE SHOT AT ME WOULD PUT A FIRE IN YOUR BELLY!
CRUSH
I'M... STILL STANDIN', ROIGHT?
BUT THERE'S A DIFFERENCE BETWEEN SURVIVING AND FIGHTING, JACK.
THAT'S PROBABLY SOMETHING WORTH CONSIDERING YOURSELF, ASH.
TERRIGENESIS MADE YOU STRONGER, BUT YOUR HEALING POWERS DON'T OFFER MUCH IN THE WAY OF OFFENSE.
I SUPPOSE...
BUT TRUTHFULLY? I'VE FELT NO DESIRE TO FIGHT.
NOT WHEN I WAS CAPTURED--WHEN JACK'S FRIENDS CAPTURED ME.
EVEN IN SIN-CONG, WITH EVERYTHING BURNING DOWN AROUND ME...
...I REALLY ONLY ACTED BECAUSE YOU ASKED.
AND I WAS CURIOUS TO SEE HOW THINGS MIGHT PAN OUT.

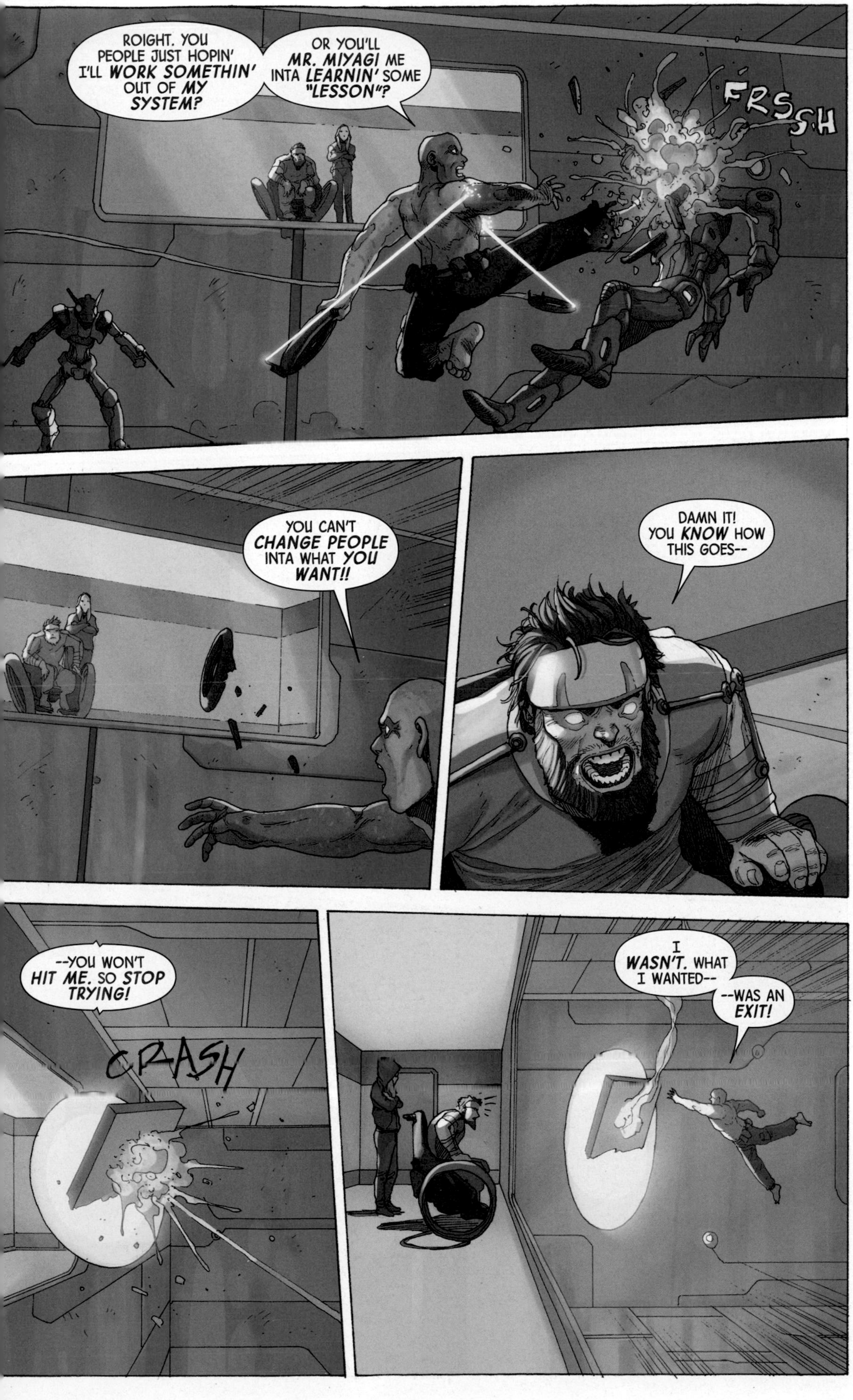
ROIGHT. YOU PEOPLE JUST HOPIN' I'LL WORK SOMETHIN' OUT OF MY SYSTEM?
OR YOU'LL MR. MIYAGI ME INTA LEARNIN' SOME "LESSON"?
FRSSH
YOU CAN'T CHANGE PEOPLE INTA WHAT YOU WANT!!
DAMN IT! YOU KNOW HOW THIS GOES--
--YOU WON'T HIT ME. SO STOP TRYING!
CRASH
I WASN'T. WHAT I WANTED--
--WAS AN EXIT!

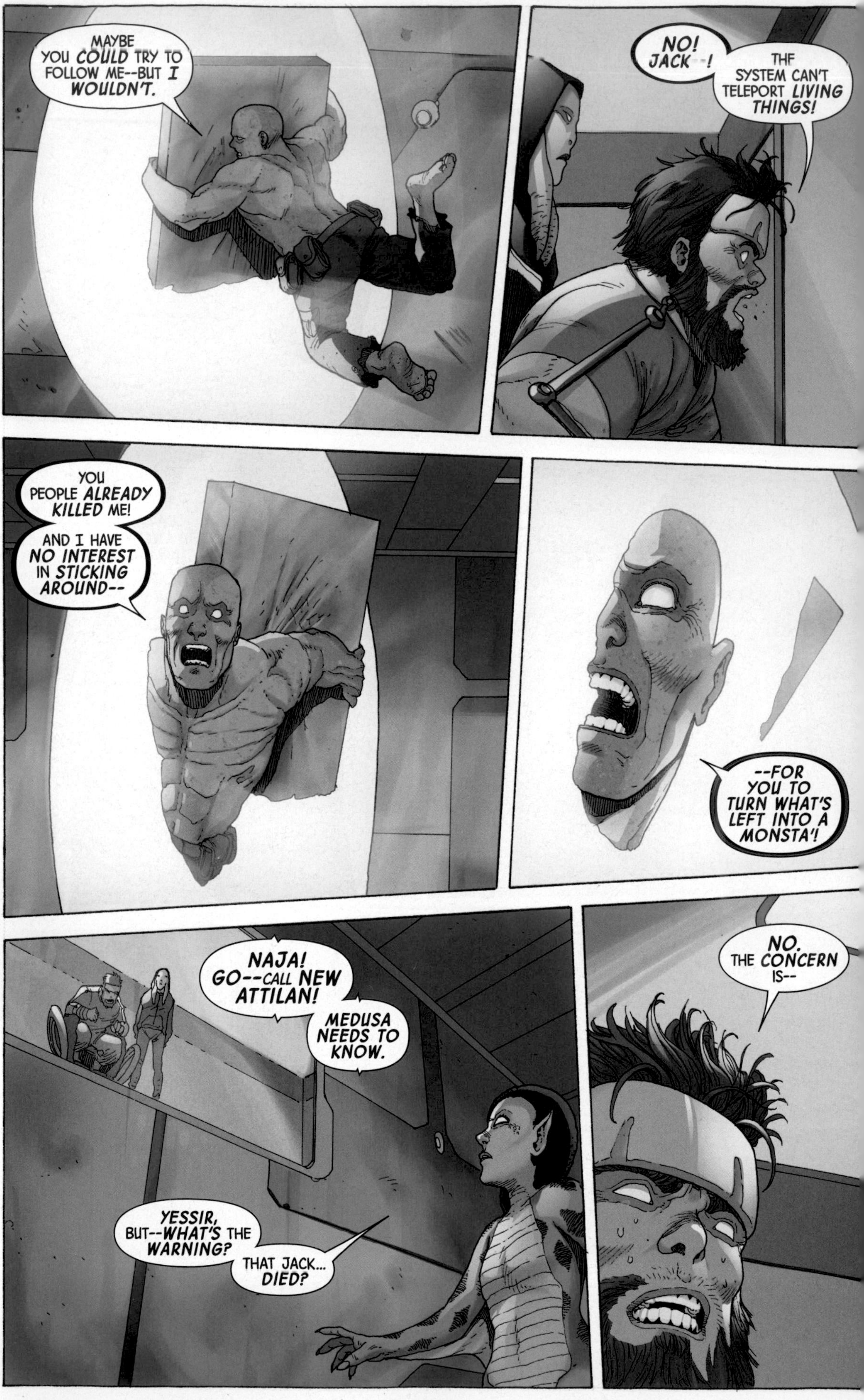
MAYBE YOU COULD TRY TO FOLLOW ME--BUT I WOULDN'T.
NO! JACK--!
THF SYSTEM CAN'T TELEPORT LIVING THINGS!
YOU PEOPLE ALREADY KILLED ME!
AND I HAVE NO INTEREST IN STICKING AROUND--
--FOR YOU TO TURN WHAT'S LEFT INTO A MONSTA'!
NAJA! GO--CALL NEW ATTILAN!
MEDUSA NEEDS TO KNOW.
YESSIR, BUT--WHAT'S THE WARNING?
THAT JACK... DIED?
NO. THE CONCERN IS--

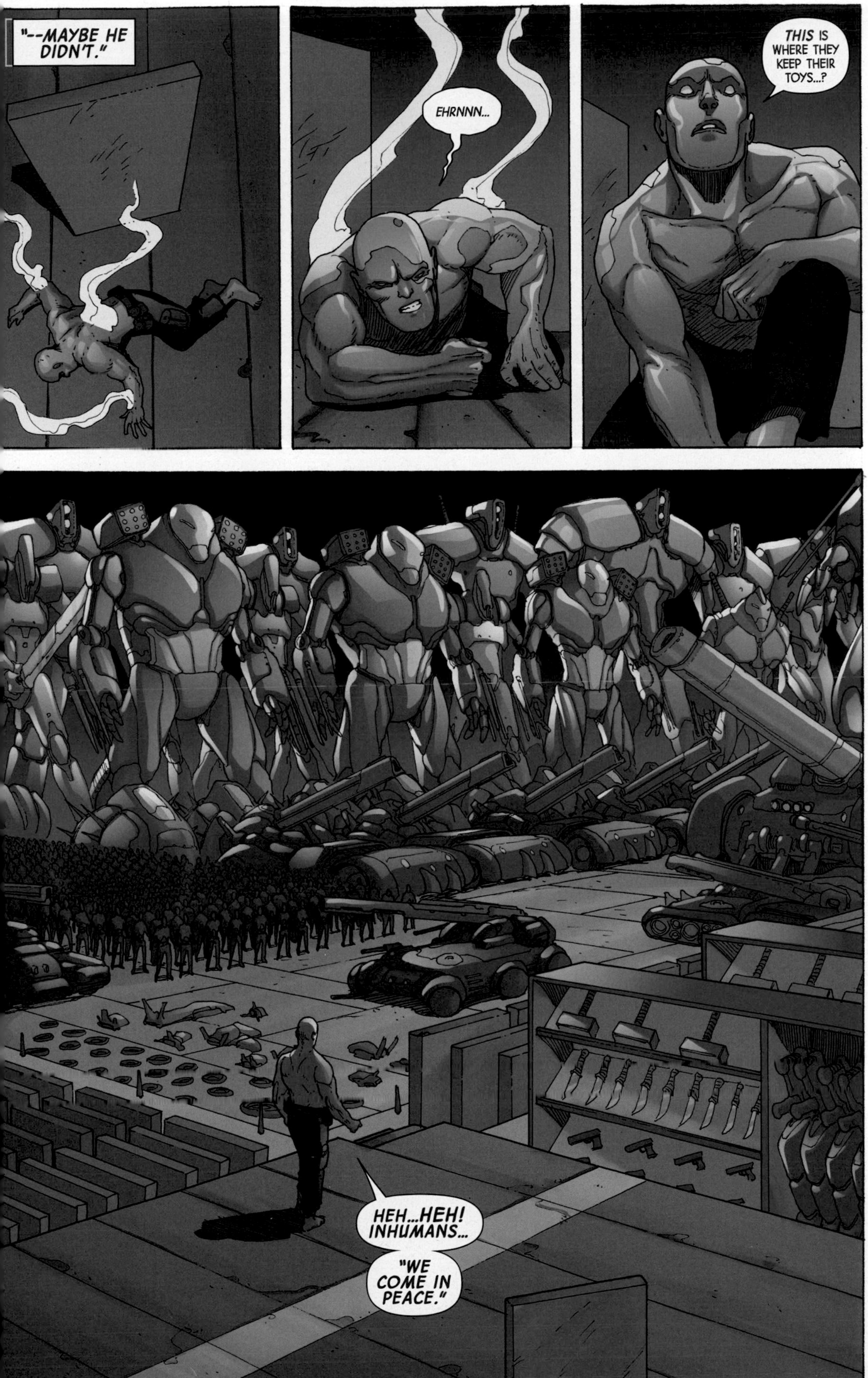
"--MAYBE HE DIDN'T."
EHRNNN...
THIS IS WHERE THEY KEEP THEIR TOYS...?
HEH...HEH! INHUMANS...
"WE COME IN PEACE."

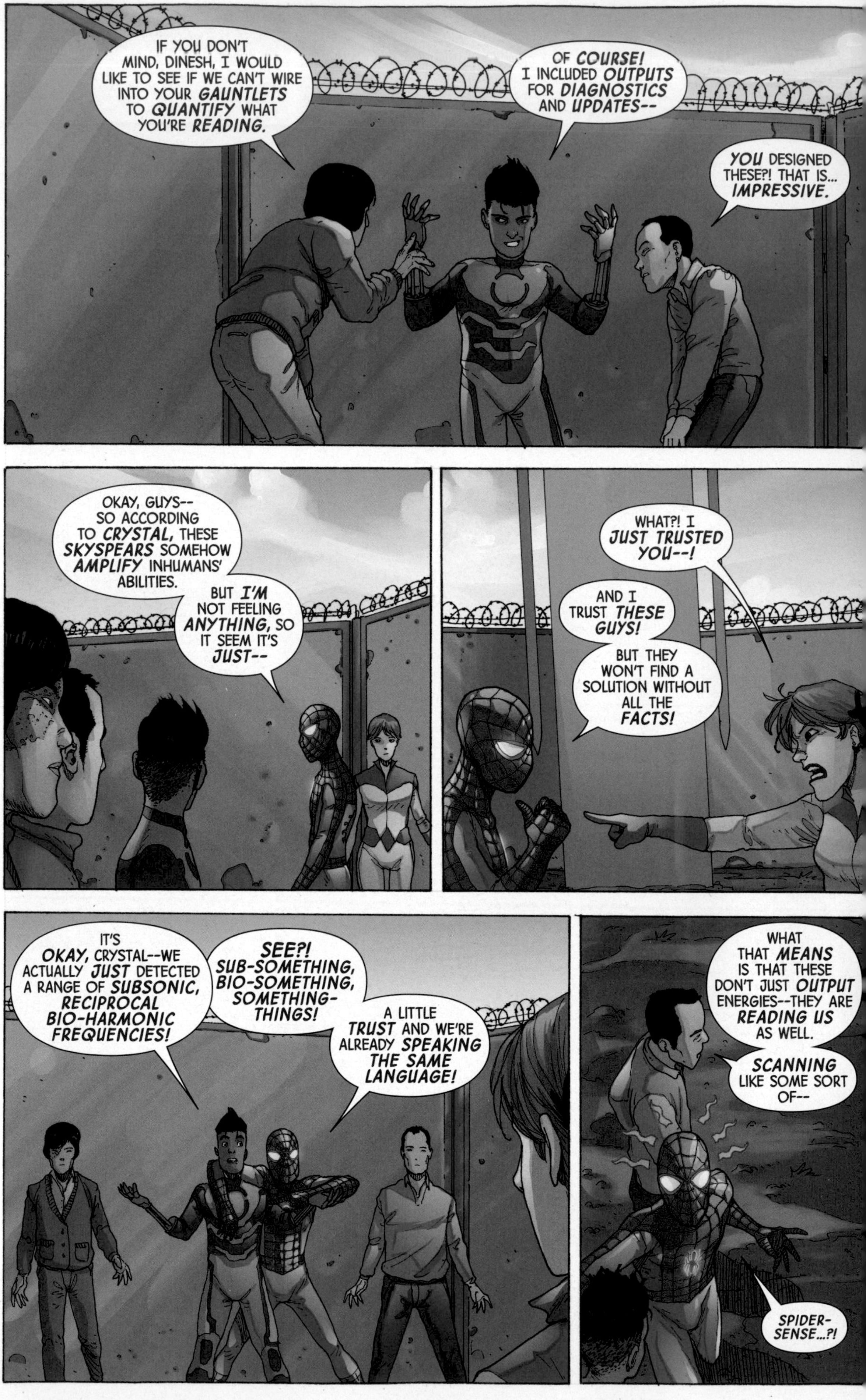
IF YOU DON'T MIND, DINESH, I WOULD LIKE TO SEE IF WE CAN'T WIRE INTO YOUR GAUNTLETS TO QUANTIFY WHAT YOU'RE READING.
OF COURSE! I INCLUDED OUTPUTS FOR DIAGNOSTICS AND UPDATES--
YOU DESIGNED THESE?! THAT IS... IMPRESSIVE.
OKAY, GUYS-- SO ACCORDING TO CRYSTAL, THESE SKYSPEARS SOMEHOW AMPLIFY INHUMANS' ABILITIES.
BUT I'M NOT FEELING ANYTHING, SO IT SEEM IT'S JUST--
WHAT?! I JUST TRUSTED YOU--!
AND I TRUST THESE GUYS!
BUT THEY WON'T FIND A SOLUTION WITHOUT ALL THE FACTS!
IT'S OKAY, CRYSTAL--WE ACTUALLY JUST DETECTED A RANGE OF SUBSONIC, RECIPROCAL BIO-HARMONIC FREQUENCIES!
SEE?! SUB-SOMETHING, BIO-SOMETHING, SOMETHING-THINGS!
A LITTLE TRUST AND WE'RE ALREADY SPEAKING THE SAME LANGUAGE!
WHAT THAT MEANS IS THAT THESE DON'T JUST OUTPUT ENERGIES--THEY ARE READING US AS WELL.
SCANNING LIKE SOME SORT OF--
SPIDER-SENSE...?!

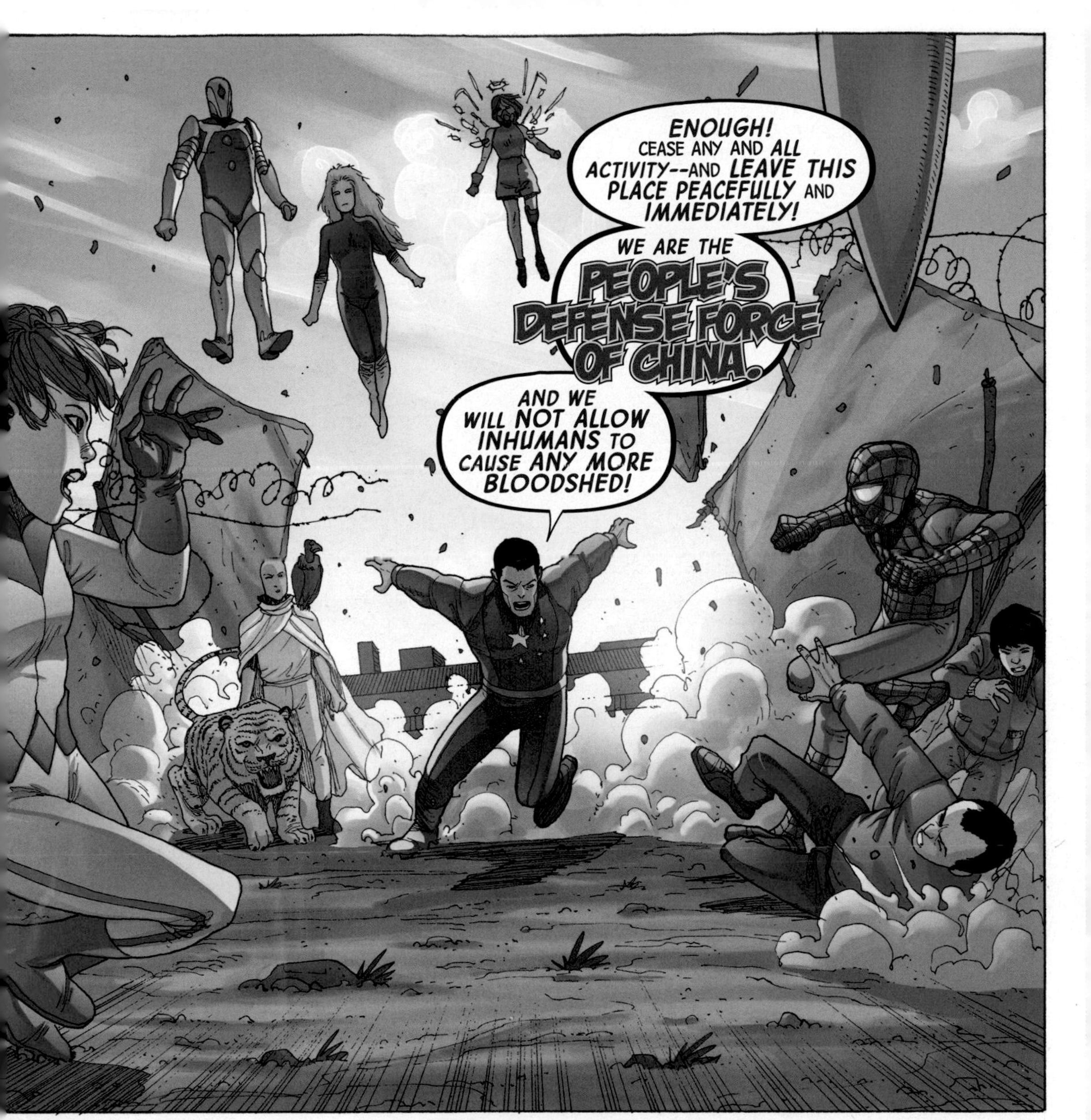
ENOUGH! CEASE ANY AND ALL ACTIVITY--AND LEAVE THIS PLACE PEACEFULLY AND IMMEDIATELY!
WE ARE THE PEOPLE'S DEFENSE FORCE OF CHINA.
AND WE WILL NOT ALLOW INHUMANS TO CAUSE ANY MORE BLOODSHED!

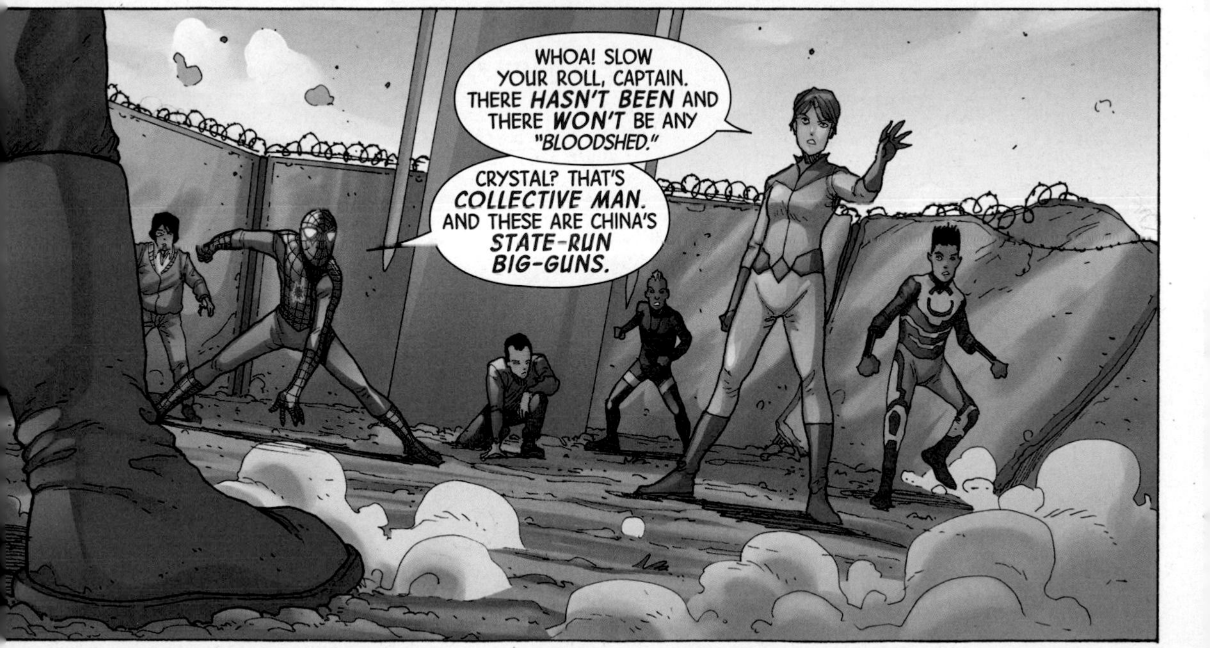
WHOA! SLOW YOUR ROLL, CAPTAIN. THERE HASN'T BEEN AND THERE WON'T BE ANY "BLOODSHED."
CRYSTAL? THAT'S COLLECTIVE MAN. AND THESE ARE CHINA'S STATE-RUN BIG-GUNS.

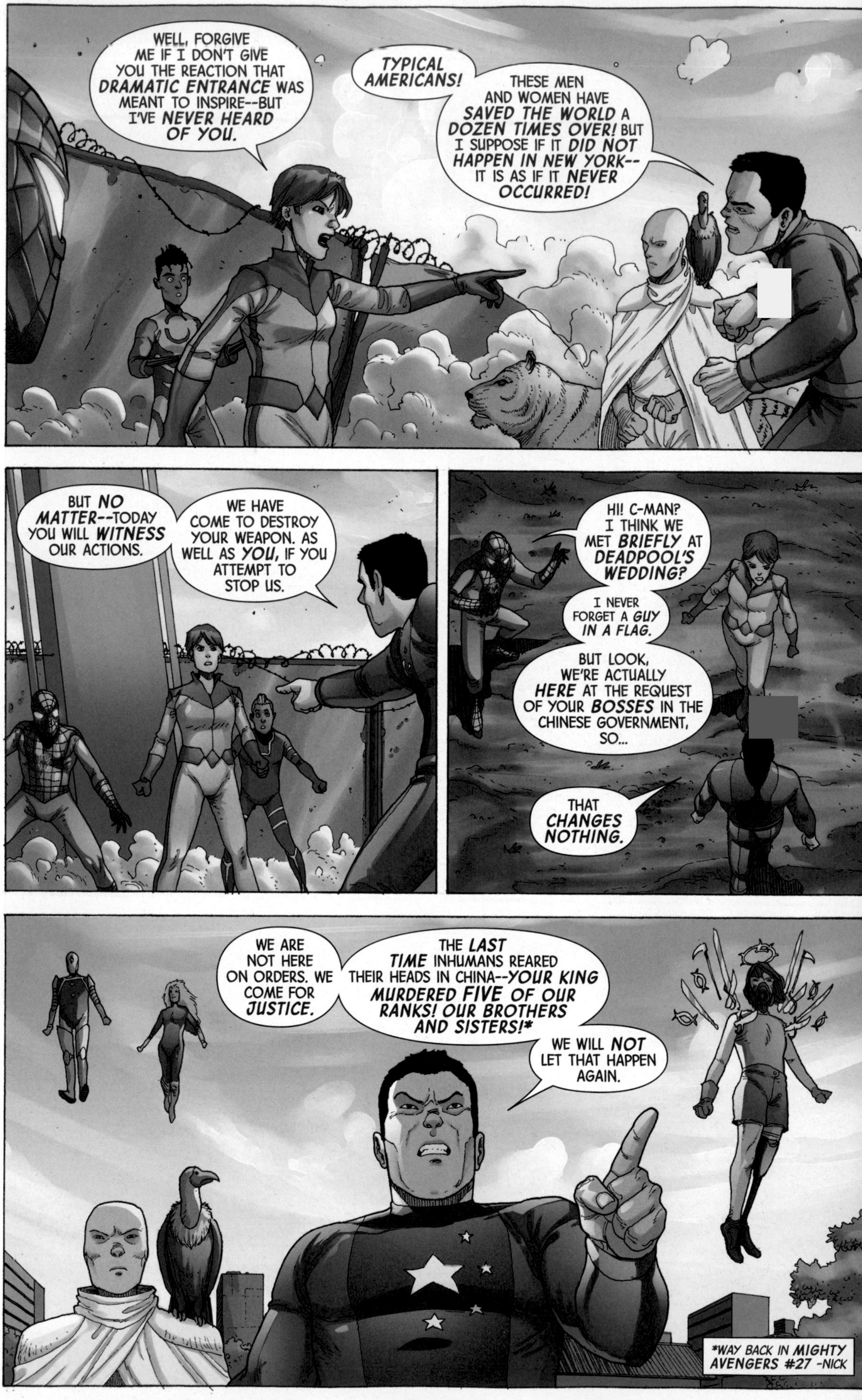
WELL, FORGIVE ME IF I DON'T GIVE YOU THE REACTION THAT DRAMATIC ENTRANCE WAS MEANT TO INSPIRE--BUT I'VE NEVER HEARD OF YOU.
TYPICAL AMERICANS!
THESE MEN AND WOMEN HAVE SAVED THE WORLD A DOZEN TIMES OVER! BUT I SUPPOSE IF IT DID NOT HAPPEN IN NEW YORK--IT IS AS IF IT NEVER OCCURRED!
BUT NO MATTER--TODAY YOU WILL WITNESS OUR ACTIONS.
WE HAVE COME TO DESTROY YOUR WEAPON. AS WELL AS YOU, IF YOU ATTEMPT TO STOP US.
HI! C-MAN? I THINK WE MET BRIEFLY AT DEADPOOL'S WEDDING?
I NEVER FORGET A GUY IN A FLAG.
BUT LOOK, WE'RE ACTUALLY HERE AT THE REQUEST OF YOUR BOSSES IN THE CHINESE GOVERNMENT, SO...
THAT CHANGES NOTHING.
WE ARE NOT HERE ON ORDERS. WE COME FOR JUSTICE.
THE LAST TIME INHUMANS REARED THEIR HEADS IN CHINA--YOUR KING MURDERED FIVE OF OUR RANKS! OUR BROTHERS AND SISTERS!*
WE WILL NOT LET THAT HAPPEN AGAIN.
*WAY BACK IN MIGHTY AVENGERS #27 -NICK

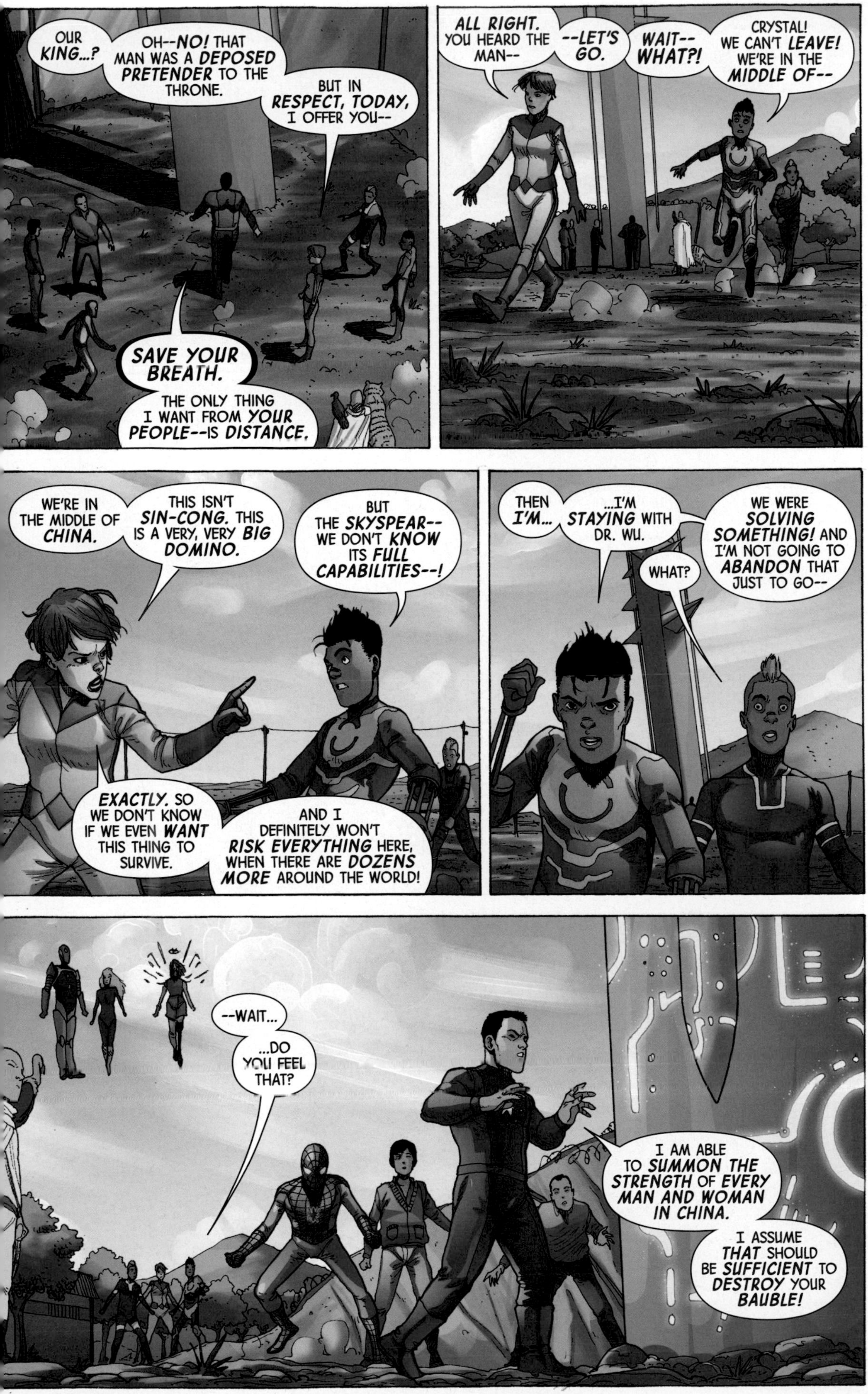
OUR KING...?
OH--NO! THAT MAN WAS A DEPOSED PRETENDER TO THE THRONE.
BUT IN RESPECT, TODAY, I OFFER YOU--
SAVE YOUR BREATH.
THE ONLY THING I WANT FROM YOUR PEOPLE--IS DISTANCE.
ALL RIGHT. YOU HEARD THE MAN--
--LET'S GO.
WAIT-- WHAT?!
CRYSTAL! WE CAN'T LEAVE! WE'RE IN THE MIDDLE OF--
WE'RE IN THE MIDDLE OF CHINA.
THIS ISN'T SIN-CONG. THIS IS A VERY, VERY BIG DOMINO.
BUT THE SKYSPEAR-- WE DON'T KNOW ITS FULL CAPABILITIES--!
EXACTLY. SO WE DON'T KNOW IF WE EVEN WANT THIS THING TO SURVIVE.
AND I DEFINITELY WON'T RISK EVERYTHING HERE, WHEN THERE ARE DOZENS MORE AROUND THE WORLD!
THEN I'M...
...I'M STAYING WITH DR. WU.
WHAT?
WE WERE SOLVING SOMETHING! AND I'M NOT GOING TO ABANDON THAT JUST TO GO--
--WAIT...
...DO YOU FEEL THAT?
I AM ABLE TO SUMMON THE STRENGTH OF EVERY MAN AND WOMAN IN CHINA.
I ASSUME THAT SHOULD BE SUFFICIENT TO DESTROY YOUR BAUBLE!

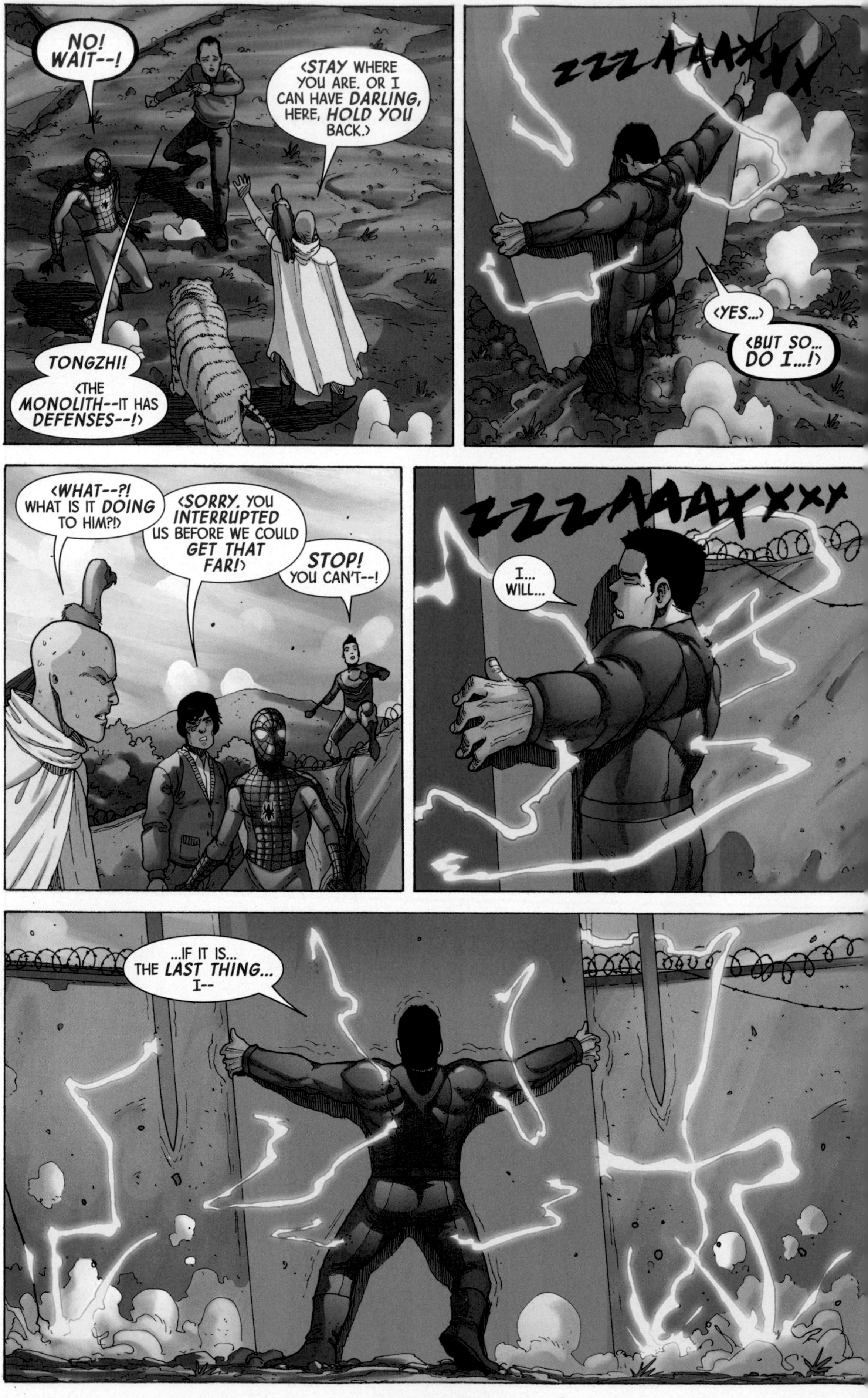
NO! WAIT--!
<STAY WHERE YOU ARE. OR I CAN HAVE DARLING, HERE, HOLD YOU BACK.>
TONGZHI!
<THE MONOLITH--IT HAS DEFENSES--!>
ZZZAAAXXX
<YES...>
<BUT SO... DO I...!>
<WHAT--?! WHAT IS IT DOING TO HIM?!>
<SORRY. YOU INTERRUPTED US BEFORE WE COULD GET THAT FAR!>
STOP! YOU CAN'T--!
ZZZAAAXXXX
I... WILL...
...IF IT IS... THE LAST THING... I--

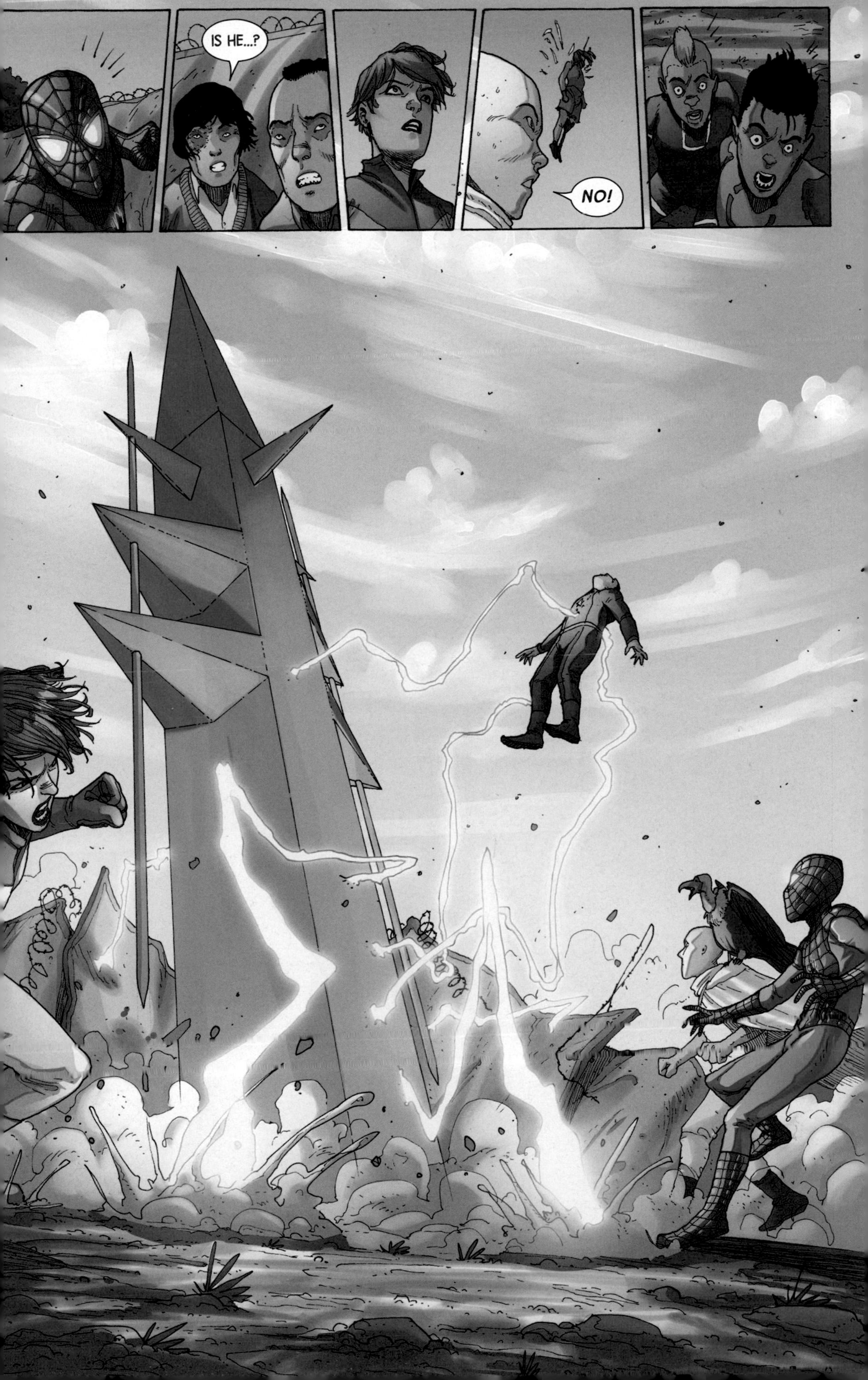
IS HE...?
NO!

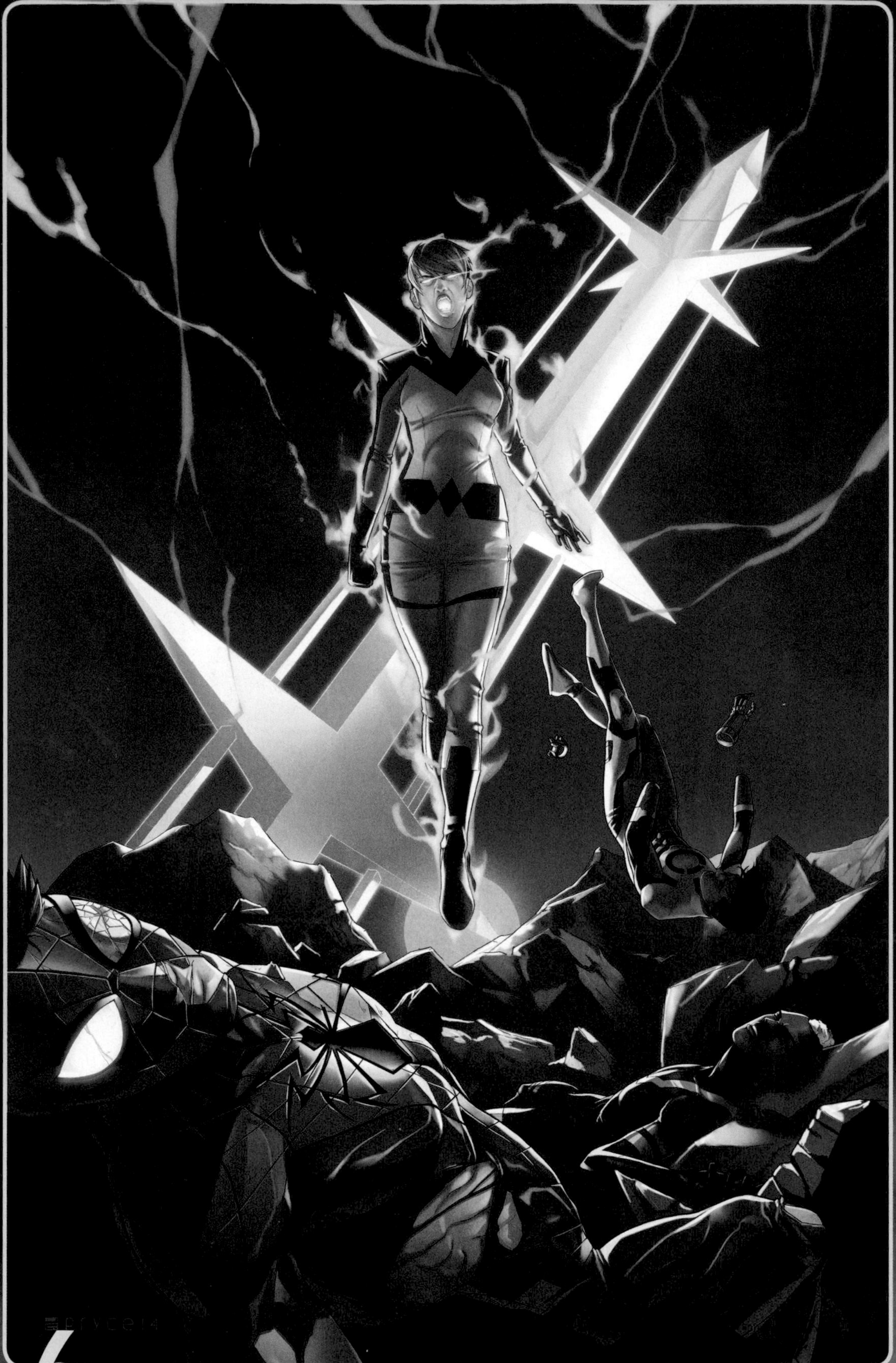

6

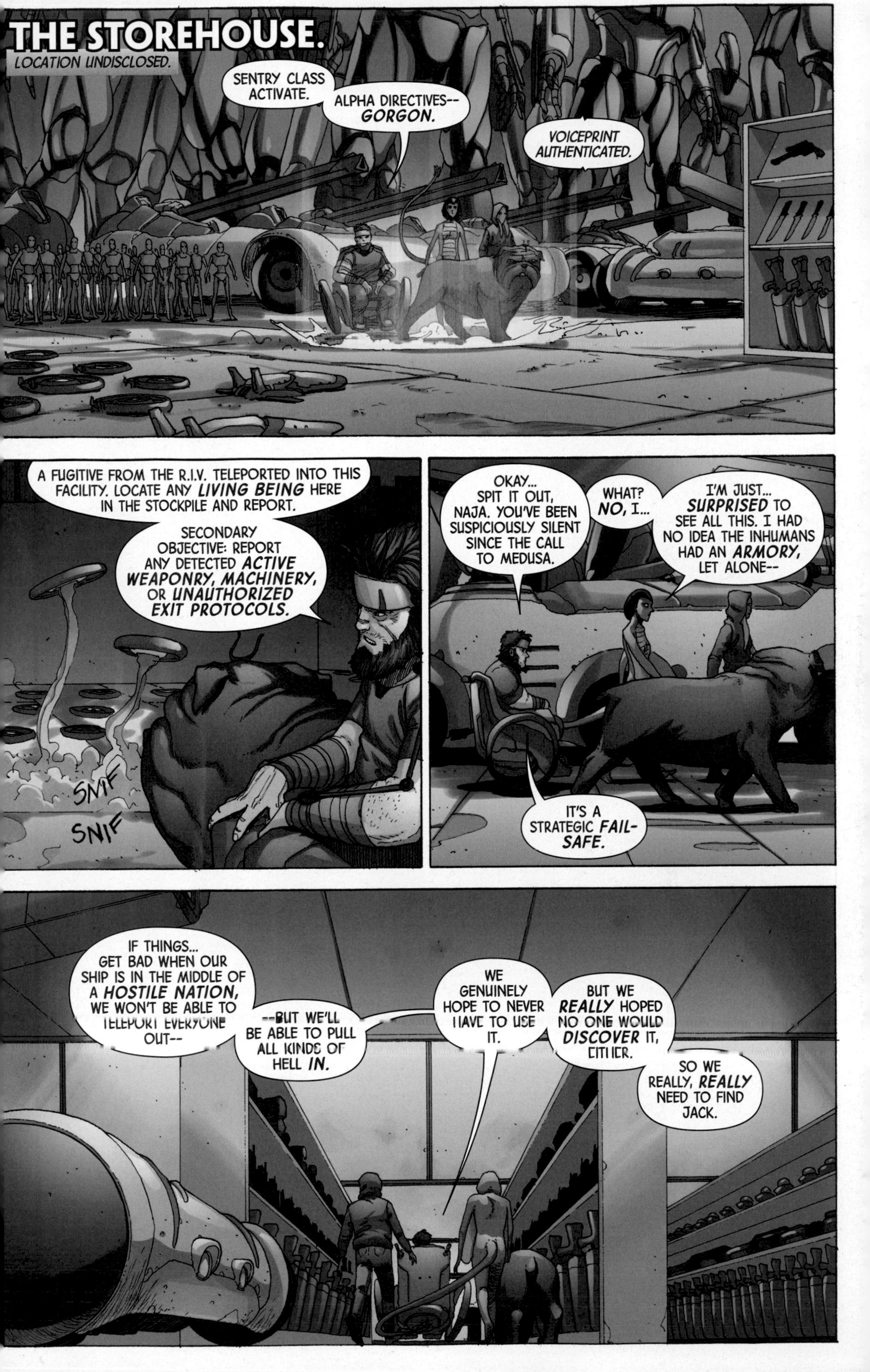
THE STOREHOUSE.
LOCATION UNDISCLOSED.
SENTRY CLASS ACTIVATE.
ALPHA DIRECTIVES-- GORGON.
VOICEPRINT AUTHENTICATED.
A FUGITIVE FROM THE R.I.V. TELEPORTED INTO THIS FACILITY. LOCATE ANY LIVING BEING HERE IN THE STOCKPILE AND REPORT.
SECONDARY OBJECTIVE: REPORT ANY DETECTED ACTIVE WEAPONRY, MACHINERY, OR UNAUTHORIZED EXIT PROTOCOLS.
SNIF
SNIF
OKAY... SPIT IT OUT, NAJA. YOU'VE BEEN SUSPICIOUSLY SILENT SINCE THE CALL TO MEDUSA.
WHAT? NO, I...
I'M JUST... SURPRISED TO SEE ALL THIS. I HAD NO IDEA THE INHUMANS HAD AN ARMORY, LET ALONE--
IT'S A STRATEGIC FAIL-SAFE.
IF THINGS... GET BAD WHEN OUR SHIP IS IN THE MIDDLE OF A HOSTILE NATION, WE WON'T BE ABLE TO TELEPORT EVERYONE OUT--
--BUT WE'LL BE ABLE TO PULL ALL KINDS OF HELL IN.
WE GENUINELY HOPE TO NEVER HAVE TO USE IT.
BUT WE REALLY HOPED NO ONE WOULD DISCOVER IT, EITHER.
SO WE REALLY, REALLY NEED TO FIND JACK.

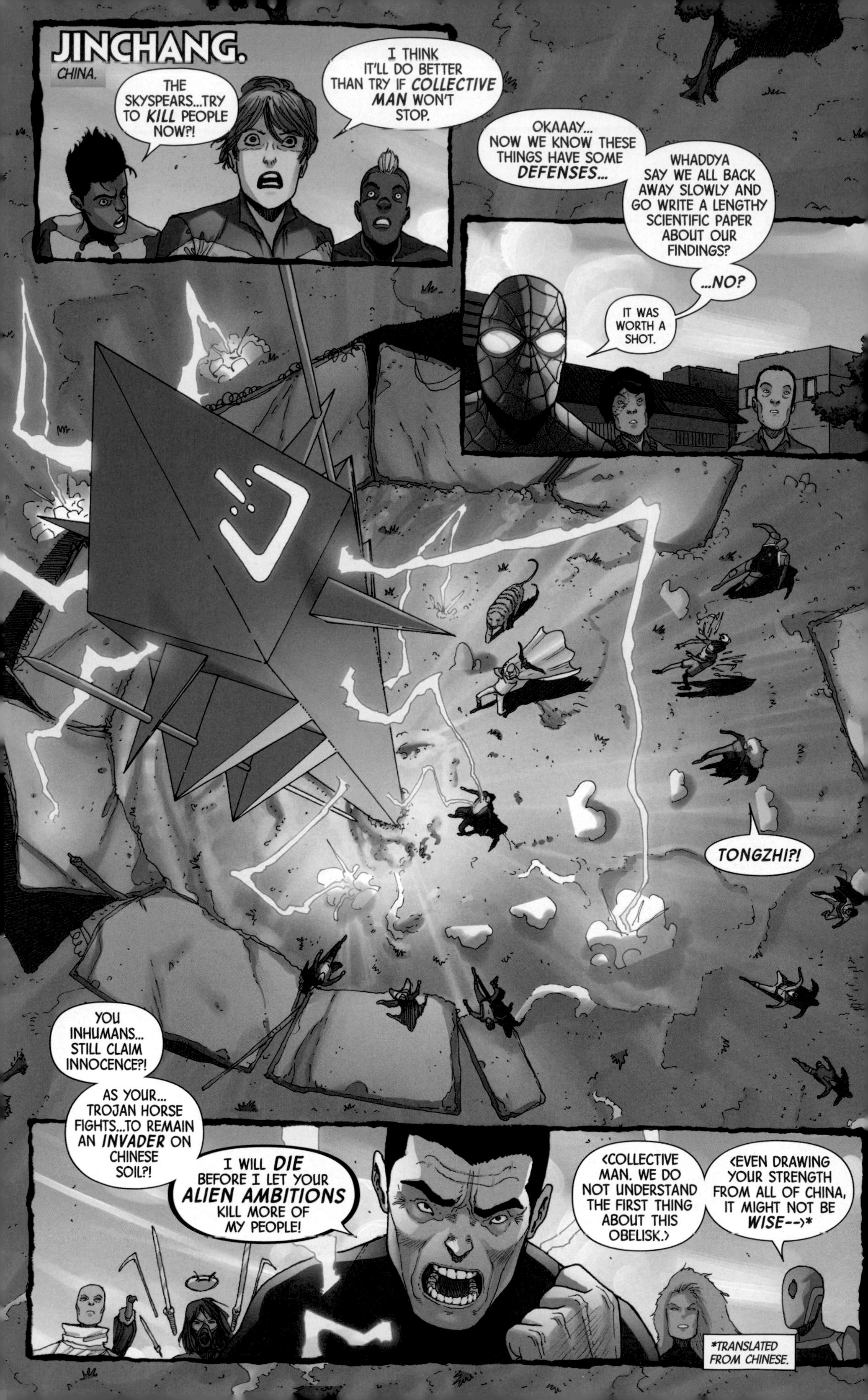
JINCHANG.
CHINA.
THE SKYSPEARS...TRY TO KILL PEOPLE NOW?!
I THINK IT'LL DO BETTER THAN TRY IF COLLECTIVE MAN WON'T STOP.
OKAAAY... NOW WE KNOW THESE THINGS HAVE SOME DEFENSES...
WHADDYA SAY WE ALL BACK AWAY SLOWLY AND GO WRITE A LENGTHY SCIENTIFIC PAPER ABOUT OUR FINDINGS?
...NO?
IT WAS WORTH A SHOT.
TONGZHI?!
YOU INHUMANS... STILL CLAIM INNOCENCE?!
AS YOUR... TROJAN HORSE FIGHTS...TO REMAIN AN INVADER ON CHINESE SOIL?!
I WILL DIE BEFORE I LET YOUR ALIEN AMBITIONS KILL MORE OF MY PEOPLE!
<COLLECTIVE MAN. WE DO NOT UNDERSTAND THE FIRST THING ABOUT THIS OBELISK.>
<EVEN DRAWING YOUR STRENGTH FROM ALL OF CHINA, IT MIGHT NOT BE WISE-->*
*TRANSLATED FROM CHINESE.

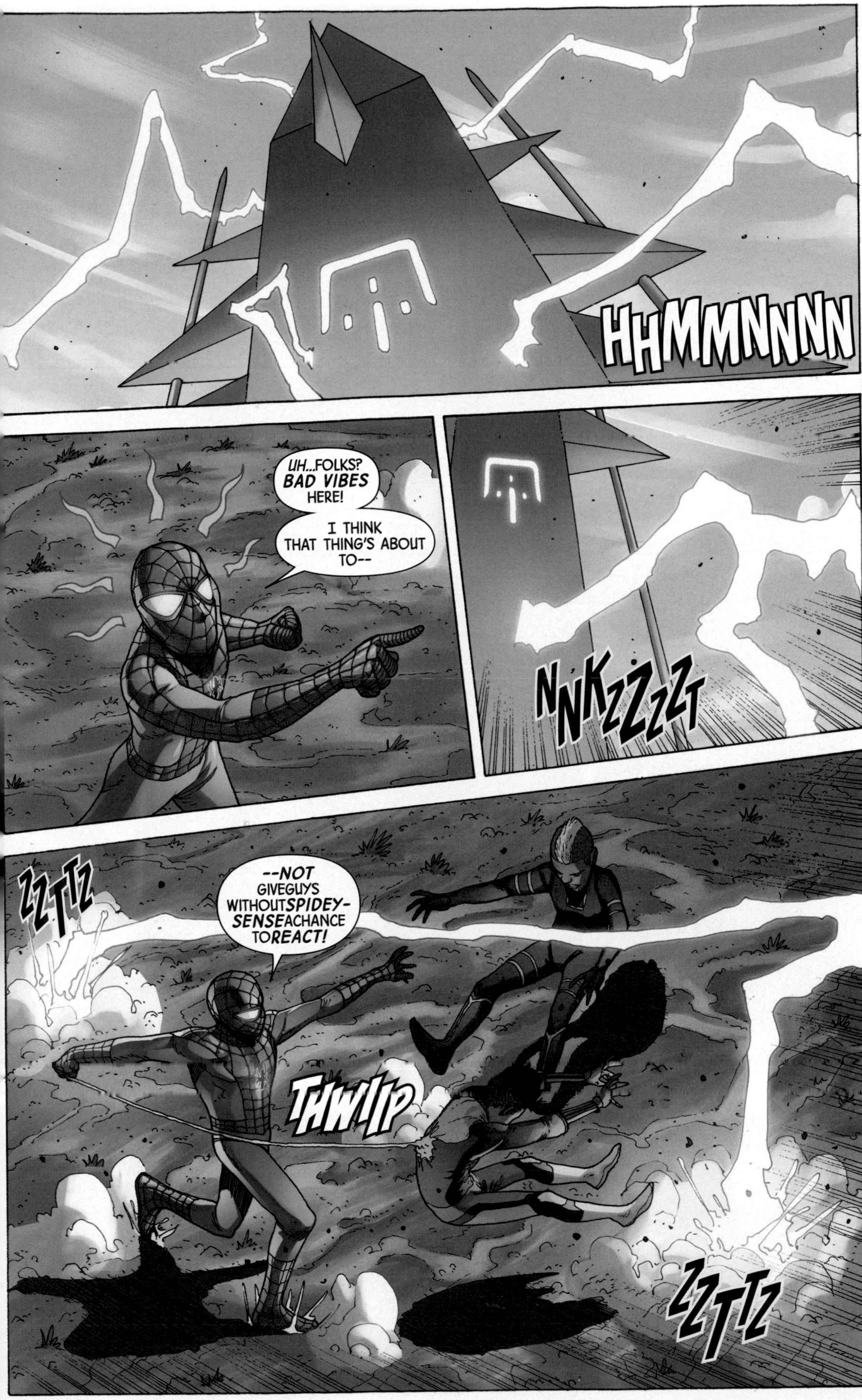
HHMMNNNNN
UH...FOLKS? BAD VIBES HERE!
I THINK THAT THING'S ABOUT TO--
NNKZZZZZT
ZZTTZ
--NOT GIVE GUYS WITHOUT SPIDEY-SENSE A CHANCE TO REACT!
THWIIP
ZZTTZ

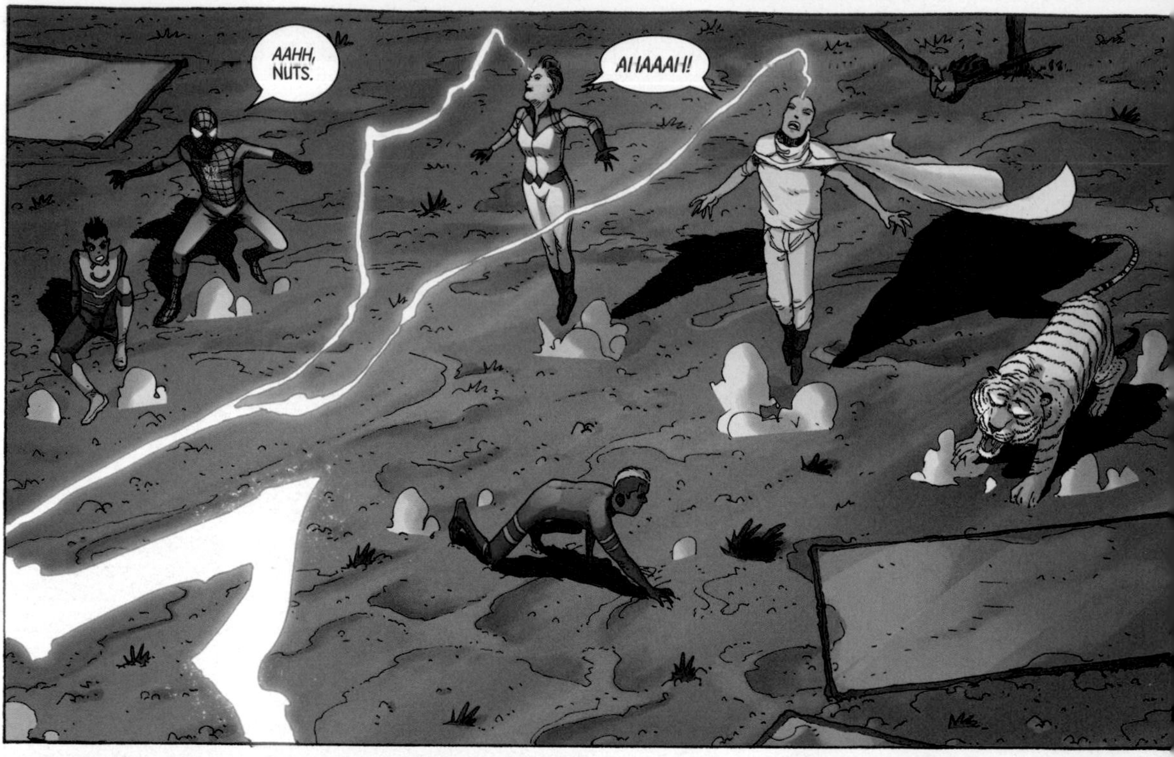
AAHH, NUTS.
AHAAAH!

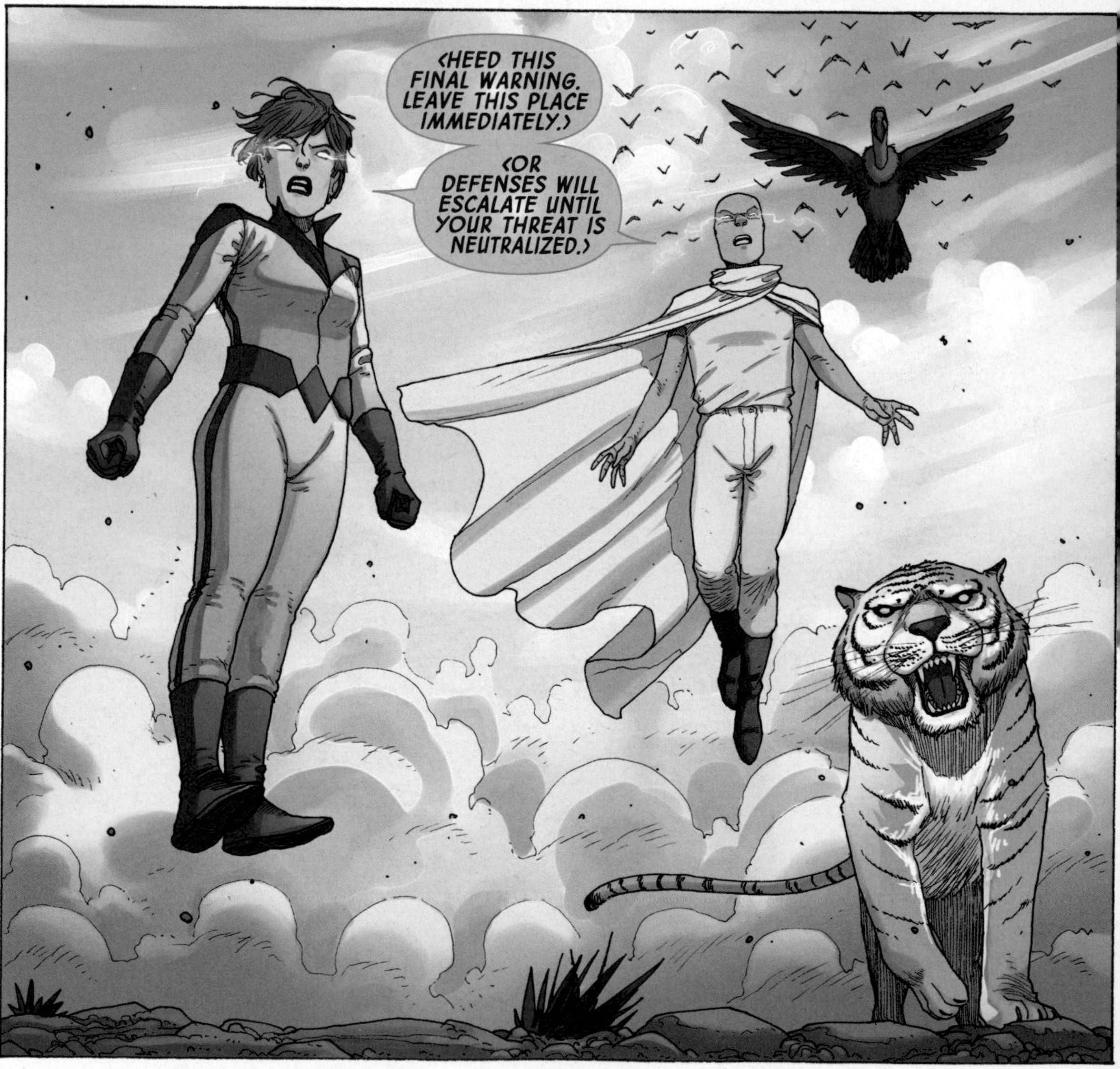
<HEED THIS FINAL WARNING. LEAVE THIS PLACE IMMEDIATELY.>
<OR DEFENSES WILL ESCALATE UNTIL YOUR THREAT IS NEUTRALIZED.>

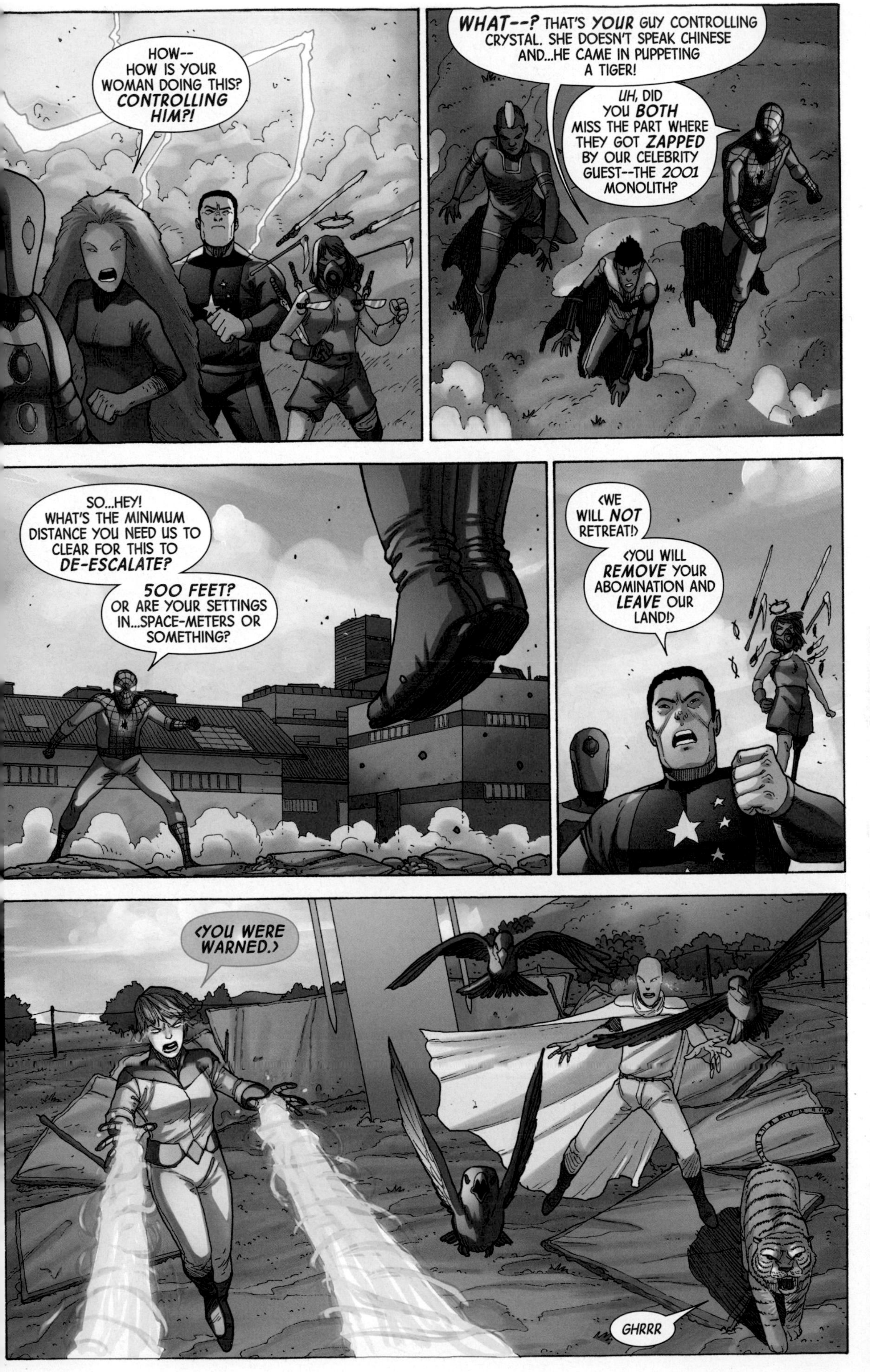
HOW-- HOW IS YOUR WOMAN DOING THIS? CONTROLLING HIM?!
WHAT--? THAT'S YOUR GUY CONTROLLING CRYSTAL. SHE DOESN'T SPEAK CHINESE AND...HE CAME IN PUPPETING A TIGER!
UH, DID YOU BOTH MISS THE PART WHERE THEY GOT ZAPPED BY OUR CELEBRITY GUEST--THE 2001 MONOLITH?
SO...HEY! WHAT'S THE MINIMUM DISTANCE YOU NEED US TO CLEAR FOR THIS TO DE-ESCALATE?
500 FEET? OR ARE YOUR SETTINGS IN...SPACE-METERS OR SOMETHING?
‹WE WILL NOT RETREAT!›
‹YOU WILL REMOVE YOUR ABOMINATION AND LEAVE OUR LAND!›
‹YOU WERE WARNED.›
GHRRR

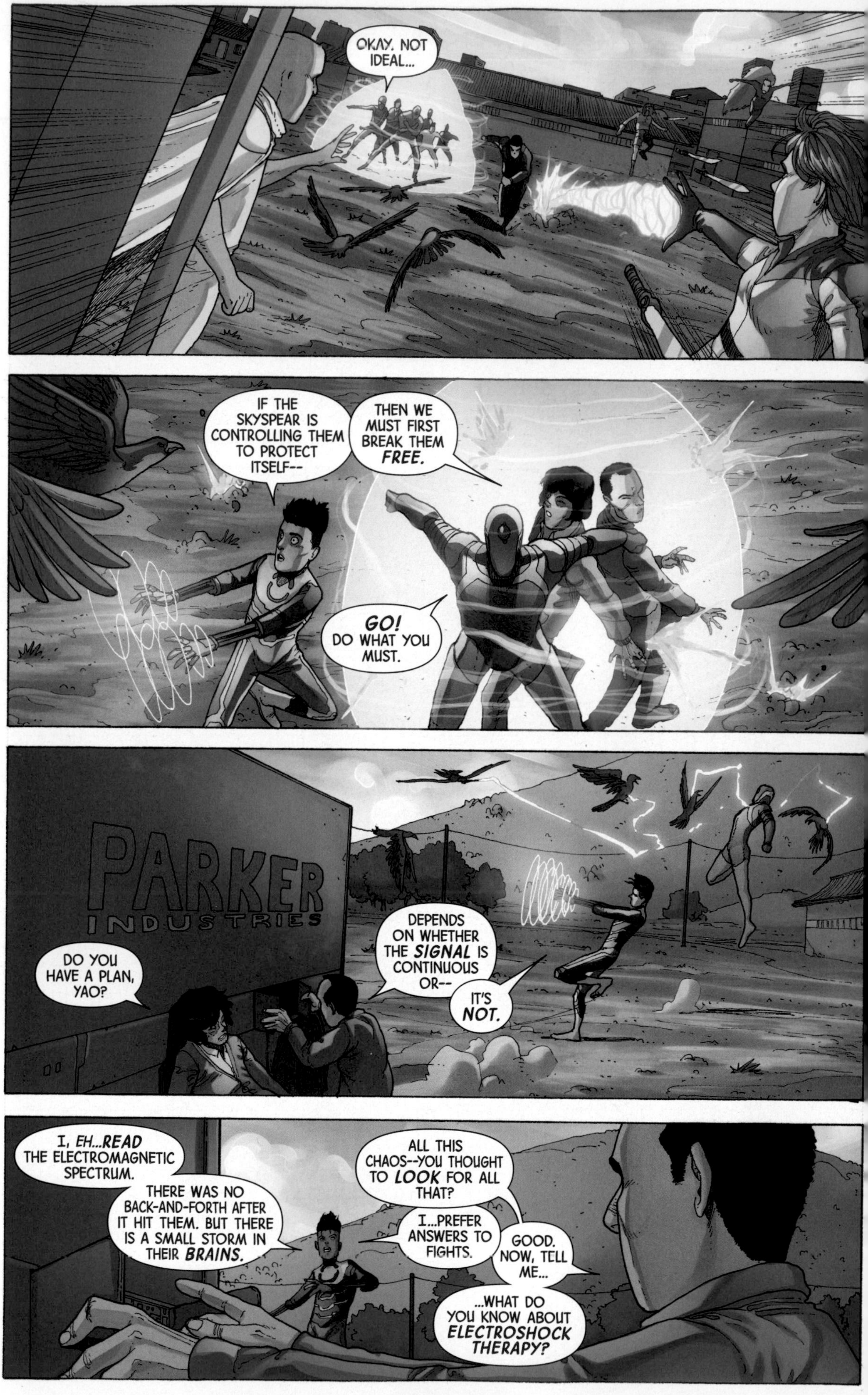
OKAY. NOT IDEAL...
IF THE SKYSPEAR IS CONTROLLING THEM TO PROTECT ITSELF--
THEN WE MUST FIRST BREAK THEM FREE.
GO! DO WHAT YOU MUST.
PARKER INDUSTRIES
DO YOU HAVE A PLAN, YAO?
DEPENDS ON WHETHER THE SIGNAL IS CONTINUOUS OR--
IT'S NOT.
I, EH...READ THE ELECTROMAGNETIC SPECTRUM.
THERE WAS NO BACK-AND-FORTH AFTER IT HIT THEM. BUT THERE IS A SMALL STORM IN THEIR BRAINS.
ALL THIS CHAOS--YOU THOUGHT TO LOOK FOR ALL THAT?
I...PREFER ANSWERS TO FIGHTS.
GOOD. NOW, TELL ME...
...WHAT DO YOU KNOW ABOUT ELECTROSHOCK THERAPY?

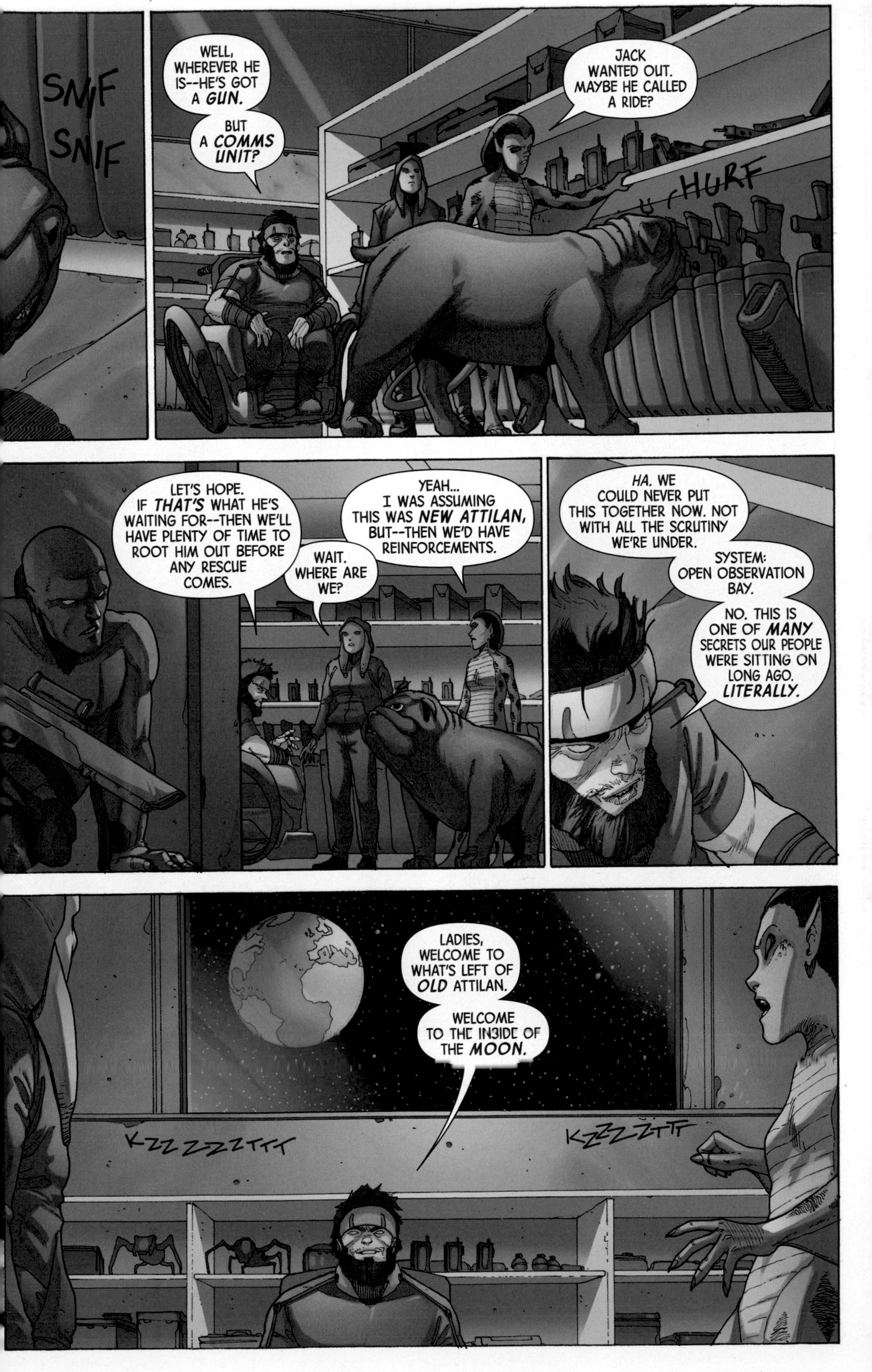
SNIF
SNIF
WELL, WHEREVER HE IS--HE'S GOT A GUN.
BUT A COMMS UNIT?
JACK WANTED OUT. MAYBE HE CALLED A RIDE?
HURF
LET'S HOPE. IF THAT'S WHAT HE'S WAITING FOR--THEN WE'LL HAVE PLENTY OF TIME TO ROOT HIM OUT BEFORE ANY RESCUE COMES.
WAIT. WHERE ARE WE?
YEAH... I WAS ASSUMING THIS WAS NEW ATTILAN, BUT--THEN WE'D HAVE REINFORCEMENTS.
HA. WE COULD NEVER PUT THIS TOGETHER NOW. NOT WITH ALL THE SCRUTINY WE'RE UNDER.
SYSTEM: OPEN OBSERVATION BAY.
NO. THIS IS ONE OF MANY SECRETS OUR PEOPLE WERE SITTING ON LONG AGO. LITERALLY.
LADIES, WELCOME TO WHAT'S LEFT OF OLD ATTILAN.
WELCOME TO THE INSIDE OF THE MOON.
KZZZZZZTTT
KZZZZTTT

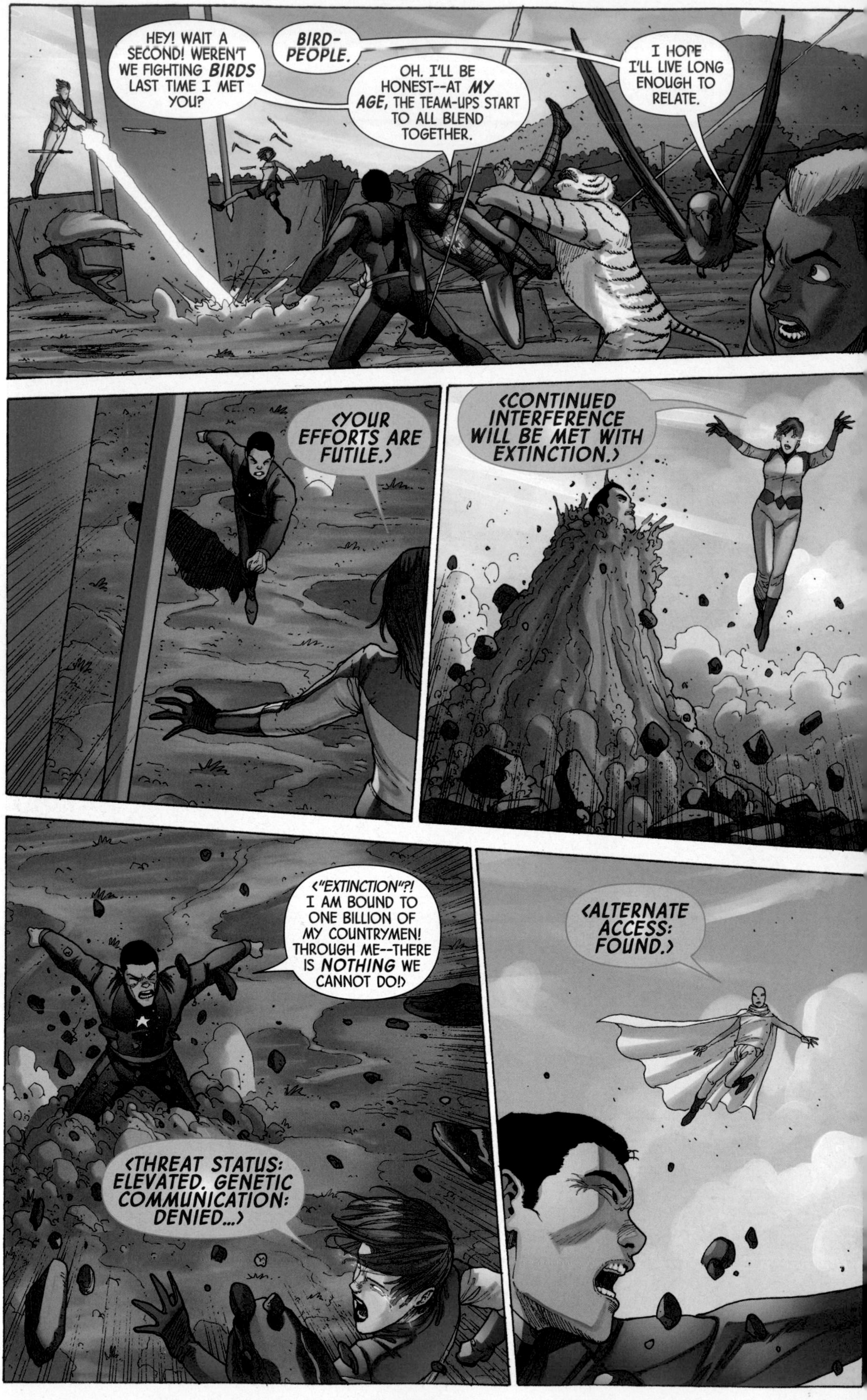

HEY! WAIT A SECOND! WEREN'T WE FIGHTING BIRDS LAST TIME I MET YOU?
BIRD-PEOPLE.
OH. I'LL BE HONEST--AT MY AGE, THE TEAM-UPS START TO ALL BLEND TOGETHER.
I HOPE I'LL LIVE LONG ENOUGH TO RELATE.
<YOUR EFFORTS ARE FUTILE.>
<CONTINUED INTERFERENCE WILL BE MET WITH EXTINCTION.>
<"EXTINCTION"?! I AM BOUND TO ONE BILLION OF MY COUNTRYMEN! THROUGH ME--THERE IS NOTHING WE CANNOT DO!>
<THREAT STATUS: ELEVATED. GENETIC COMMUNICATION: DENIED...>
<ALTERNATE ACCESS: FOUND.>

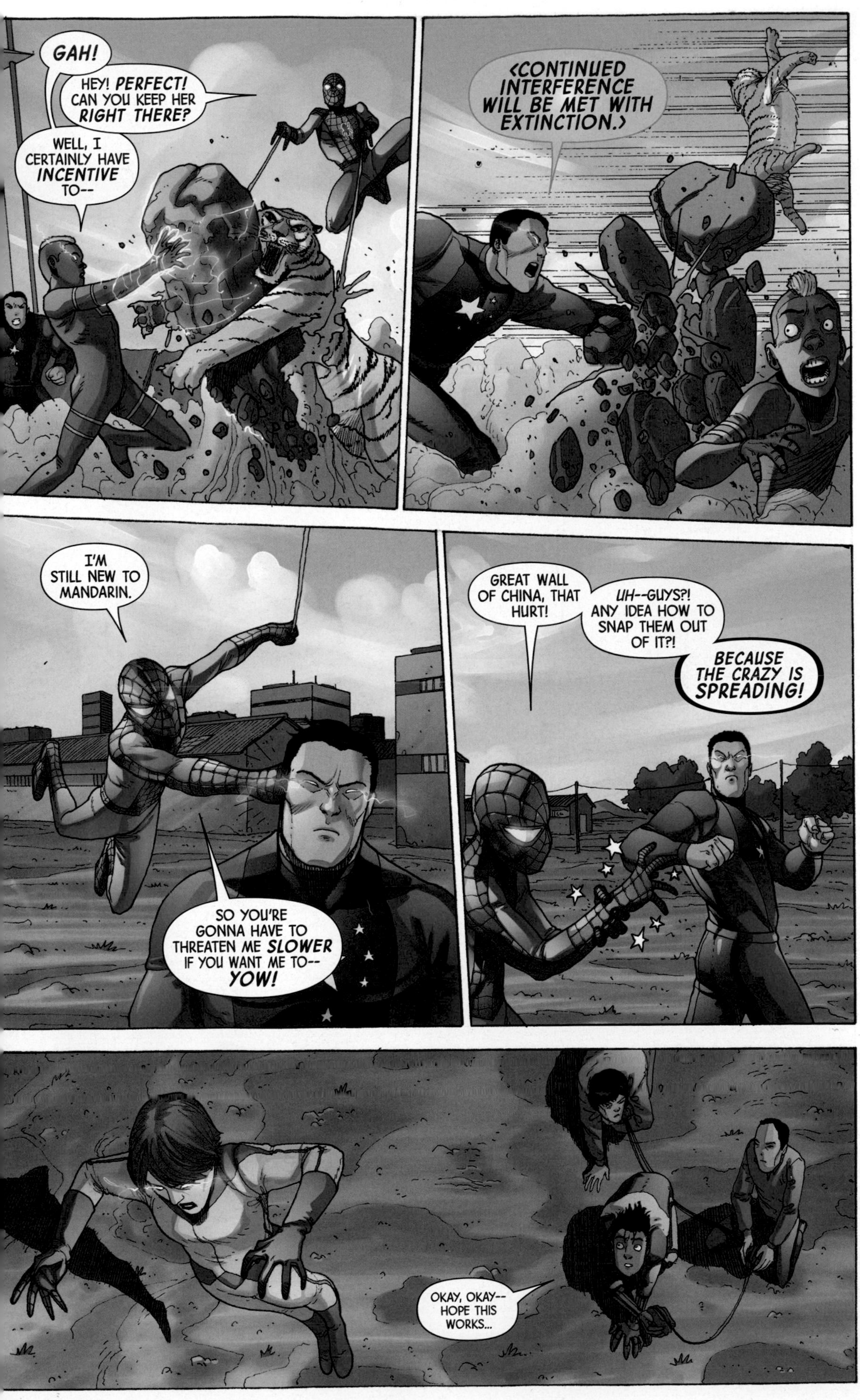
GAH!
HEY! PERFECT! CAN YOU KEEP HER RIGHT THERE?
WELL, I CERTAINLY HAVE INCENTIVE TO--
<CONTINUED INTERFERENCE WILL BE MET WITH EXTINCTION.>
I'M STILL NEW TO MANDARIN.
SO YOU'RE GONNA HAVE TO THREATEN ME SLOWER IF YOU WANT ME TO-- YOW!
GREAT WALL OF CHINA, THAT HURT!
UH--GUYS?! ANY IDEA HOW TO SNAP THEM OUT OF IT?!
BECAUSE THE CRAZY IS SPREADING!
OKAY, OKAY-- HOPE THIS WORKS...

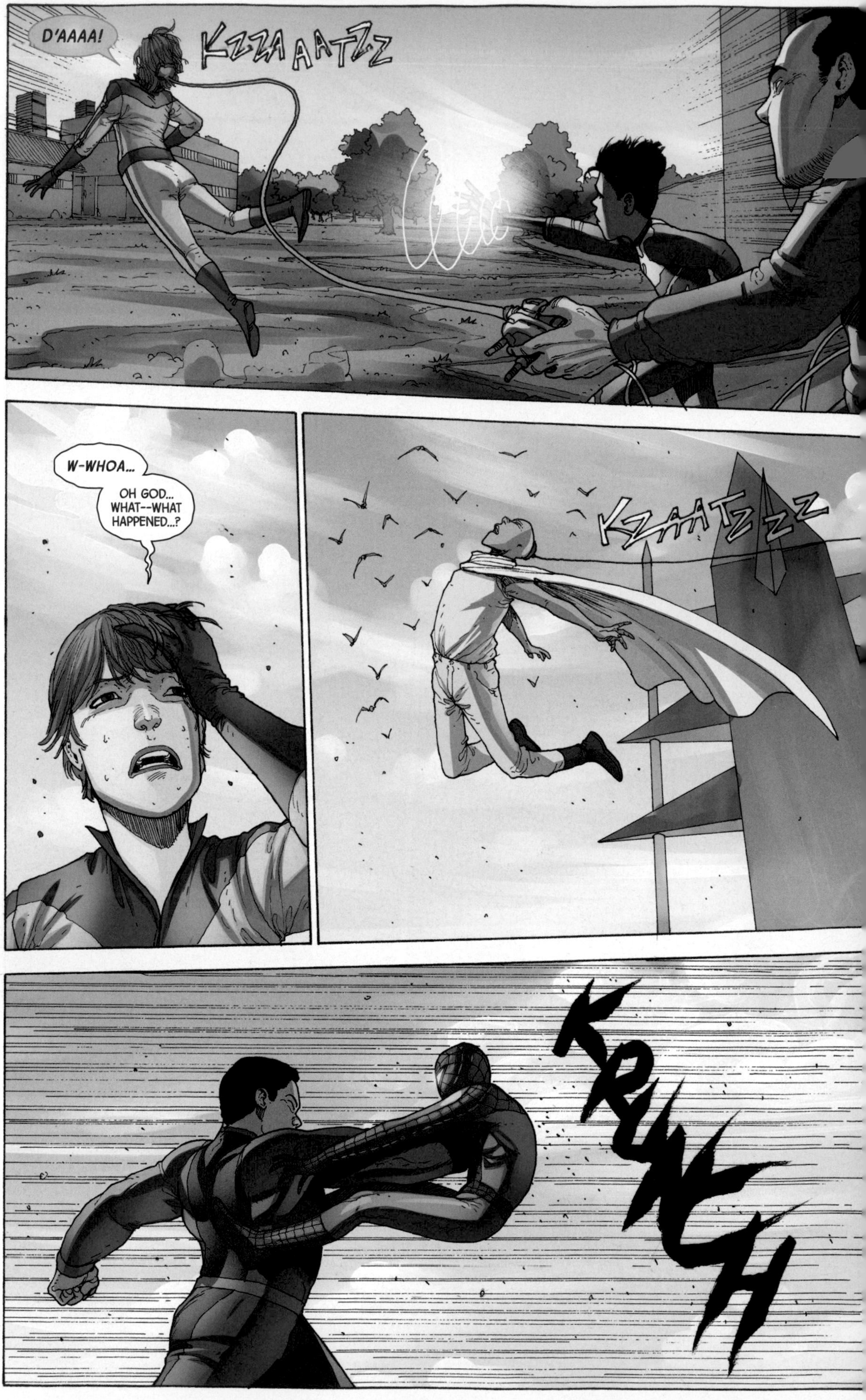
D'AAAA!
KZZAAATZZ
W-WHOA...
OH GOD... WHAT--WHAT HAPPENED...?
KZAAATZZZ
KRUNCH

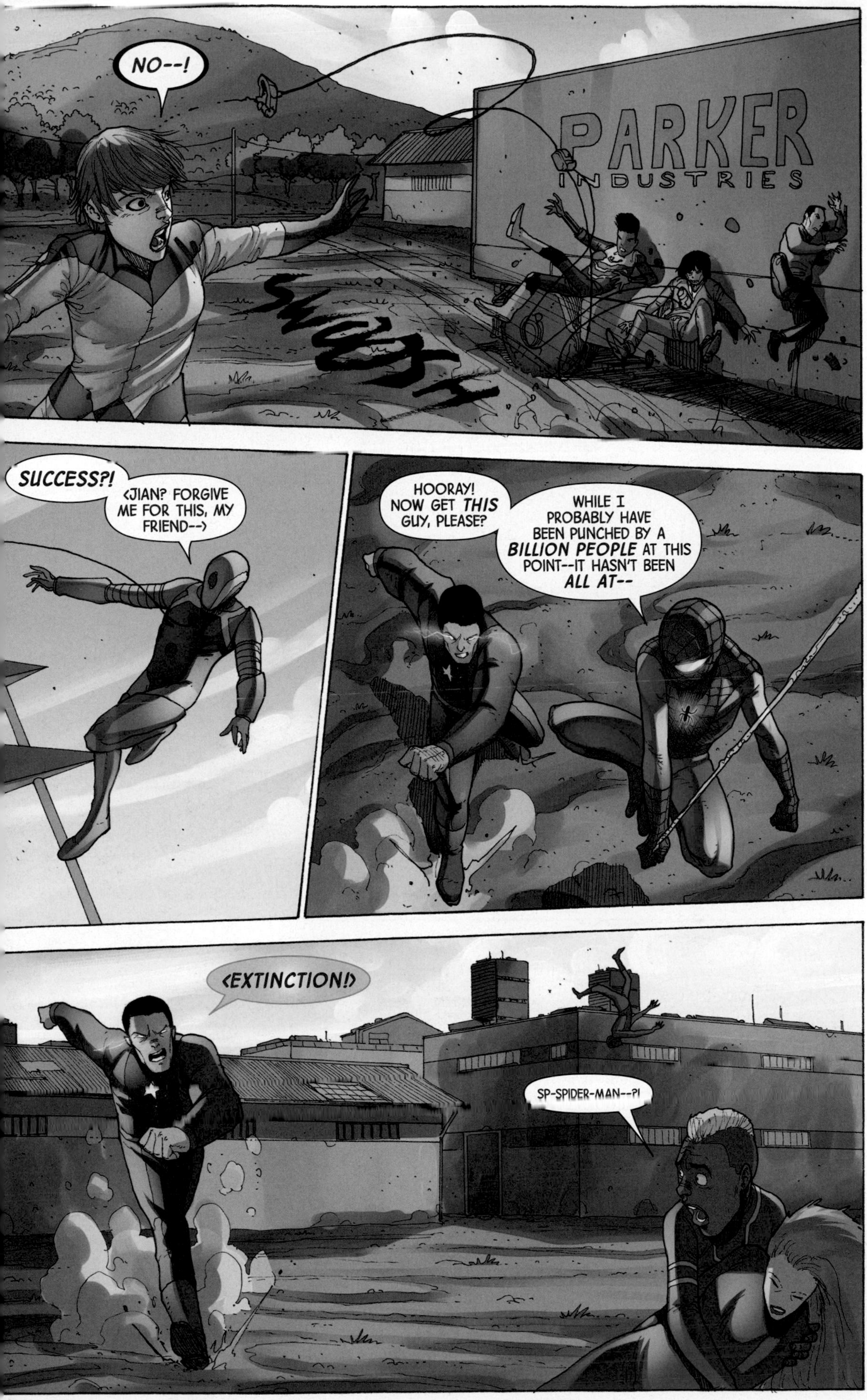
NO--!
PARKER INDUSTRIES
SWOOSH
SUCCESS?!
<JIAN? FORGIVE ME FOR THIS, MY FRIEND-->
HOORAY! NOW GET THIS GUY, PLEASE?
WHILE I PROBABLY HAVE BEEN PUNCHED BY A BILLION PEOPLE AT THIS POINT--IT HASN'T BEEN ALL AT--
<EXTINCTION!>
SP-SPIDER-MAN--?!

HURAAAGGH!

KzATZzzZTzz

IS EVERYONE... ...ALL RIGHT?!

HRNHH...?

UH... DEFINITELY NOT.

APPARENTLY I GOT PUNCHED SO HARD...I'M SEEING QUINTUPLE.

WHAT THE--?!

<DID--DID OUR DEVICE--?!>

<RELAX. THEY ARE THE COLLECTIVE MAN.>

<FIVE BROTHERS. INITIALLY ONLY ABLE TO COMBINE THEIR STRENGTH. UNTIL SOME YEARS AGO-->

<EXTINCTION!>

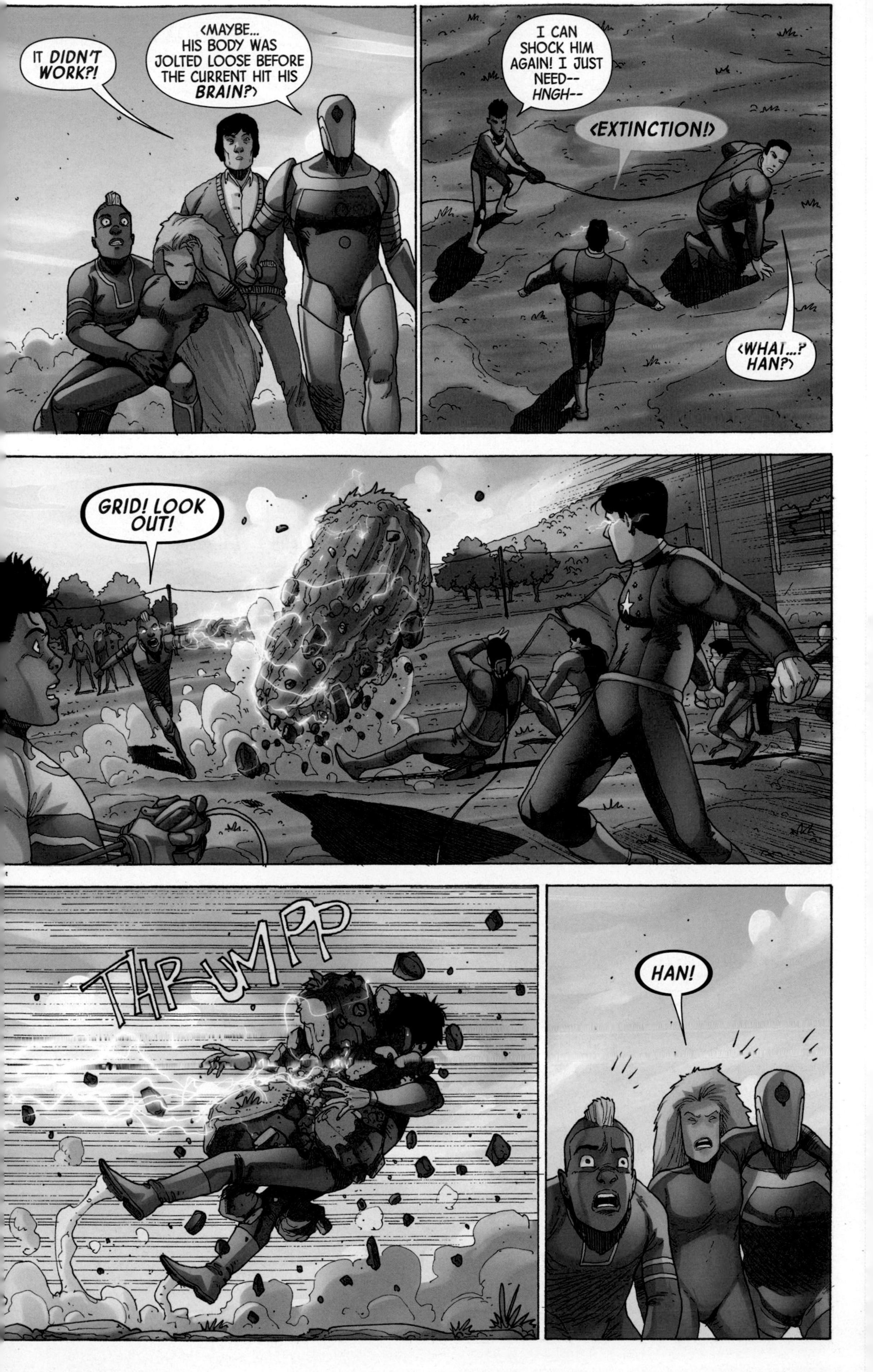
IT DIDN'T WORK?!
<MAYBE... HIS BODY WAS JOLTED LOOSE BEFORE THE CURRENT HIT HIS BRAIN?>
I CAN SHOCK HIM AGAIN! I JUST NEED-- HNGH--
<EXTINCTION!>
<WHAT...? HAN?>
GRID! LOOK OUT!
THRUMPP
HAN!

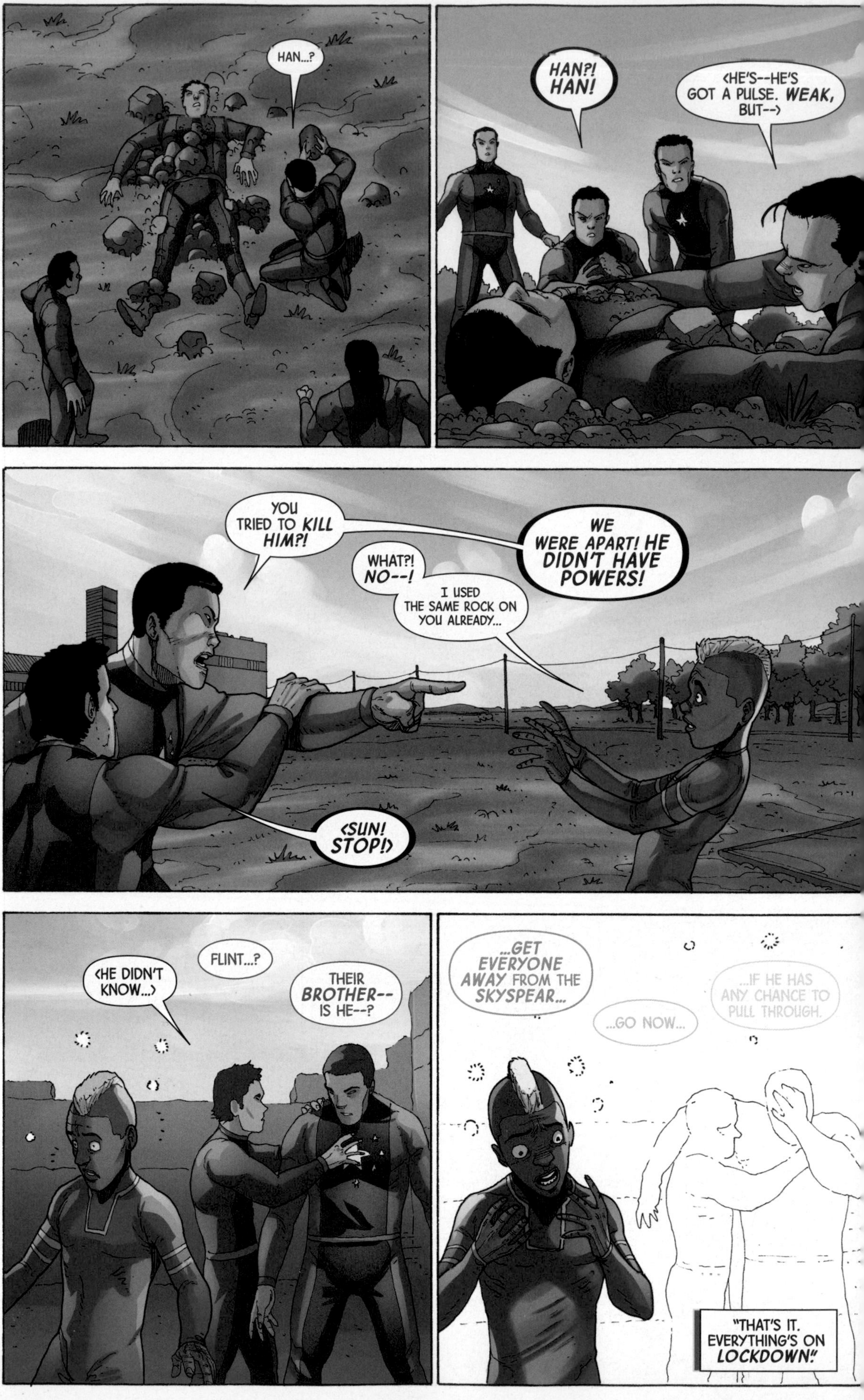
HAN...?
HAN?! HAN!
<HE'S--HE'S GOT A PULSE. WEAK, BUT-->
YOU TRIED TO KILL HIM?!
WE WERE APART! HE DIDN'T HAVE POWERS!
WHAT?! NO--!
I USED THE SAME ROCK ON YOU ALREADY...
<SUN! STOP!>
<HE DIDN'T KNOW...>
FLINT...?
THEIR BROTHER-- IS HE--?
...GET EVERYONE AWAY FROM THE SKYSPEAR...
...GO NOW...
...IF HE HAS ANY CHANCE TO PULL THROUGH.
"THAT'S IT. EVERYTHING'S ON LOCKDOWN."

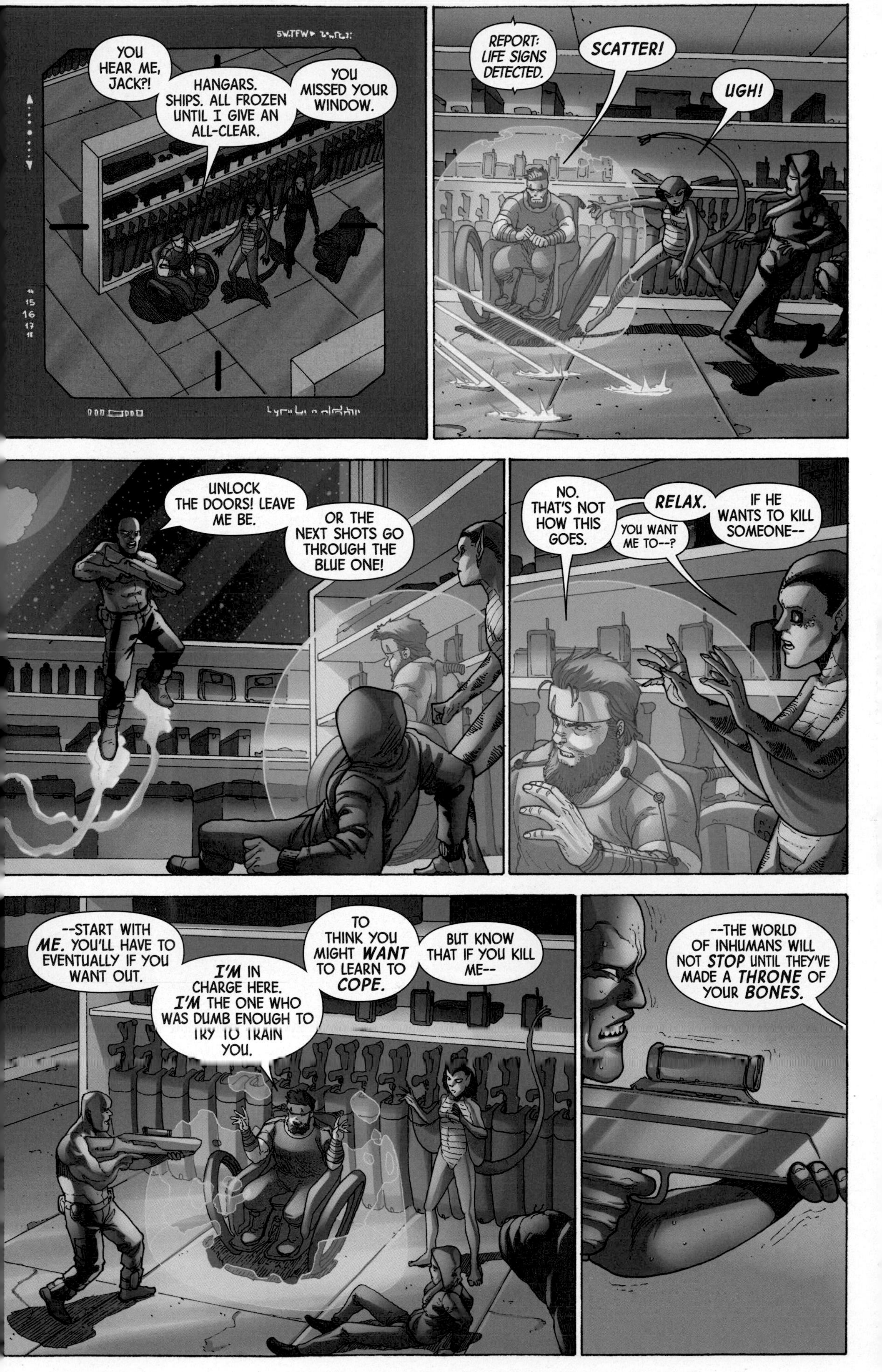
YOU HEAR ME, JACK?!
HANGARS. SHIPS. ALL FROZEN UNTIL I GIVE AN ALL-CLEAR.
YOU MISSED YOUR WINDOW.
REPORT: LIFE SIGNS DETECTED.
SCATTER!
UGH!
UNLOCK THE DOORS! LEAVE ME BE.
OR THE NEXT SHOTS GO THROUGH THE BLUE ONE!
NO. THAT'S NOT HOW THIS GOES.
RELAX.
YOU WANT ME TO--?
IF HE WANTS TO KILL SOMEONE--
--START WITH ME. YOU'LL HAVE TO EVENTUALLY IF YOU WANT OUT.
I'M IN CHARGE HERE. I'M THE ONE WHO WAS DUMB ENOUGH TO TRY TO TRAIN YOU.
TO THINK YOU MIGHT WANT TO LEARN TO COPE.
BUT KNOW THAT IF YOU KILL ME--
--THE WORLD OF INHUMANS WILL NOT STOP UNTIL THEY'VE MADE A THRONE OF YOUR BONES.

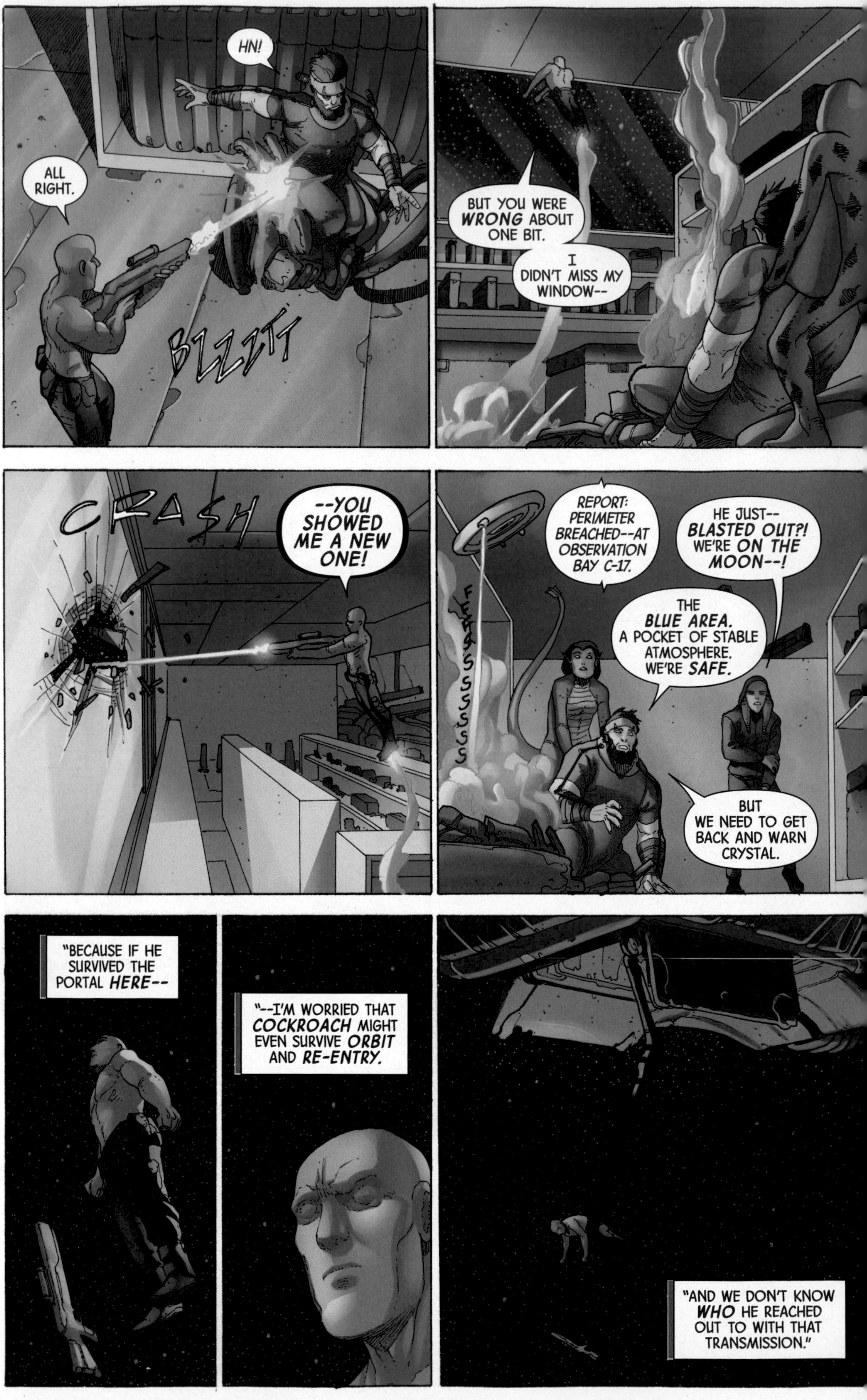
HN!
ALL RIGHT.
BZZZTT
BUT YOU WERE WRONG ABOUT ONE BIT.
I DIDN'T MISS MY WINDOW--
CRASH
--YOU SHOWED ME A NEW ONE!
REPORT: PERIMETER BREACHED--AT OBSERVATION BAY C-17.
FSSSSSSSSS
HE JUST-- BLASTED OUT?! WE'RE ON THE MOON--!
THE BLUE AREA. A POCKET OF STABLE ATMOSPHERE. WE'RE SAFE.
BUT WE NEED TO GET BACK AND WARN CRYSTAL.
"BECAUSE IF HE SURVIVED THE PORTAL HERE--
"--I'M WORRIED THAT COCKROACH MIGHT EVEN SURVIVE ORBIT AND RE-ENTRY.
"AND WE DON'T KNOW WHO HE REACHED OUT TO WITH THAT TRANSMISSION."

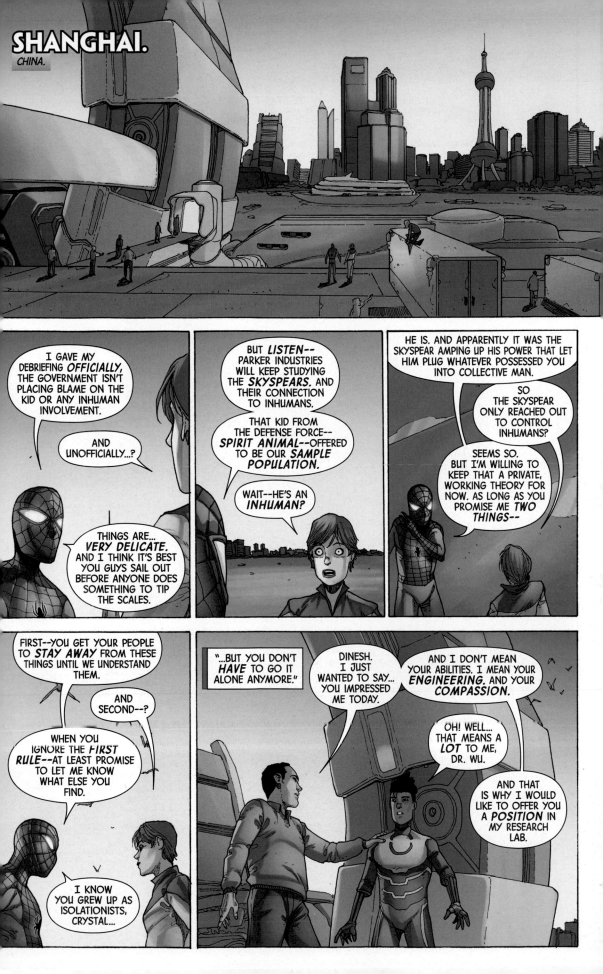

SHANGHAI.
CHINA.

I GAVE MY DEBRIEFING *OFFICIALLY*, THE GOVERNMENT ISN'T PLACING BLAME ON THE KID OR ANY INHUMAN INVOLVEMENT.

AND UNOFFICIALLY...?

THINGS ARE... *VERY DELICATE.* AND I THINK IT'S BEST YOU GUYS SAIL OUT BEFORE ANYONE DOES SOMETHING TO TIP THE SCALES.

BUT *LISTEN*-- PARKER INDUSTRIES WILL KEEP STUDYING THE *SKYSPEARS.* AND THEIR CONNECTION TO INHUMANS.

THAT KID FROM THE DEFENSE FORCE-- *SPIRIT ANIMAL*--OFFERED TO BE OUR *SAMPLE POPULATION.*

WAIT--HE'S AN *INHUMAN?*

HE IS. AND APPARENTLY IT WAS THE SKYSPEAR AMPING UP HIS POWER THAT LET HIM PLUG WHATEVER POSSESSED YOU INTO COLLECTIVE MAN.

SO THE SKYSPEAR ONLY REACHED OUT TO CONTROL INHUMANS?

SEEMS SO. BUT I'M WILLING TO KEEP THAT A PRIVATE, WORKING THEORY FOR NOW. AS LONG AS YOU PROMISE ME *TWO THINGS*--

FIRST--YOU GET YOUR PEOPLE TO *STAY AWAY* FROM THESE THINGS UNTIL WE UNDERSTAND THEM.

AND SECOND--?

WHEN YOU IGNORE THE *FIRST RULE*--AT LEAST PROMISE TO LET ME KNOW WHAT ELSE YOU FIND.

I KNOW YOU GREW UP AS ISOLATIONISTS, CRYSTAL...

"...BUT YOU DON'T *HAVE* TO GO IT ALONE ANYMORE."

DINESH. I JUST WANTED TO SAY... YOU IMPRESSED ME TODAY.

AND I DON'T MEAN YOUR ABILITIES. I MEAN YOUR *ENGINEERING.* AND YOUR *COMPASSION.*

OH! WELL... THAT MEANS A *LOT* TO ME, DR. WU.

AND THAT IS WHY I WOULD LIKE TO OFFER YOU A *POSITION* IN MY RESEARCH LAB.

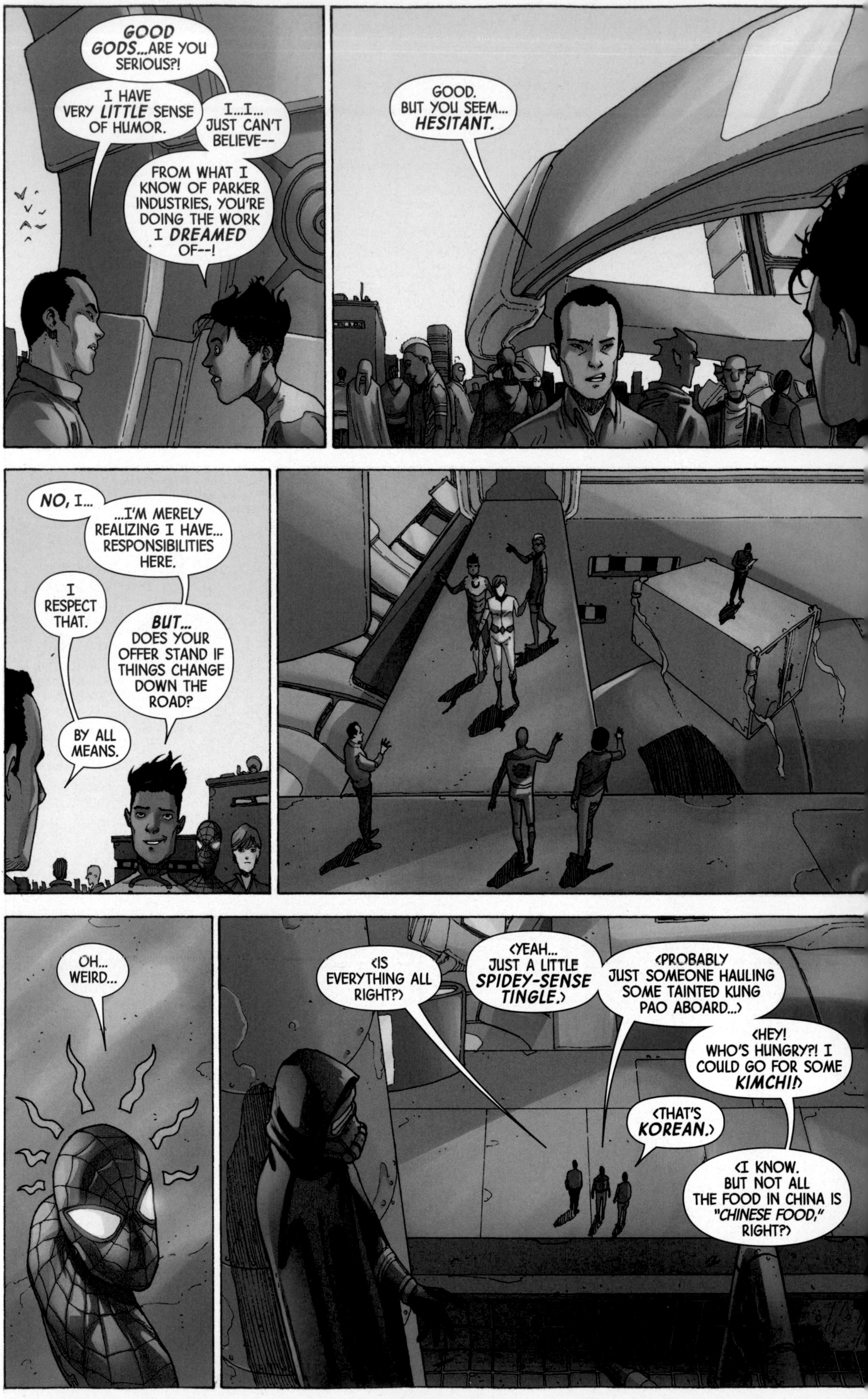
GOOD GODS...ARE YOU SERIOUS?!
I HAVE VERY LITTLE SENSE OF HUMOR.
I...I... JUST CAN'T BELIEVE--
FROM WHAT I KNOW OF PARKER INDUSTRIES, YOU'RE DOING THE WORK I DREAMED OF--!
GOOD. BUT YOU SEEM... HESITANT.
NO, I...
...I'M MERELY REALIZING I HAVE... RESPONSIBILITIES HERE.
I RESPECT THAT.
BUT... DOES YOUR OFFER STAND IF THINGS CHANGE DOWN THE ROAD?
BY ALL MEANS.
OH... WEIRD...
<IS EVERYTHING ALL RIGHT?>
<YEAH... JUST A LITTLE SPIDEY-SENSE TINGLE.>
<PROBABLY JUST SOMEONE HAULING SOME TAINTED KUNG PAO ABOARD...>
<HEY! WHO'S HUNGRY?! I COULD GO FOR SOME KIMCHI!>
<THAT'S KOREAN.>
<I KNOW. BUT NOT ALL THE FOOD IN CHINA IS "CHINESE FOOD," RIGHT?>

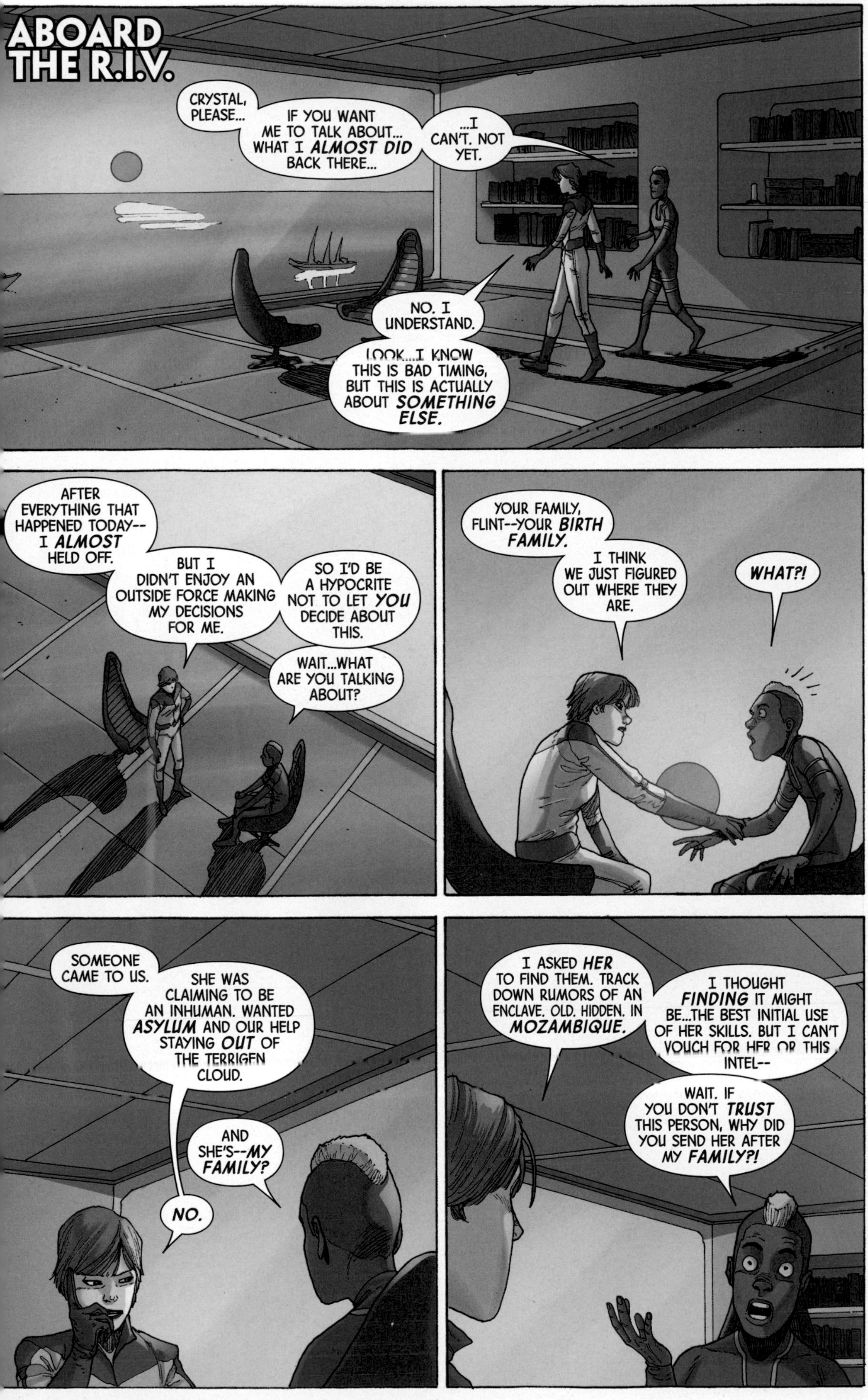
ABOARD THE R.I.V.
CRYSTAL, PLEASE...
IF YOU WANT ME TO TALK ABOUT... WHAT I ALMOST DID BACK THERE...
...I CAN'T. NOT YET.
NO. I UNDERSTAND.
LOOK...I KNOW THIS IS BAD TIMING, BUT THIS IS ACTUALLY ABOUT SOMETHING ELSE.
AFTER EVERYTHING THAT HAPPENED TODAY-- I ALMOST HELD OFF.
BUT I DIDN'T ENJOY AN OUTSIDE FORCE MAKING MY DECISIONS FOR ME.
SO I'D BE A HYPOCRITE NOT TO LET YOU DECIDE ABOUT THIS.
WAIT...WHAT ARE YOU TALKING ABOUT?
YOUR FAMILY, FLINT--YOUR BIRTH FAMILY.
I THINK WE JUST FIGURED OUT WHERE THEY ARE.
WHAT?!
SOMEONE CAME TO US.
SHE WAS CLAIMING TO BE AN INHUMAN. WANTED ASYLUM AND OUR HELP STAYING OUT OF THE TERRIGEN CLOUD.
AND SHE'S--MY FAMILY?
NO.
I ASKED HER TO FIND THEM. TRACK DOWN RUMORS OF AN ENCLAVE. OLD. HIDDEN. IN MOZAMBIQUE.
I THOUGHT FINDING IT MIGHT BE...THE BEST INITIAL USE OF HER SKILLS. BUT I CAN'T VOUCH FOR HER OR THIS INTEL--
WAIT. IF YOU DON'T TRUST THIS PERSON, WHY DID YOU SEND HER AFTER MY FAMILY?!

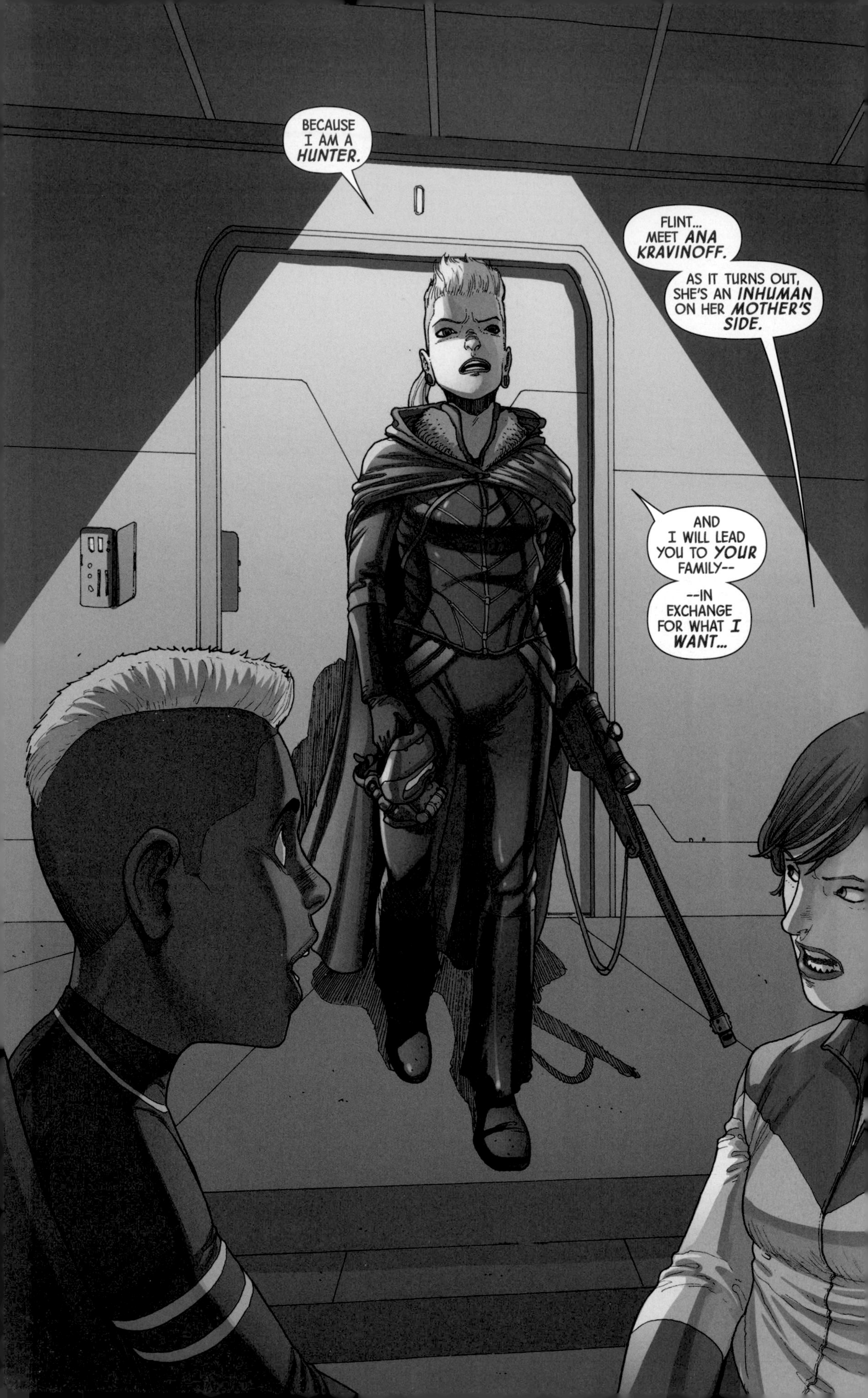
BECAUSE I AM A HUNTER.
FLINT... MEET ANA KRAVINOFF.
AS IT TURNS OUT, SHE'S AN INHUMAN ON HER MOTHER'S SIDE.
AND I WILL LEAD YOU TO YOUR FAMILY--
--IN EXCHANGE FOR WHAT I WANT...

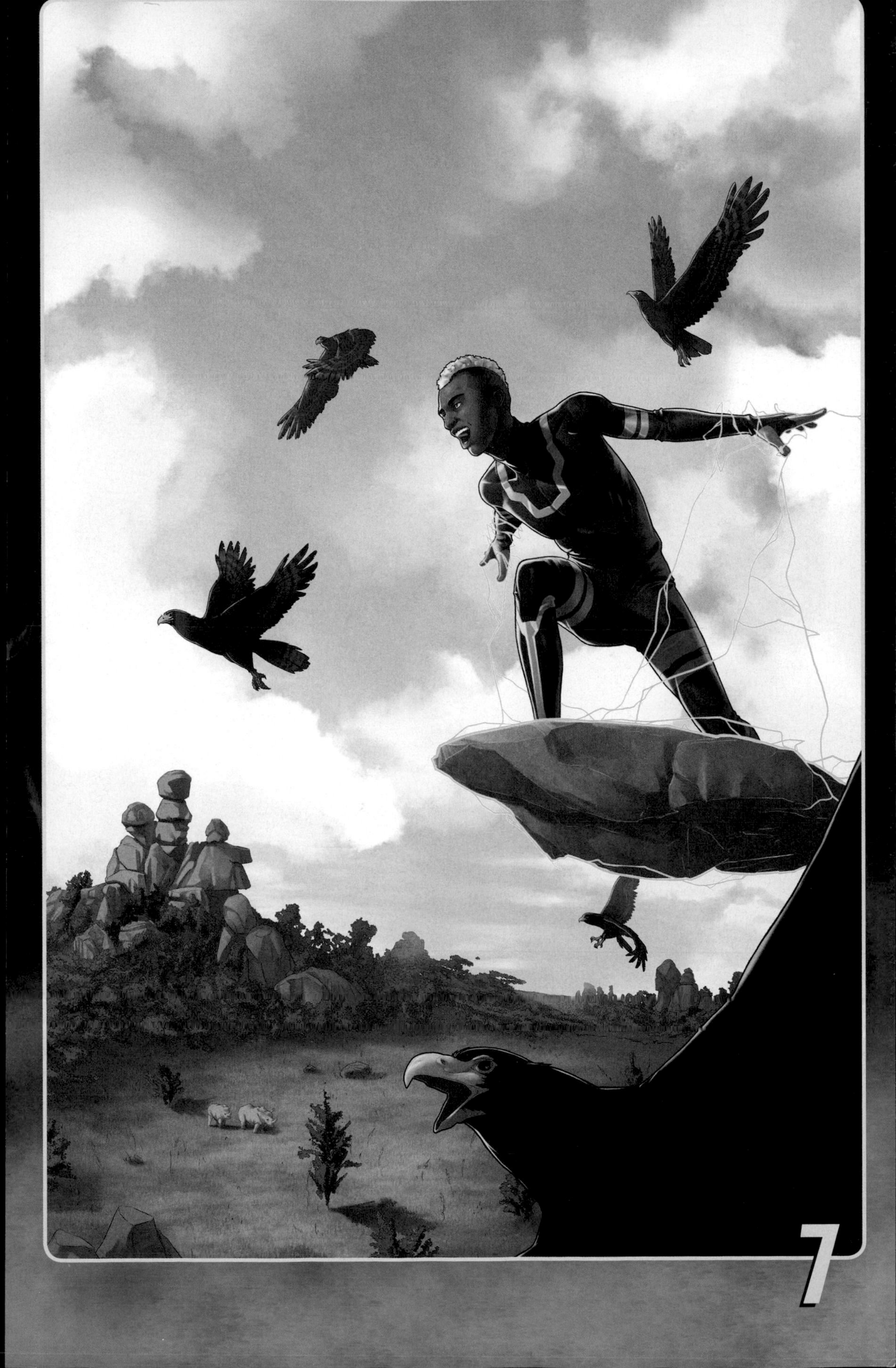

7

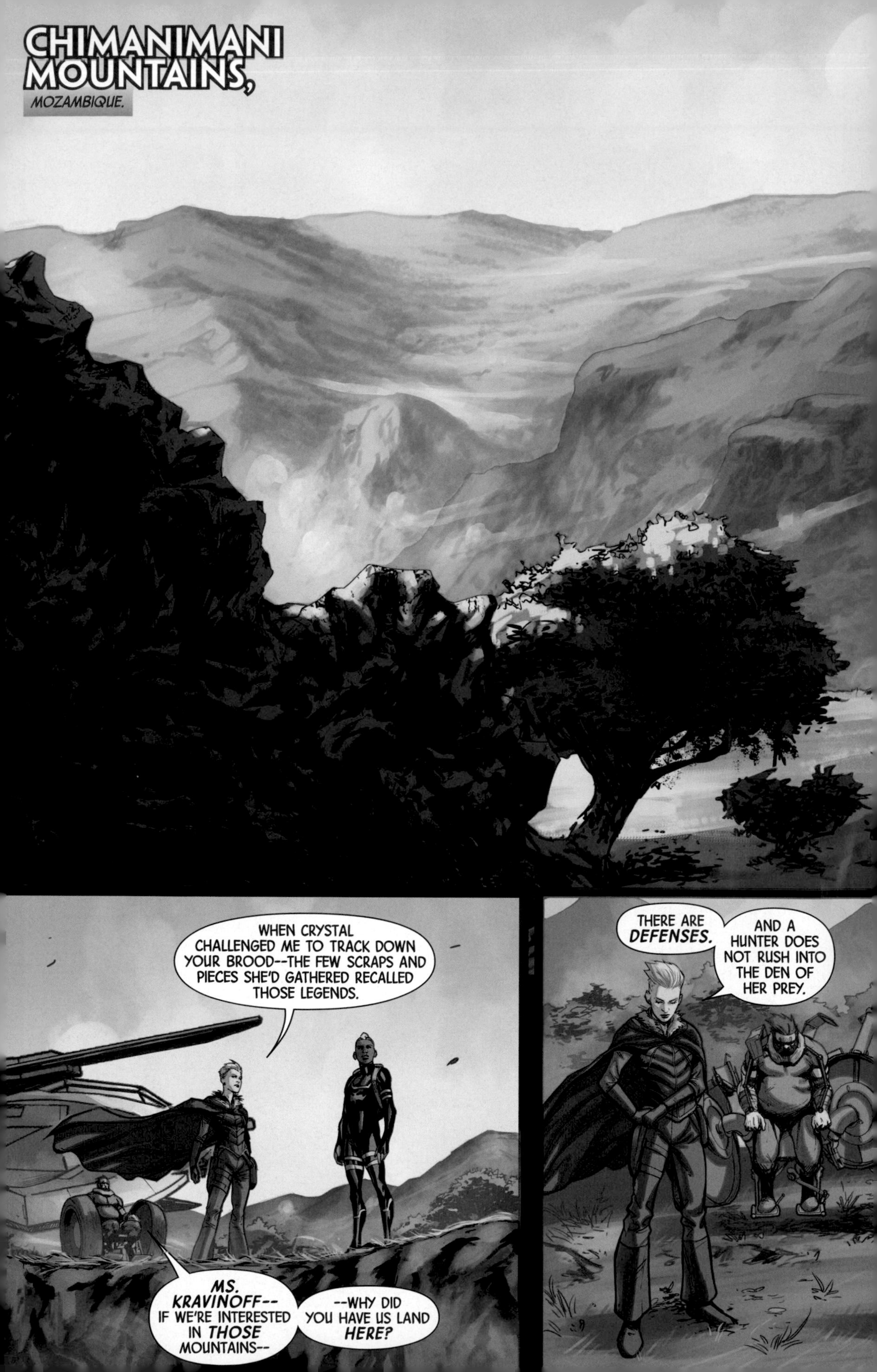
CHIMANIMANI MOUNTAINS,
MOZAMBIQUE.
WHEN CRYSTAL CHALLENGED ME TO TRACK DOWN YOUR BROOD--THE FEW SCRAPS AND PIECES SHE'D GATHERED RECALLED THOSE LEGENDS.
MS. KRAVINOFF-- IF WE'RE INTERESTED IN THOSE MOUNTAINS--
--WHY DID YOU HAVE US LAND HERE?
THERE ARE DEFENSES.
AND A HUNTER DOES NOT RUSH INTO THE DEN OF HER PREY.

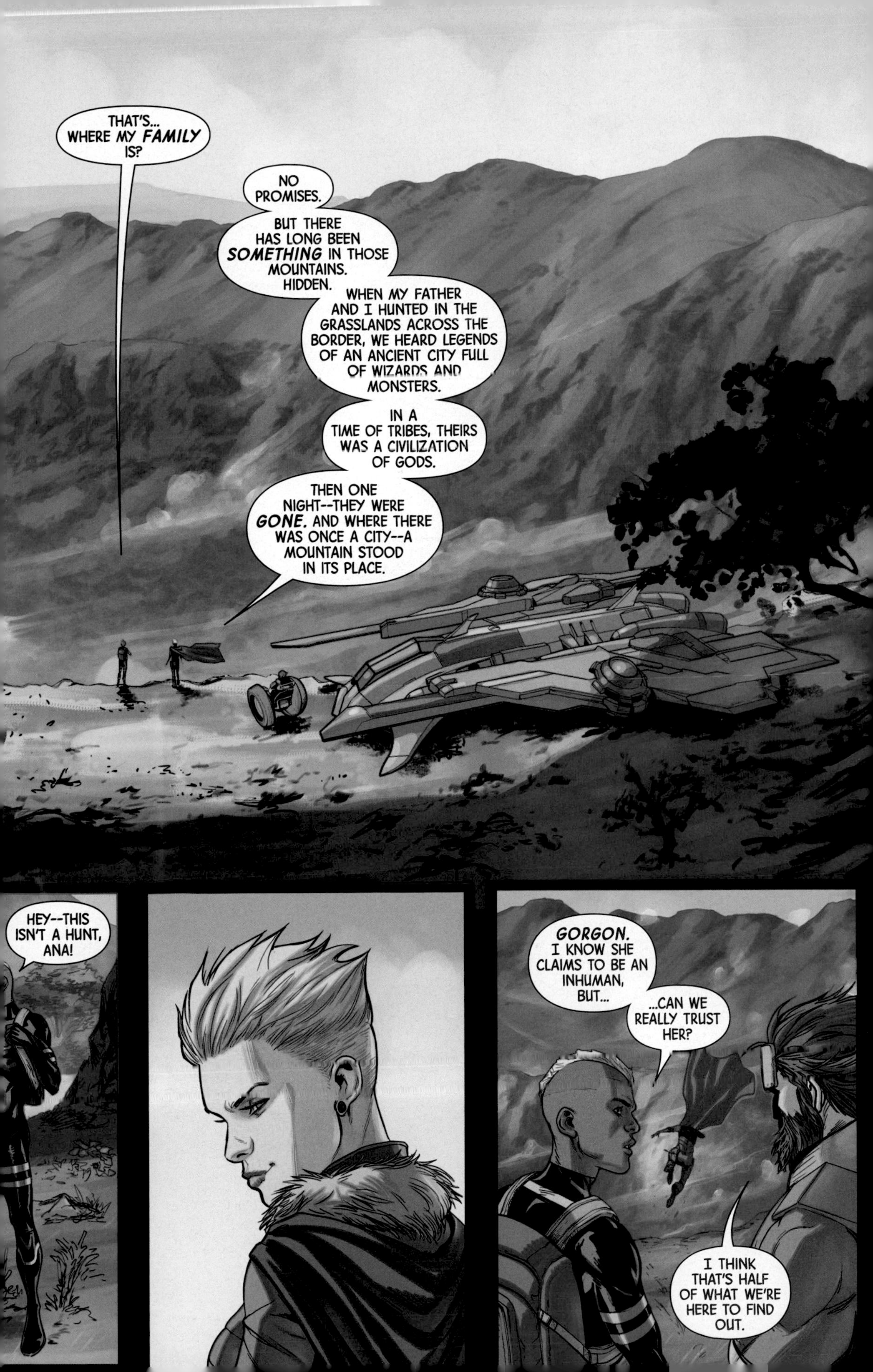
THAT'S... WHERE MY FAMILY IS?
NO PROMISES.
BUT THERE HAS LONG BEEN SOMETHING IN THOSE MOUNTAINS. HIDDEN.
WHEN MY FATHER AND I HUNTED IN THE GRASSLANDS ACROSS THE BORDER, WE HEARD LEGENDS OF AN ANCIENT CITY FULL OF WIZARDS AND MONSTERS.
IN A TIME OF TRIBES, THEIRS WAS A CIVILIZATION OF GODS.
THEN ONE NIGHT--THEY WERE GONE. AND WHERE THERE WAS ONCE A CITY--A MOUNTAIN STOOD IN ITS PLACE.
HEY--THIS ISN'T A HUNT, ANA!
GORGON. I KNOW SHE CLAIMS TO BE AN INHUMAN, BUT...
...CAN WE REALLY TRUST HER?
I THINK THAT'S HALF OF WHAT WE'RE HERE TO FIND OUT.

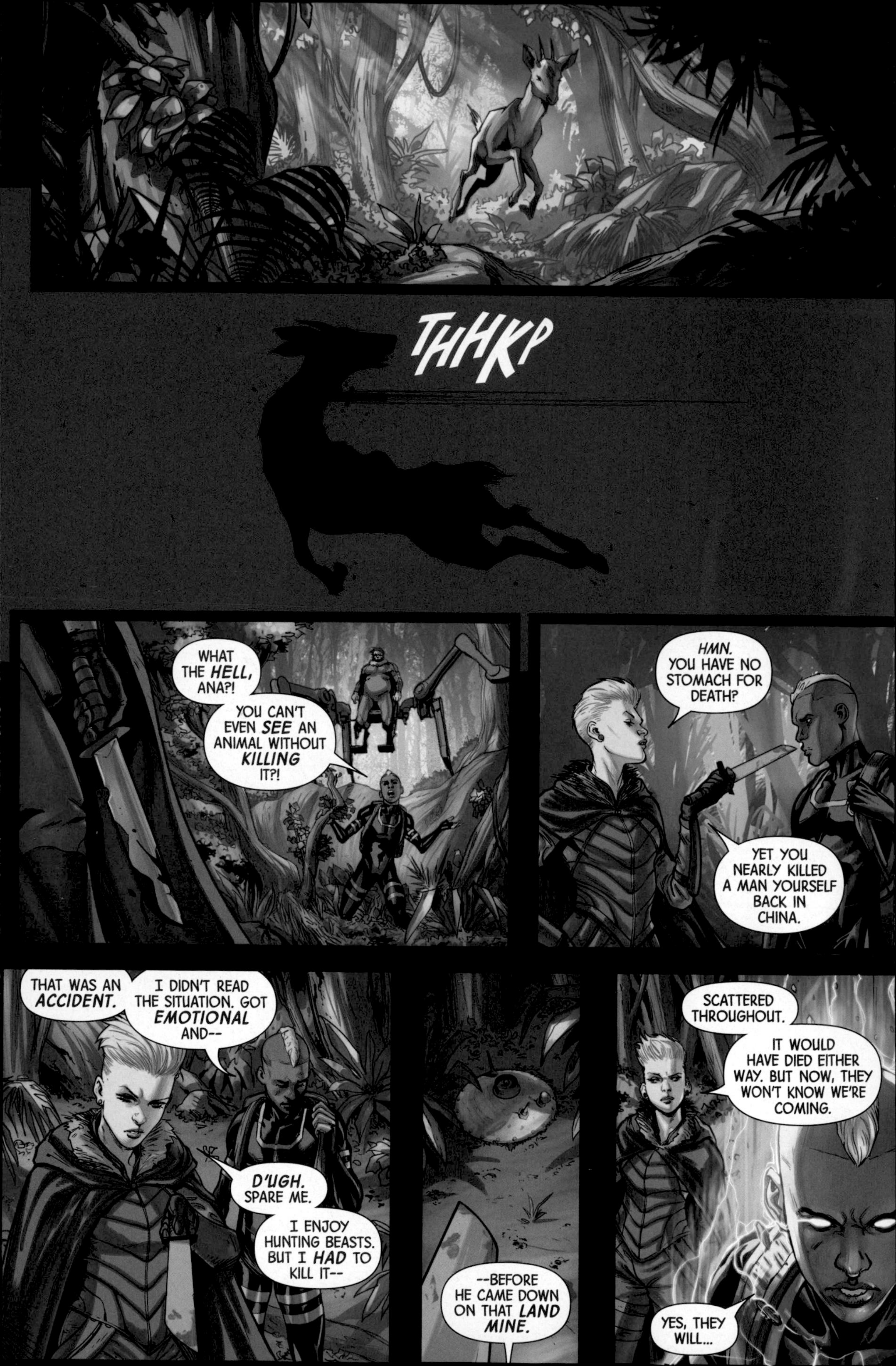
THHKP
WHAT THE HELL, ANA?!
YOU CAN'T EVEN SEE AN ANIMAL WITHOUT KILLING IT?!
HMN. YOU HAVE NO STOMACH FOR DEATH?
YET YOU NEARLY KILLED A MAN YOURSELF BACK IN CHINA.
THAT WAS AN ACCIDENT.
I DIDN'T READ THE SITUATION. GOT EMOTIONAL AND--
D'UGH. SPARE ME.
I ENJOY HUNTING BEASTS. BUT I HAD TO KILL IT--
--BEFORE HE CAME DOWN ON THAT LAND MINE.
SCATTERED THROUGHOUT.
IT WOULD HAVE DIED EITHER WAY. BUT NOW, THEY WON'T KNOW WE'RE COMING.
YES, THEY WILL...

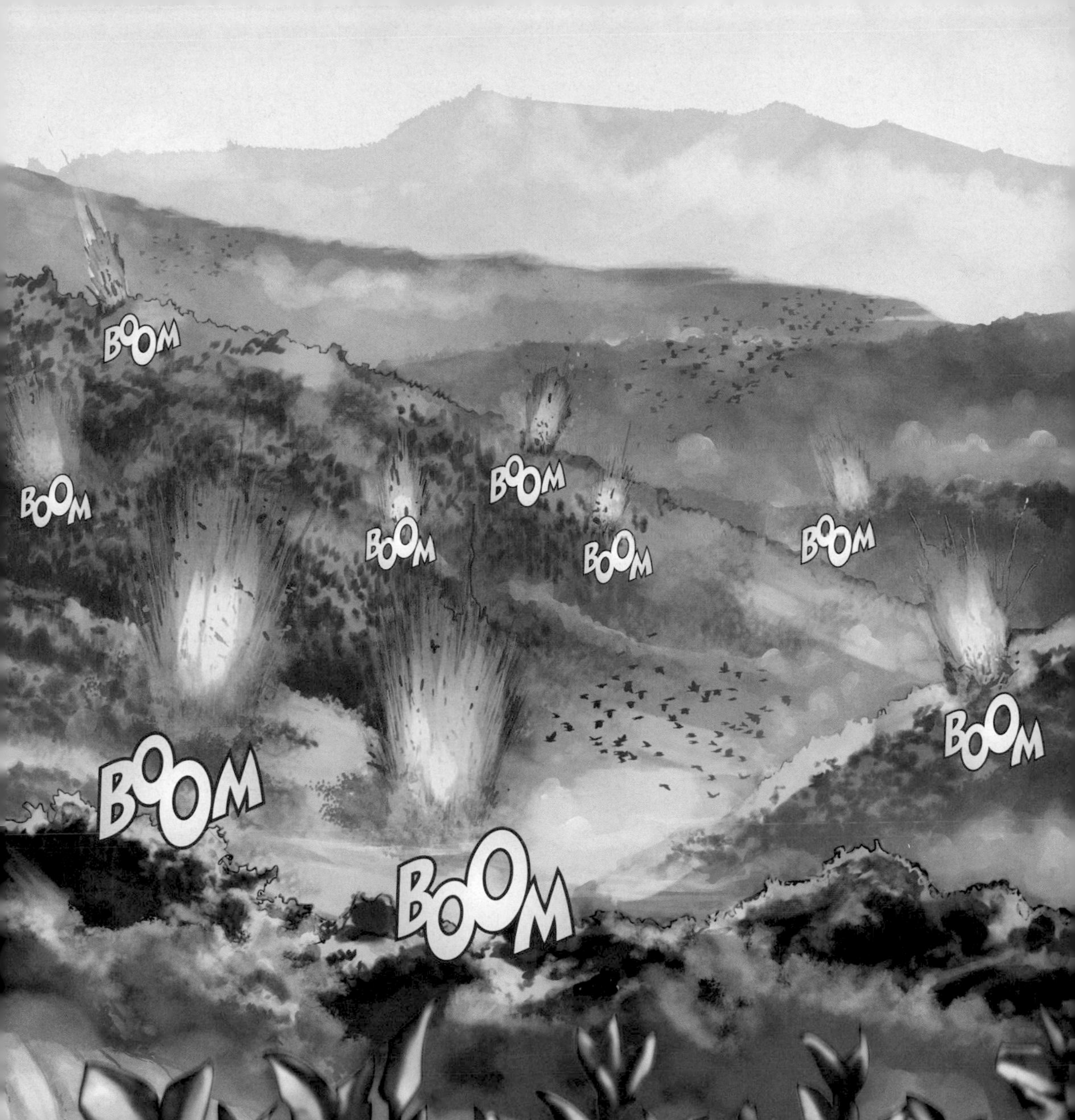
BOOM
BOOM
BOOM
BOOM
BOOM
BOOM
BOOM
BOOM
BOOM
BOOM

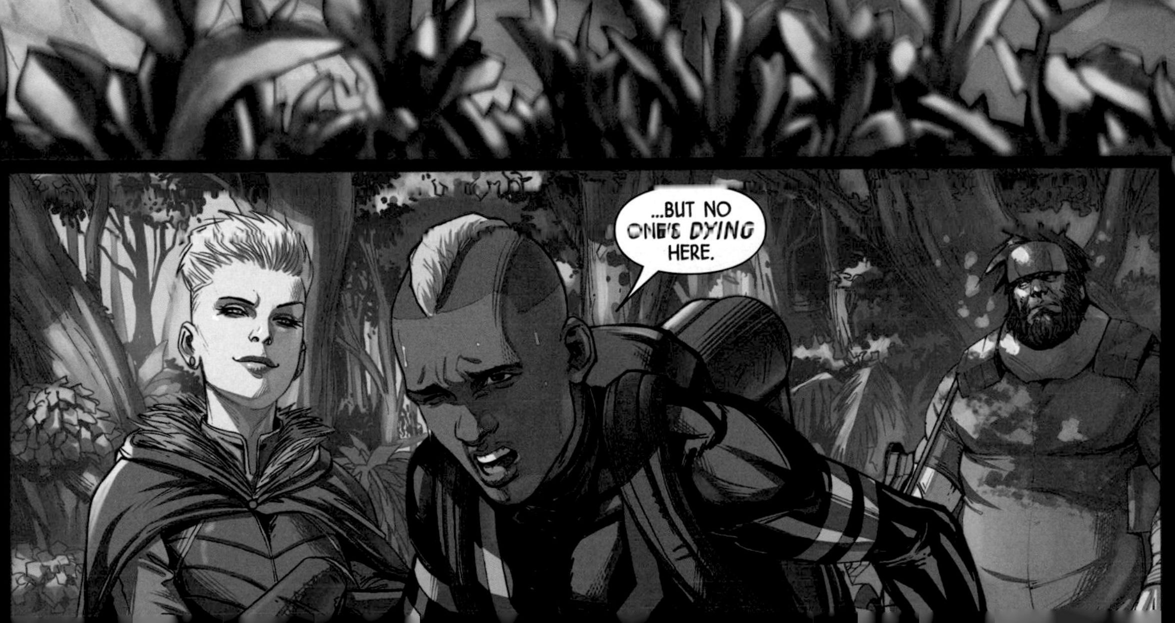
...BUT NO ONE'S DYING HERE.

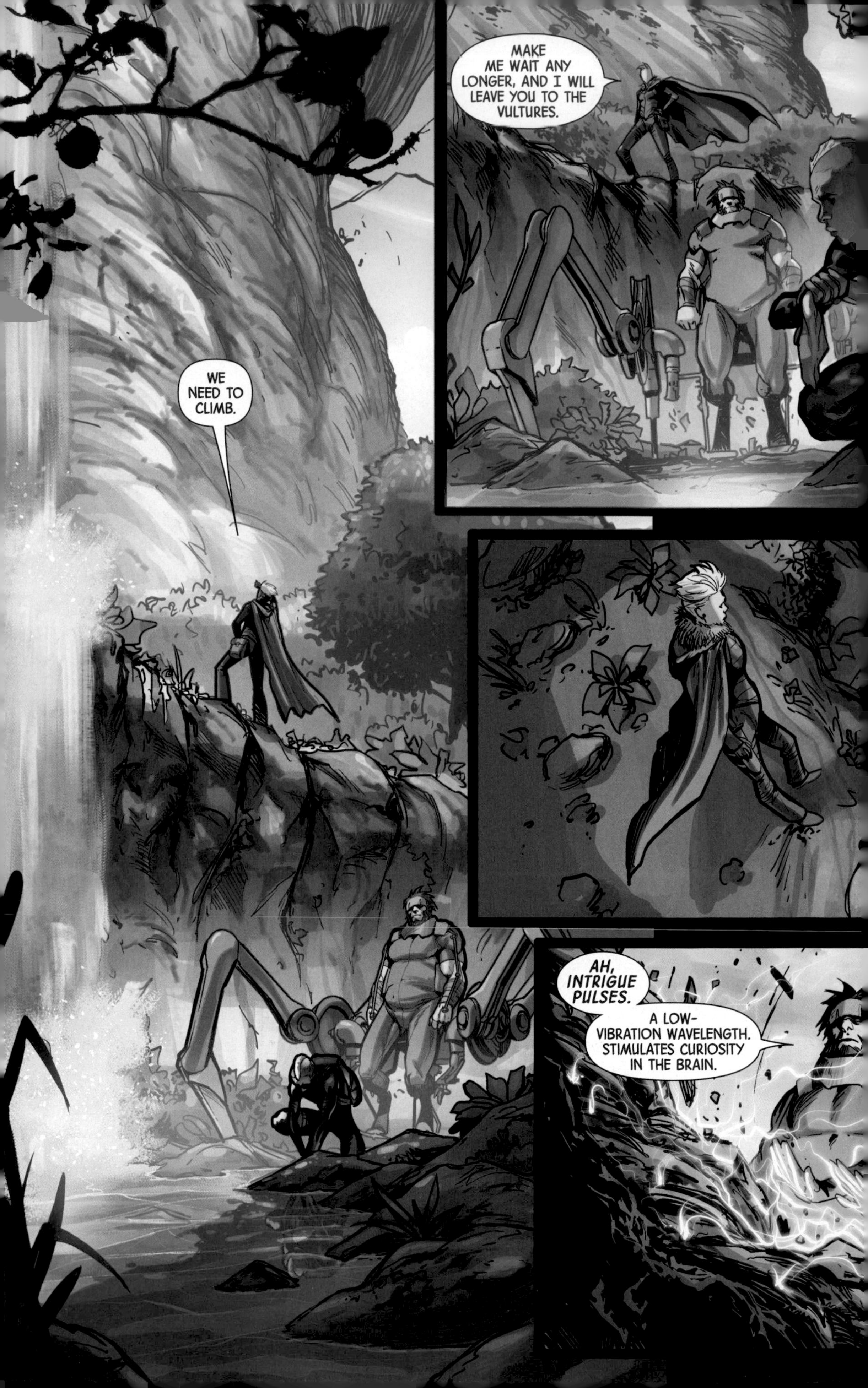
WE NEED TO CLIMB.
MAKE ME WAIT ANY LONGER, AND I WILL LEAVE YOU TO THE VULTURES.
AH, INTRIGUE PULSES.
A LOW-VIBRATION WAVELENGTH. STIMULATES CURIOSITY IN THE BRAIN.

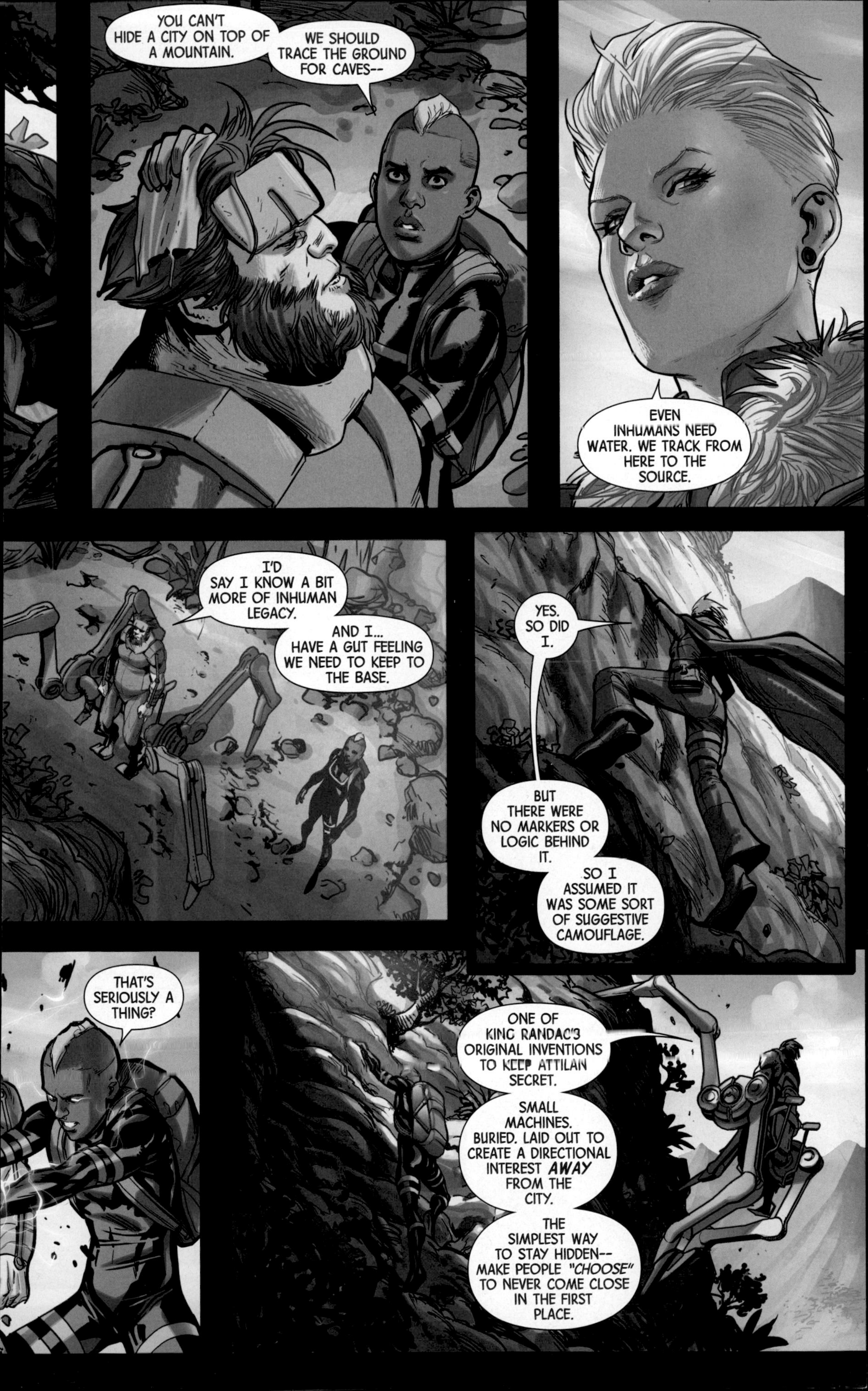
YOU CAN'T HIDE A CITY ON TOP OF A MOUNTAIN.
WE SHOULD TRACE THE GROUND FOR CAVES--
EVEN INHUMANS NEED WATER. WE TRACK FROM HERE TO THE SOURCE.
I'D SAY I KNOW A BIT MORE OF INHUMAN LEGACY.
AND I... HAVE A GUT FEELING WE NEED TO KEEP TO THE BASE.
YES. SO DID I.
BUT THERE WERE NO MARKERS OR LOGIC BEHIND IT.
SO I ASSUMED IT WAS SOME SORT OF SUGGESTIVE CAMOUFLAGE.
THAT'S SERIOUSLY A THING?
ONE OF KING RANDAC'S ORIGINAL INVENTIONS TO KEEP ATTILAN SECRET.
SMALL MACHINES. BURIED. LAID OUT TO CREATE A DIRECTIONAL INTEREST AWAY FROM THE CITY.
THE SIMPLEST WAY TO STAY HIDDEN-- MAKE PEOPLE "CHOOSE" TO NEVER COME CLOSE IN THE FIRST PLACE.

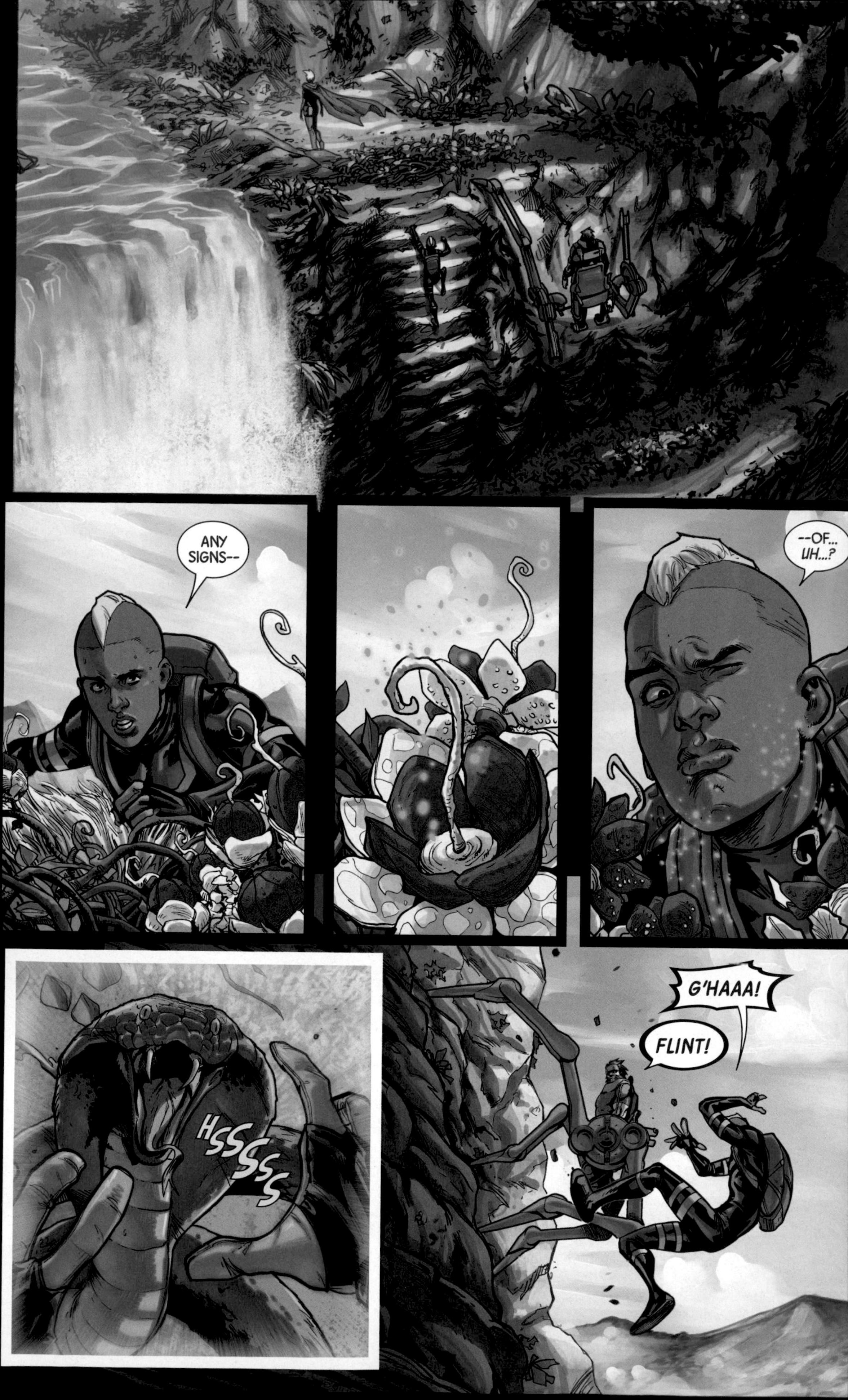
ANY SIGNS--
--OF... UH...?
HSSSSS
G'HAAA!
FLINT!

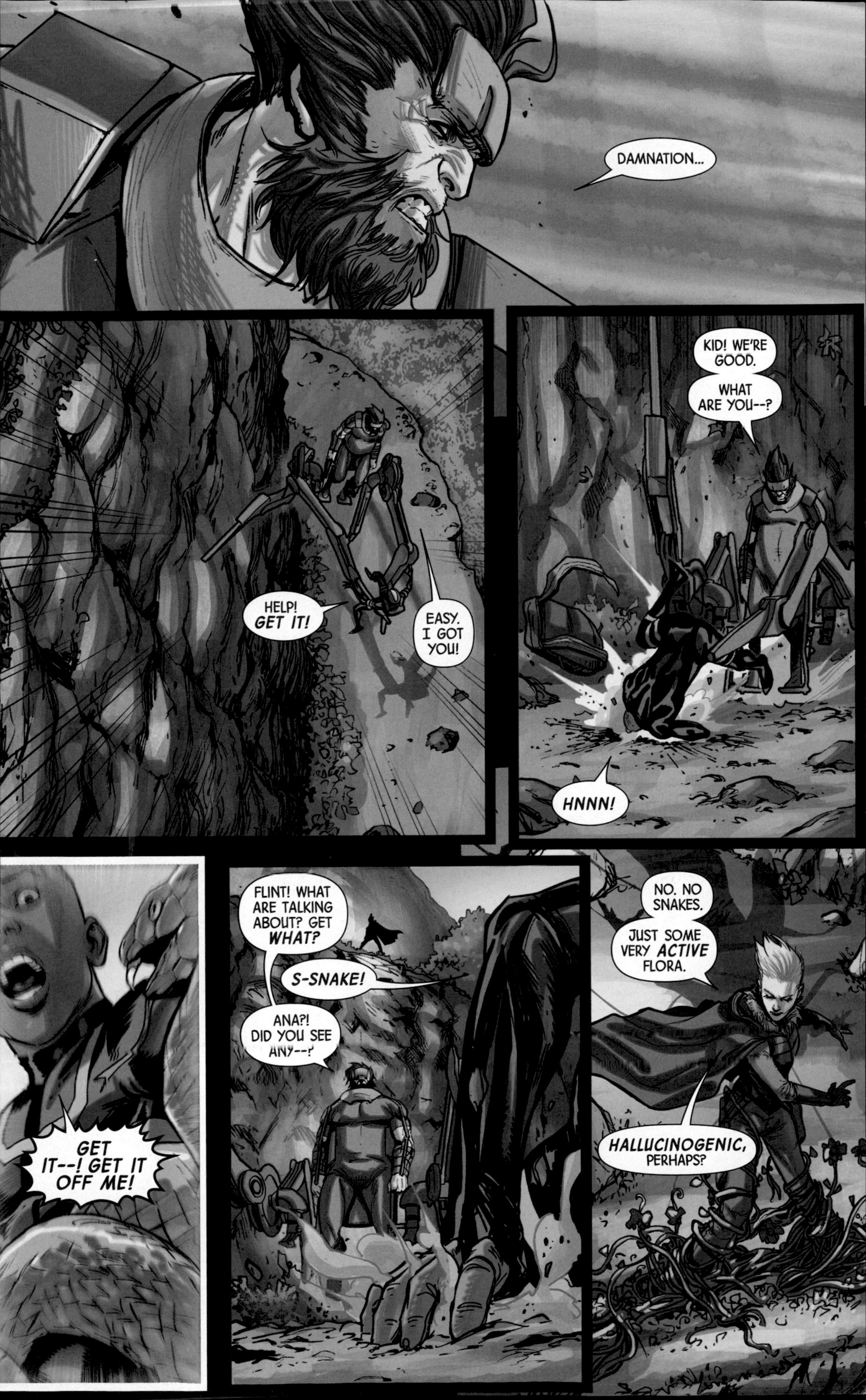
DAMNATION...
HELP! GET IT!
EASY. I GOT YOU!
KID! WE'RE GOOD.
WHAT ARE YOU--?
HNNN!
GET IT--! GET IT OFF ME!
FLINT! WHAT ARE TALKING ABOUT? GET WHAT?
S-SNAKE!
ANA?! DID YOU SEE ANY--?
NO. NO SNAKES.
JUST SOME VERY ACTIVE FLORA.
HALLUCINOGENIC, PERHAPS?

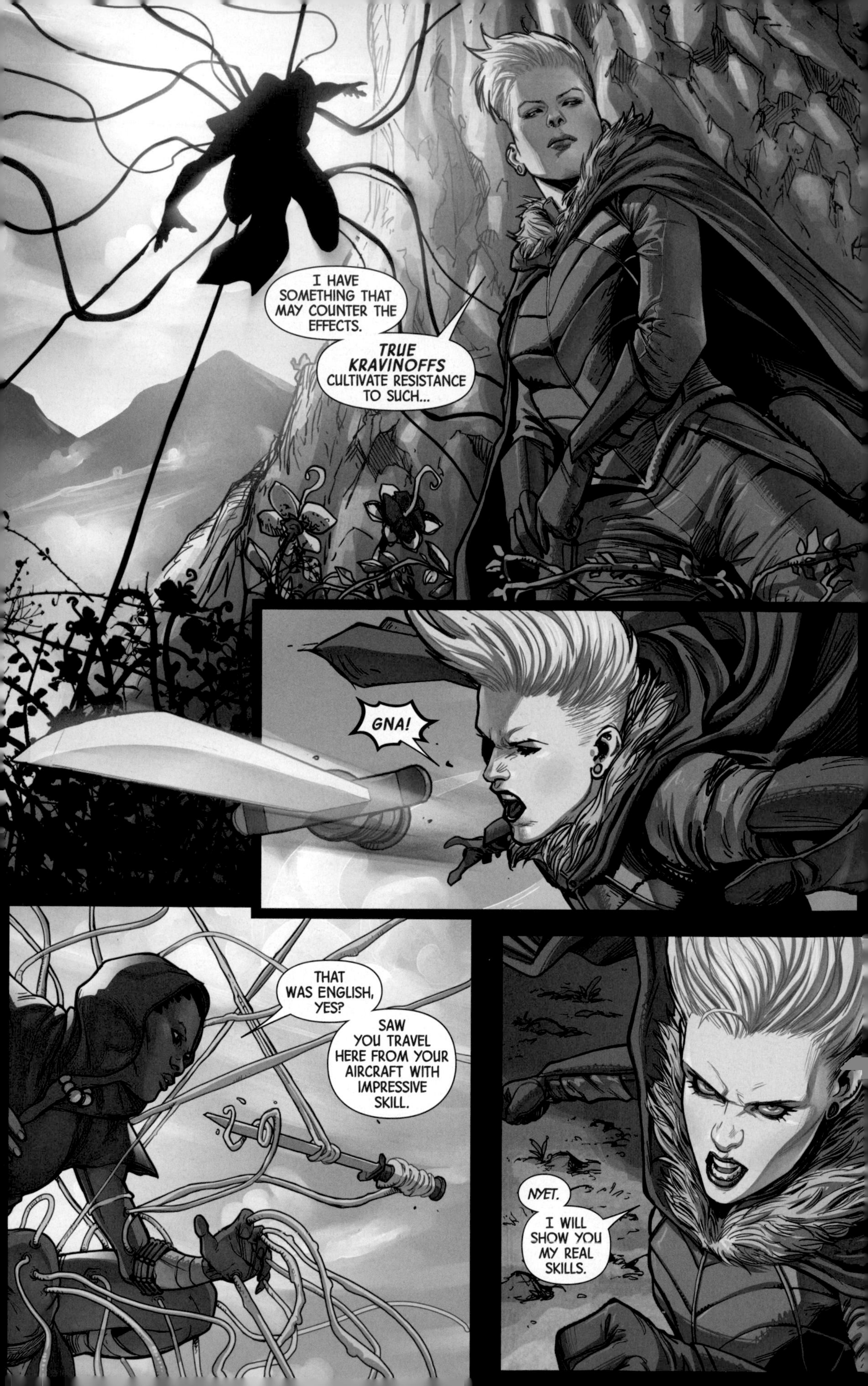
I HAVE SOMETHING THAT MAY COUNTER THE EFFECTS.
TRUE KRAVINOFFS CULTIVATE RESISTANCE TO SUCH...
GNA!
THAT WAS ENGLISH, YES?
SAW YOU TRAVEL HERE FROM YOUR AIRCRAFT WITH IMPRESSIVE SKILL.
NYET.
I WILL SHOW YOU MY REAL SKILLS.

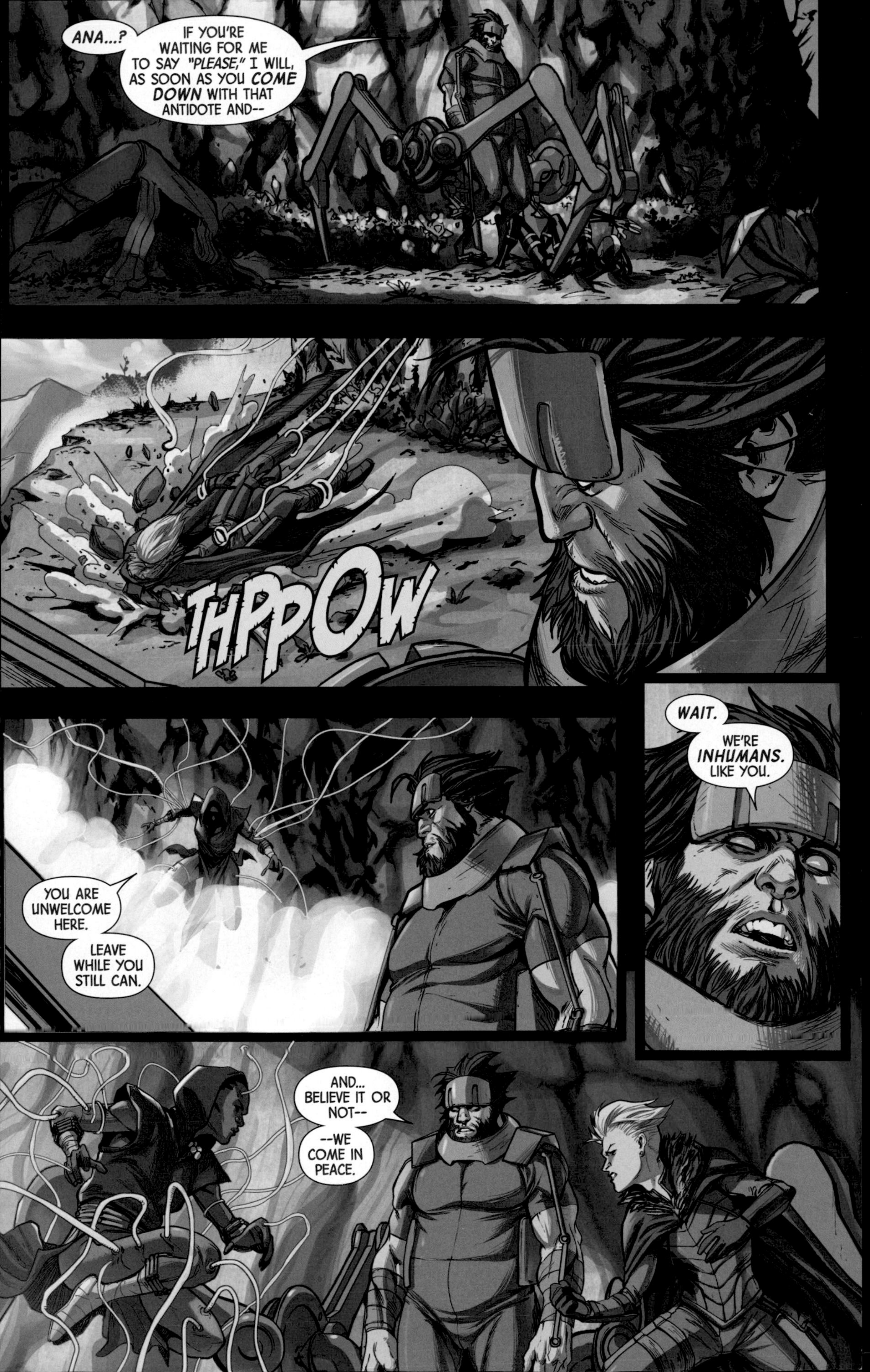
ANA...?
IF YOU'RE WAITING FOR ME TO SAY "PLEASE," I WILL, AS SOON AS YOU COME DOWN WITH THAT ANTIDOTE AND--
THPPOW
WAIT.
WE'RE INHUMANS. LIKE YOU.
YOU ARE UNWELCOME HERE.
LEAVE WHILE YOU STILL CAN.
AND... BELIEVE IT OR NOT--
--WE COME IN PEACE.

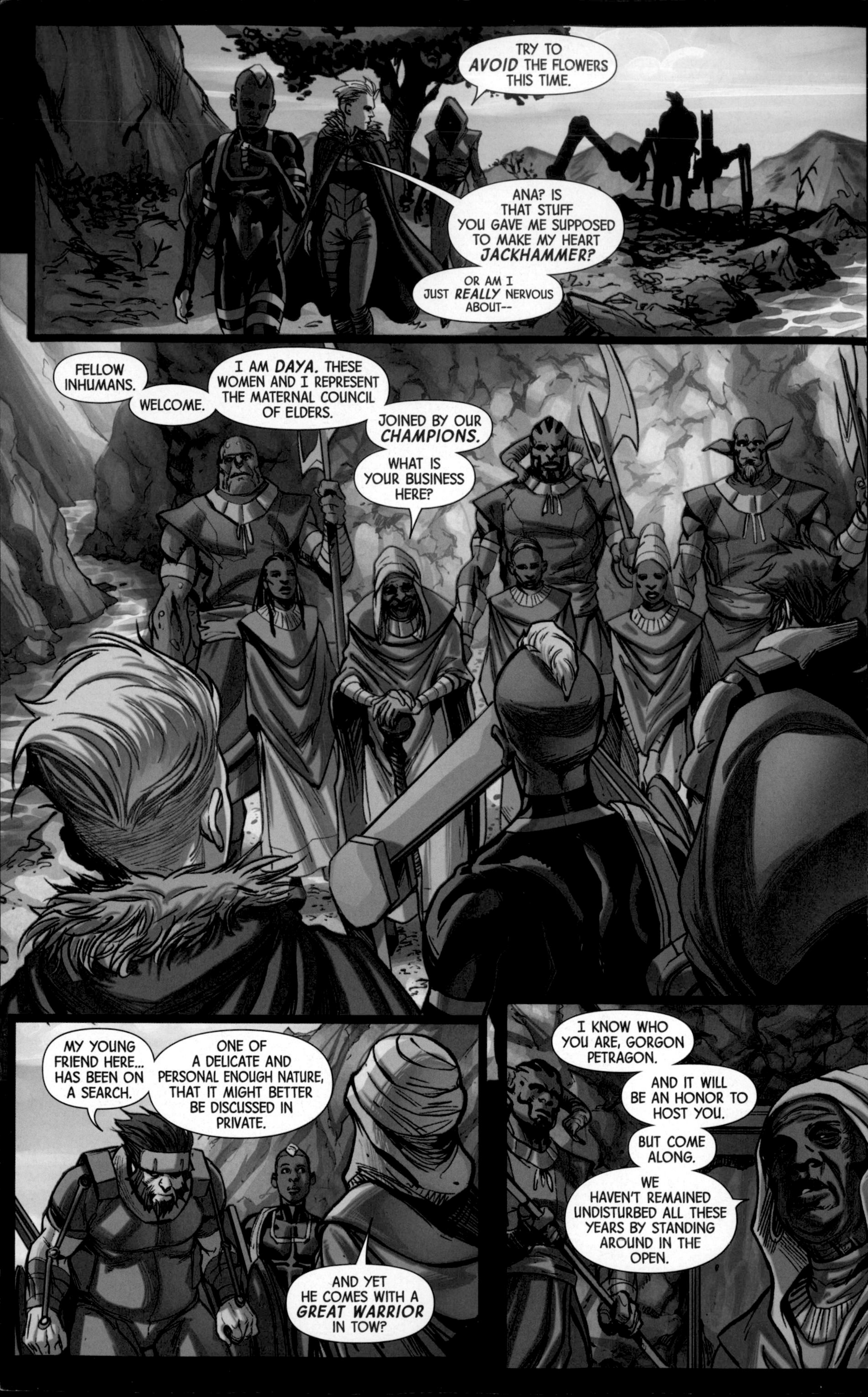
TRY TO AVOID THE FLOWERS THIS TIME.
ANA? IS THAT STUFF YOU GAVE ME SUPPOSED TO MAKE MY HEART JACKHAMMER?
OR AM I JUST REALLY NERVOUS ABOUT--
FELLOW INHUMANS.
WELCOME.
I AM DAYA. THESE WOMEN AND I REPRESENT THE MATERNAL COUNCIL OF ELDERS.
JOINED BY OUR CHAMPIONS.
WHAT IS YOUR BUSINESS HERE?
MY YOUNG FRIEND HERE... HAS BEEN ON A SEARCH.
ONE OF A DELICATE AND PERSONAL ENOUGH NATURE, THAT IT MIGHT BETTER BE DISCUSSED IN PRIVATE.
AND YET HE COMES WITH A GREAT WARRIOR IN TOW?
I KNOW WHO YOU ARE, GORGON PETRAGON.
AND IT WILL BE AN HONOR TO HOST YOU.
BUT COME ALONG.
WE HAVEN'T REMAINED UNDISTURBED ALL THESE YEARS BY STANDING AROUND IN THE OPEN.

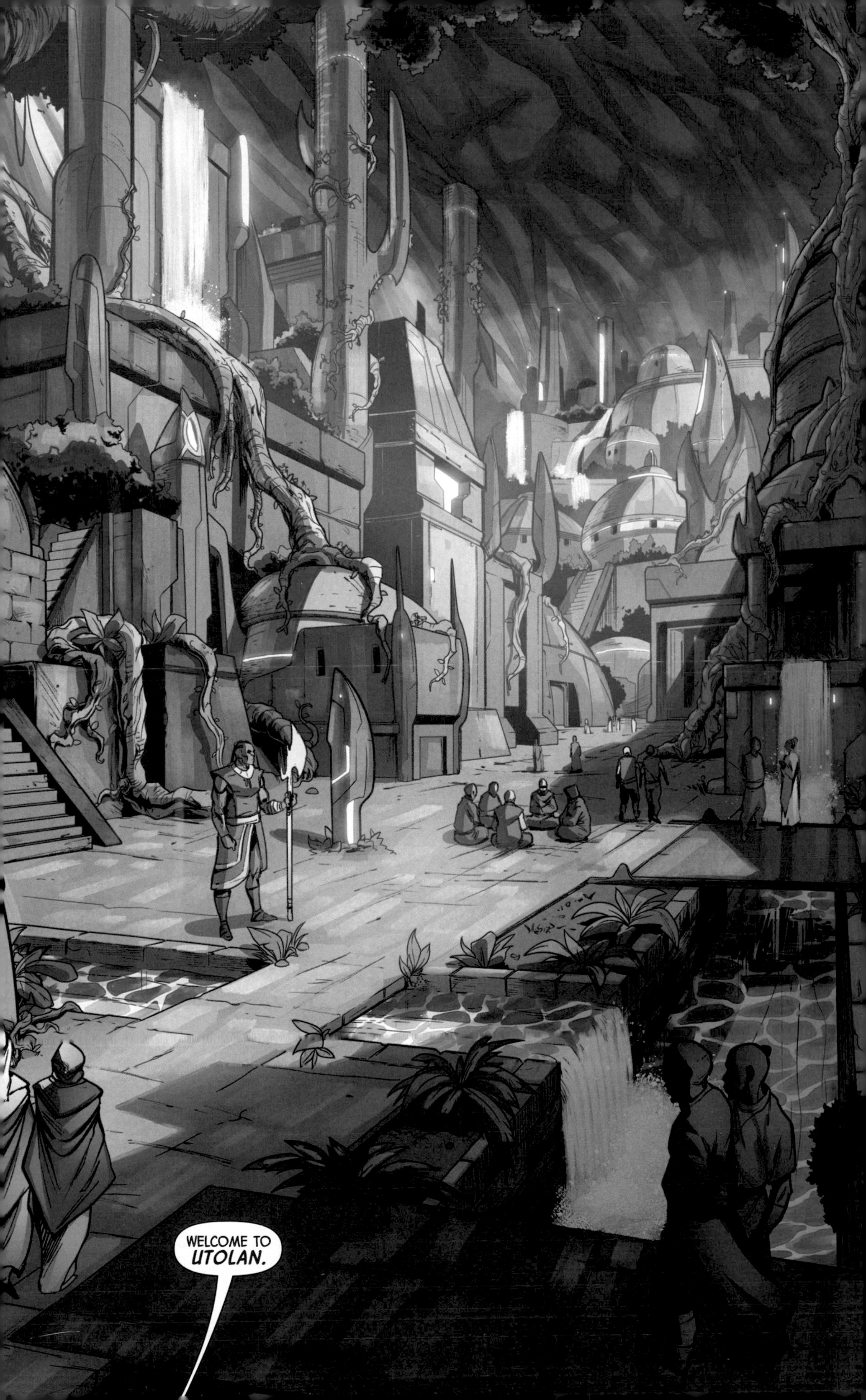
WELCOME TO UTOLAN.

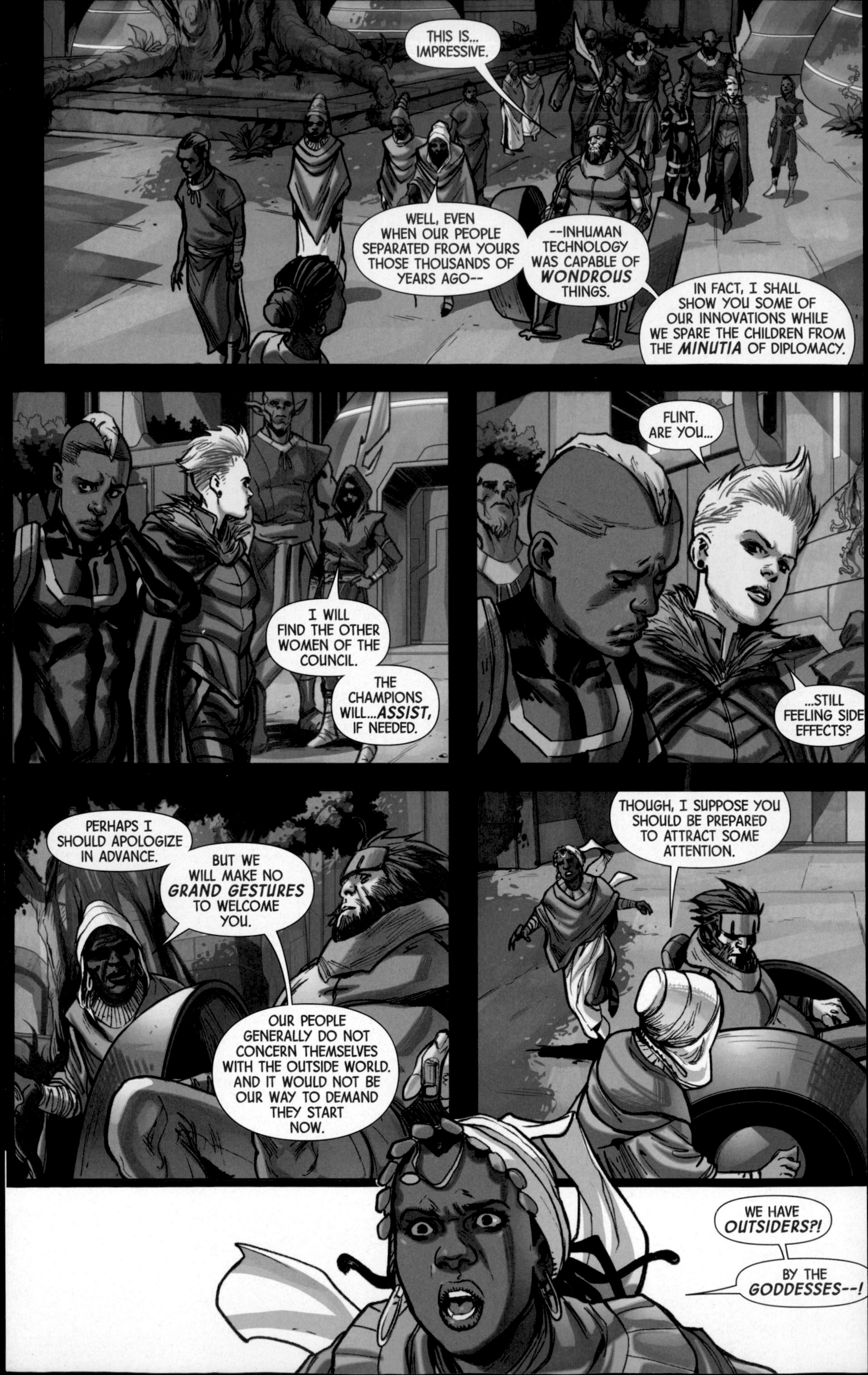
THIS IS... IMPRESSIVE.
WELL, EVEN WHEN OUR PEOPLE SEPARATED FROM YOURS THOSE THOUSANDS OF YEARS AGO--
--INHUMAN TECHNOLOGY WAS CAPABLE OF WONDROUS THINGS.
IN FACT, I SHALL SHOW YOU SOME OF OUR INNOVATIONS WHILE WE SPARE THE CHILDREN FROM THE MINUTIA OF DIPLOMACY.
I WILL FIND THE OTHER WOMEN OF THE COUNCIL.
THE CHAMPIONS WILL...ASSIST, IF NEEDED.
FLINT. ARE YOU...
...STILL FEELING SIDE EFFECTS?
PERHAPS I SHOULD APOLOGIZE IN ADVANCE.
BUT WE WILL MAKE NO GRAND GESTURES TO WELCOME YOU.
OUR PEOPLE GENERALLY DO NOT CONCERN THEMSELVES WITH THE OUTSIDE WORLD. AND IT WOULD NOT BE OUR WAY TO DEMAND THEY START NOW.
THOUGH, I SUPPOSE YOU SHOULD BE PREPARED TO ATTRACT SOME ATTENTION.
WE HAVE OUTSIDERS?!
BY THE GODDESSES--!

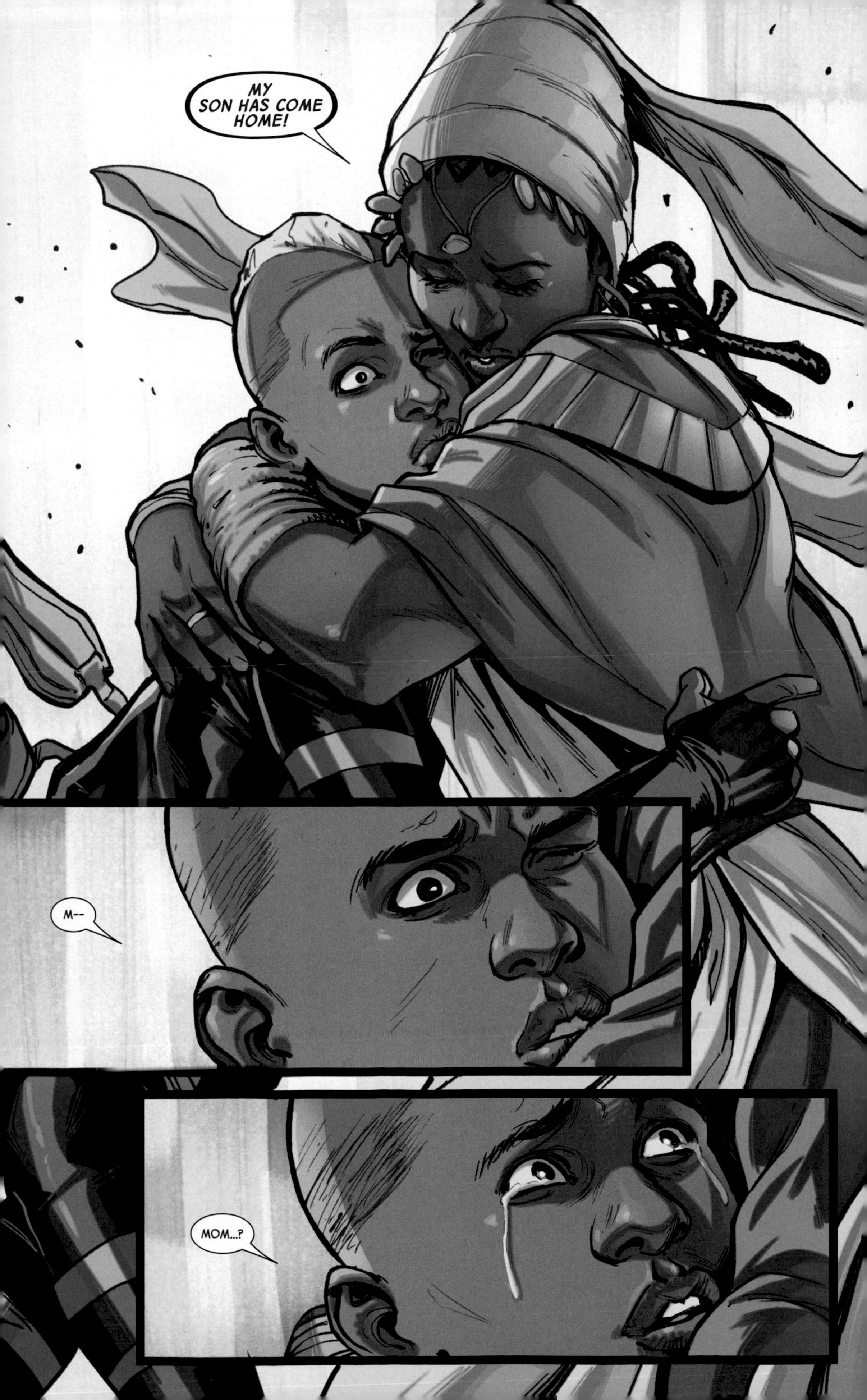
MY SON HAS COME HOME!
M--
MOM...?

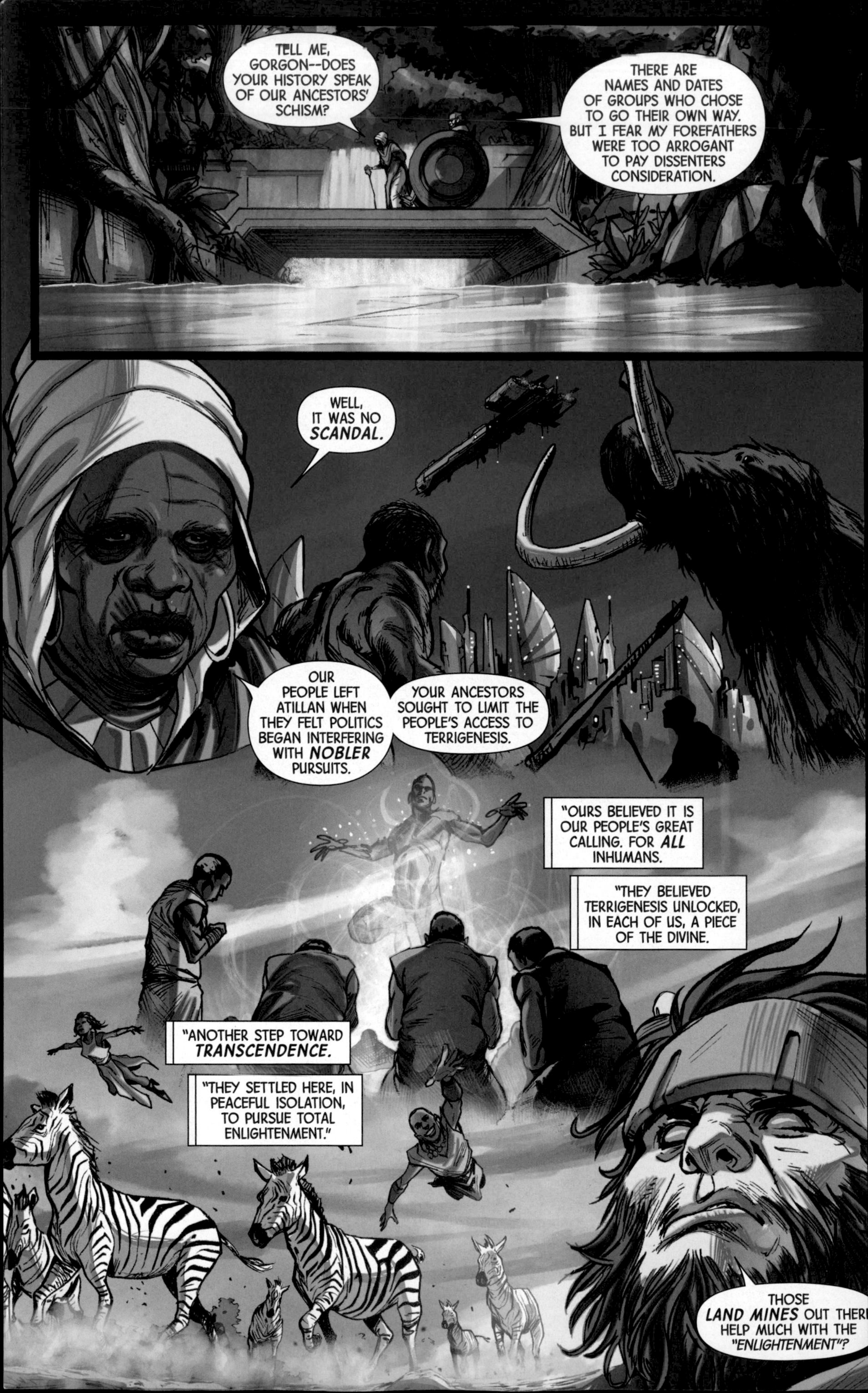
TELL ME, GORGON--DOES YOUR HISTORY SPEAK OF OUR ANCESTORS' SCHISM?
THERE ARE NAMES AND DATES OF GROUPS WHO CHOSE TO GO THEIR OWN WAY. BUT I FEAR MY FOREFATHERS WERE TOO ARROGANT TO PAY DISSENTERS CONSIDERATION.
WELL, IT WAS NO SCANDAL.
OUR PEOPLE LEFT ATILLAN WHEN THEY FELT POLITICS BEGAN INTERFERING WITH NOBLER PURSUITS.
YOUR ANCESTORS SOUGHT TO LIMIT THE PEOPLE'S ACCESS TO TERRIGENESIS.
"OURS BELIEVED IT IS OUR PEOPLE'S GREAT CALLING. FOR ALL INHUMANS.
"THEY BELIEVED TERRIGENESIS UNLOCKED, IN EACH OF US, A PIECE OF THE DIVINE.
"ANOTHER STEP TOWARD TRANSCENDENCE.
"THEY SETTLED HERE, IN PEACEFUL ISOLATION, TO PURSUE TOTAL ENLIGHTENMENT."
THOSE LAND MINES OUT THERE HELP MUCH WITH THE "ENLIGHTENMENT"?

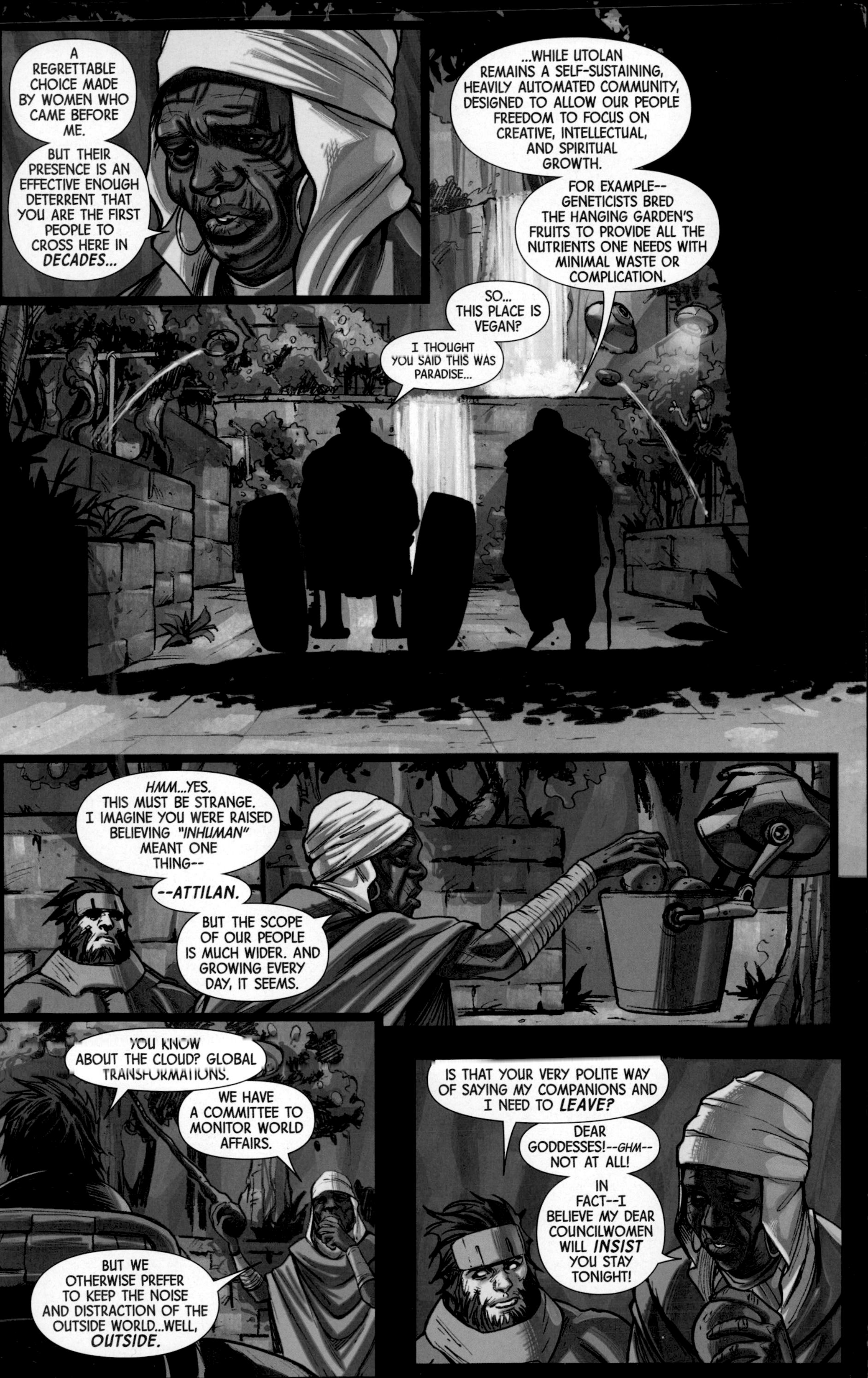
A REGRETTABLE CHOICE MADE BY WOMEN WHO CAME BEFORE ME.
BUT THEIR PRESENCE IS AN EFFECTIVE ENOUGH DETERRENT THAT YOU ARE THE FIRST PEOPLE TO CROSS HERE IN DECADES...
...WHILE UTOLAN REMAINS A SELF-SUSTAINING, HEAVILY AUTOMATED COMMUNITY, DESIGNED TO ALLOW OUR PEOPLE FREEDOM TO FOCUS ON CREATIVE, INTELLECTUAL, AND SPIRITUAL GROWTH.
FOR EXAMPLE--GENETICISTS BRED THE HANGING GARDEN'S FRUITS TO PROVIDE ALL THE NUTRIENTS ONE NEEDS WITH MINIMAL WASTE OR COMPLICATION.
SO... THIS PLACE IS VEGAN?
I THOUGHT YOU SAID THIS WAS PARADISE...
HMM...YES. THIS MUST BE STRANGE. I IMAGINE YOU WERE RAISED BELIEVING "INHUMAN" MEANT ONE THING--
--ATTILAN.
BUT THE SCOPE OF OUR PEOPLE IS MUCH WIDER. AND GROWING EVERY DAY, IT SEEMS.
YOU KNOW ABOUT THE CLOUD? GLOBAL TRANSFORMATIONS.
WE HAVE A COMMITTEE TO MONITOR WORLD AFFAIRS.
BUT WE OTHERWISE PREFER TO KEEP THE NOISE AND DISTRACTION OF THE OUTSIDE WORLD...WELL, OUTSIDE.
IS THAT YOUR VERY POLITE WAY OF SAYING MY COMPANIONS AND I NEED TO LEAVE?
DEAR GODDESSES!--GHM--NOT AT ALL!
IN FACT--I BELIEVE MY DEAR COUNCILWOMEN WILL INSIST YOU STAY TONIGHT!

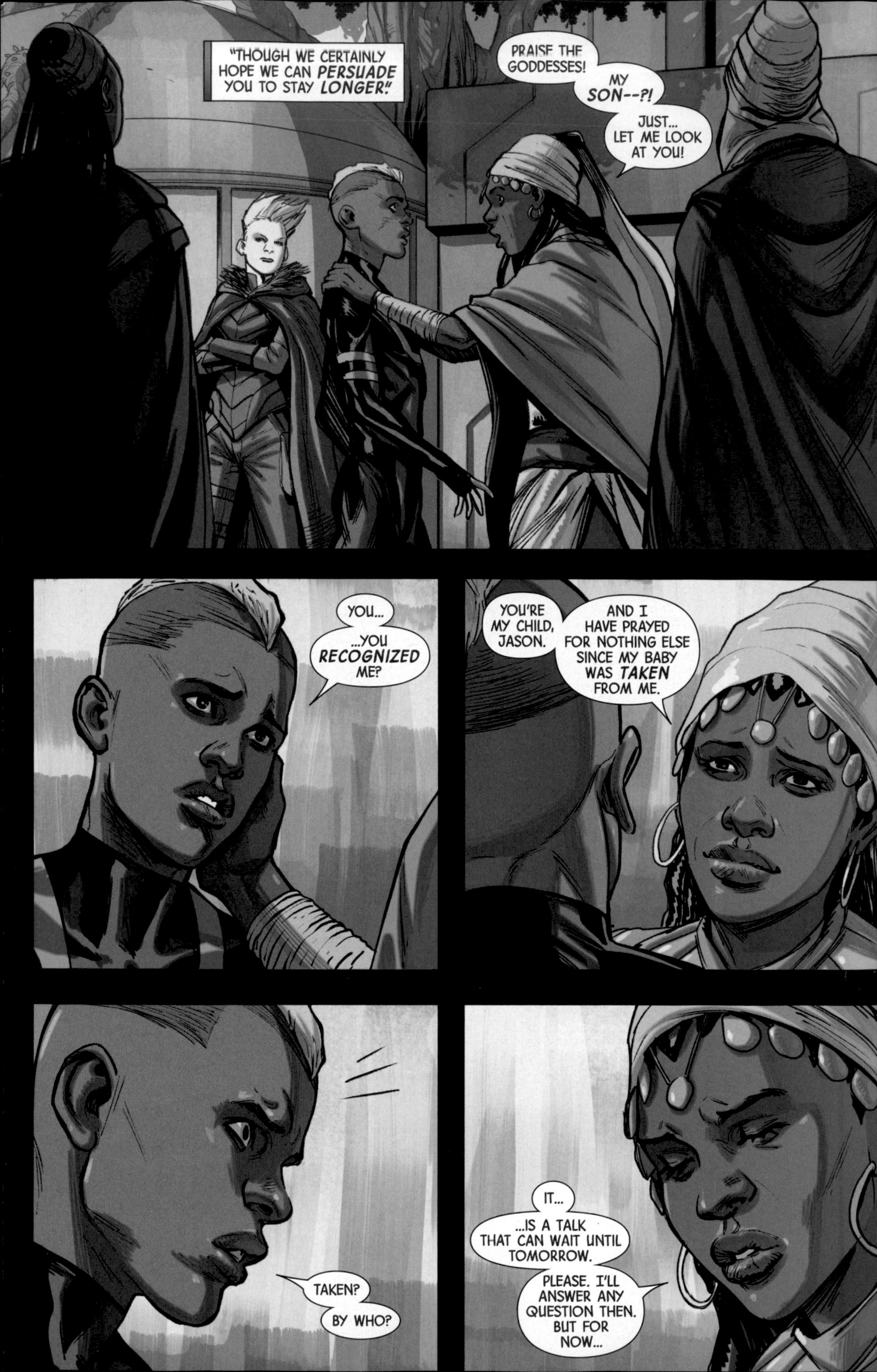
"THOUGH WE CERTAINLY HOPE WE CAN PERSUADE YOU TO STAY LONGER."
PRAISE THE GODDESSES!
MY SON--?!
JUST... LET ME LOOK AT YOU!
YOU...
...YOU RECOGNIZED ME?
YOU'RE MY CHILD, JASON.
AND I HAVE PRAYED FOR NOTHING ELSE SINCE MY BABY WAS TAKEN FROM ME.
TAKEN?
BY WHO?
IT...
...IS A TALK THAT CAN WAIT UNTIL TOMORROW.
PLEASE. I'LL ANSWER ANY QUESTION THEN. BUT FOR NOW...

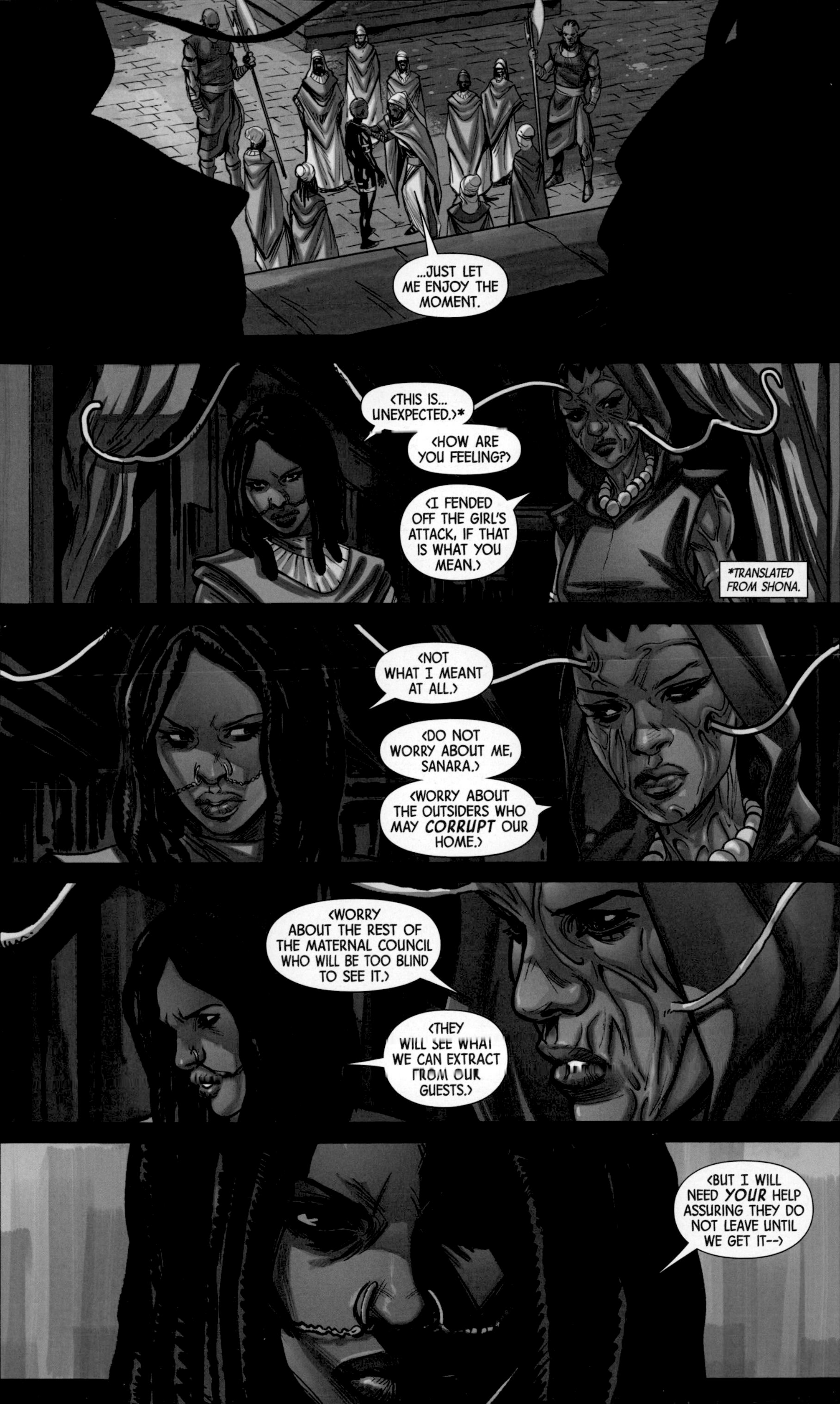
...JUST LET ME ENJOY THE MOMENT.
<THIS IS... UNEXPECTED.>*
<HOW ARE YOU FEELING?>
<I FENDED OFF THE GIRL'S ATTACK, IF THAT IS WHAT YOU MEAN.>
*TRANSLATED FROM SHONA.
<NOT WHAT I MEANT AT ALL.>
<DO NOT WORRY ABOUT ME, SANARA.>
<WORRY ABOUT THE OUTSIDERS WHO MAY CORRUPT OUR HOME.>
<WORRY ABOUT THE REST OF THE MATERNAL COUNCIL WHO WILL BE TOO BLIND TO SEE IT.>
<THEY WILL SEE WHAT WE CAN EXTRACT FROM OUR GUESTS.>
<BUT I WILL NEED YOUR HELP ASSURING THEY DO NOT LEAVE UNTIL WE GET IT-->

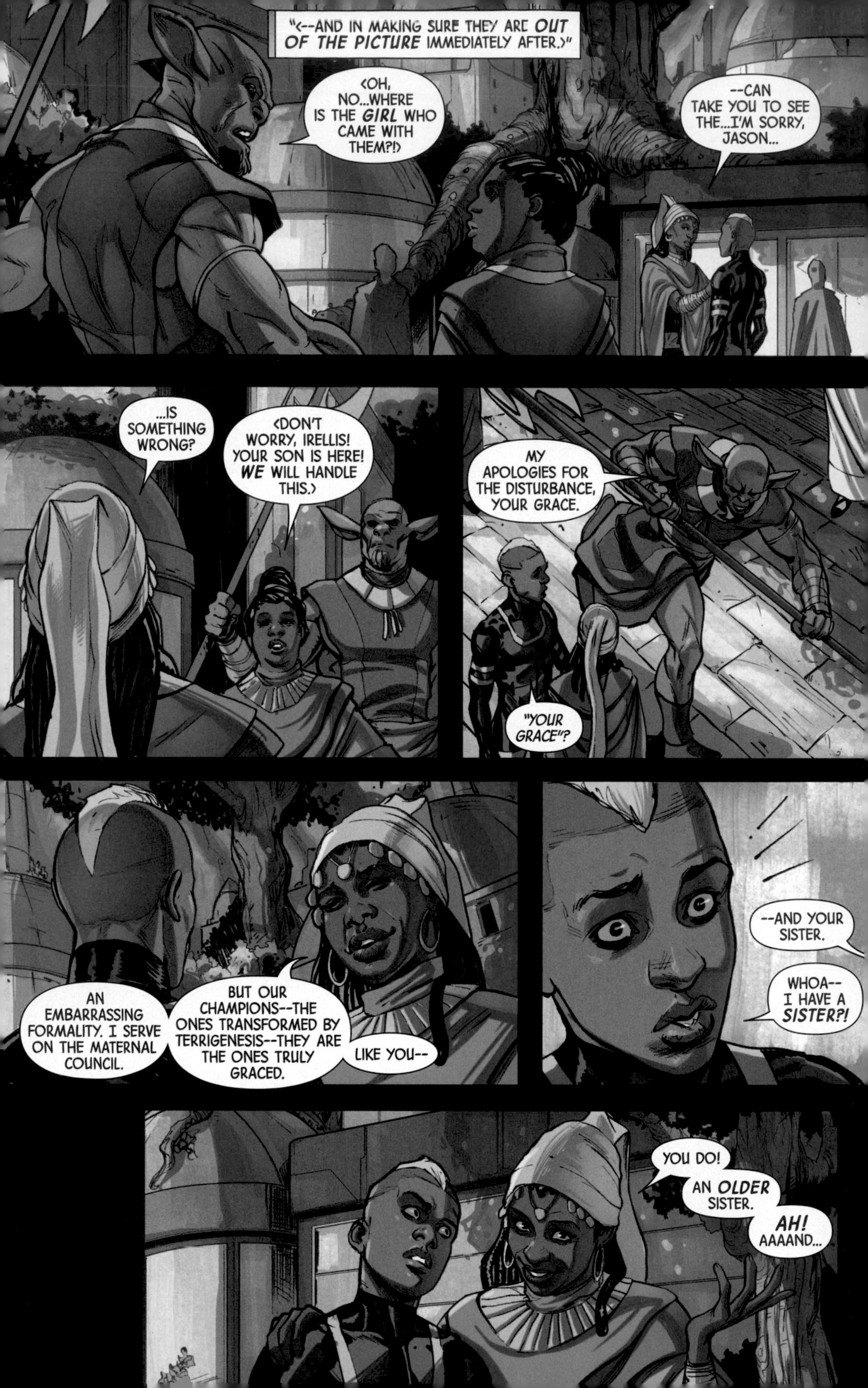
"<--AND IN MAKING SURE THEY ARE OUT OF THE PICTURE IMMEDIATELY AFTER.>"
<OH, NO...WHERE IS THE GIRL WHO CAME WITH THEM?!>
--CAN TAKE YOU TO SEE THE...I'M SORRY, JASON...
...IS SOMETHING WRONG?
<DON'T WORRY, IRELLIS! YOUR SON IS HERE! WE WILL HANDLE THIS.>
MY APOLOGIES FOR THE DISTURBANCE, YOUR GRACE.
"YOUR GRACE"?
AN EMBARRASSING FORMALITY. I SERVE ON THE MATERNAL COUNCIL.
BUT OUR CHAMPIONS--THE ONES TRANSFORMED BY TERRIGENESIS--THEY ARE THE ONES TRULY GRACED.
LIKE YOU--
--AND YOUR SISTER.
WHOA-- I HAVE A SISTER?!
YOU DO!
AN OLDER SISTER.
AH! AAAAND...

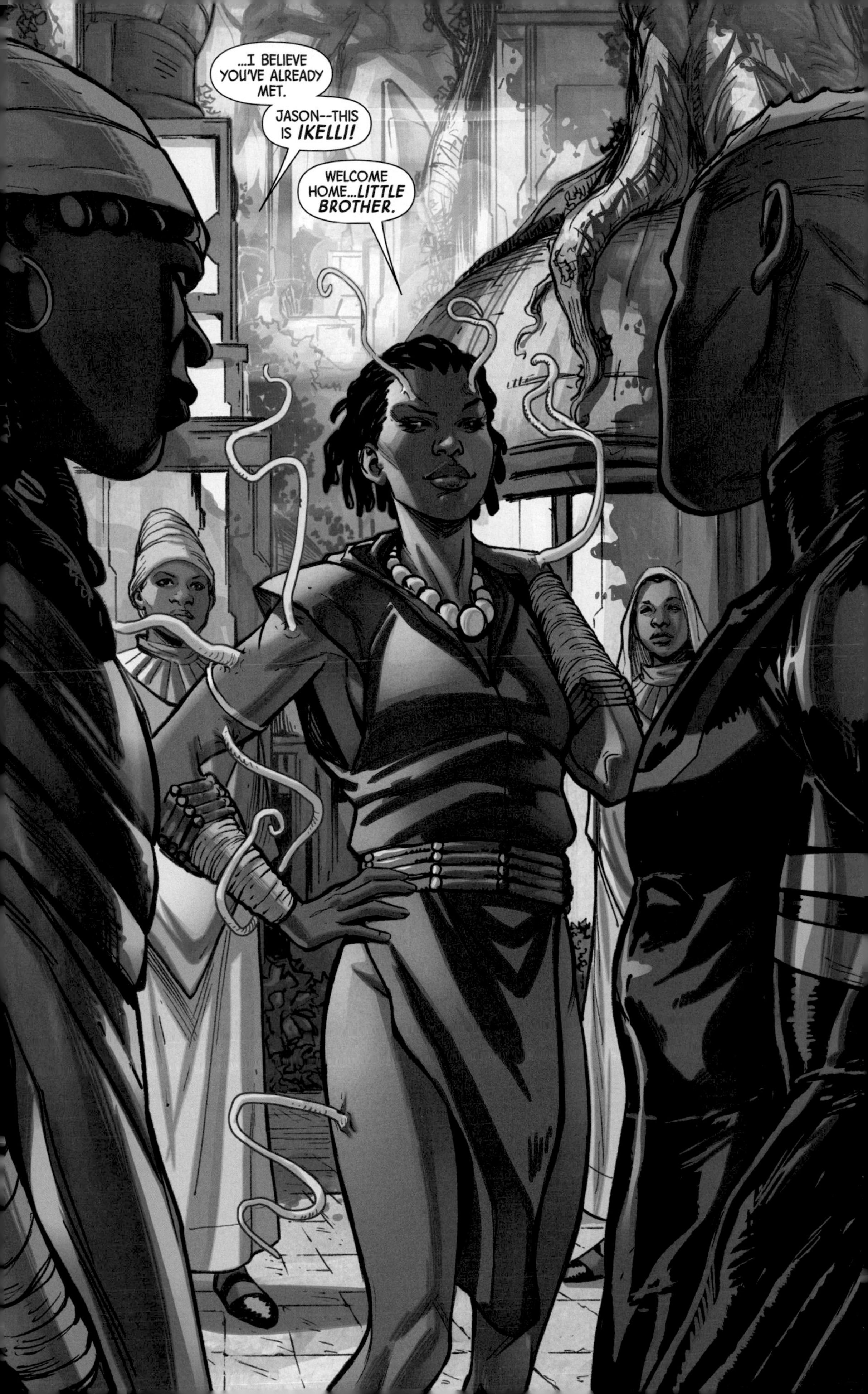
...I BELIEVE YOU'VE ALREADY MET.
JASON--THIS IS IKELLI!
WELCOME HOME...LITTLE BROTHER.

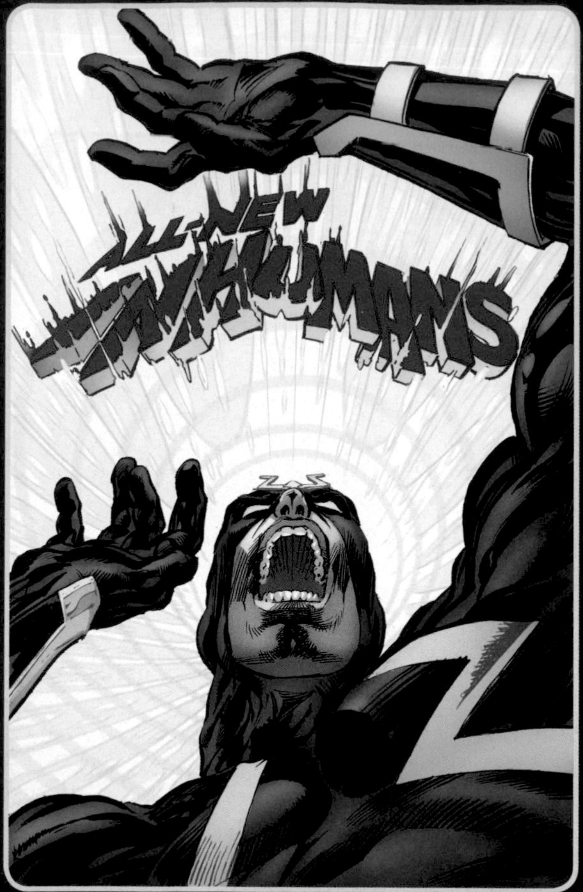
ALL-NEW INHUMANS

#5 CLASSIC VARIANT BY
NEAL ADAMS & EDGAR DELGADO

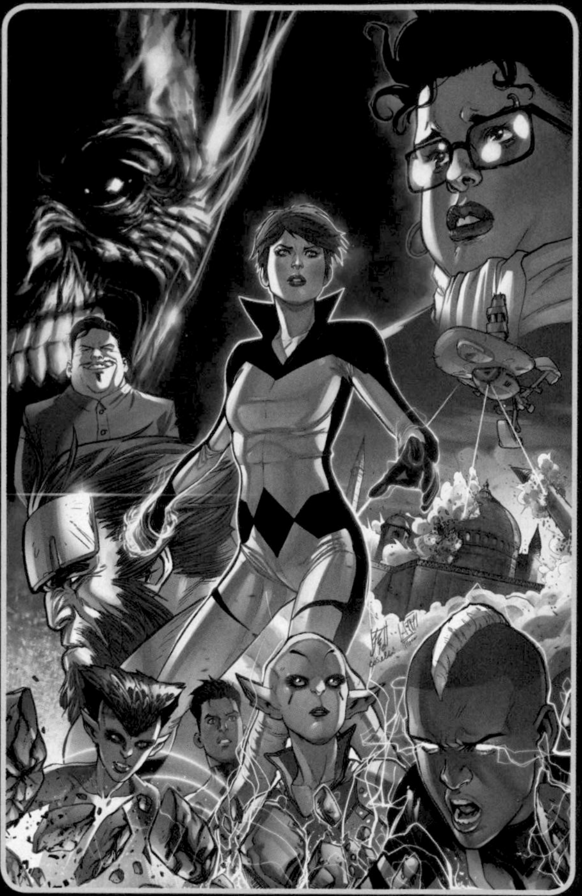

#5 STORY THUS FAR VARIANT BY
STEFANO CASELLI & ANDRES MOSSA

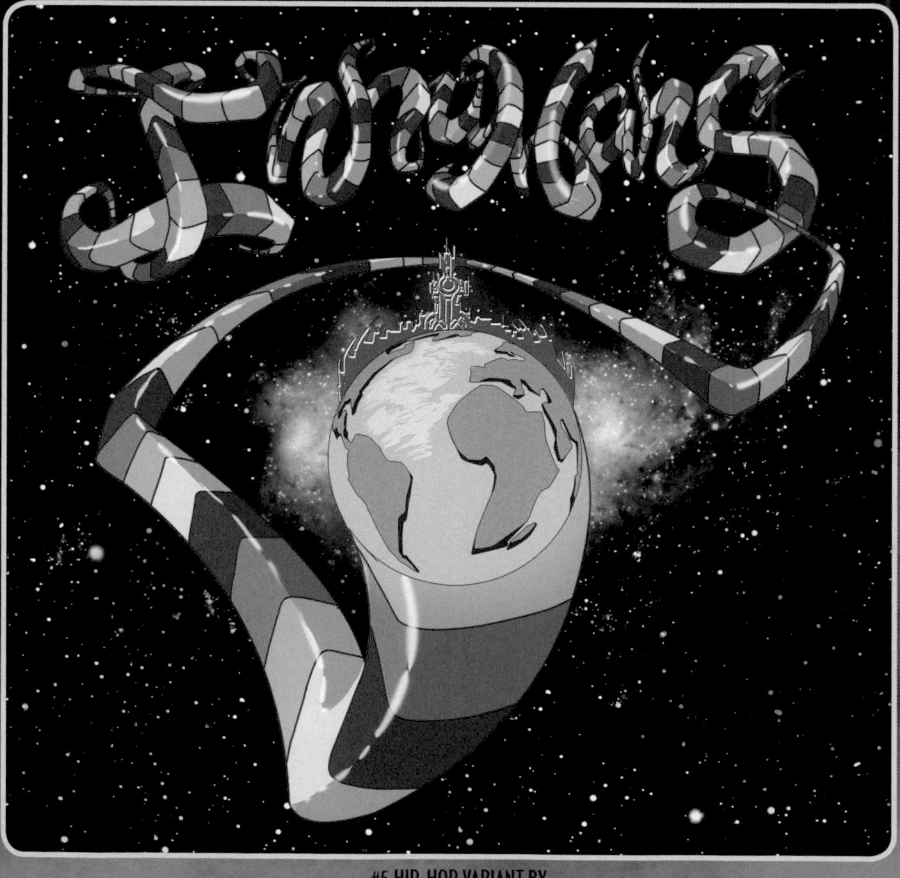

#5 HIP-HOP VARIANT BY
DAMION SCOTT

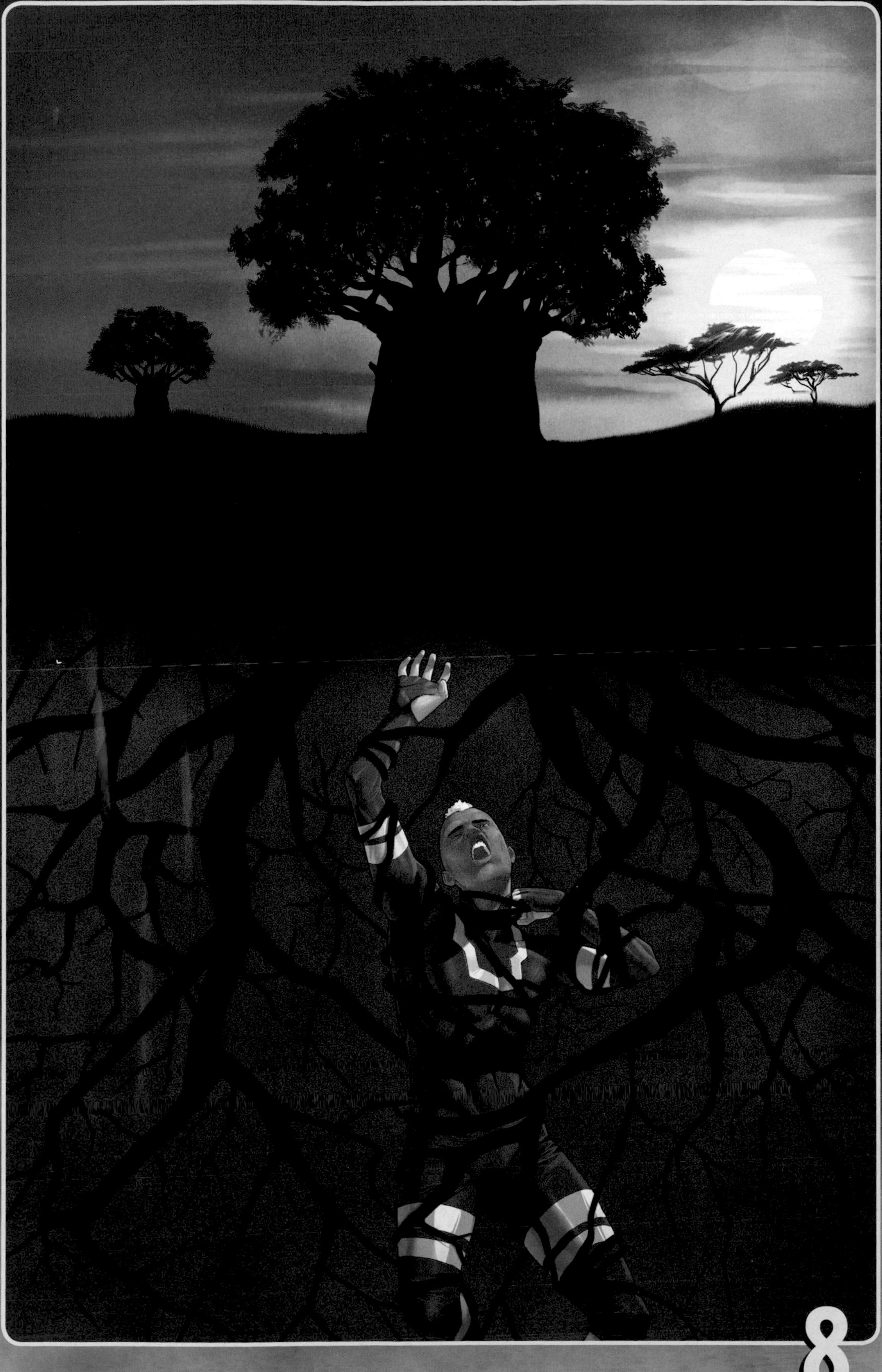

8

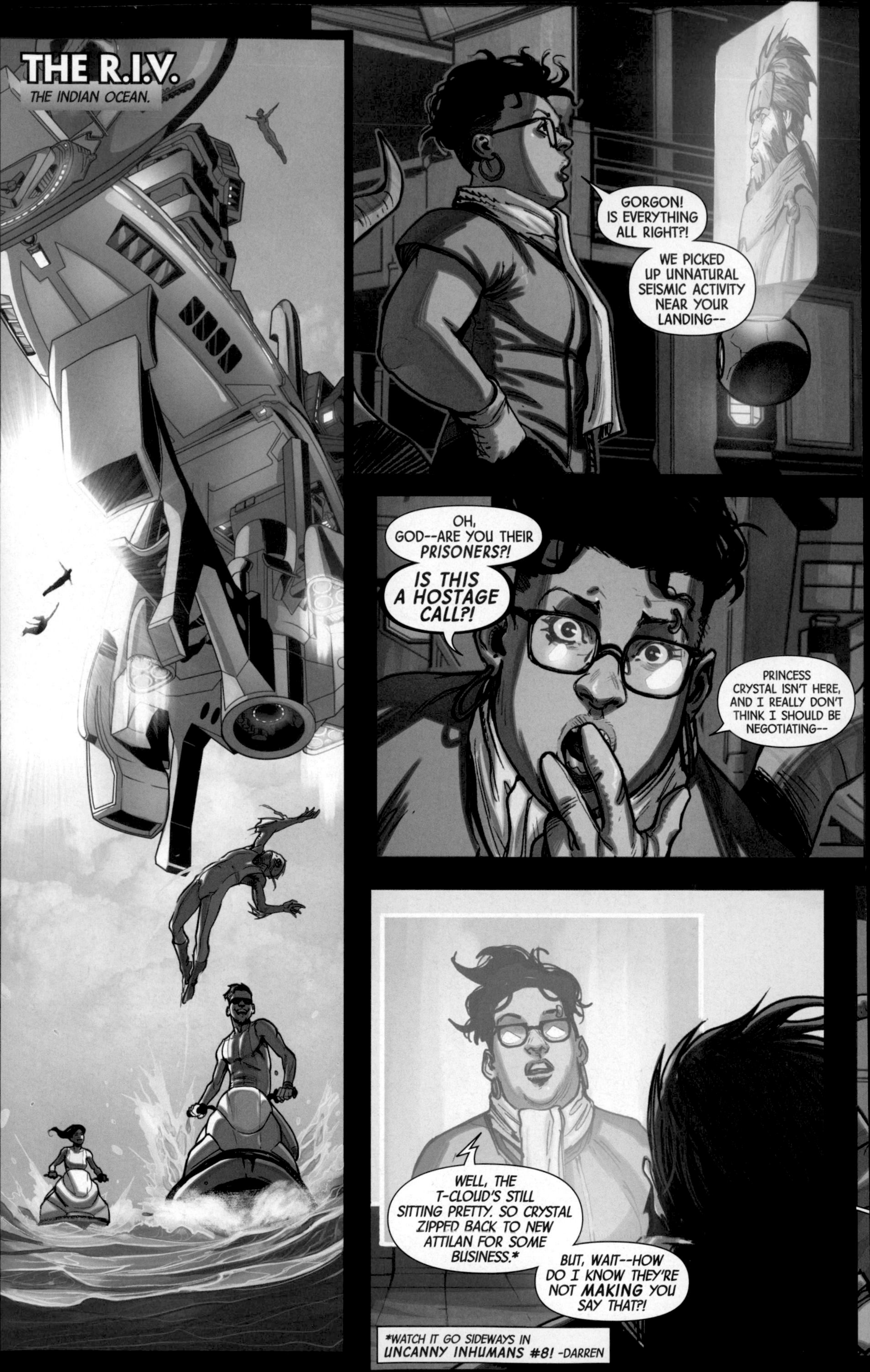
THE R.I.V.
THE INDIAN OCEAN.
GORGON! IS EVERYTHING ALL RIGHT?!
WE PICKED UP UNNATURAL SEISMIC ACTIVITY NEAR YOUR LANDING--
OH, GOD--ARE YOU THEIR PRISONERS?!
IS THIS A HOSTAGE CALL?!
PRINCESS CRYSTAL ISN'T HERE, AND I REALLY DON'T THINK I SHOULD BE NEGOTIATING--
WELL, THE T-CLOUD'S STILL SITTING PRETTY. SO CRYSTAL ZIPPED BACK TO NEW ATTILAN FOR SOME BUSINESS.*
BUT, WAIT--HOW DO I KNOW THEY'RE NOT MAKING YOU SAY THAT?!
*WATCH IT GO SIDEWAYS IN UNCANNY INHUMANS #8! -DARREN

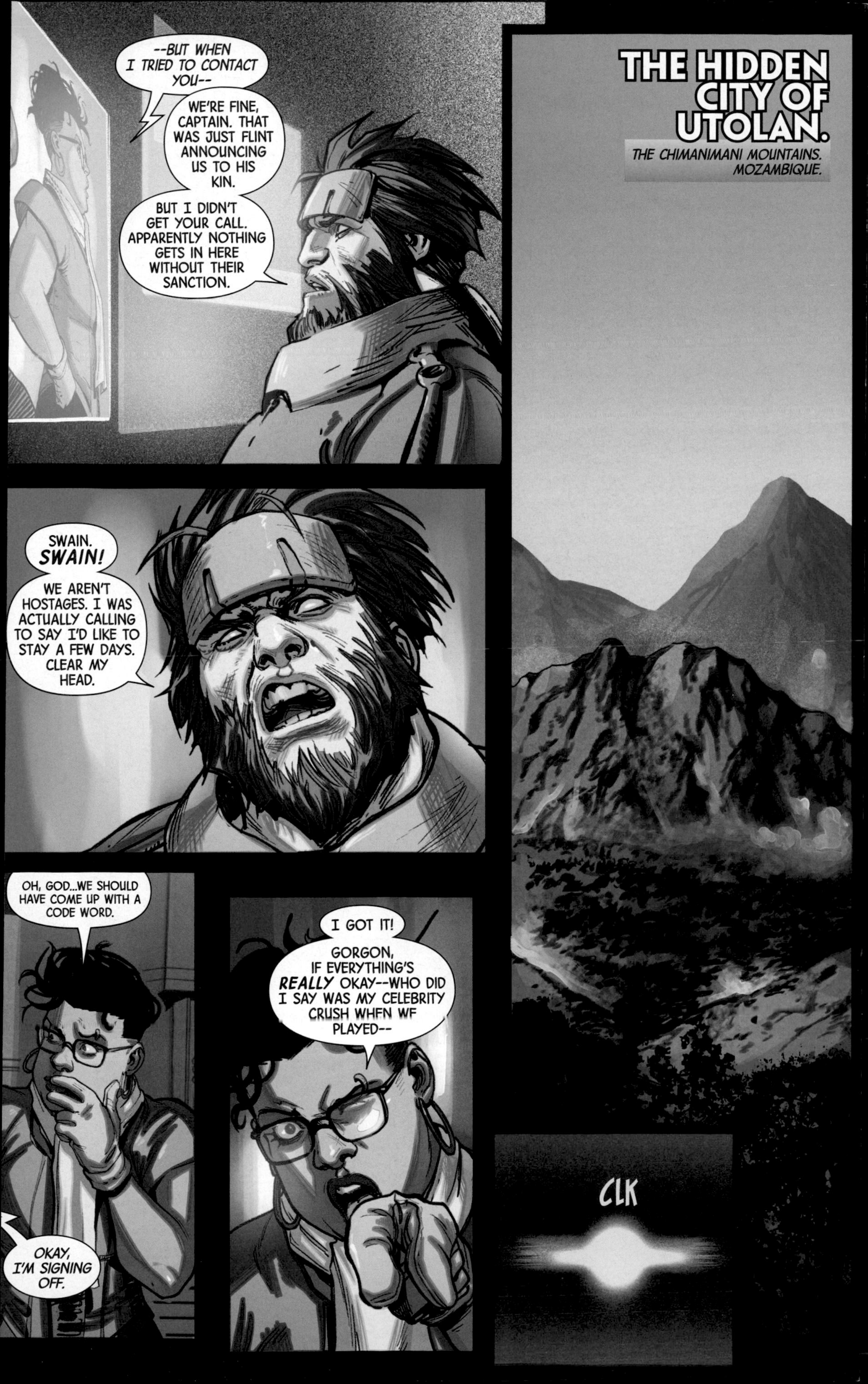
--BUT WHEN I TRIED TO CONTACT YOU--
WE'RE FINE, CAPTAIN. THAT WAS JUST FLINT ANNOUNCING US TO HIS KIN.
BUT I DIDN'T GET YOUR CALL. APPARENTLY NOTHING GETS IN HERE WITHOUT THEIR SANCTION.
SWAIN. SWAIN!
WE AREN'T HOSTAGES. I WAS ACTUALLY CALLING TO SAY I'D LIKE TO STAY A FEW DAYS. CLEAR MY HEAD.
OH, GOD...WE SHOULD HAVE COME UP WITH A CODE WORD.
I GOT IT!
GORGON, IF EVERYTHING'S REALLY OKAY--WHO DID I SAY WAS MY CELEBRITY CRUSH WHEN WE PLAYED--
OKAY, I'M SIGNING OFF.
THE HIDDEN CITY OF UTOLAN.
THE CHIMANIMANI MOUNTAINS. MOZAMBIQUE.
CLK

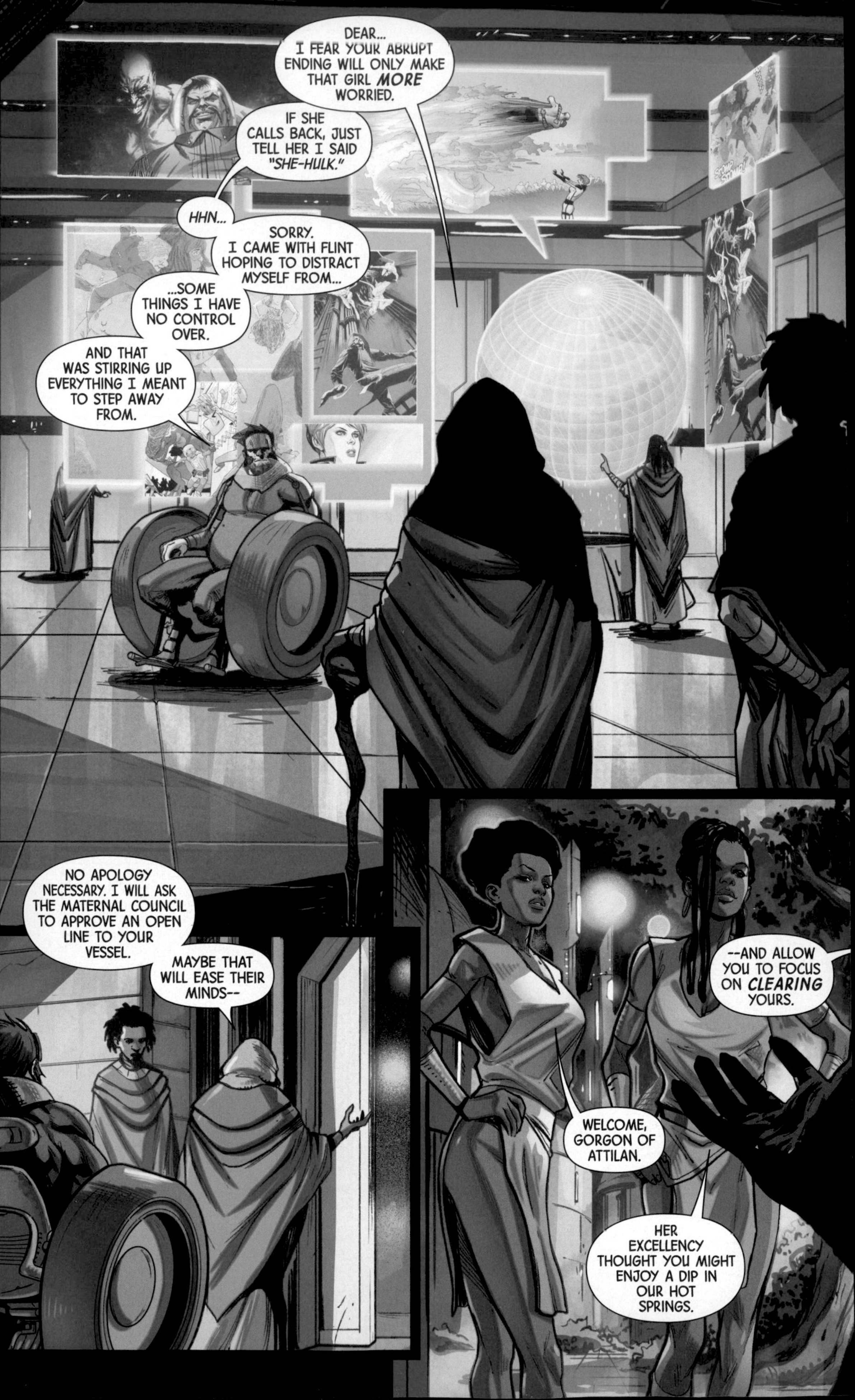
DEAR... I FEAR YOUR ABRUPT ENDING WILL ONLY MAKE THAT GIRL *MORE* WORRIED.
IF SHE CALLS BACK, JUST TELL HER I SAID "*SHE-HULK.*"
HHN...
SORRY. I CAME WITH FLINT HOPING TO DISTRACT MYSELF FROM...
...SOME THINGS I HAVE NO CONTROL OVER.
AND THAT WAS STIRRING UP EVERYTHING I MEANT TO STEP AWAY FROM.
NO APOLOGY NECESSARY. I WILL ASK THE MATERNAL COUNCIL TO APPROVE AN OPEN LINE TO YOUR VESSEL.
MAYBE THAT WILL EASE THEIR MINDS--
--AND ALLOW YOU TO FOCUS ON *CLEARING* YOURS.
WELCOME, GORGON OF ATTILAN.
HER EXCELLENCY THOUGHT YOU MIGHT ENJOY A DIP IN OUR HOT SPRINGS.

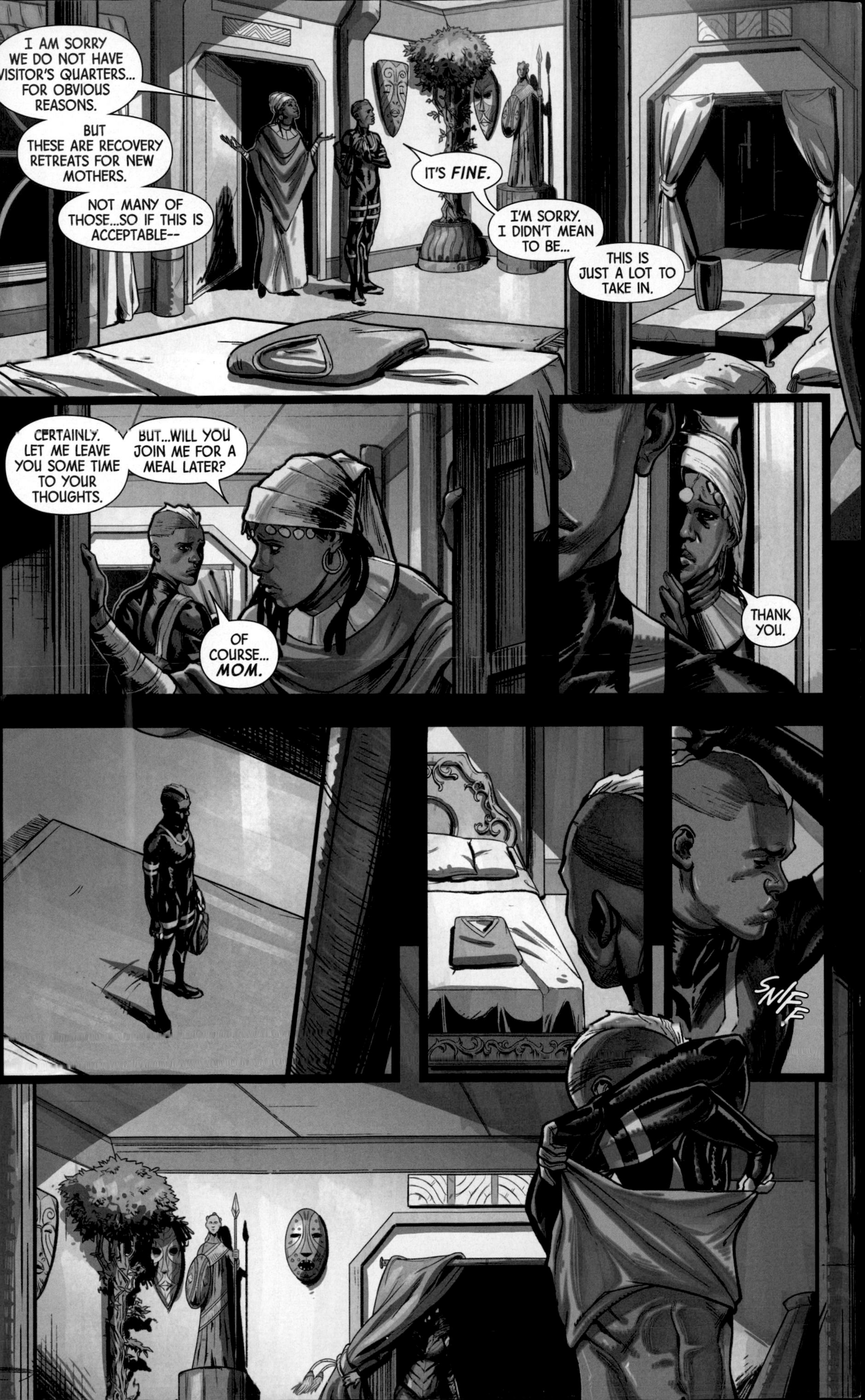
I AM SORRY WE DO NOT HAVE VISITOR'S QUARTERS... FOR OBVIOUS REASONS.
BUT THESE ARE RECOVERY RETREATS FOR NEW MOTHERS.
NOT MANY OF THOSE...SO IF THIS IS ACCEPTABLE--
IT'S FINE.
I'M SORRY. I DIDN'T MEAN TO BE...
THIS IS JUST A LOT TO TAKE IN.
CERTAINLY. LET ME LEAVE YOU SOME TIME TO YOUR THOUGHTS.
BUT...WILL YOU JOIN ME FOR A MEAL LATER?
OF COURSE... MOM.
THANK YOU.
SNIFF

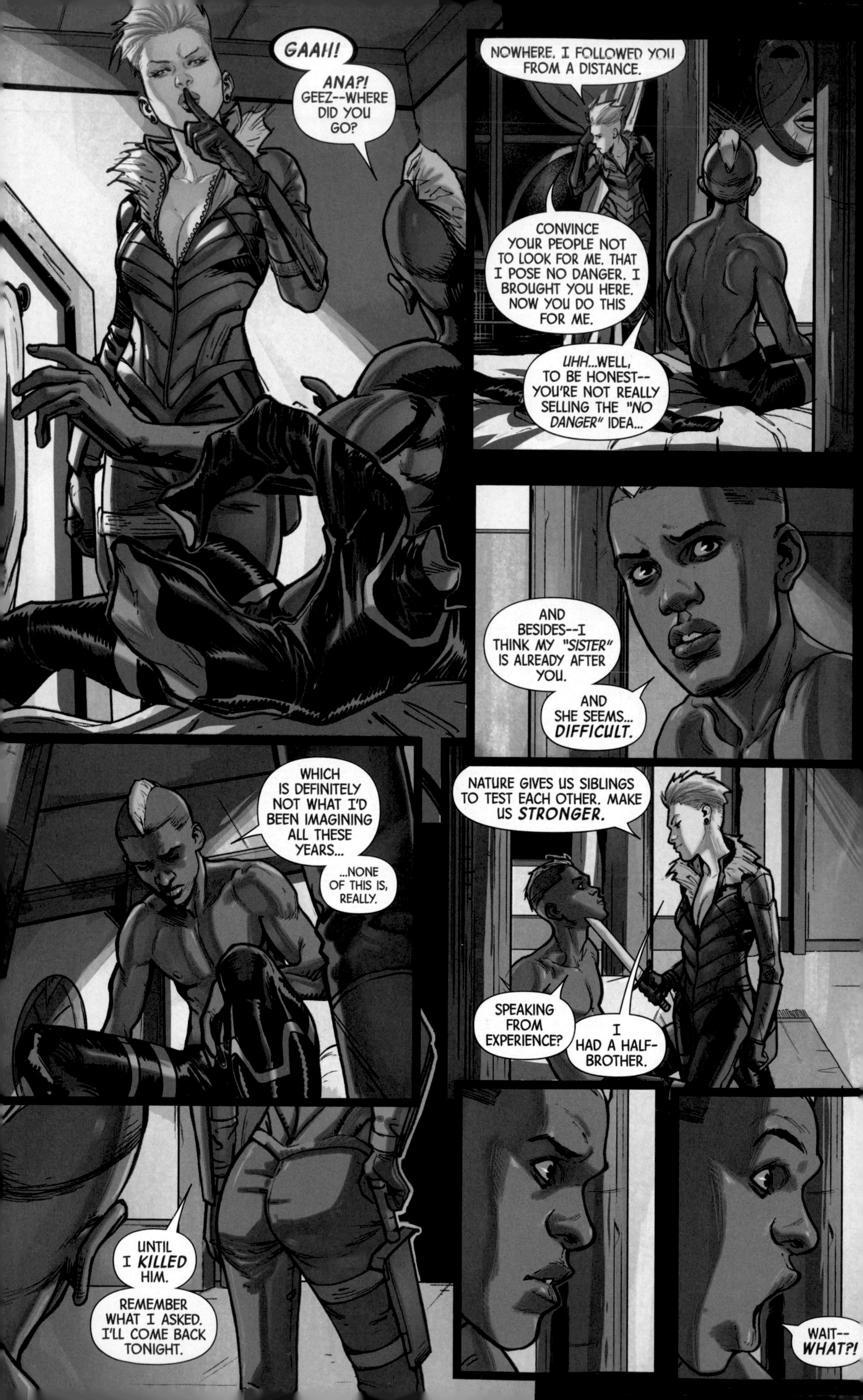
GAAH!
ANA?! GEEZ--WHERE DID YOU GO?
NOWHERE. I FOLLOWED YOU FROM A DISTANCE.
CONVINCE YOUR PEOPLE NOT TO LOOK FOR ME. THAT I POSE NO DANGER. I BROUGHT YOU HERE. NOW YOU DO THIS FOR ME.
UHH...WELL, TO BE HONEST--YOU'RE NOT REALLY SELLING THE "NO DANGER" IDEA...
AND BESIDES--I THINK MY "SISTER" IS ALREADY AFTER YOU.
AND SHE SEEMS... DIFFICULT.
WHICH IS DEFINITELY NOT WHAT I'D BEEN IMAGINING ALL THESE YEARS...
...NONE OF THIS IS, REALLY.
NATURE GIVES US SIBLINGS TO TEST EACH OTHER. MAKE US STRONGER.
SPEAKING FROM EXPERIENCE?
I HAD A HALF-BROTHER.
UNTIL I KILLED HIM.
REMEMBER WHAT I ASKED. I'LL COME BACK TONIGHT.
WAIT--WHAT?!

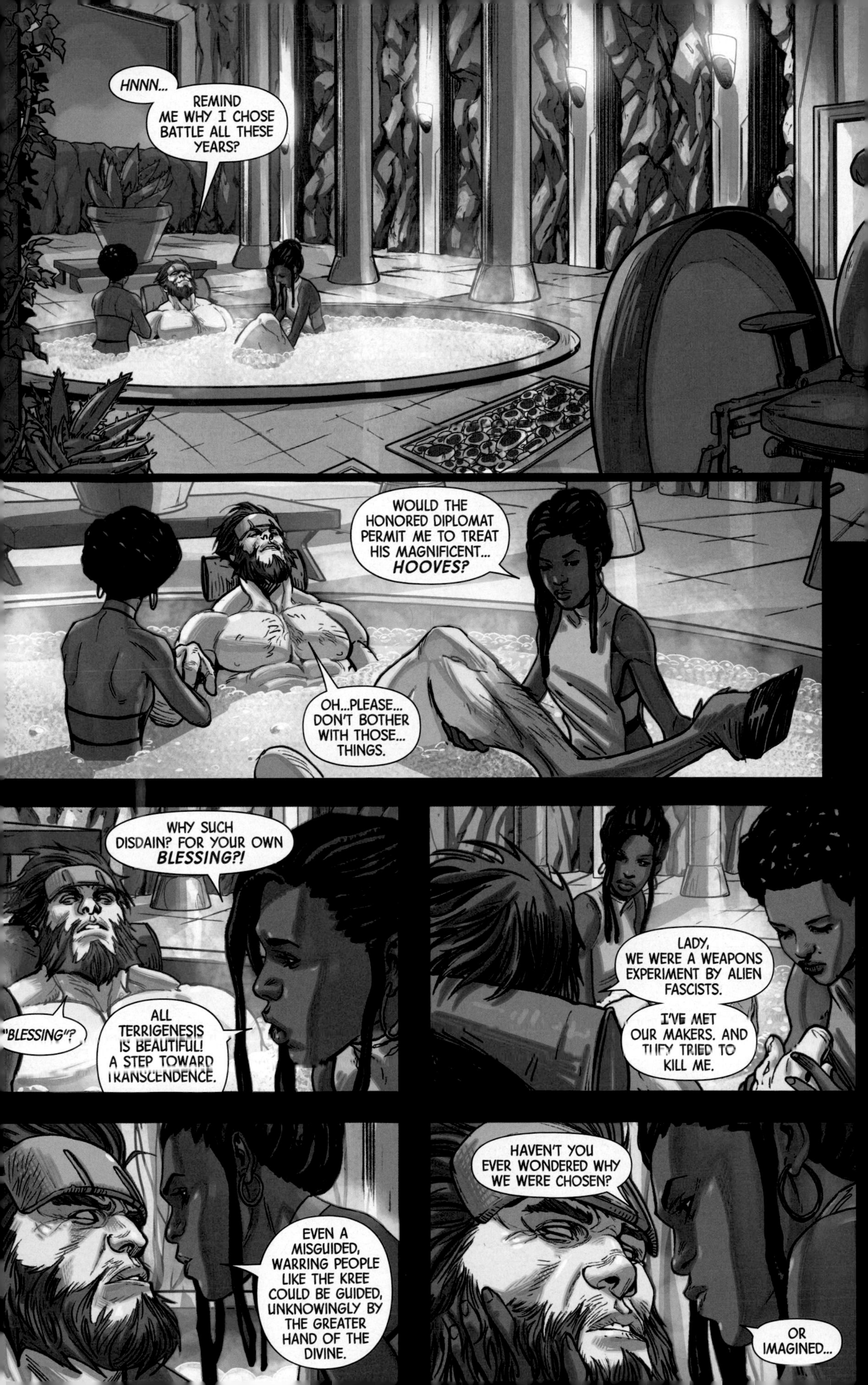
HNNN...
REMIND ME WHY I CHOSE BATTLE ALL THESE YEARS?
WOULD THE HONORED DIPLOMAT PERMIT ME TO TREAT HIS MAGNIFICENT... HOOVES?
OH...PLEASE... DON'T BOTHER WITH THOSE... THINGS.
WHY SUCH DISDAIN? FOR YOUR OWN BLESSING?!
"BLESSING"?
ALL TERRIGENESIS IS BEAUTIFUL! A STEP TOWARD TRANSCENDENCE.
LADY, WE WERE A WEAPONS EXPERIMENT BY ALIEN FASCISTS.
I'VE MET OUR MAKERS. AND THEY TRIED TO KILL ME.
EVEN A MISGUIDED, WARRING PEOPLE LIKE THE KREE COULD BE GUIDED, UNKNOWINGLY BY THE GREATER HAND OF THE DIVINE.
HAVEN'T YOU EVER WONDERED WHY WE WERE CHOSEN?
OR IMAGINED...

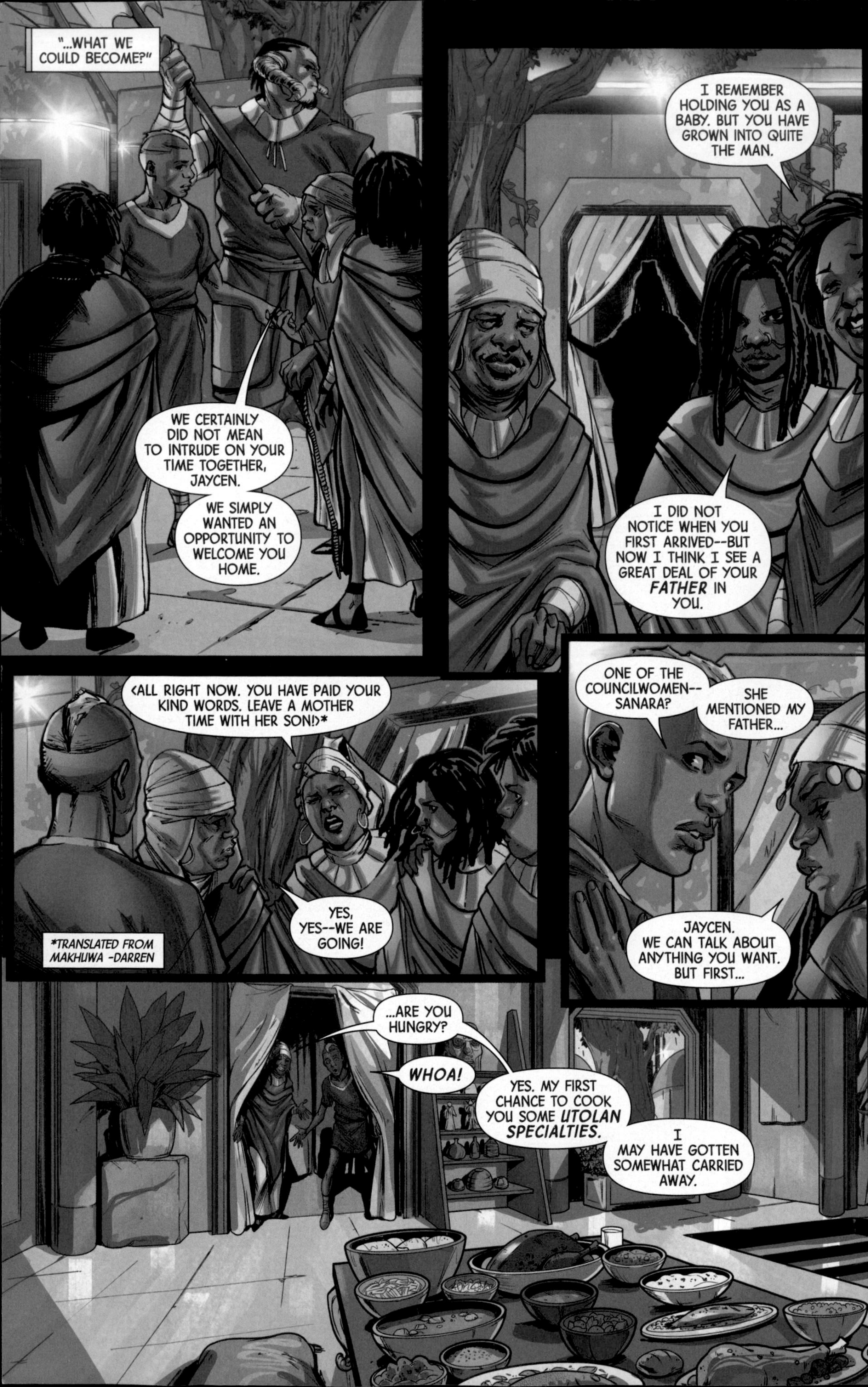
"...WHAT WE COULD BECOME?"
WE CERTAINLY DID NOT MEAN TO INTRUDE ON YOUR TIME TOGETHER, JAYCEN.
WE SIMPLY WANTED AN OPPORTUNITY TO WELCOME YOU HOME.
I REMEMBER HOLDING YOU AS A BABY. BUT YOU HAVE GROWN INTO QUITE THE MAN.
I DID NOT NOTICE WHEN YOU FIRST ARRIVED--BUT NOW I THINK I SEE A GREAT DEAL OF YOUR *FATHER* IN YOU.
<ALL RIGHT NOW. YOU HAVE PAID YOUR KIND WORDS. LEAVE A MOTHER TIME WITH HER SON!>*
YES, YES--WE ARE GOING!
*TRANSLATED FROM MAKHUWA -DARREN
ONE OF THE COUNCILWOMEN--SANARA?
SHE MENTIONED MY FATHER...
JAYCEN. WE CAN TALK ABOUT ANYTHING YOU WANT. BUT FIRST...
...ARE YOU HUNGRY?
WHOA!
YES. MY FIRST CHANCE TO COOK YOU SOME *UTOLAN SPECIALTIES.*
I MAY HAVE GOTTEN SOMEWHAT CARRIED AWAY.

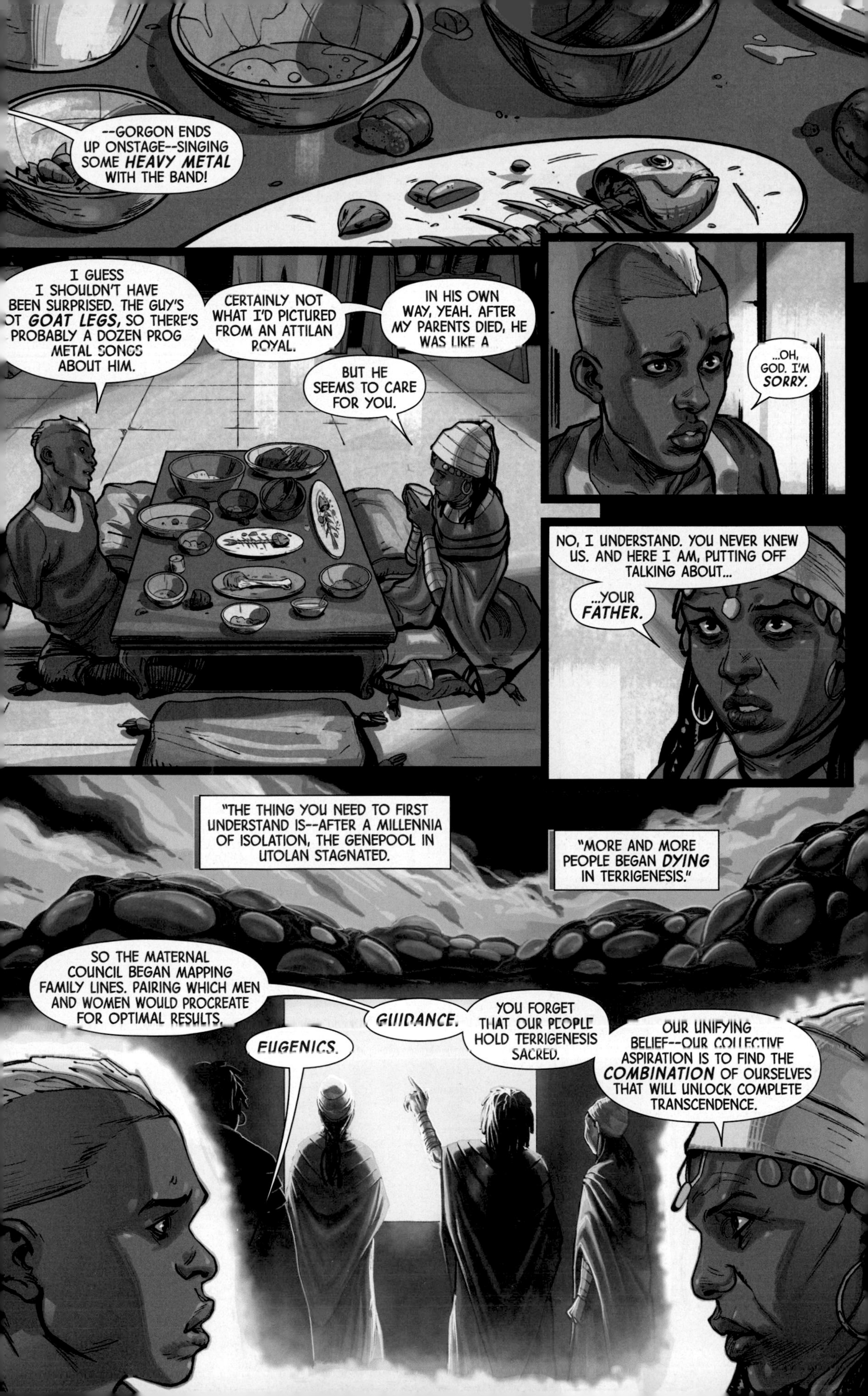
--GORGON ENDS UP ONSTAGE--SINGING SOME HEAVY METAL WITH THE BAND!
I GUESS I SHOULDN'T HAVE BEEN SURPRISED. THE GUY'S GOT GOAT LEGS, SO THERE'S PROBABLY A DOZEN PROG METAL SONGS ABOUT HIM.
CERTAINLY NOT WHAT I'D PICTURED FROM AN ATTILAN ROYAL.
BUT HE SEEMS TO CARE FOR YOU.
IN HIS OWN WAY, YEAH. AFTER MY PARENTS DIED, HE WAS LIKE A
...OH, GOD. I'M SORRY.
NO, I UNDERSTAND. YOU NEVER KNEW US. AND HERE I AM, PUTTING OFF TALKING ABOUT...
...YOUR FATHER.
"THE THING YOU NEED TO FIRST UNDERSTAND IS--AFTER A MILLENNIA OF ISOLATION, THE GENEPOOL IN UTOLAN STAGNATED.
"MORE AND MORE PEOPLE BEGAN DYING IN TERRIGENESIS."
SO THE MATERNAL COUNCIL BEGAN MAPPING FAMILY LINES. PAIRING WHICH MEN AND WOMEN WOULD PROCREATE FOR OPTIMAL RESULTS.
EUGENICS.
GUIDANCE.
YOU FORGET THAT OUR PEOPLE HOLD TERRIGENESIS SACRED.
OUR UNIFYING BELIEF--OUR COLLECTIVE ASPIRATION IS TO FIND THE COMBINATION OF OURSELVES THAT WILL UNLOCK COMPLETE TRANSCENDENCE.

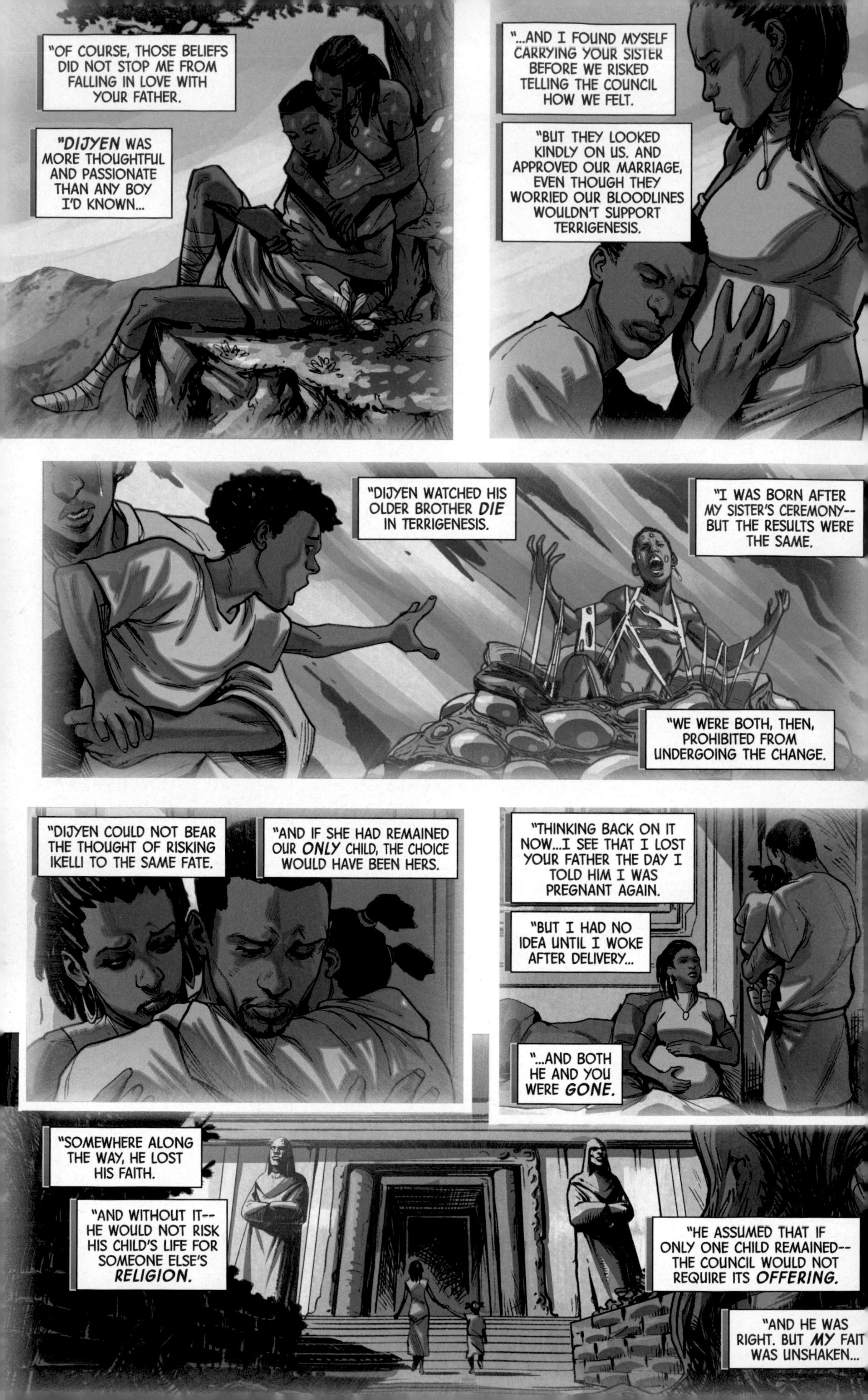
"OF COURSE, THOSE BELIEFS DID NOT STOP ME FROM FALLING IN LOVE WITH YOUR FATHER.
"DIJYEN WAS MORE THOUGHTFUL AND PASSIONATE THAN ANY BOY I'D KNOWN...
"...AND I FOUND MYSELF CARRYING YOUR SISTER BEFORE WE RISKED TELLING THE COUNCIL HOW WE FELT.
"BUT THEY LOOKED KINDLY ON US. AND APPROVED OUR MARRIAGE, EVEN THOUGH THEY WORRIED OUR BLOODLINES WOULDN'T SUPPORT TERRIGENESIS.
"DIJYEN WATCHED HIS OLDER BROTHER DIE IN TERRIGENESIS.
"I WAS BORN AFTER MY SISTER'S CEREMONY--BUT THE RESULTS WERE THE SAME.
"WE WERE BOTH, THEN, PROHIBITED FROM UNDERGOING THE CHANGE.
"DIJYEN COULD NOT BEAR THE THOUGHT OF RISKING IKELLI TO THE SAME FATE.
"AND IF SHE HAD REMAINED OUR ONLY CHILD, THE CHOICE WOULD HAVE BEEN HERS.
"THINKING BACK ON IT NOW...I SEE THAT I LOST YOUR FATHER THE DAY I TOLD HIM I WAS PREGNANT AGAIN.
"BUT I HAD NO IDEA UNTIL I WOKE AFTER DELIVERY...
"...AND BOTH HE AND YOU WERE GONE.
"SOMEWHERE ALONG THE WAY, HE LOST HIS FAITH.
"AND WITHOUT IT--HE WOULD NOT RISK HIS CHILD'S LIFE FOR SOMEONE ELSE'S RELIGION.
"HE ASSUMED THAT IF ONLY ONE CHILD REMAINED--THE COUNCIL WOULD NOT REQUIRE ITS OFFERING.
"AND HE WAS RIGHT. BUT MY FAIT WAS UNSHAKEN...

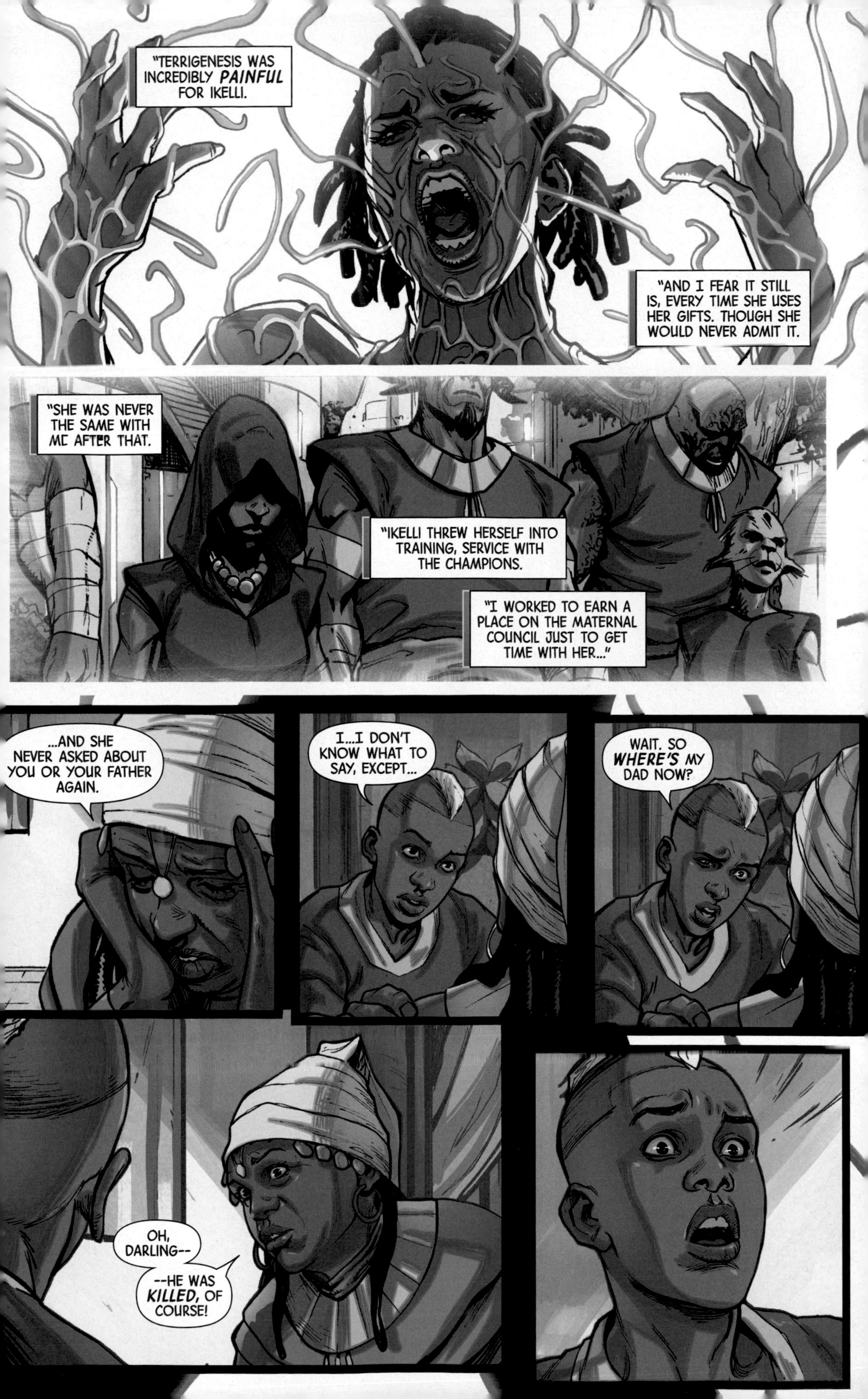
"TERRIGENESIS WAS INCREDIBLY PAINFUL FOR IKELLI.
"AND I FEAR IT STILL IS, EVERY TIME SHE USES HER GIFTS. THOUGH SHE WOULD NEVER ADMIT IT.
"SHE WAS NEVER THE SAME WITH ME AFTER THAT.
"IKELLI THREW HERSELF INTO TRAINING, SERVICE WITH THE CHAMPIONS.
"I WORKED TO EARN A PLACE ON THE MATERNAL COUNCIL JUST TO GET TIME WITH HER..."
...AND SHE NEVER ASKED ABOUT YOU OR YOUR FATHER AGAIN.
I...I DON'T KNOW WHAT TO SAY, EXCEPT...
WAIT. SO WHERE'S MY DAD NOW?
OH, DARLING--
--HE WAS KILLED, OF COURSE!

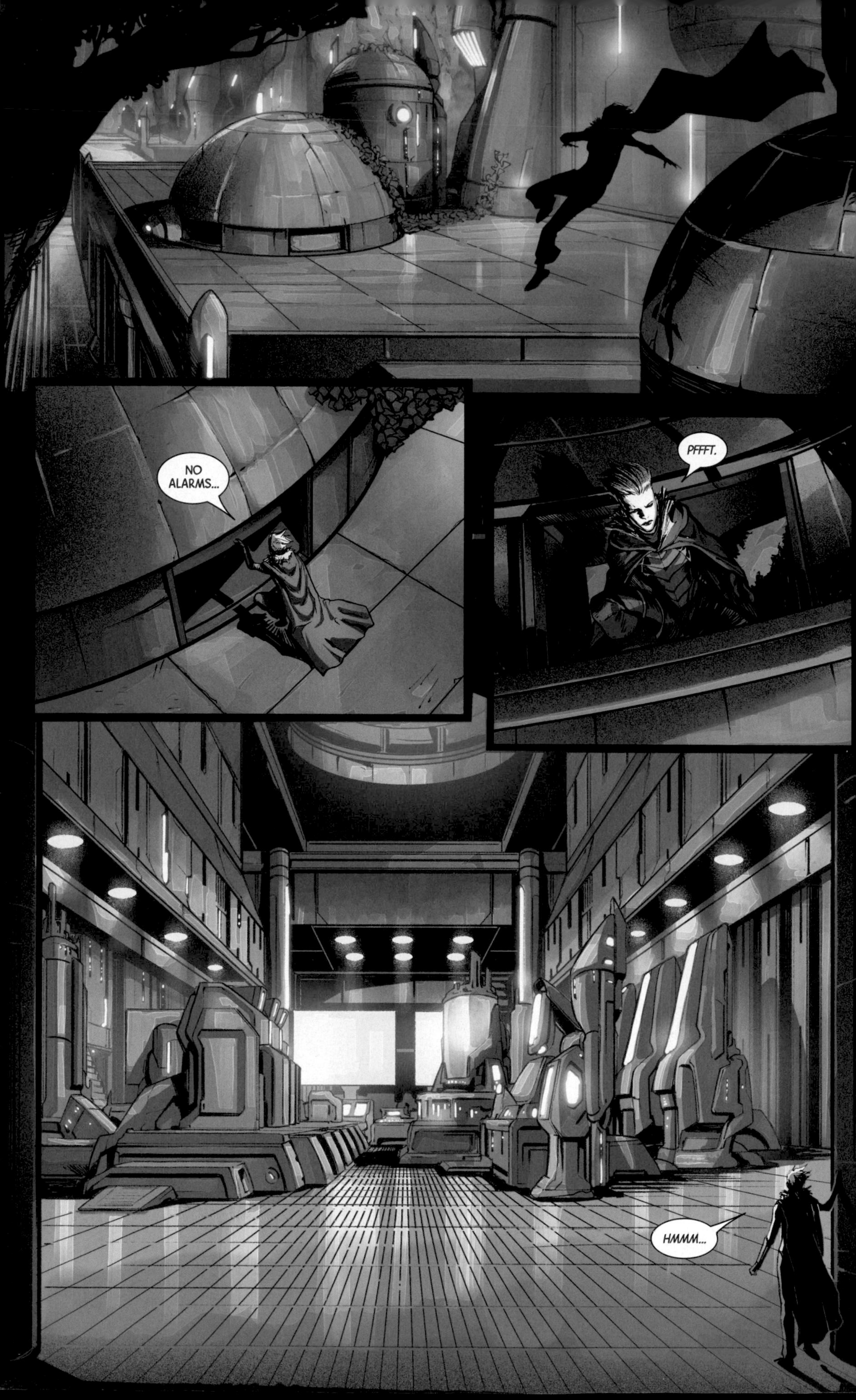

NO ALARMS...
PFFFT.
HMMM...

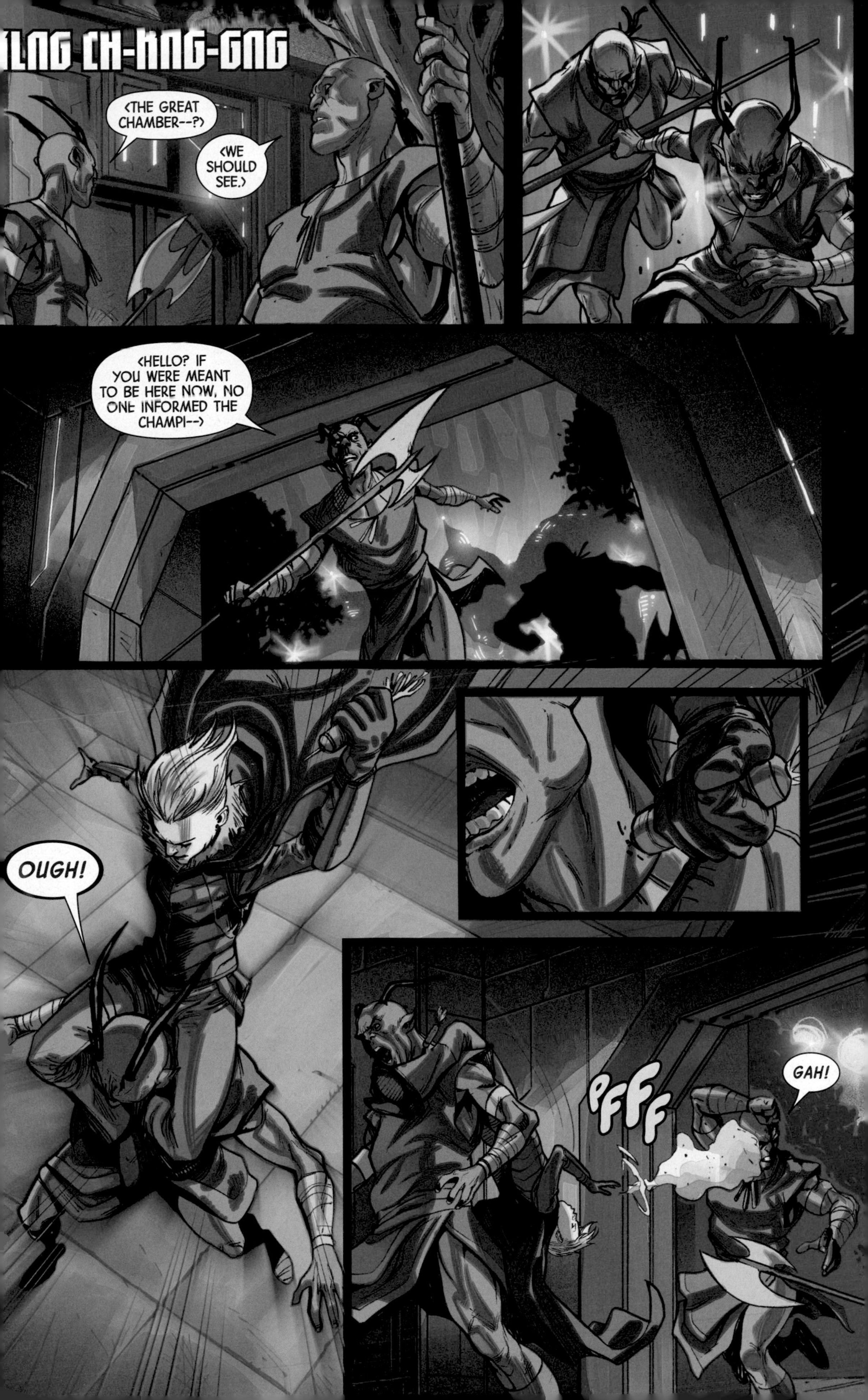

CHAMBER--?>
<WE SHOULD SEE.>
<HELLO? IF YOU WERE MEANT TO BE HERE NOW, NO ONE INFORMED THE CHAMPI-->
OUGH!
PFFF
GAH!

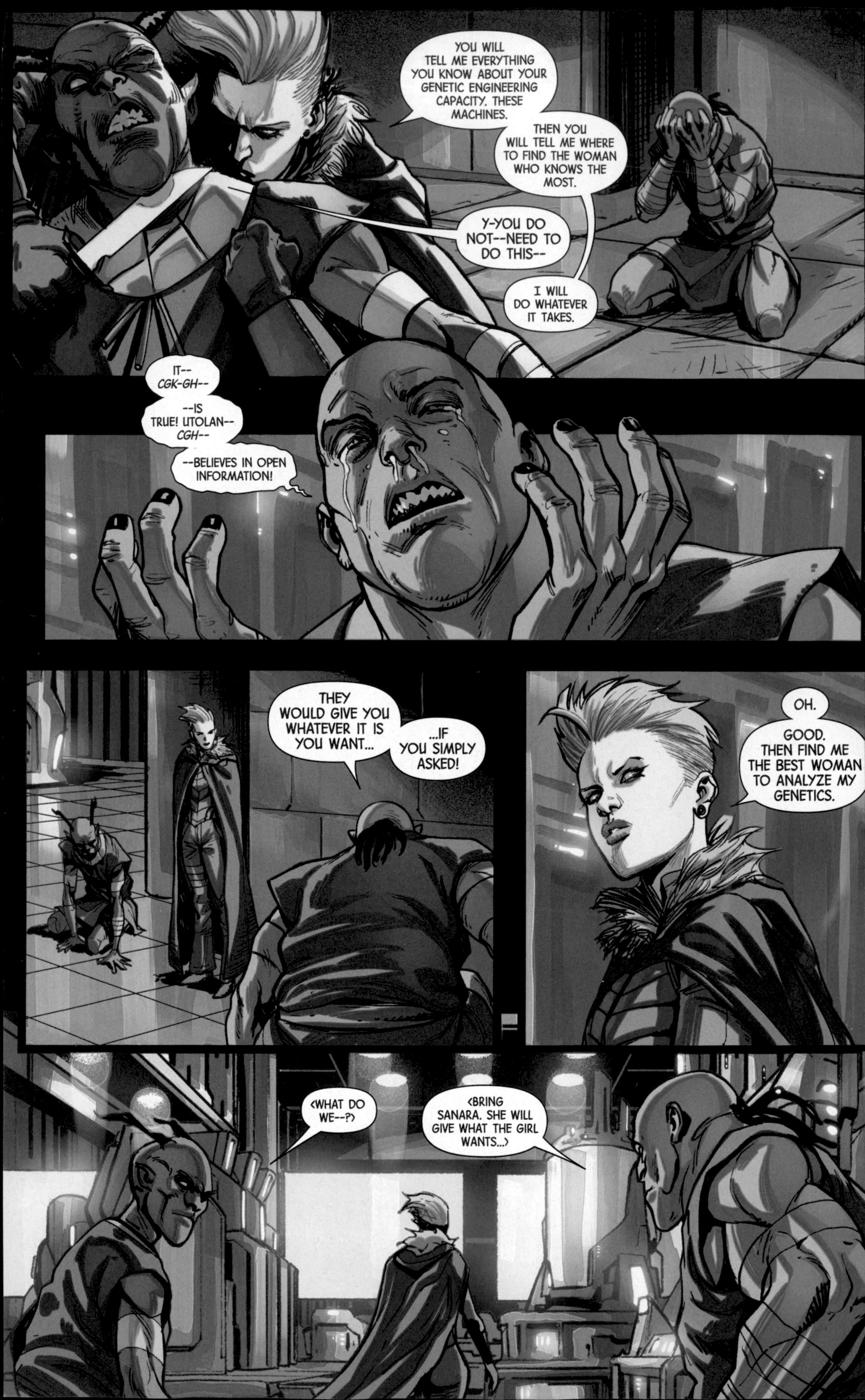
YOU WILL TELL ME EVERYTHING YOU KNOW ABOUT YOUR GENETIC ENGINEERING CAPACITY. THESE MACHINES.
THEN YOU WILL TELL ME WHERE TO FIND THE WOMAN WHO KNOWS THE MOST.
Y-YOU DO NOT--NEED TO DO THIS--
I WILL DO WHATEVER IT TAKES.
IT-- CGK-GH--
--IS TRUE! UTOLAN-- CGH--
--BELIEVES IN OPEN INFORMATION!
THEY WOULD GIVE YOU WHATEVER IT IS YOU WANT...
...IF YOU SIMPLY ASKED!
OH.
GOOD. THEN FIND ME THE BEST WOMAN TO ANALYZE MY GENETICS.
<WHAT DO WE--?>
<BRING SANARA. SHE WILL GIVE WHAT THE GIRL WANTS...>

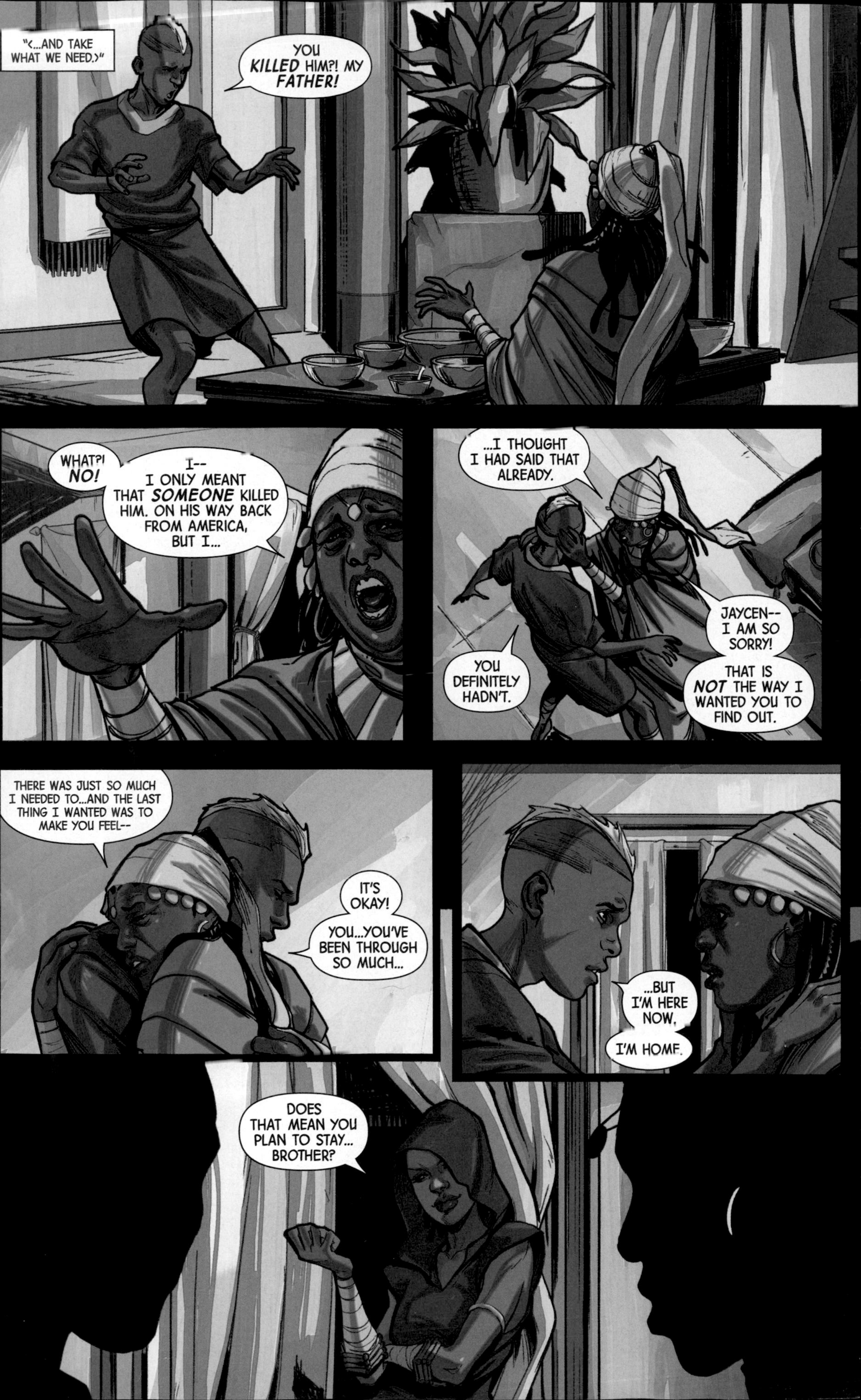
"<...AND TAKE WHAT WE NEED.>"
YOU KILLED HIM?! MY FATHER!
WHAT?! NO!
I-- I ONLY MEANT THAT SOMEONE KILLED HIM. ON HIS WAY BACK FROM AMERICA, BUT I...
...I THOUGHT I HAD SAID THAT ALREADY.
YOU DEFINITELY HADN'T.
JAYCEN-- I AM SO SORRY!
THAT IS NOT THE WAY I WANTED YOU TO FIND OUT.
THERE WAS JUST SO MUCH I NEEDED TO...AND THE LAST THING I WANTED WAS TO MAKE YOU FEEL--
IT'S OKAY!
YOU...YOU'VE BEEN THROUGH SO MUCH...
...BUT I'M HERE NOW.
I'M HOME.
DOES THAT MEAN YOU PLAN TO STAY... BROTHER?

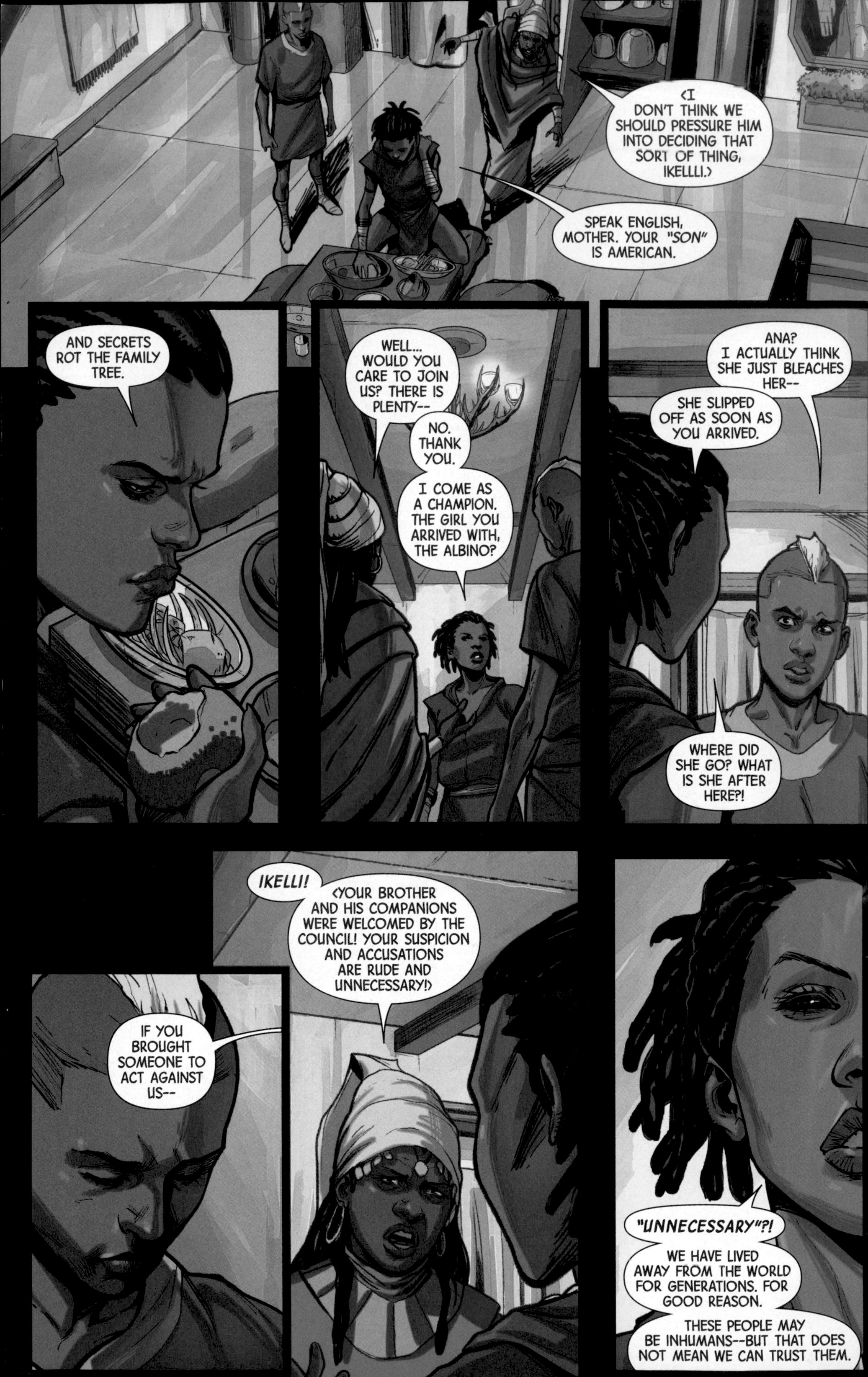
<I DON'T THINK WE SHOULD PRESSURE HIM INTO DECIDING THAT SORT OF THING, IKELLLI.>
SPEAK ENGLISH, MOTHER. YOUR "SON" IS AMERICAN.
AND SECRETS ROT THE FAMILY TREE.
WELL... WOULD YOU CARE TO JOIN US? THERE IS PLENTY--
NO. THANK YOU.
I COME AS A CHAMPION. THE GIRL YOU ARRIVED WITH, THE ALBINO?
ANA? I ACTUALLY THINK SHE JUST BLEACHES HER--
SHE SLIPPED OFF AS SOON AS YOU ARRIVED.
WHERE DID SHE GO? WHAT IS SHE AFTER HERE?!
IF YOU BROUGHT SOMEONE TO ACT AGAINST US--
IKELLI!
<YOUR BROTHER AND HIS COMPANIONS WERE WELCOMED BY THE COUNCIL! YOUR SUSPICION AND ACCUSATIONS ARE RUDE AND UNNECESSARY!>
"UNNECESSARY"?!
WE HAVE LIVED AWAY FROM THE WORLD FOR GENERATIONS. FOR GOOD REASON.
THESE PEOPLE MAY BE INHUMANS--BUT THAT DOES NOT MEAN WE CAN TRUST THEM.

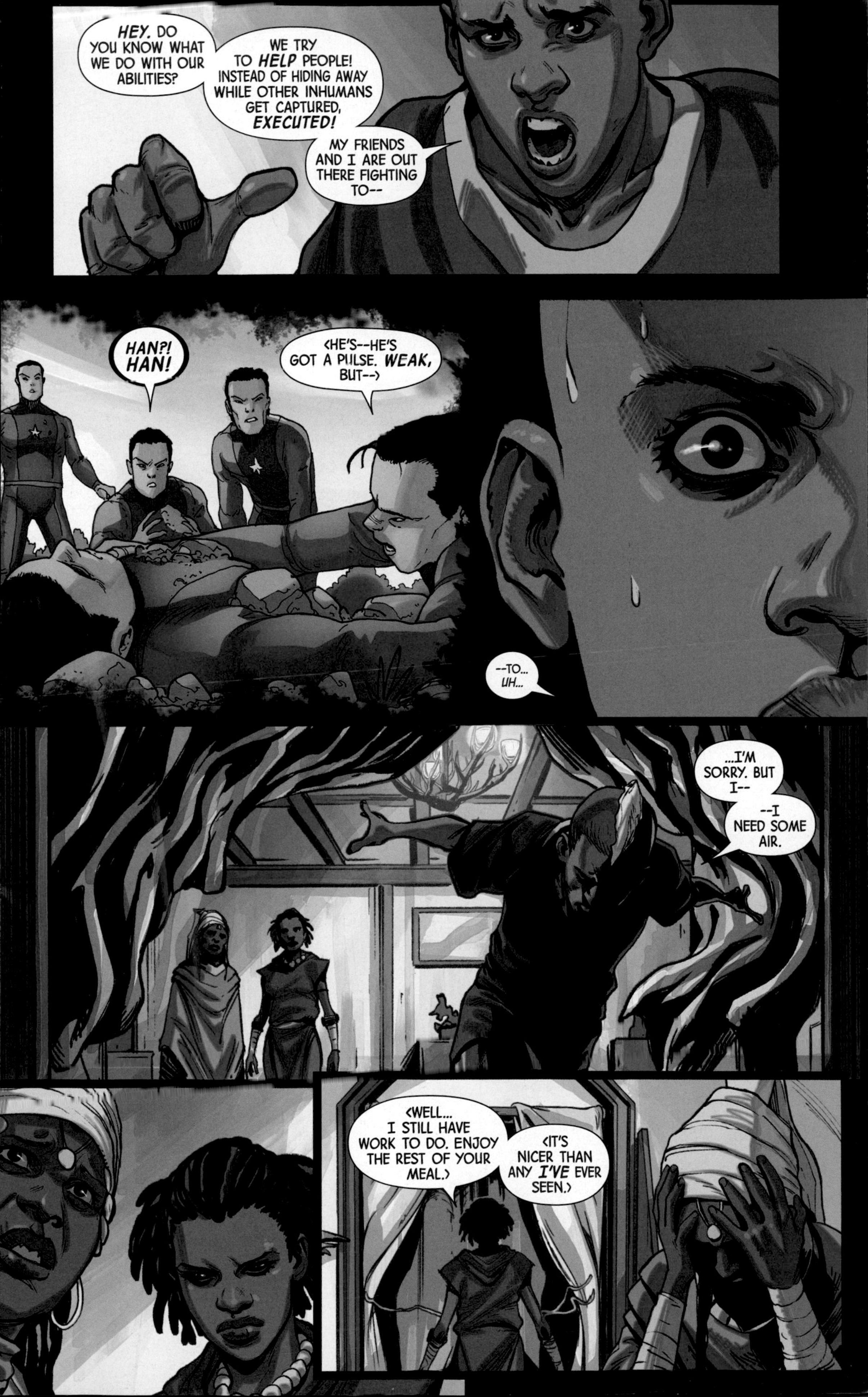
HEY. DO YOU KNOW WHAT WE DO WITH OUR ABILITIES?
WE TRY TO HELP PEOPLE! INSTEAD OF HIDING AWAY WHILE OTHER INHUMANS GET CAPTURED, EXECUTED!
MY FRIENDS AND I ARE OUT THERE FIGHTING TO--
HAN?! HAN!
<HE'S--HE'S GOT A PULSE. WEAK, BUT-->
--TO... UH...
...I'M SORRY. BUT I--
--I NEED SOME AIR.
<WELL... I STILL HAVE WORK TO DO. ENJOY THE REST OF YOUR MEAL.>
<IT'S NICER THAN ANY I'VE EVER SEEN.>

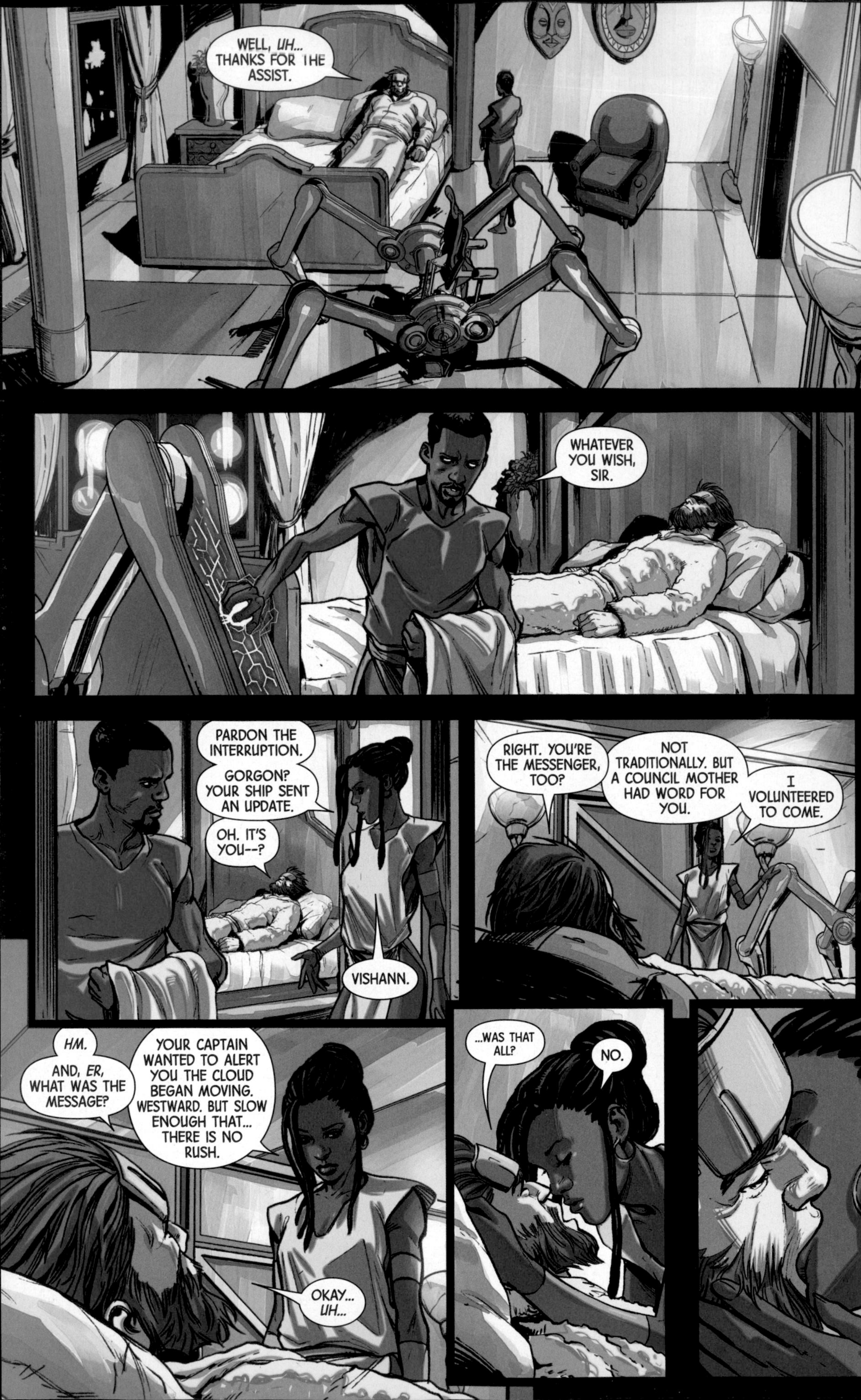
WELL, UH... THANKS FOR THE ASSIST.
WHATEVER YOU WISH, SIR.
PARDON THE INTERRUPTION.
GORGON? YOUR SHIP SENT AN UPDATE.
OH. IT'S YOU--?
VISHANN.
RIGHT. YOU'RE THE MESSENGER, TOO?
NOT TRADITIONALLY. BUT A COUNCIL MOTHER HAD WORD FOR YOU.
I VOLUNTEERED TO COME.
HM.
AND, ER, WHAT WAS THE MESSAGE?
YOUR CAPTAIN WANTED TO ALERT YOU THE CLOUD BEGAN MOVING. WESTWARD. BUT SLOW ENOUGH THAT... THERE IS NO RUSH.
OKAY... UH...
...WAS THAT ALL?
NO.

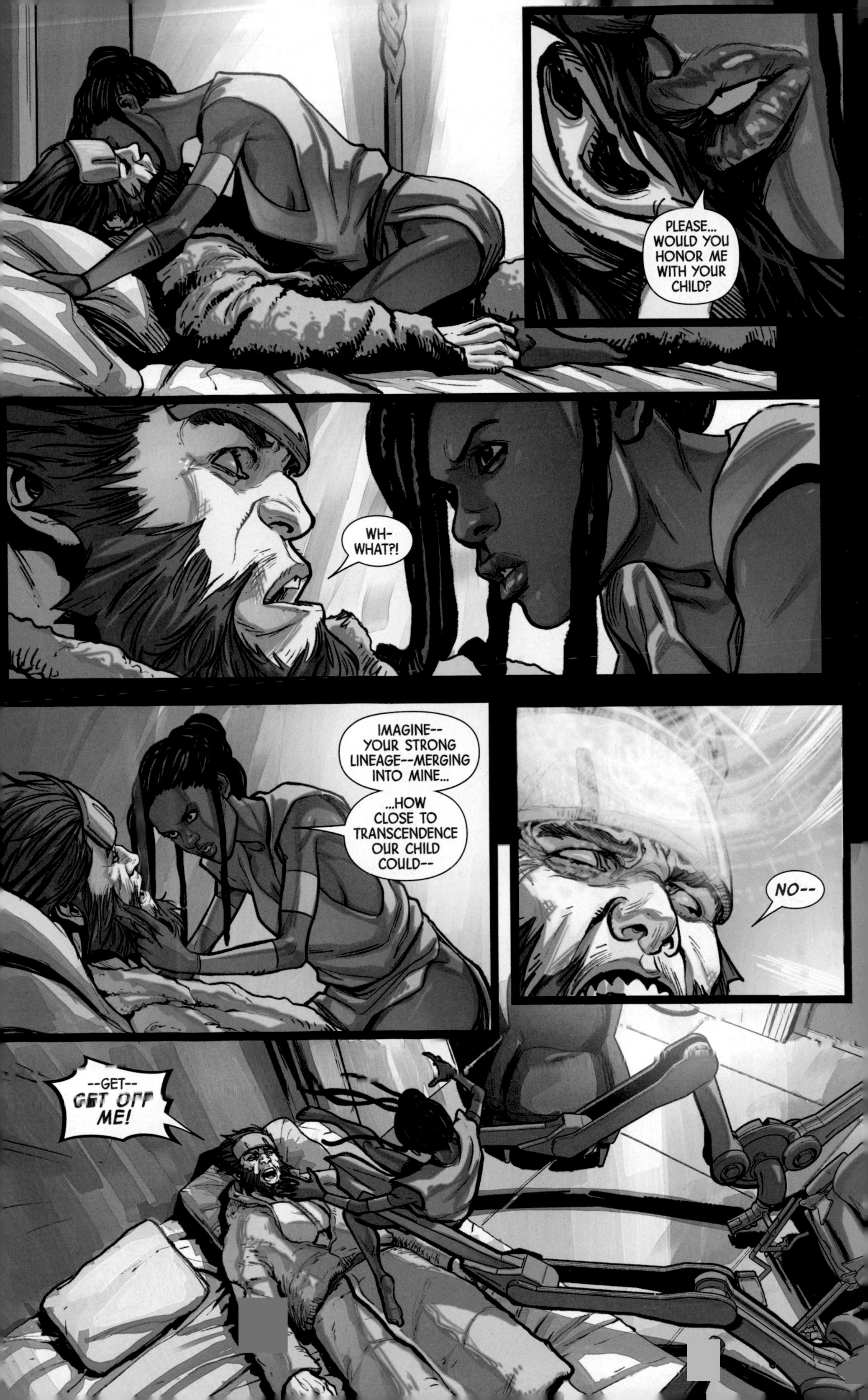
PLEASE... WOULD YOU HONOR ME WITH YOUR CHILD?
WH- WHAT?!
IMAGINE-- YOUR STRONG LINEAGE--MERGING INTO MINE...
...HOW CLOSE TO TRANSCENDENCE OUR CHILD COULD--
NO--
--GET-- GET OFF ME!

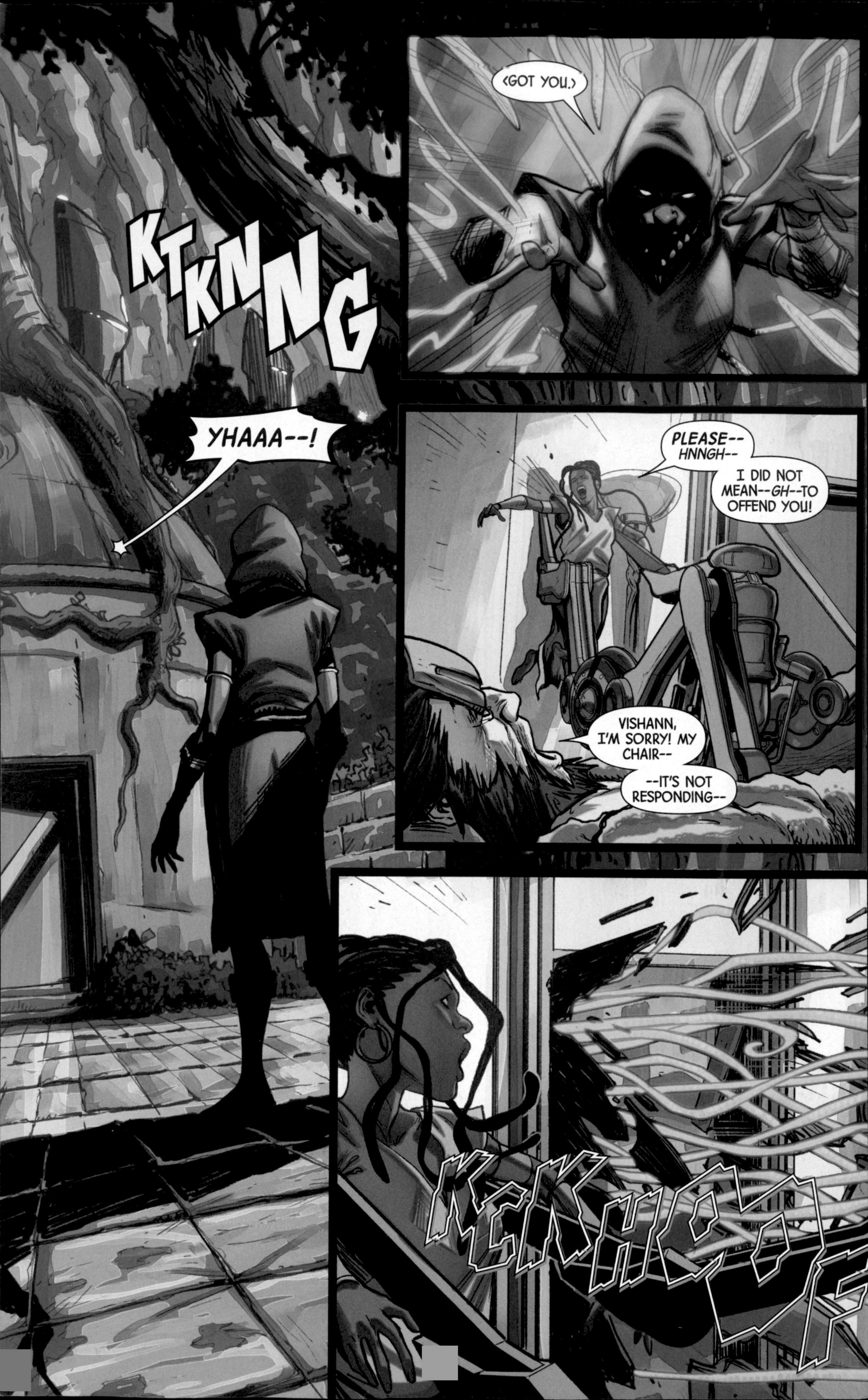
KTKNNG
YHAAA--!
‹GOT YOU.›
PLEASE-- HNNGH--
I DID NOT MEAN--GH--TO OFFEND YOU!
VISHANN, I'M SORRY! MY CHAIR--
--IT'S NOT RESPONDING--

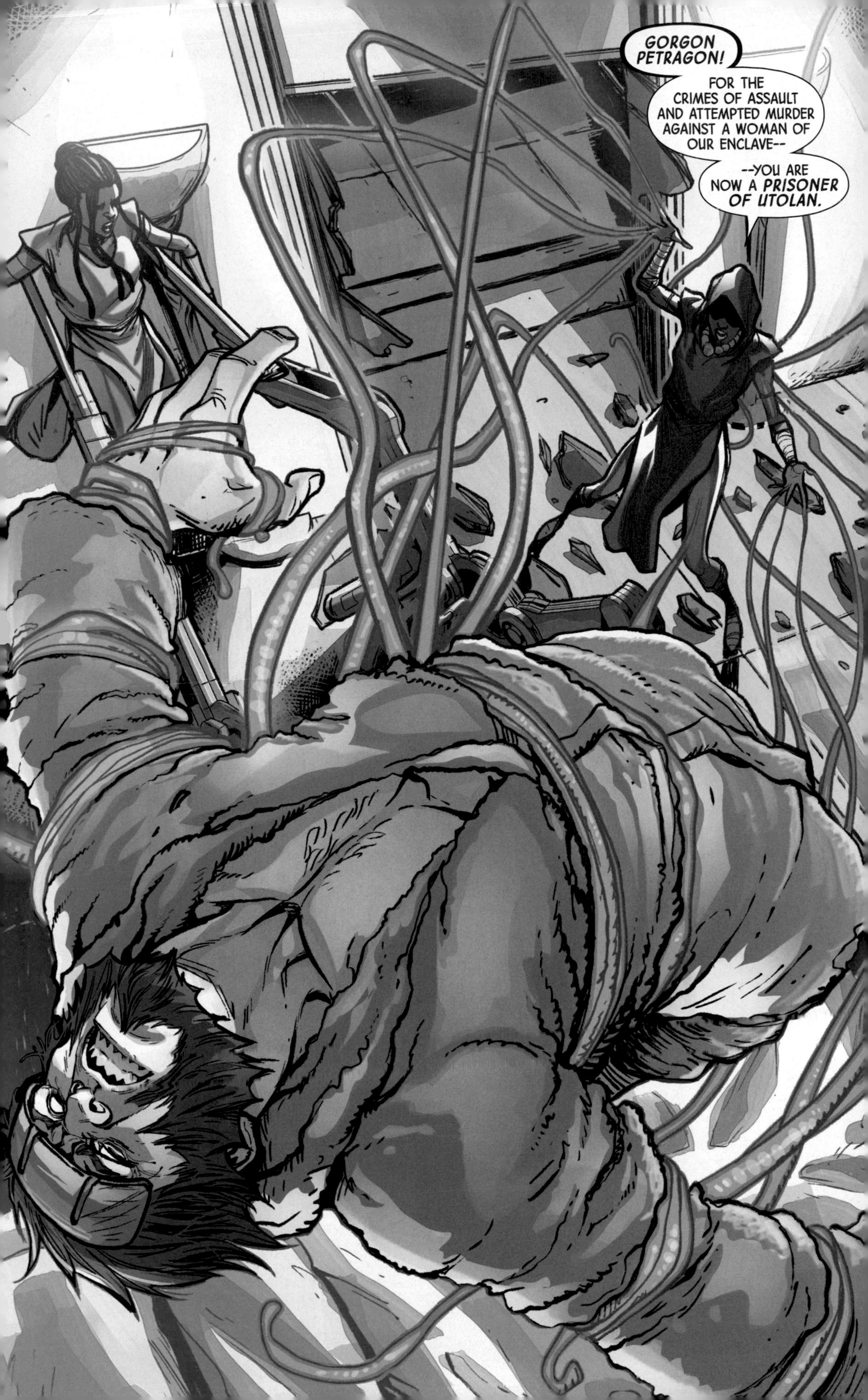
GORGON PETRAGON!
FOR THE CRIMES OF ASSAULT AND ATTEMPTED MURDER AGAINST A WOMAN OF OUR ENCLAVE--
--YOU ARE NOW A *PRISONER OF UTOLAN.*

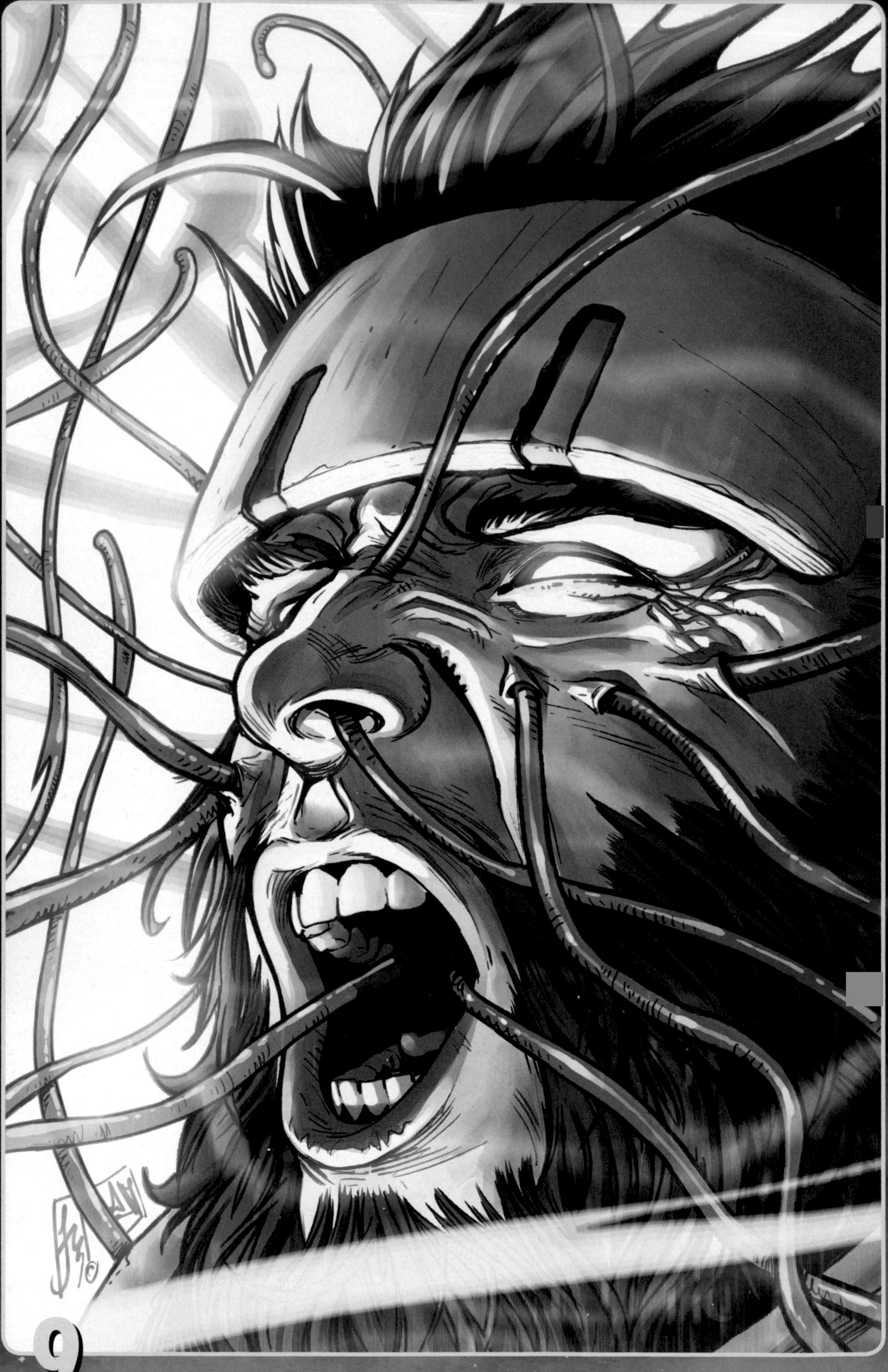

9

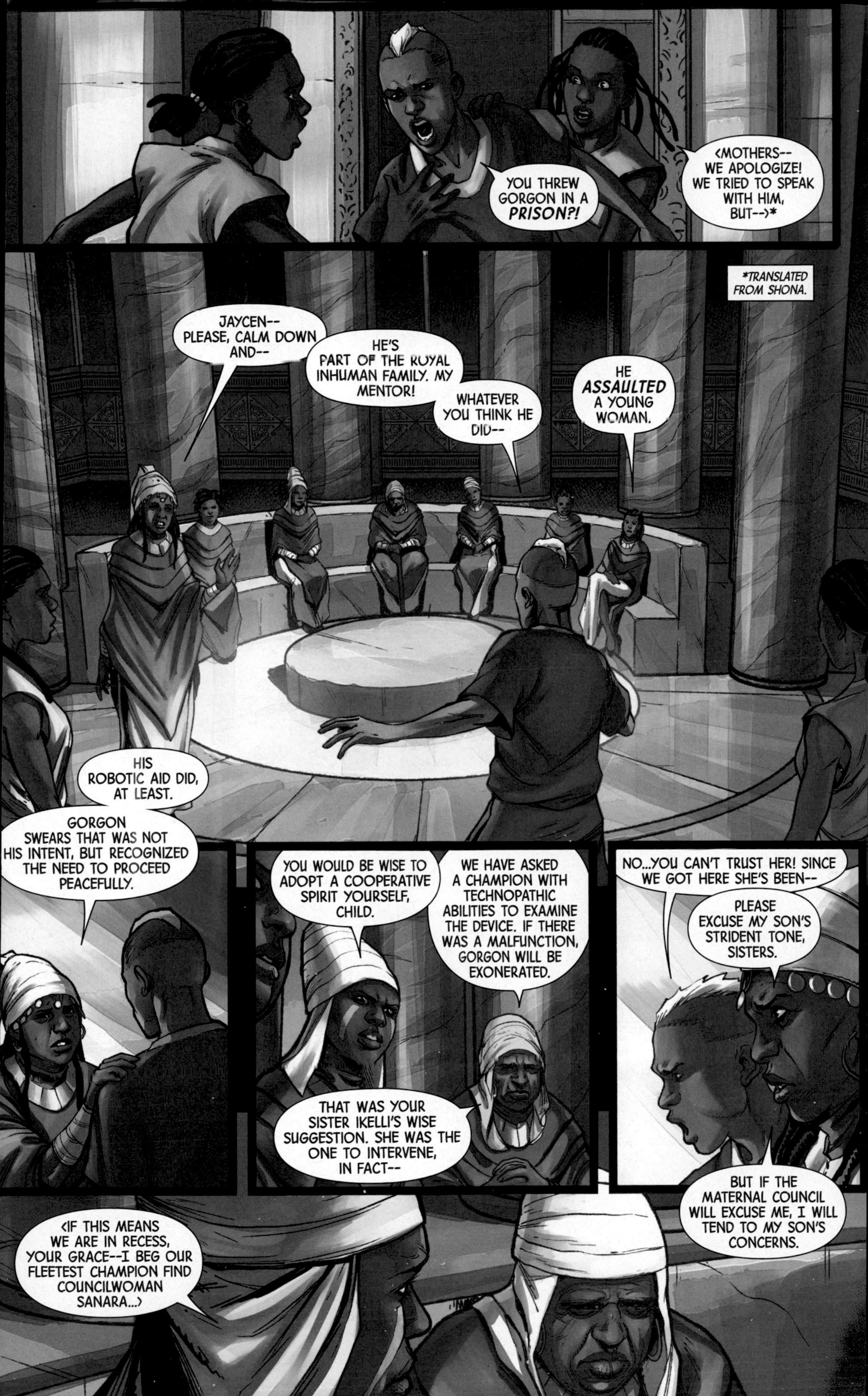
YOU THREW GORGON IN A PRISON?!
<MOTHERS-- WE APOLOGIZE! WE TRIED TO SPEAK WITH HIM, BUT-->*
*TRANSLATED FROM SHONA.
JAYCEN-- PLEASE, CALM DOWN AND--
HE'S PART OF THE ROYAL INHUMAN FAMILY. MY MENTOR!
WHATEVER YOU THINK HE DID--
HE ASSAULTED A YOUNG WOMAN.
HIS ROBOTIC AID DID, AT LEAST.
GORGON SWEARS THAT WAS NOT HIS INTENT, BUT RECOGNIZED THE NEED TO PROCEED PEACEFULLY.
YOU WOULD BE WISE TO ADOPT A COOPERATIVE SPIRIT YOURSELF, CHILD.
WE HAVE ASKED A CHAMPION WITH TECHNOPATHIC ABILITIES TO EXAMINE THE DEVICE. IF THERE WAS A MALFUNCTION, GORGON WILL BE EXONERATED.
THAT WAS YOUR SISTER IKELLI'S WISE SUGGESTION. SHE WAS THE ONE TO INTERVENE, IN FACT--
NO...YOU CAN'T TRUST HER! SINCE WE GOT HERE SHE'S BEEN--
PLEASE EXCUSE MY SON'S STRIDENT TONE, SISTERS.
BUT IF THE MATERNAL COUNCIL WILL EXCUSE ME, I WILL TEND TO MY SON'S CONCERNS.
<IF THIS MEANS WE ARE IN RECESS, YOUR GRACE--I BEG OUR FLEETEST CHAMPION FIND COUNCILWOMAN SANARA...>

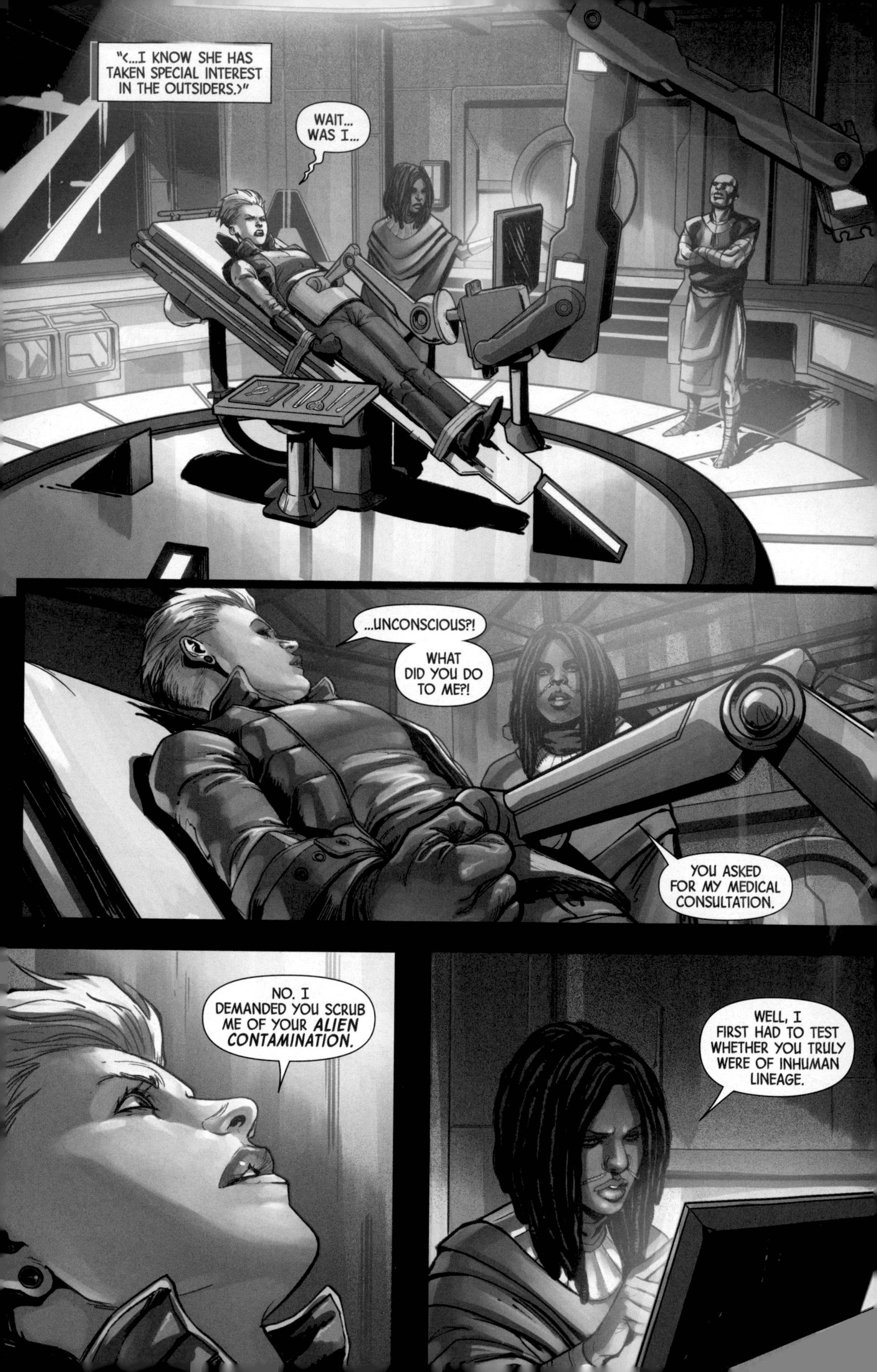
"<...I KNOW SHE HAS TAKEN SPECIAL INTEREST IN THE OUTSIDERS.>"
WAIT... WAS I...
...UNCONSCIOUS?!
WHAT DID YOU DO TO ME?!
YOU ASKED FOR MY MEDICAL CONSULTATION.
NO. I DEMANDED YOU SCRUB ME OF YOUR ALIEN CONTAMINATION.
WELL, I FIRST HAD TO TEST WHETHER YOU TRULY WERE OF INHUMAN LINEAGE.

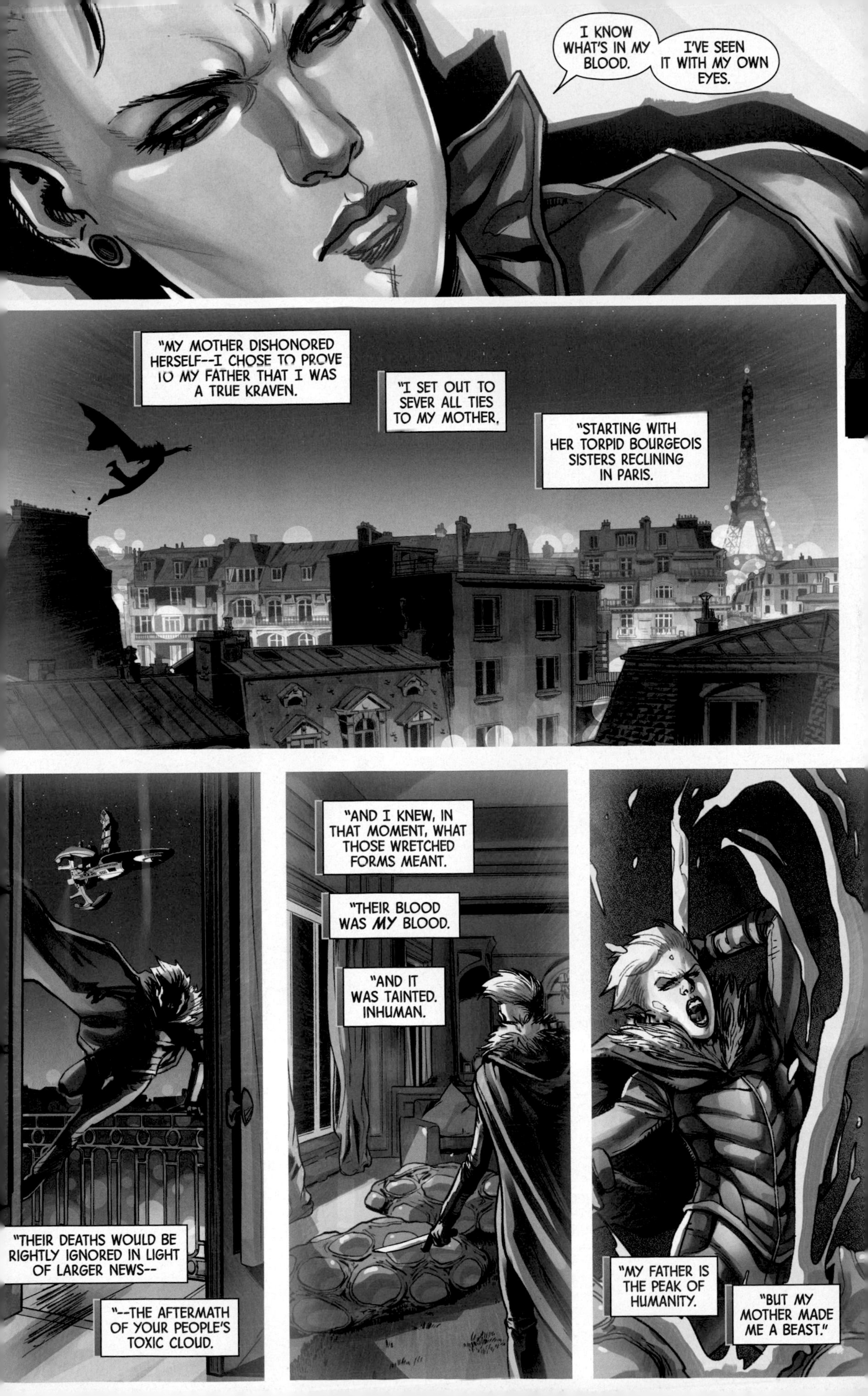

I KNOW WHAT'S IN MY BLOOD.
I'VE SEEN IT WITH MY OWN EYES.
"MY MOTHER DISHONORED HERSELF--I CHOSE TO PROVE TO MY FATHER THAT I WAS A TRUE KRAVEN.
"I SET OUT TO SEVER ALL TIES TO MY MOTHER,
"STARTING WITH HER TORPID BOURGEOIS SISTERS RECLINING IN PARIS.
"THEIR DEATHS WOULD BE RIGHTLY IGNORED IN LIGHT OF LARGER NEWS--
"--THE AFTERMATH OF YOUR PEOPLE'S TOXIC CLOUD.
"AND I KNEW, IN THAT MOMENT, WHAT THOSE WRETCHED FORMS MEANT.
"THEIR BLOOD WAS *MY* BLOOD.
"AND IT WAS TAINTED. INHUMAN.
"MY FATHER IS THE PEAK OF HUMANITY.
"BUT MY MOTHER MADE ME A BEAST."

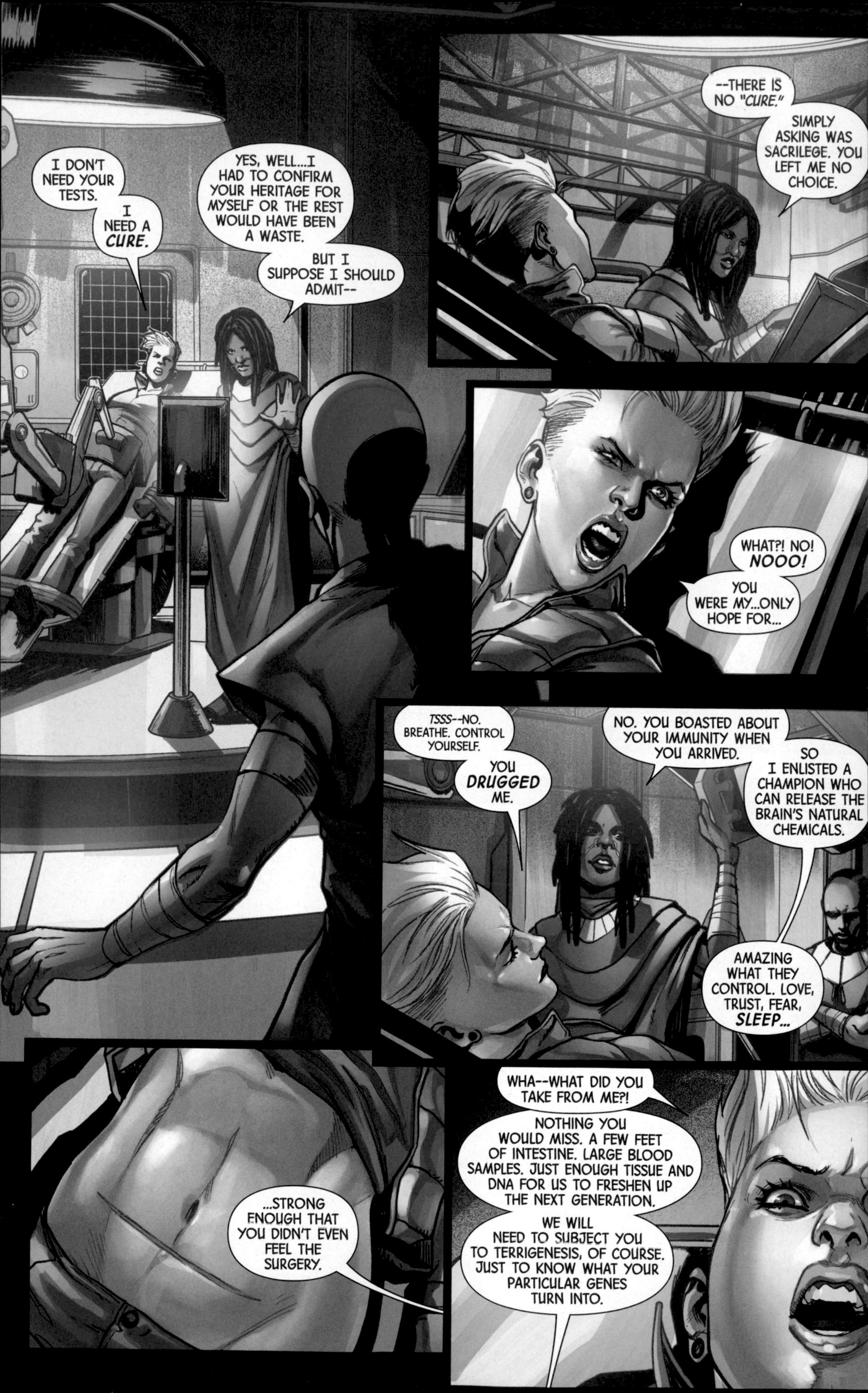
I DON'T NEED YOUR TESTS.
I NEED A *CURE.*
YES, WELL...I HAD TO CONFIRM YOUR HERITAGE FOR MYSELF OR THE REST WOULD HAVE BEEN A WASTE.
BUT I SUPPOSE I SHOULD ADMIT--
--THERE IS NO "*CURE.*"
SIMPLY ASKING WAS SACRILEGE. YOU LEFT ME NO CHOICE.
WHAT?! NO! ***NOOO!***
YOU WERE MY...ONLY HOPE FOR...
TSSS--NO. BREATHE. CONTROL YOURSELF.
YOU ***DRUGGED*** ME.
NO. YOU BOASTED ABOUT YOUR IMMUNITY WHEN YOU ARRIVED.
SO I ENLISTED A CHAMPION WHO CAN RELEASE THE BRAIN'S NATURAL CHEMICALS.
AMAZING WHAT THEY CONTROL. LOVE, TRUST, FEAR, ***SLEEP...***
...STRONG ENOUGH THAT YOU DIDN'T EVEN FEEL THE SURGERY.
WHA--WHAT DID YOU TAKE FROM ME?!
NOTHING YOU WOULD MISS. A FEW FEET OF INTESTINE. LARGE BLOOD SAMPLES. JUST ENOUGH TISSUE AND DNA FOR US TO FRESHEN UP THE NEXT GENERATION.
WE WILL NEED TO SUBJECT YOU TO TERRIGENESIS, OF COURSE. JUST TO KNOW WHAT YOUR PARTICULAR GENES TURN INTO.

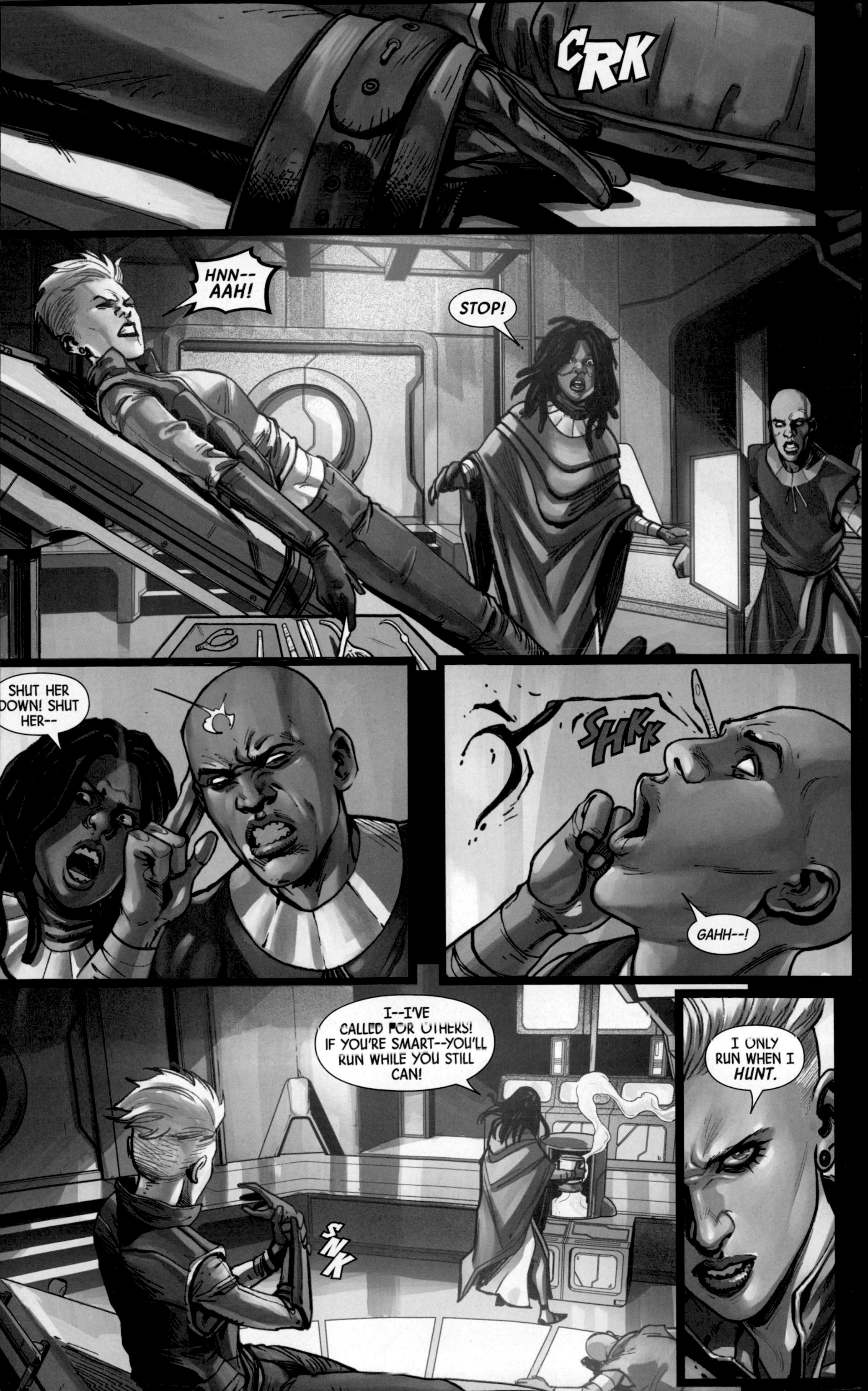
CRK
HNN--AAH!
STOP!
SHUT HER DOWN! SHUT HER--
SHKK
GAHH--!
I--I'VE CALLED FOR OTHERS! IF YOU'RE SMART--YOU'LL RUN WHILE YOU STILL CAN!
SNK
I ONLY RUN WHEN I HUNT.

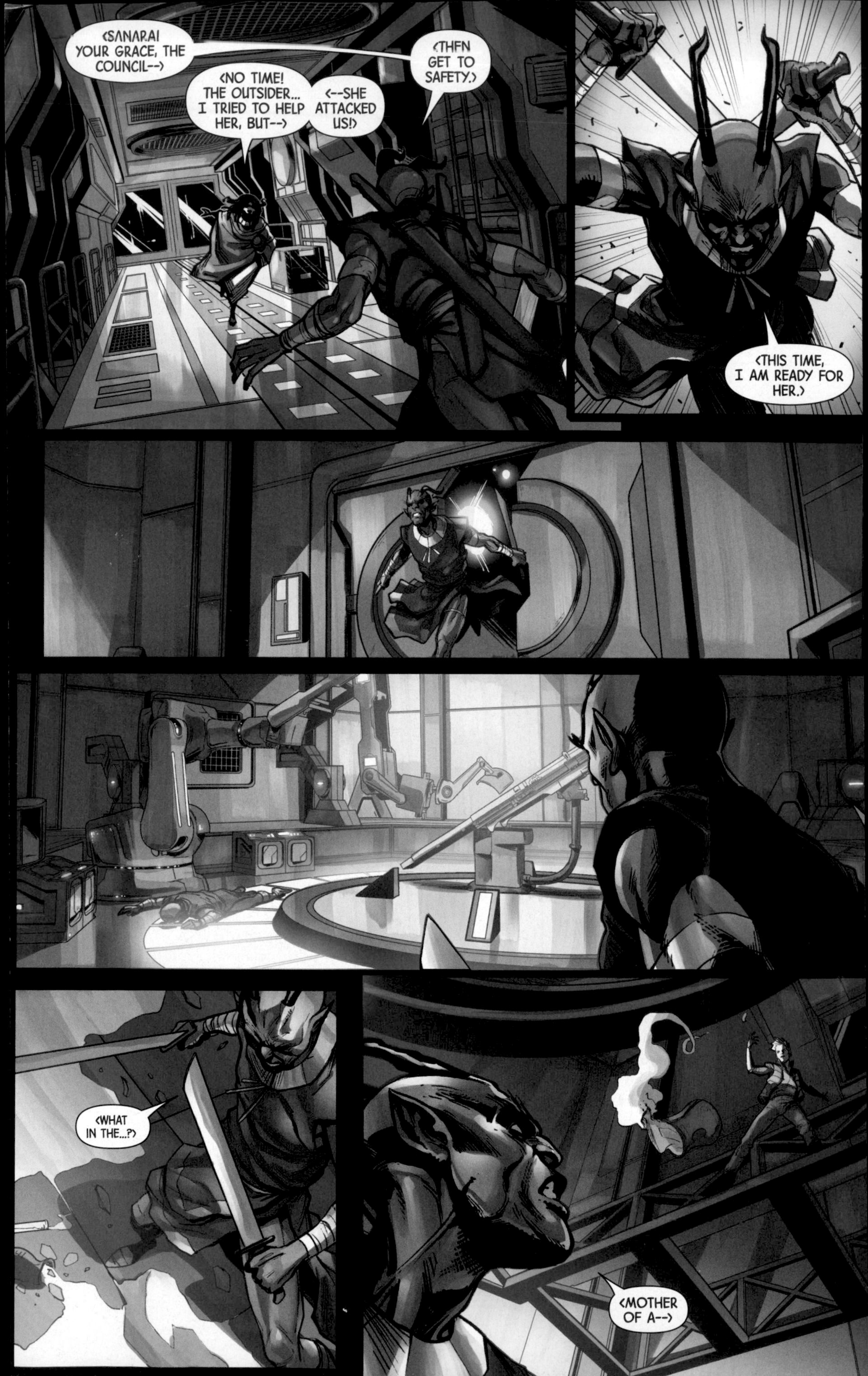
<SANARAI YOUR GRACE, THE COUNCIL-->
<NO TIME! THE OUTSIDER... I TRIED TO HELP HER, BUT-->
<--SHE ATTACKED US!>
<THEN GET TO SAFETY.>
<THIS TIME, I AM READY FOR HER.>
<WHAT IN THE...?>
<MOTHER OF A-->

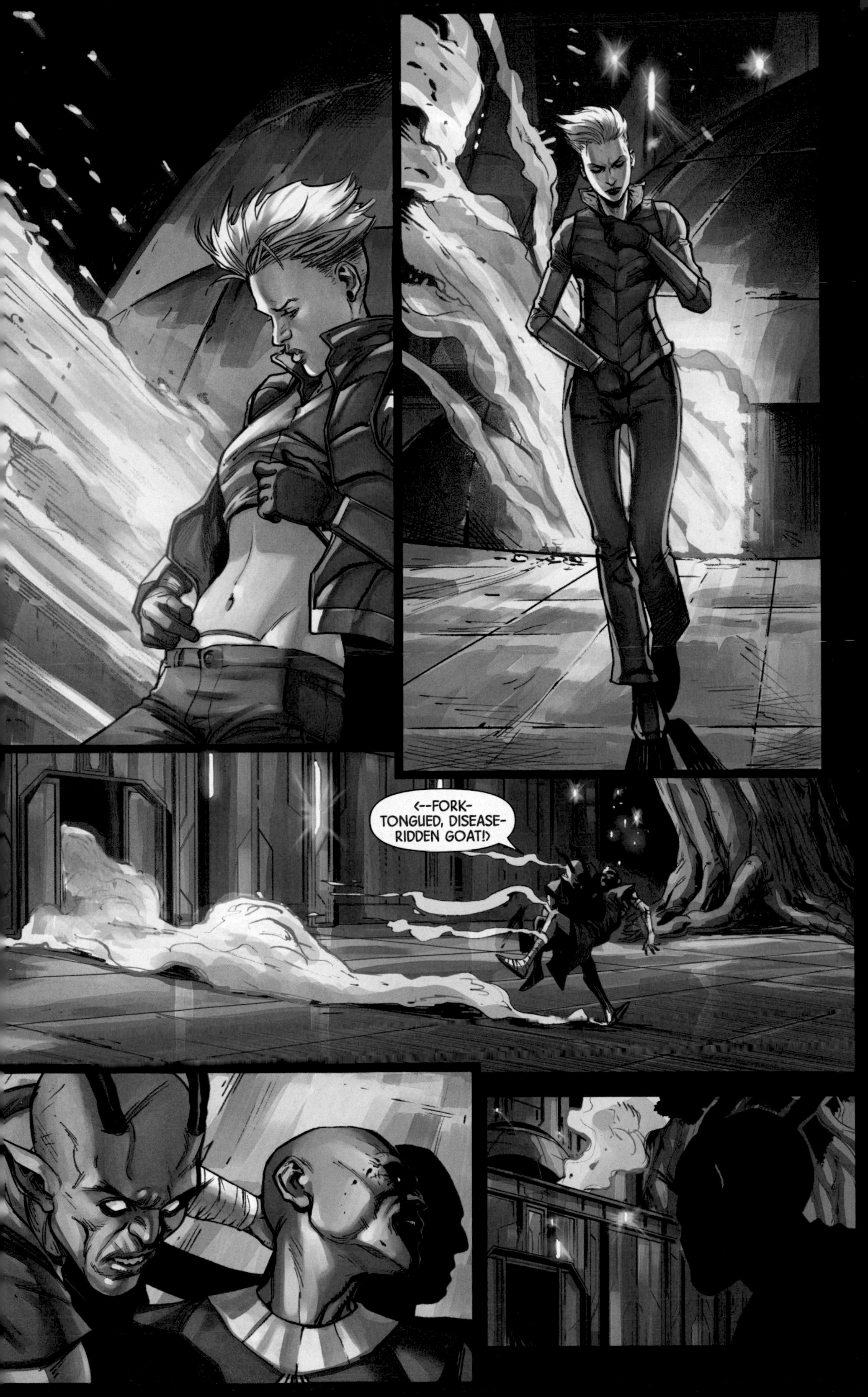
<--FORK-TONGUED, DISEASE-RIDDEN GOAT!>

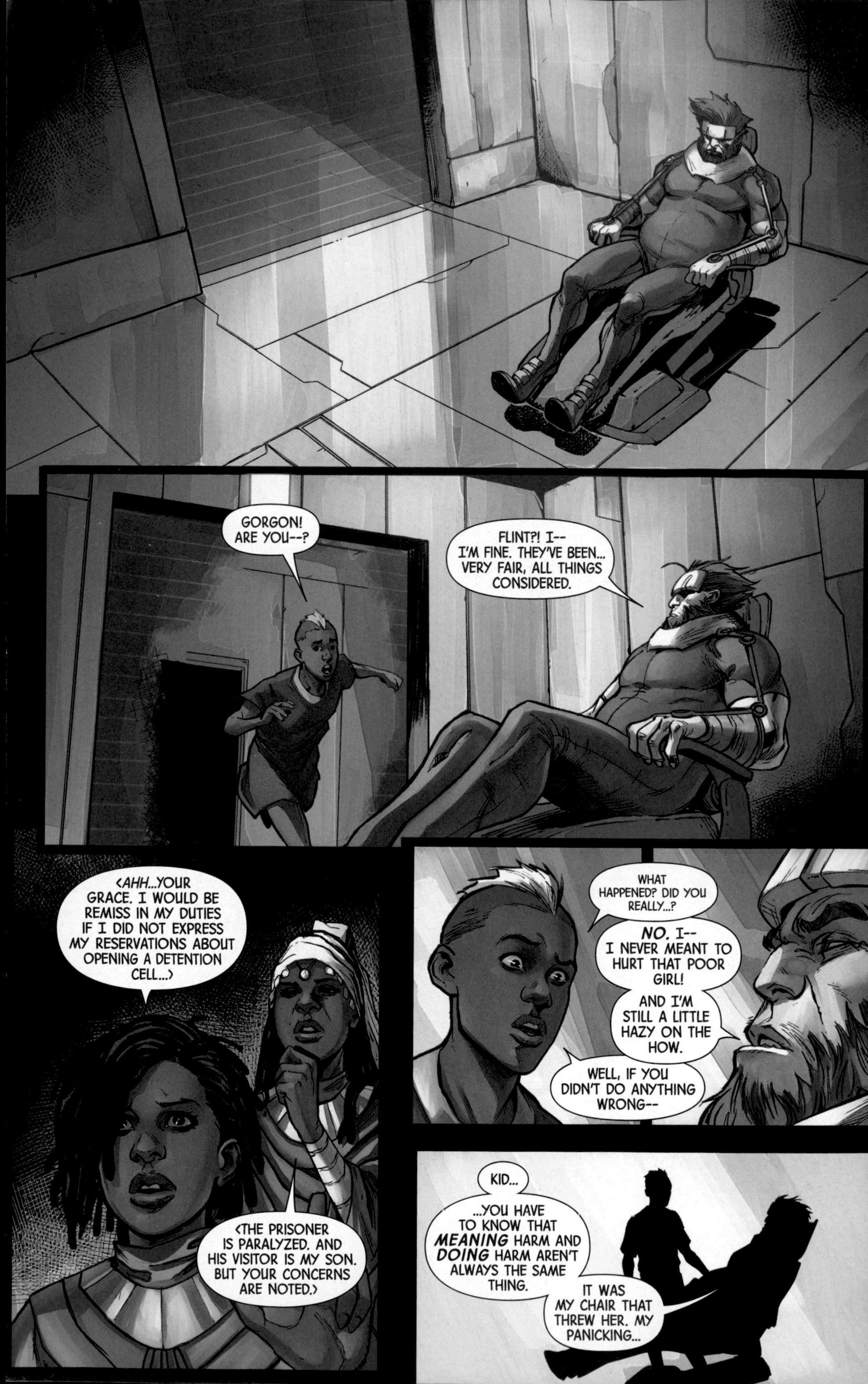
GORGON! ARE YOU--?
FLINT?! I-- I'M FINE. THEY'VE BEEN... VERY FAIR, ALL THINGS CONSIDERED.
<AHH...YOUR GRACE. I WOULD BE REMISS IN MY DUTIES IF I DID NOT EXPRESS MY RESERVATIONS ABOUT OPENING A DETENTION CELL...>
<THE PRISONER IS PARALYZED. AND HIS VISITOR IS MY SON. BUT YOUR CONCERNS ARE NOTED.>
WHAT HAPPENED? DID YOU REALLY...?
NO. I-- I NEVER MEANT TO HURT THAT POOR GIRL!
AND I'M STILL A LITTLE HAZY ON THE HOW.
WELL, IF YOU DIDN'T DO ANYTHING WRONG--
KID...
...YOU HAVE TO KNOW THAT *MEANING* HARM AND *DOING* HARM AREN'T ALWAYS THE SAME THING.
IT WAS MY CHAIR THAT THREW HER. MY PANICKING...

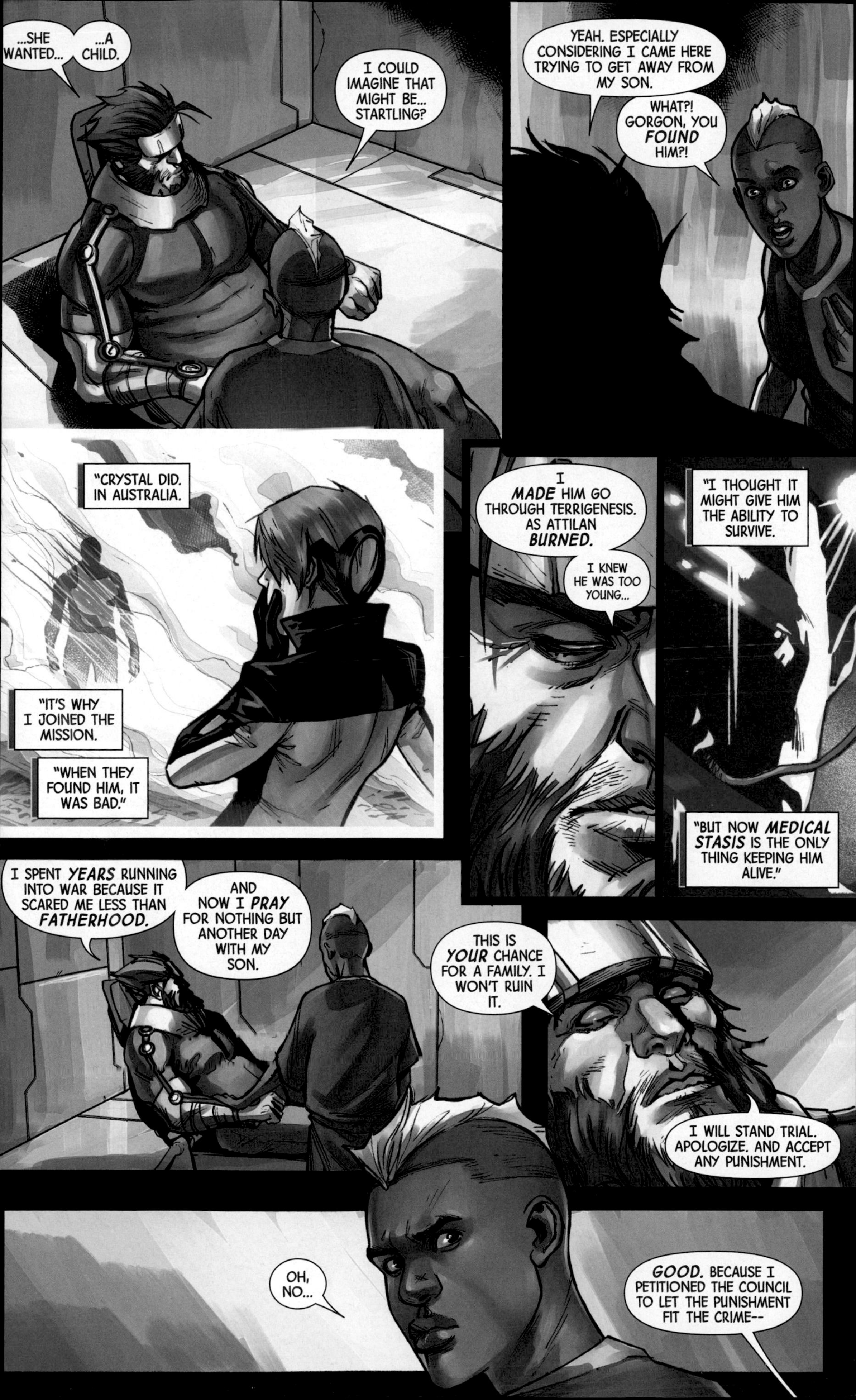
...SHE WANTED...
...A CHILD.
I COULD IMAGINE THAT MIGHT BE... STARTLING?
YEAH. ESPECIALLY CONSIDERING I CAME HERE TRYING TO GET AWAY FROM MY SON.
WHAT?! GORGON, YOU FOUND HIM?!
"CRYSTAL DID. IN AUSTRALIA.
"IT'S WHY I JOINED THE MISSION.
"WHEN THEY FOUND HIM, IT WAS BAD."
I MADE HIM GO THROUGH TERRIGENESIS. AS ATTILAN BURNED.
I KNEW HE WAS TOO YOUNG...
"I THOUGHT IT MIGHT GIVE HIM THE ABILITY TO SURVIVE.
"BUT NOW MEDICAL STASIS IS THE ONLY THING KEEPING HIM ALIVE."
I SPENT YEARS RUNNING INTO WAR BECAUSE IT SCARED ME LESS THAN FATHERHOOD.
AND NOW I PRAY FOR NOTHING BUT ANOTHER DAY WITH MY SON.
THIS IS YOUR CHANCE FOR A FAMILY. I WON'T RUIN IT.
I WILL STAND TRIAL. APOLOGIZE. AND ACCEPT ANY PUNISHMENT.
OH, NO...
GOOD. BECAUSE I PETITIONED THE COUNCIL TO LET THE PUNISHMENT FIT THE CRIME--

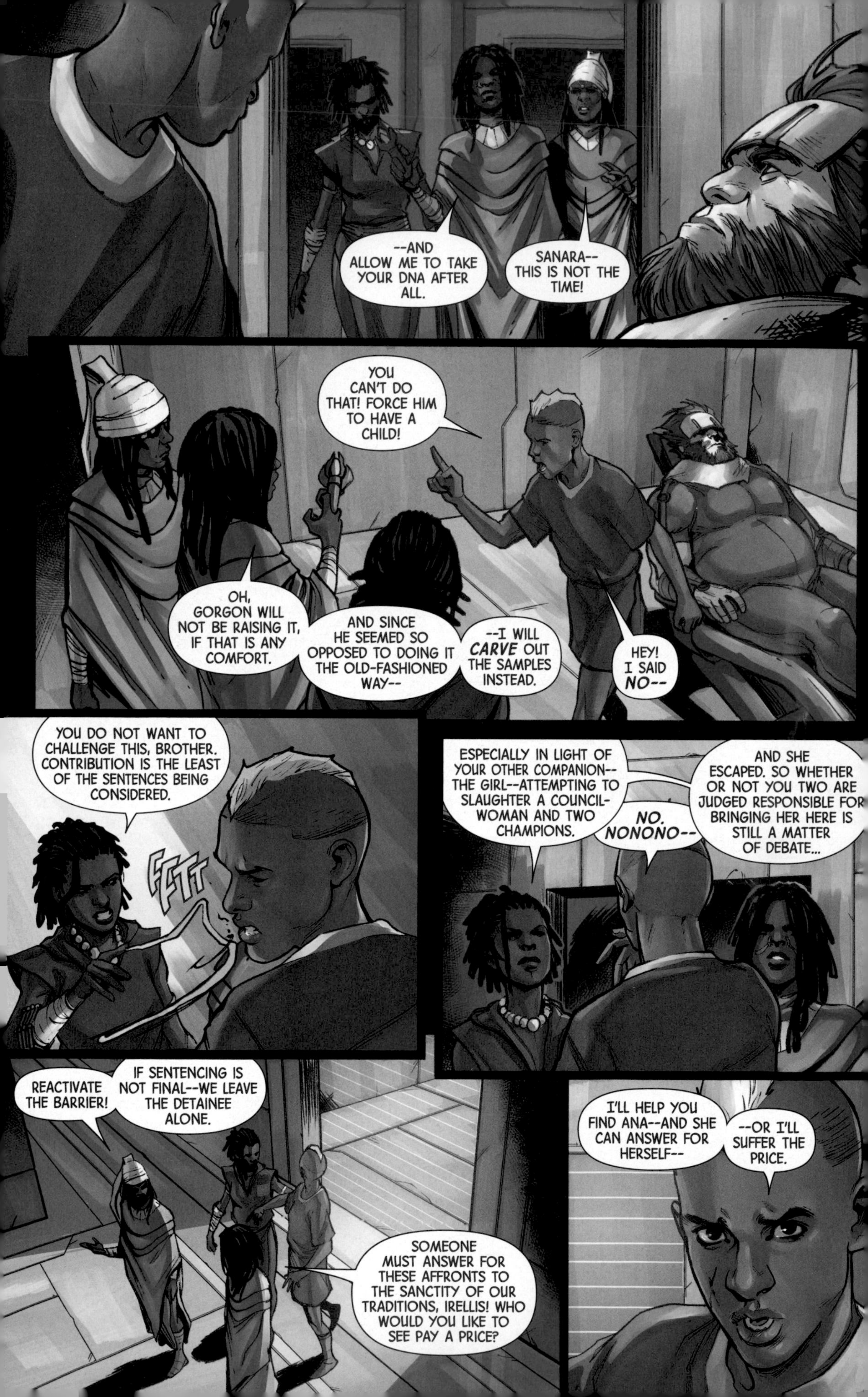
--AND ALLOW ME TO TAKE YOUR DNA AFTER ALL.
SANARA-- THIS IS NOT THE TIME!
YOU CAN'T DO THAT! FORCE HIM TO HAVE A CHILD!
OH, GORGON WILL NOT BE RAISING IT, IF THAT IS ANY COMFORT.
AND SINCE HE SEEMED SO OPPOSED TO DOING IT THE OLD-FASHIONED WAY--
--I WILL CARVE OUT THE SAMPLES INSTEAD.
HEY! I SAID NO--
YOU DO NOT WANT TO CHALLENGE THIS, BROTHER. CONTRIBUTION IS THE LEAST OF THE SENTENCES BEING CONSIDERED.
FFTT
ESPECIALLY IN LIGHT OF YOUR OTHER COMPANION--THE GIRL--ATTEMPTING TO SLAUGHTER A COUNCIL-WOMAN AND TWO CHAMPIONS.
NO. NONONO--
AND SHE ESCAPED. SO WHETHER OR NOT YOU TWO ARE JUDGED RESPONSIBLE FOR BRINGING HER HERE IS STILL A MATTER OF DEBATE...
REACTIVATE THE BARRIER!
IF SENTENCING IS NOT FINAL--WE LEAVE THE DETAINEE ALONE.
SOMEONE MUST ANSWER FOR THESE AFFRONTS TO THE SANCTITY OF OUR TRADITIONS, IRELLIS! WHO WOULD YOU LIKE TO SEE PAY A PRICE?
I'LL HELP YOU FIND ANA--AND SHE CAN ANSWER FOR HERSELF--
--OR I'LL SUFFER THE PRICE.

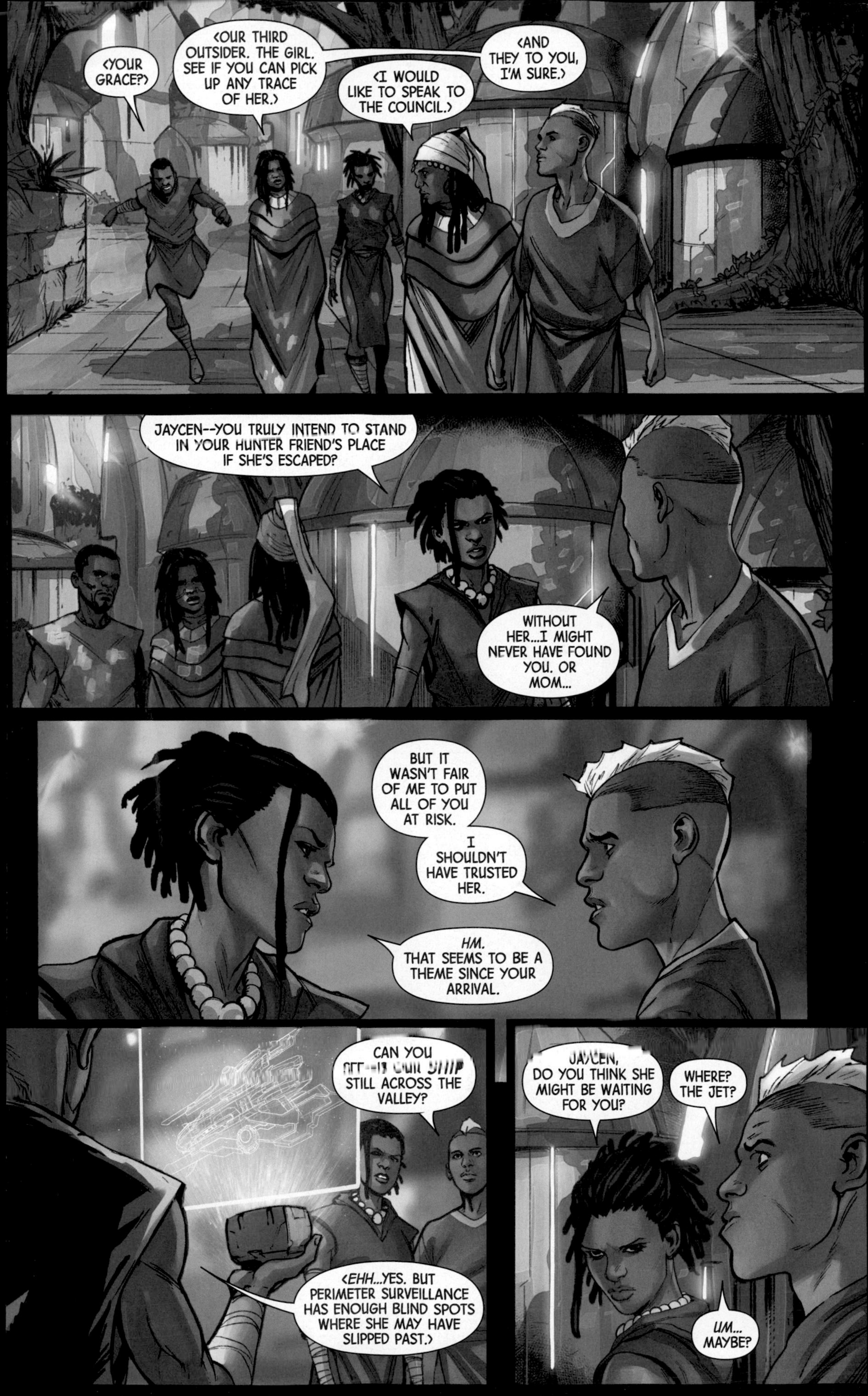

<YOUR GRACE?>
<OUR THIRD OUTSIDER. THE GIRL. SEE IF YOU CAN PICK UP ANY TRACE OF HER.>
<I WOULD LIKE TO SPEAK TO THE COUNCIL.>
<AND THEY TO YOU, I'M SURE.>
JAYCEN--YOU TRULY INTEND TO STAND IN YOUR HUNTER FRIEND'S PLACE IF SHE'S ESCAPED?
WITHOUT HER...I MIGHT NEVER HAVE FOUND YOU. OR MOM...
BUT IT WASN'T FAIR OF ME TO PUT ALL OF YOU AT RISK.
I SHOULDN'T HAVE TRUSTED HER.
HM. THAT SEEMS TO BE A THEME SINCE YOUR ARRIVAL.
CAN YOU
STILL ACROSS THE VALLEY?
<*EHH*...YES. BUT PERIMETER SURVEILLANCE HAS ENOUGH BLIND SPOTS WHERE SHE MAY HAVE SLIPPED PAST.>
JAYCEN, DO YOU THINK SHE MIGHT BE WAITING FOR YOU?
WHERE? THE JET?
UM... MAYBE?

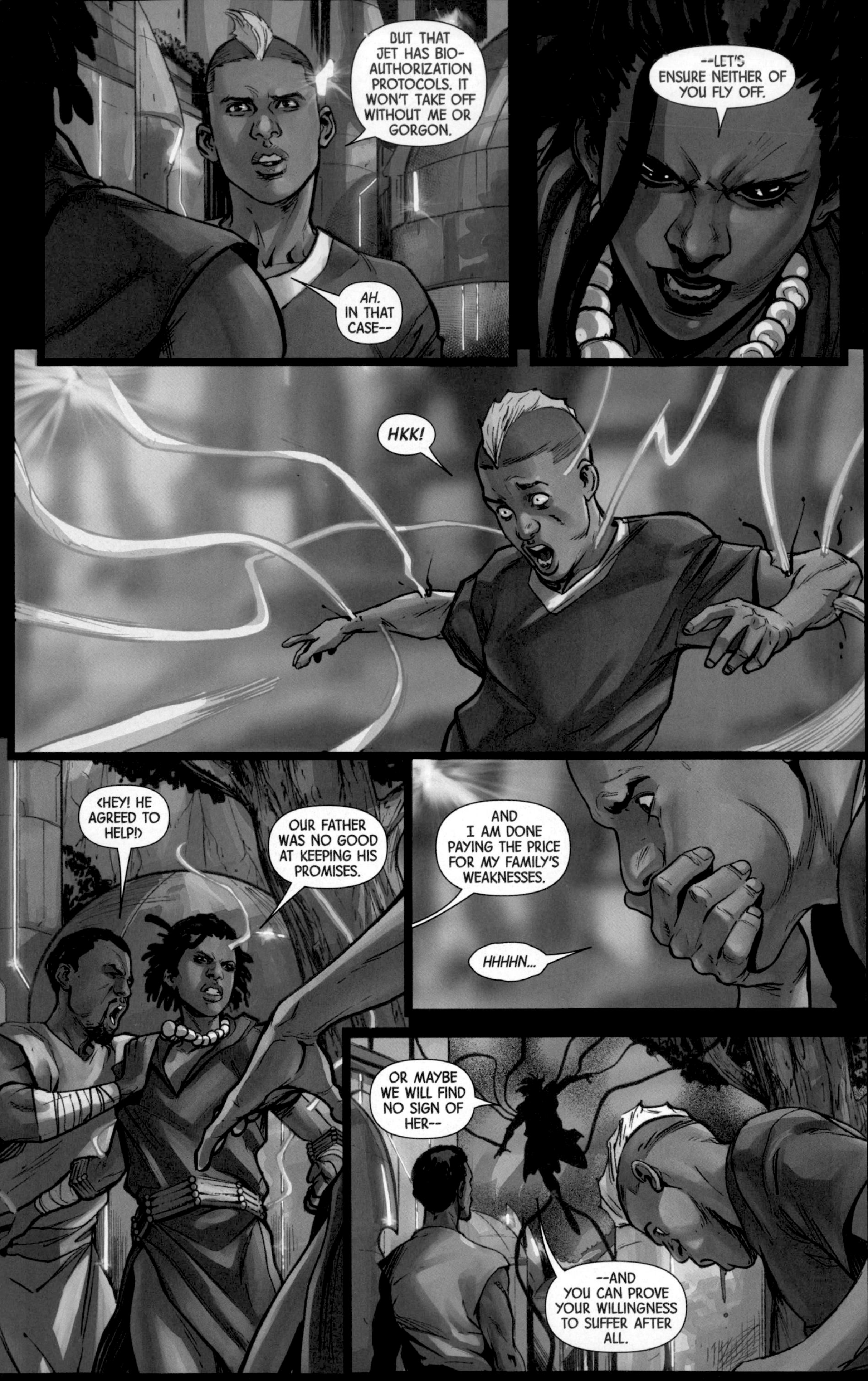
BUT THAT JET HAS BIO-AUTHORIZATION PROTOCOLS. IT WON'T TAKE OFF WITHOUT ME OR GORGON.
AH. IN THAT CASE--
--LET'S ENSURE NEITHER OF YOU FLY OFF.
HKK!
<HEY! HE AGREED TO HELP!>
OUR FATHER WAS NO GOOD AT KEEPING HIS PROMISES.
AND I AM DONE PAYING THE PRICE FOR MY FAMILY'S WEAKNESSES.
HHHHN...
OR MAYBE WE WILL FIND NO SIGN OF HER--
--AND YOU CAN PROVE YOUR WILLINGNESS TO SUFFER AFTER ALL.

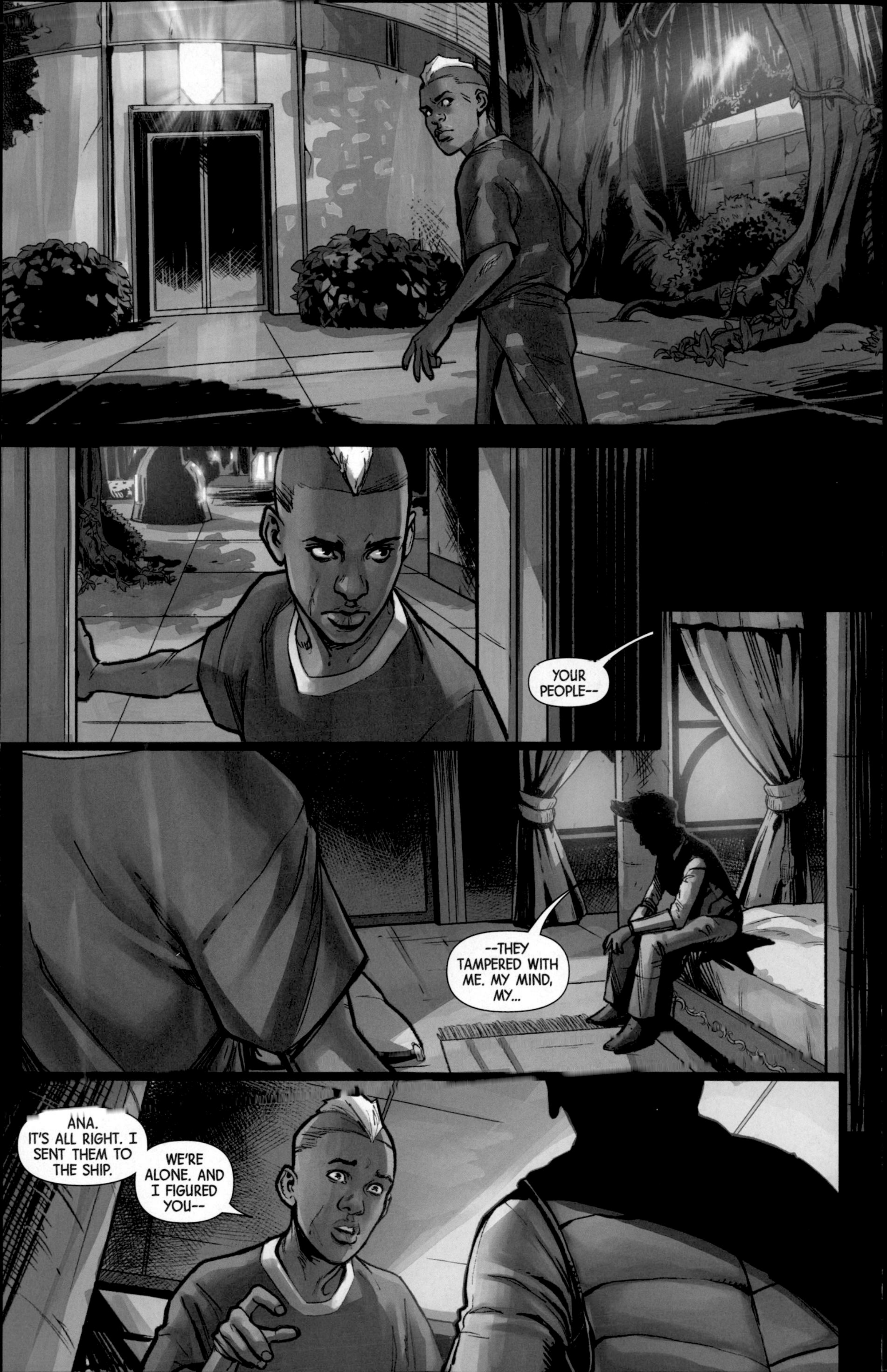
YOUR PEOPLE--
--THEY TAMPERED WITH ME. MY MIND, MY...
ANA. IT'S ALL RIGHT. I SENT THEM TO THE SHIP.
WE'RE ALONE. AND I FIGURED YOU--

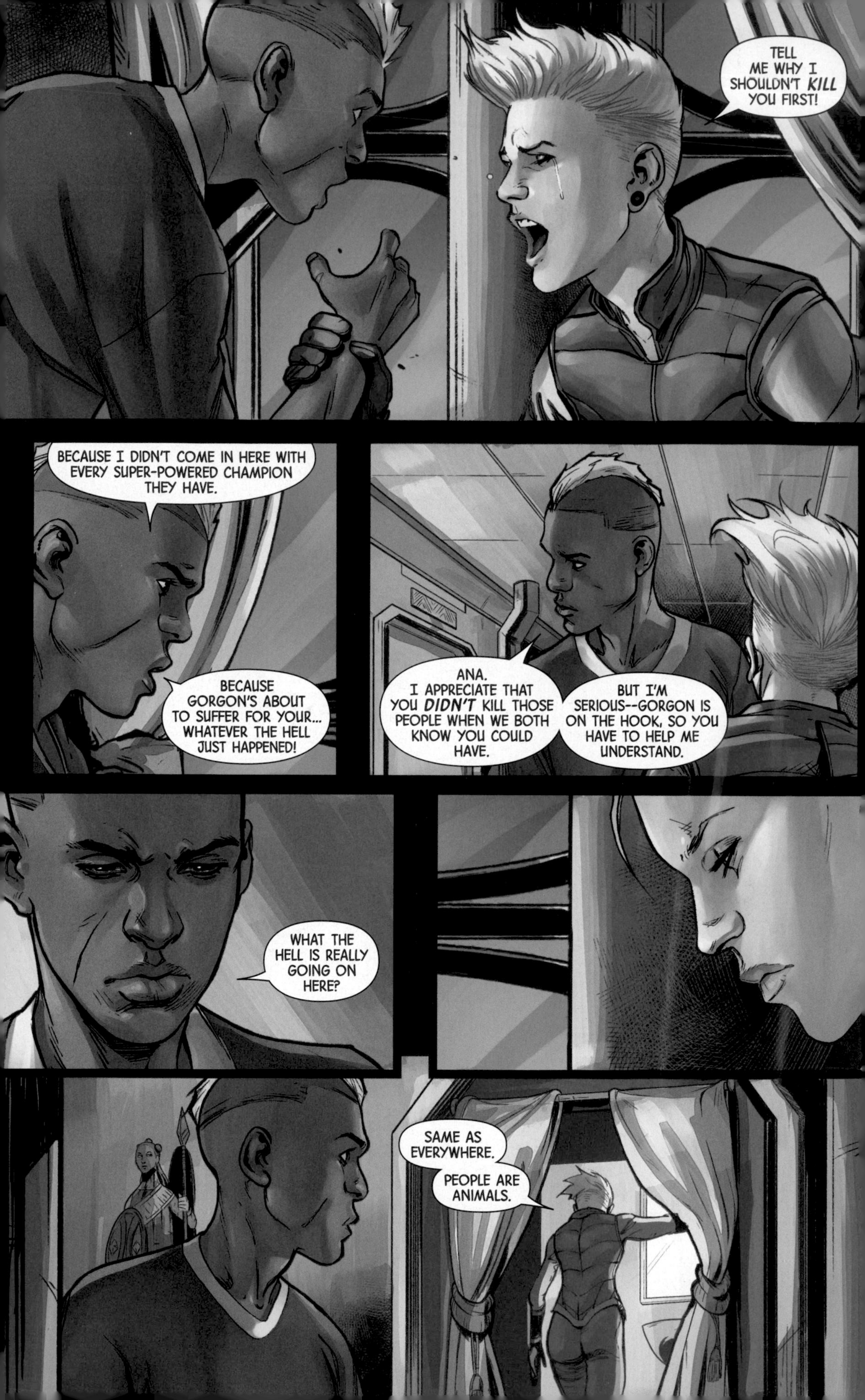
TELL ME WHY I SHOULDN'T KILL YOU FIRST!
BECAUSE I DIDN'T COME IN HERE WITH EVERY SUPER-POWERED CHAMPION THEY HAVE.
BECAUSE GORGON'S ABOUT TO SUFFER FOR YOUR... WHATEVER THE HELL JUST HAPPENED!
ANA. I APPRECIATE THAT YOU DIDN'T KILL THOSE PEOPLE WHEN WE BOTH KNOW YOU COULD HAVE.
BUT I'M SERIOUS--GORGON IS ON THE HOOK, SO YOU HAVE TO HELP ME UNDERSTAND.
WHAT THE HELL IS REALLY GOING ON HERE?
SAME AS EVERYWHERE.
PEOPLE ARE ANIMALS.

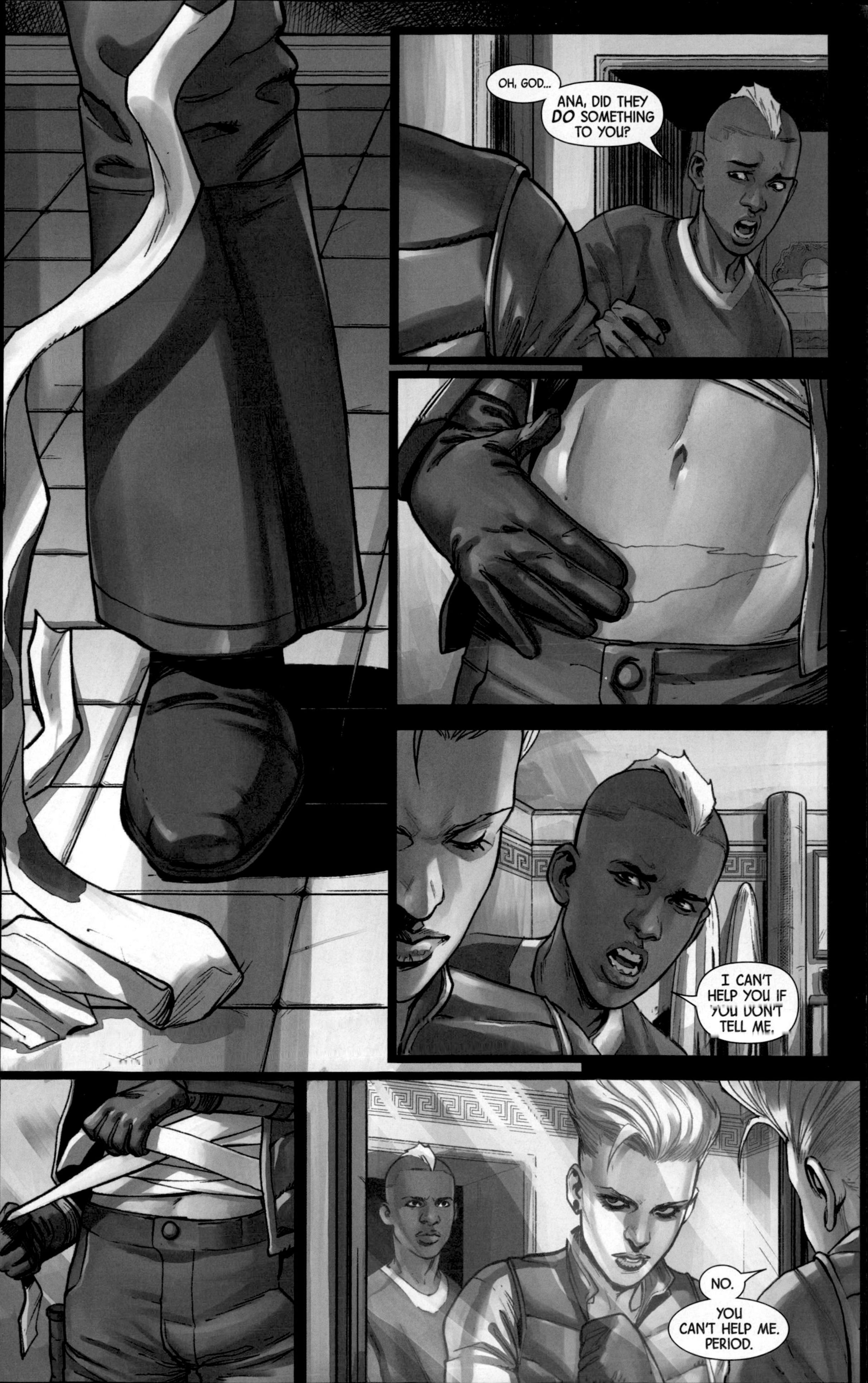
OH, GOD...
ANA, DID THEY DO SOMETHING TO YOU?
I CAN'T HELP YOU IF YOU DON'T TELL ME.
NO.
YOU CAN'T HELP ME. PERIOD.

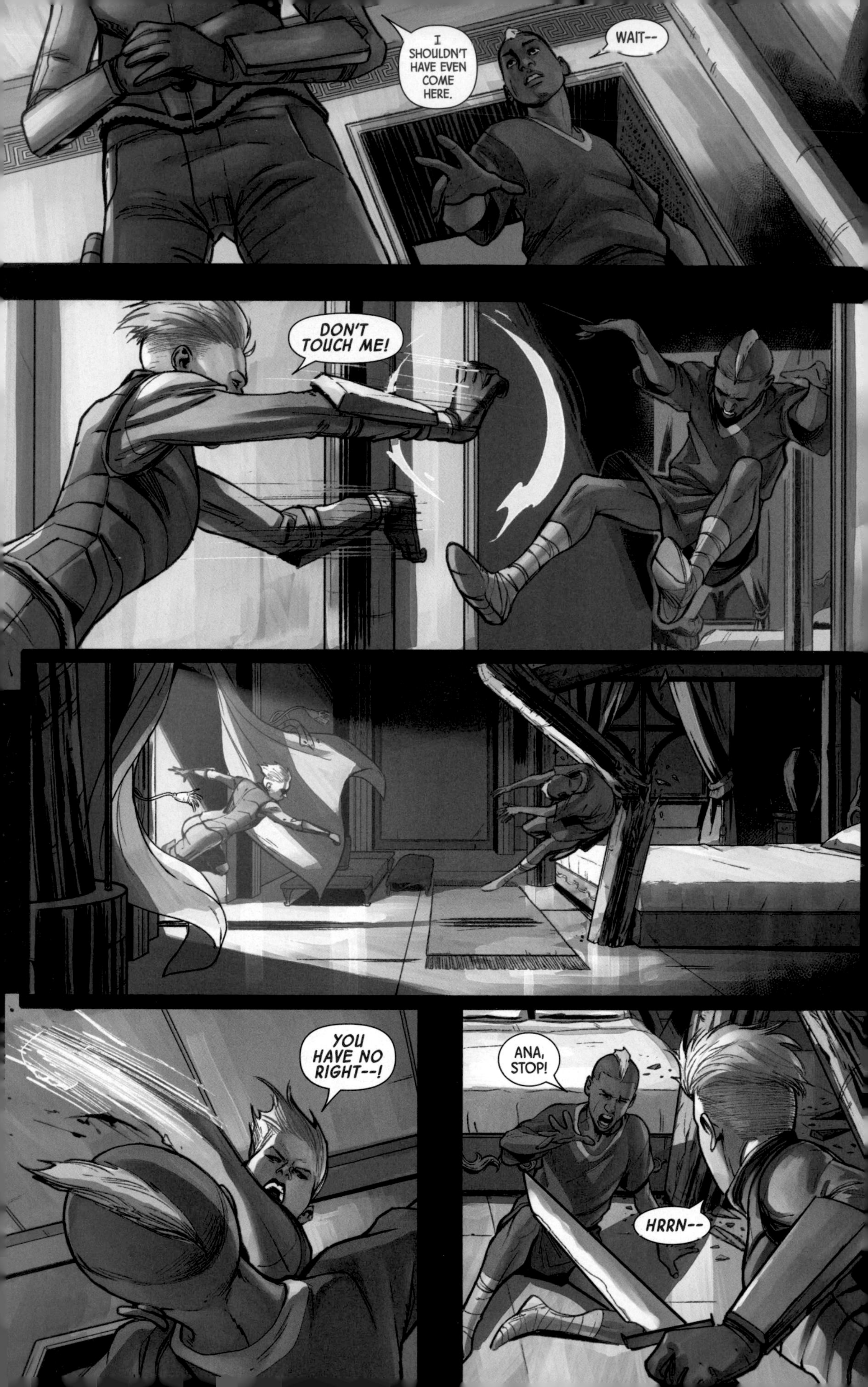
I SHOULDN'T HAVE EVEN COME HERE.
WAIT--
DON'T TOUCH ME!
YOU HAVE NO RIGHT--!
ANA, STOP!
HRRN--

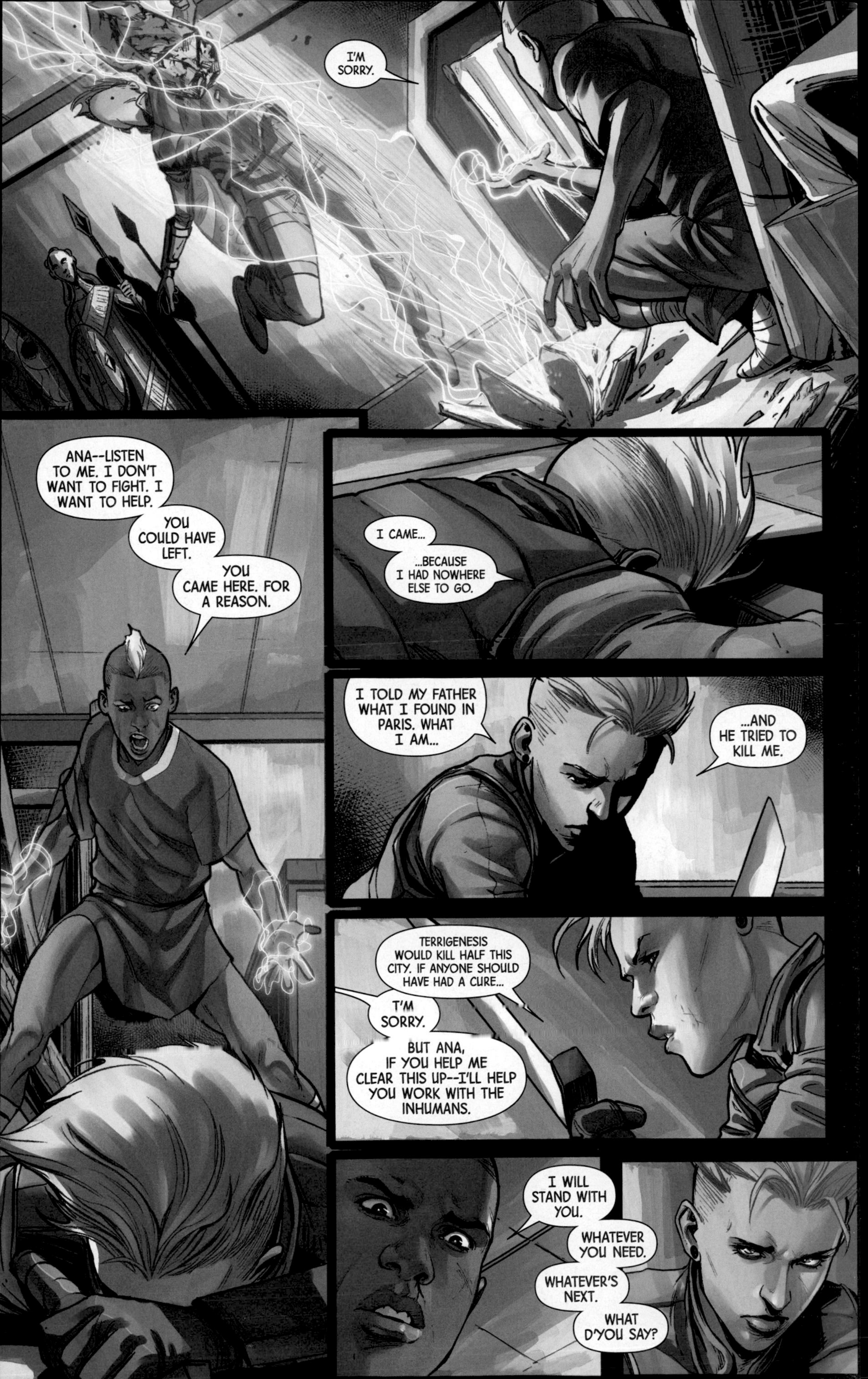
I'M SORRY.
ANA--LISTEN TO ME. I DON'T WANT TO FIGHT. I WANT TO HELP.
YOU COULD HAVE LEFT.
YOU CAME HERE. FOR A REASON.
I CAME...
...BECAUSE I HAD NOWHERE ELSE TO GO.
I TOLD MY FATHER WHAT I FOUND IN PARIS. WHAT I AM...
...AND HE TRIED TO KILL ME.
TERRIGENESIS WOULD KILL HALF THIS CITY. IF ANYONE SHOULD HAVE HAD A CURE...
I'M SORRY.
BUT ANA, IF YOU HELP ME CLEAR THIS UP--I'LL HELP YOU WORK WITH THE INHUMANS.
I WILL STAND WITH YOU.
WHATEVER YOU NEED.
WHATEVER'S NEXT.
WHAT D'YOU SAY?

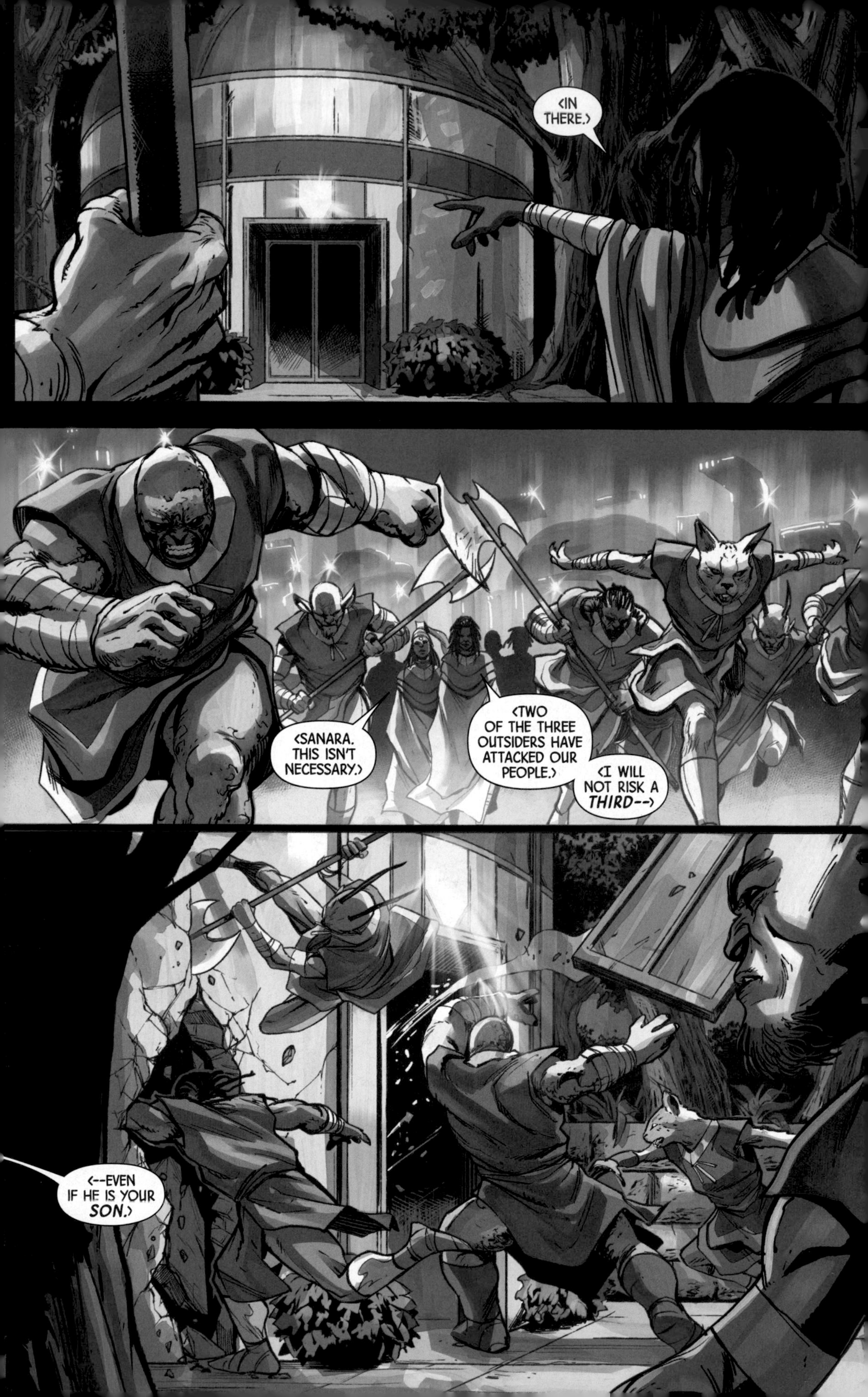
<IN THERE.>
<SANARA. THIS ISN'T NECESSARY.>
<TWO OF THE THREE OUTSIDERS HAVE ATTACKED OUR PEOPLE.>
<I WILL NOT RISK A *THIRD*-->
<--EVEN IF HE IS YOUR *SON*.>

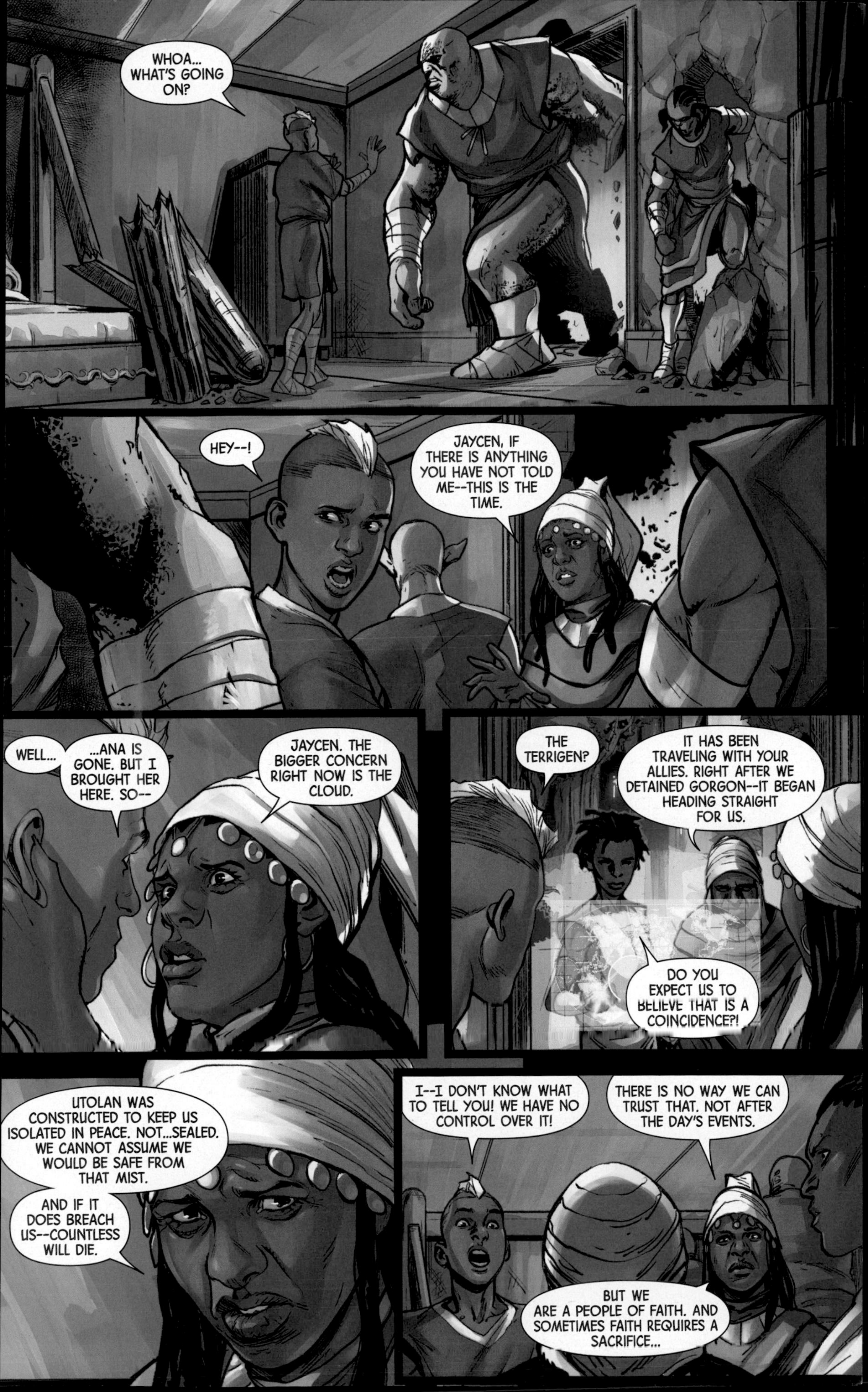
WHOA... WHAT'S GOING ON?
HEY--!
JAYCEN, IF THERE IS ANYTHING YOU HAVE NOT TOLD ME--THIS IS THE TIME.
WELL...
...ANA IS GONE. BUT I BROUGHT HER HERE. SO--
JAYCEN. THE BIGGER CONCERN RIGHT NOW IS THE CLOUD.
THE TERRIGEN?
IT HAS BEEN TRAVELING WITH YOUR ALLIES. RIGHT AFTER WE DETAINED GORGON--IT BEGAN HEADING STRAIGHT FOR US.
DO YOU EXPECT US TO BELIEVE THAT IS A COINCIDENCE?!
UTOLAN WAS CONSTRUCTED TO KEEP US ISOLATED IN PEACE. NOT...SEALED. WE CANNOT ASSUME WE WOULD BE SAFE FROM THAT MIST.
AND IF IT DOES BREACH US--COUNTLESS WILL DIE.
I--I DON'T KNOW WHAT TO TELL YOU! WE HAVE NO CONTROL OVER IT!
THERE IS NO WAY WE CAN TRUST THAT. NOT AFTER THE DAY'S EVENTS.
BUT WE ARE A PEOPLE OF FAITH. AND SOMETIMES FAITH REQUIRES A SACRIFICE...

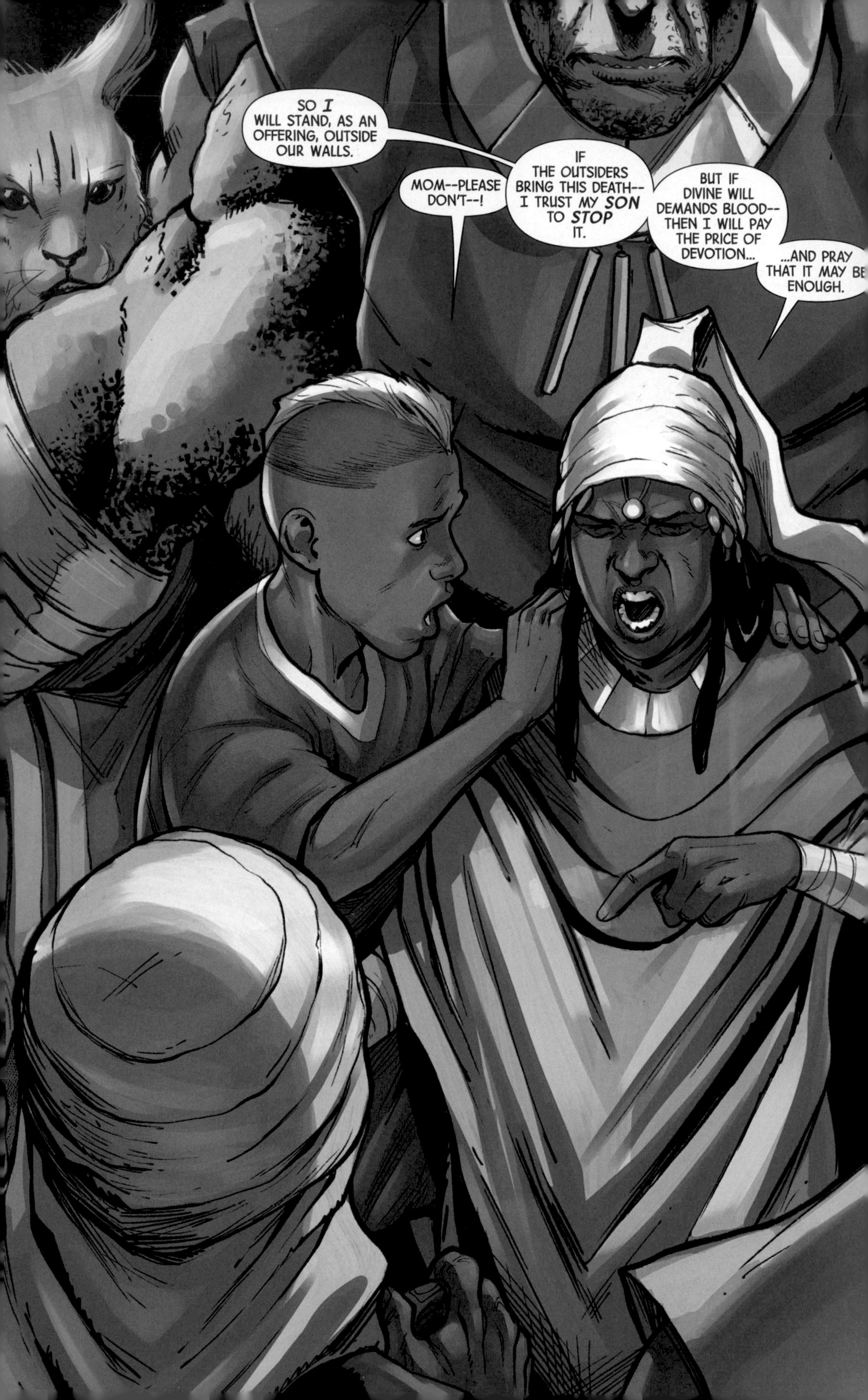

SO I WILL STAND, AS AN OFFERING, OUTSIDE OUR WALLS.
IF THE OUTSIDERS BRING THIS DEATH-- I TRUST MY SON TO STOP IT.
MOM--PLEASE DON'T--!
BUT IF DIVINE WILL DEMANDS BLOOD-- THEN I WILL PAY THE PRICE OF DEVOTION...
...AND PRAY THAT IT MAY BE ENOUGH.

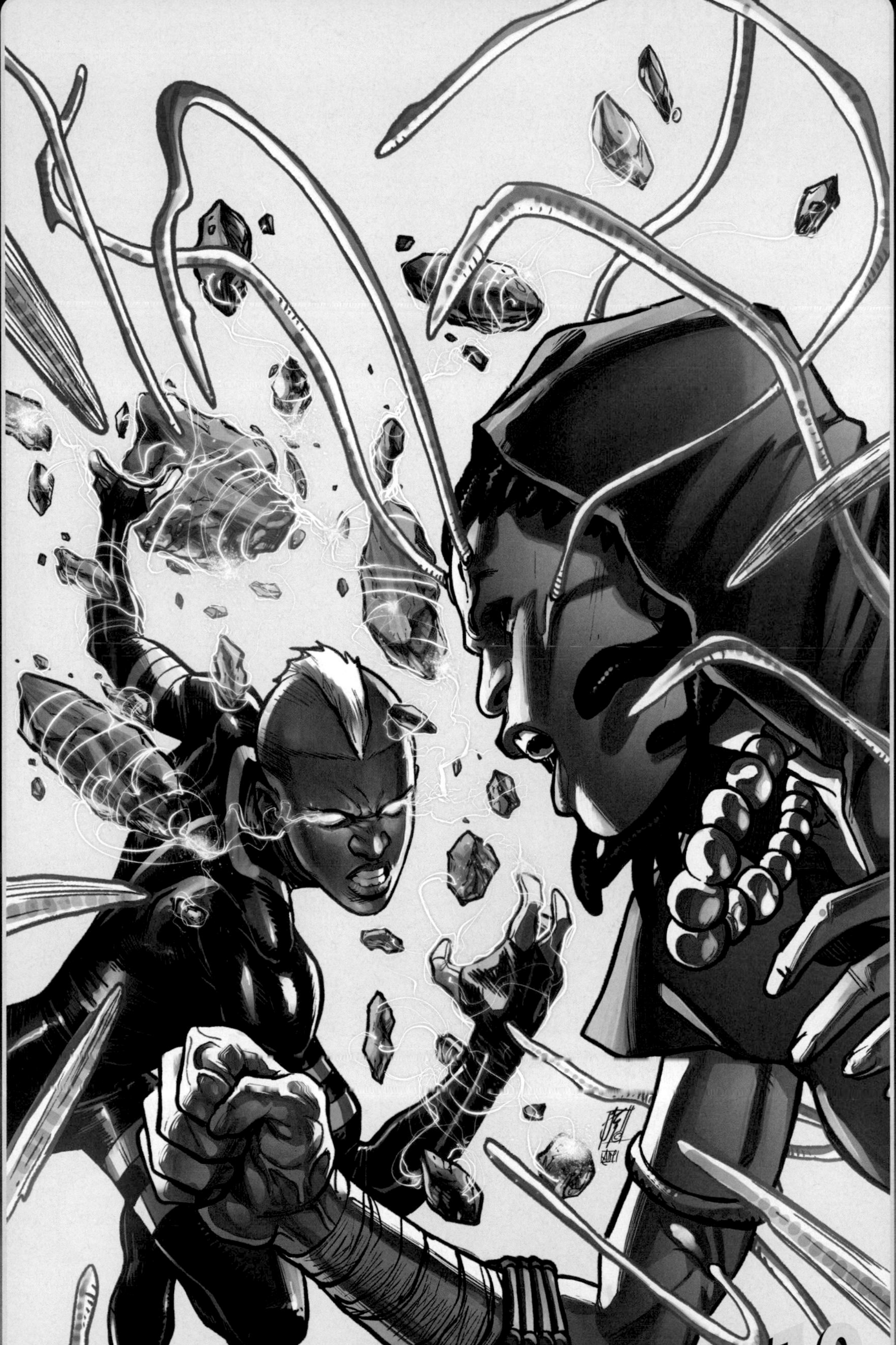

10

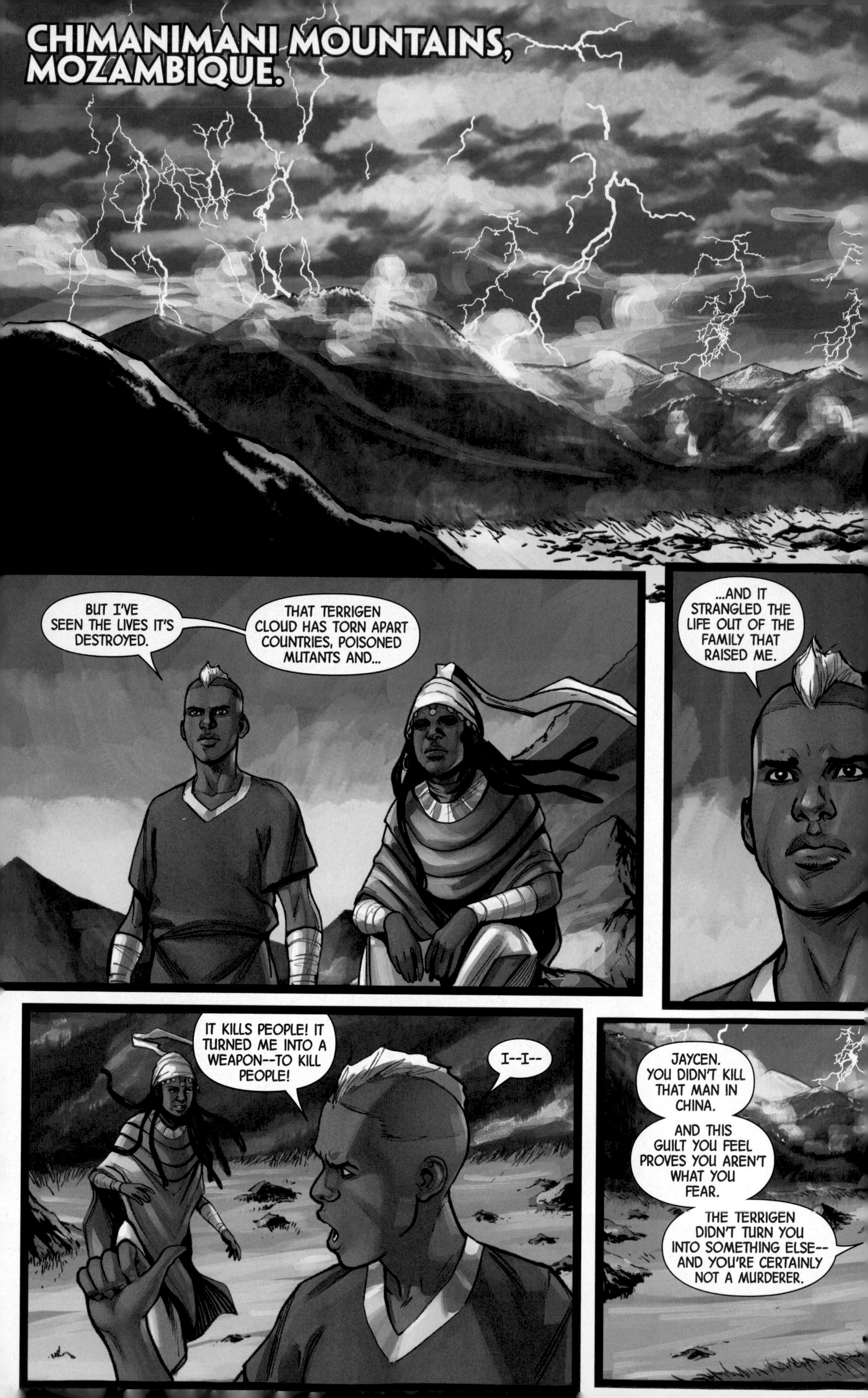

CHIMANIMANI MOUNTAINS, MOZAMBIQUE.
BUT I'VE SEEN THE LIVES IT'S DESTROYED.
THAT TERRIGEN CLOUD HAS TORN APART COUNTRIES, POISONED MUTANTS AND...
...AND IT STRANGLED THE LIFE OUT OF THE FAMILY THAT RAISED ME.
IT KILLS PEOPLE! IT TURNED ME INTO A WEAPON--TO KILL PEOPLE!
I--I--
JAYCEN. YOU DIDN'T KILL THAT MAN IN CHINA.
AND THIS GUILT YOU FEEL PROVES YOU AREN'T WHAT YOU FEAR.
THE TERRIGEN DIDN'T TURN YOU INTO SOMETHING ELSE-- AND YOU'RE CERTAINLY NOT A MURDERER.

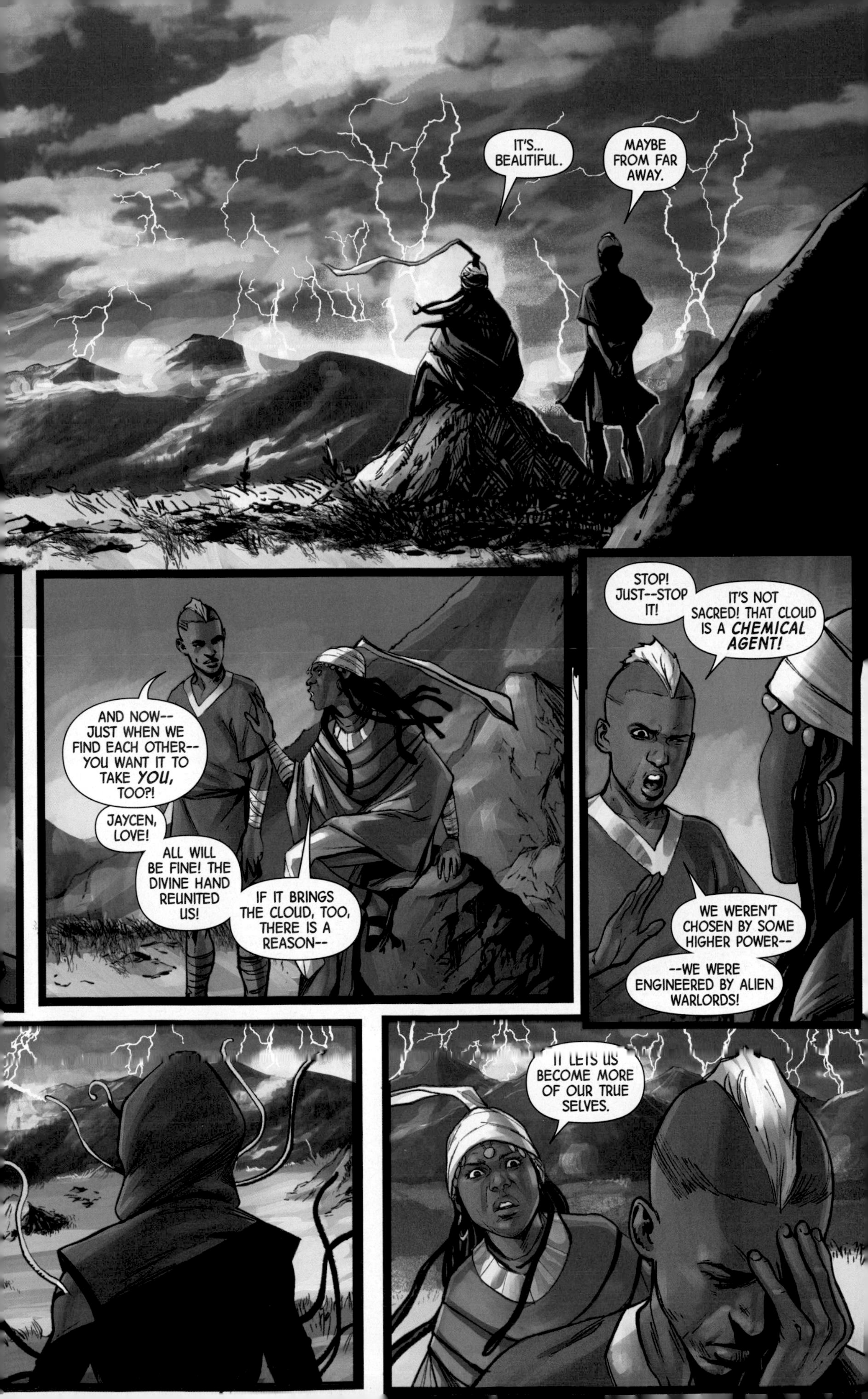
IT'S... BEAUTIFUL.
MAYBE FROM FAR AWAY.
AND NOW-- JUST WHEN WE FIND EACH OTHER-- YOU WANT IT TO TAKE *YOU,* TOO?!
JAYCEN, LOVE!
ALL WILL BE FINE! THE DIVINE HAND REUNITED US!
IF IT BRINGS THE CLOUD, TOO, THERE IS A REASON--
STOP! JUST--STOP IT!
IT'S NOT SACRED! THAT CLOUD IS A *CHEMICAL AGENT!*
WE WEREN'T CHOSEN BY SOME HIGHER POWER--
--WE WERE ENGINEERED BY ALIEN WARLORDS!
IT LETS US BECOME MORE OF OUR TRUE SELVES.

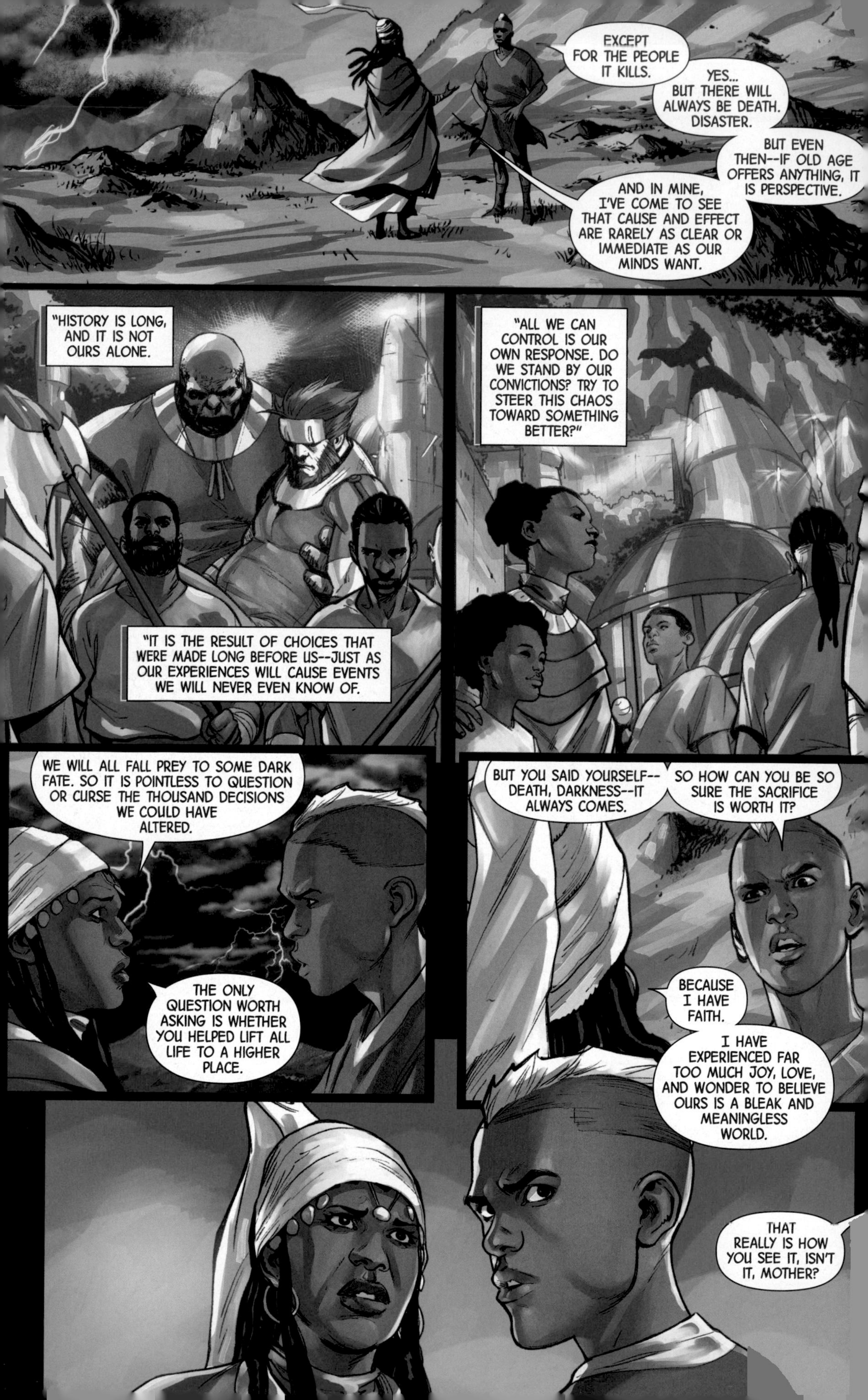
EXCEPT FOR THE PEOPLE IT KILLS.
YES... BUT THERE WILL ALWAYS BE DEATH. DISASTER.
BUT EVEN THEN--IF OLD AGE OFFERS ANYTHING, IT IS PERSPECTIVE.
AND IN MINE, I'VE COME TO SEE THAT CAUSE AND EFFECT ARE RARELY AS CLEAR OR IMMEDIATE AS OUR MINDS WANT.
"HISTORY IS LONG, AND IT IS NOT OURS ALONE.
"IT IS THE RESULT OF CHOICES THAT WERE MADE LONG BEFORE US--JUST AS OUR EXPERIENCES WILL CAUSE EVENTS WE WILL NEVER EVEN KNOW OF.
"ALL WE CAN CONTROL IS OUR OWN RESPONSE. DO WE STAND BY OUR CONVICTIONS? TRY TO STEER THIS CHAOS TOWARD SOMETHING BETTER?"
WE WILL ALL FALL PREY TO SOME DARK FATE. SO IT IS POINTLESS TO QUESTION OR CURSE THE THOUSAND DECISIONS WE COULD HAVE ALTERED.
THE ONLY QUESTION WORTH ASKING IS WHETHER YOU HELPED LIFT ALL LIFE TO A HIGHER PLACE.
BUT YOU SAID YOURSELF--DEATH, DARKNESS--IT ALWAYS COMES.
SO HOW CAN YOU BE SO SURE THE SACRIFICE IS WORTH IT?
BECAUSE I HAVE FAITH.
I HAVE EXPERIENCED FAR TOO MUCH JOY, LOVE, AND WONDER TO BELIEVE OURS IS A BLEAK AND MEANINGLESS WORLD.
THAT REALLY IS HOW YOU SEE IT, ISN'T IT, MOTHER?

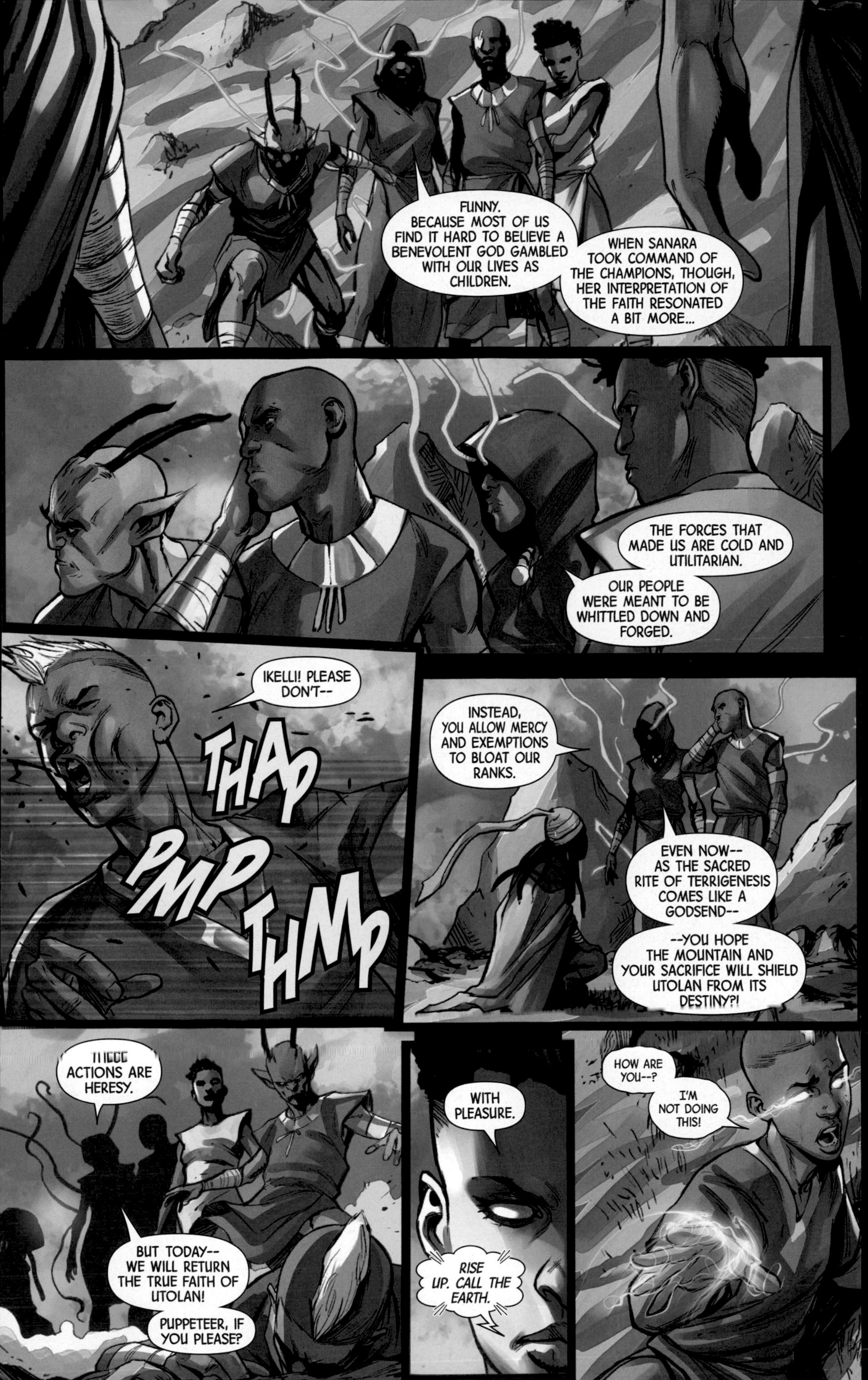
FUNNY. BECAUSE MOST OF US FIND IT HARD TO BELIEVE A BENEVOLENT GOD GAMBLED WITH OUR LIVES AS CHILDREN.
WHEN SANARA TOOK COMMAND OF THE CHAMPIONS, THOUGH, HER INTERPRETATION OF THE FAITH RESONATED A BIT MORE...
THE FORCES THAT MADE US ARE COLD AND UTILITARIAN.
OUR PEOPLE WERE MEANT TO BE WHITTLED DOWN AND FORGED.
IKELLI! PLEASE DON'T--
THAP
PMP
THMP
INSTEAD, YOU ALLOW MERCY AND EXEMPTIONS TO BLOAT OUR RANKS.
EVEN NOW-- AS THE SACRED RITE OF TERRIGENESIS COMES LIKE A GODSEND--
--YOU HOPE THE MOUNTAIN AND YOUR SACRIFICE WILL SHIELD UTOLAN FROM ITS DESTINY?!
ACTIONS ARE HERESY.
BUT TODAY-- WE WILL RETURN THE TRUE FAITH OF UTOLAN!
PUPPETEER, IF YOU PLEASE?
WITH PLEASURE.
RISE UP. CALL THE EARTH.
HOW ARE YOU--?
I'M NOT DOING THIS!

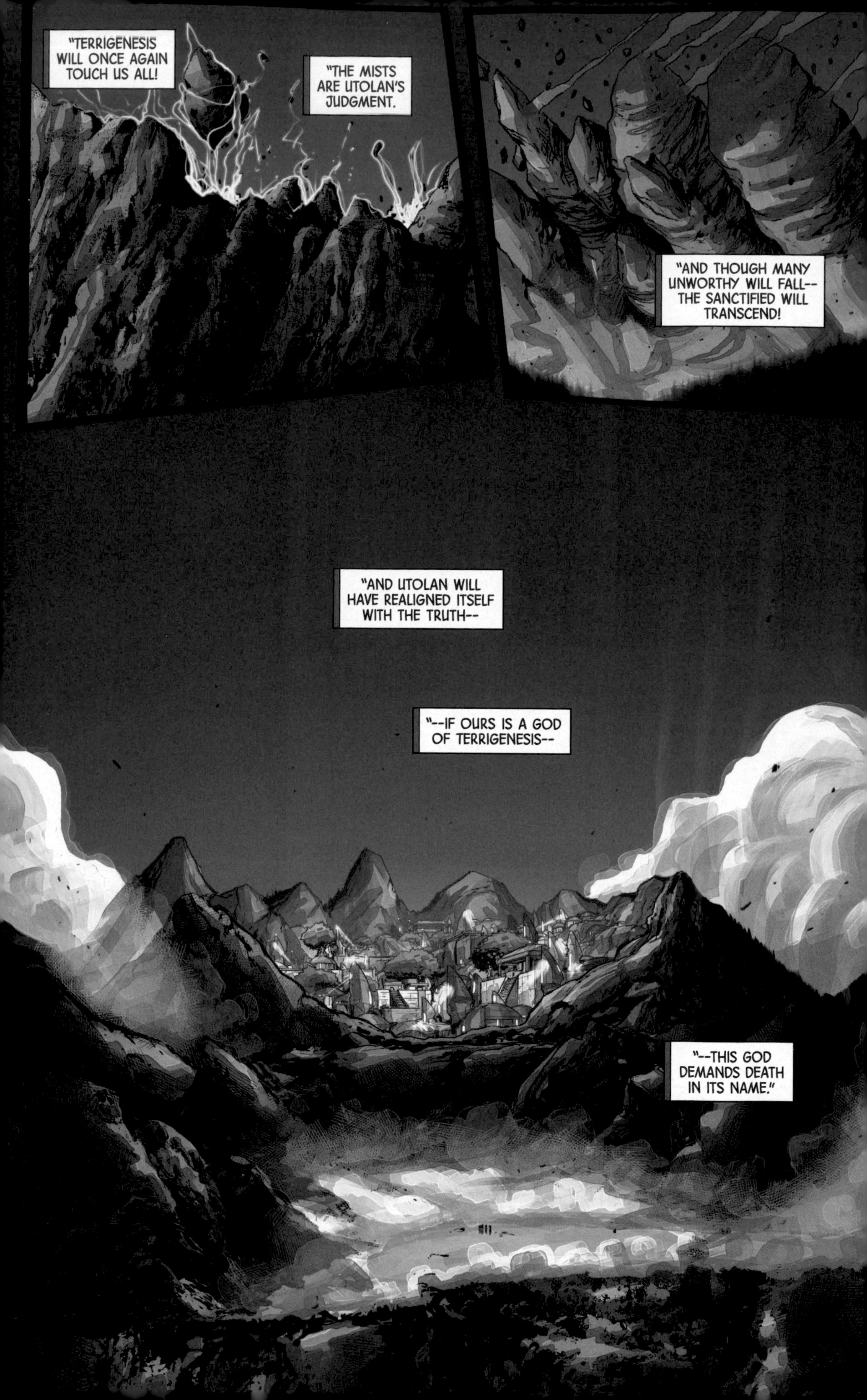
"TERRIGENESIS WILL ONCE AGAIN TOUCH US ALL!
"THE MISTS ARE UTOLAN'S JUDGMENT.
"AND THOUGH MANY UNWORTHY WILL FALL-- THE SANCTIFIED WILL TRANSCEND!
"AND UTOLAN WILL HAVE REALIGNED ITSELF WITH THE TRUTH--
"--IF OURS IS A GOD OF TERRIGENESIS--
"--THIS GOD DEMANDS DEATH IN ITS NAME."

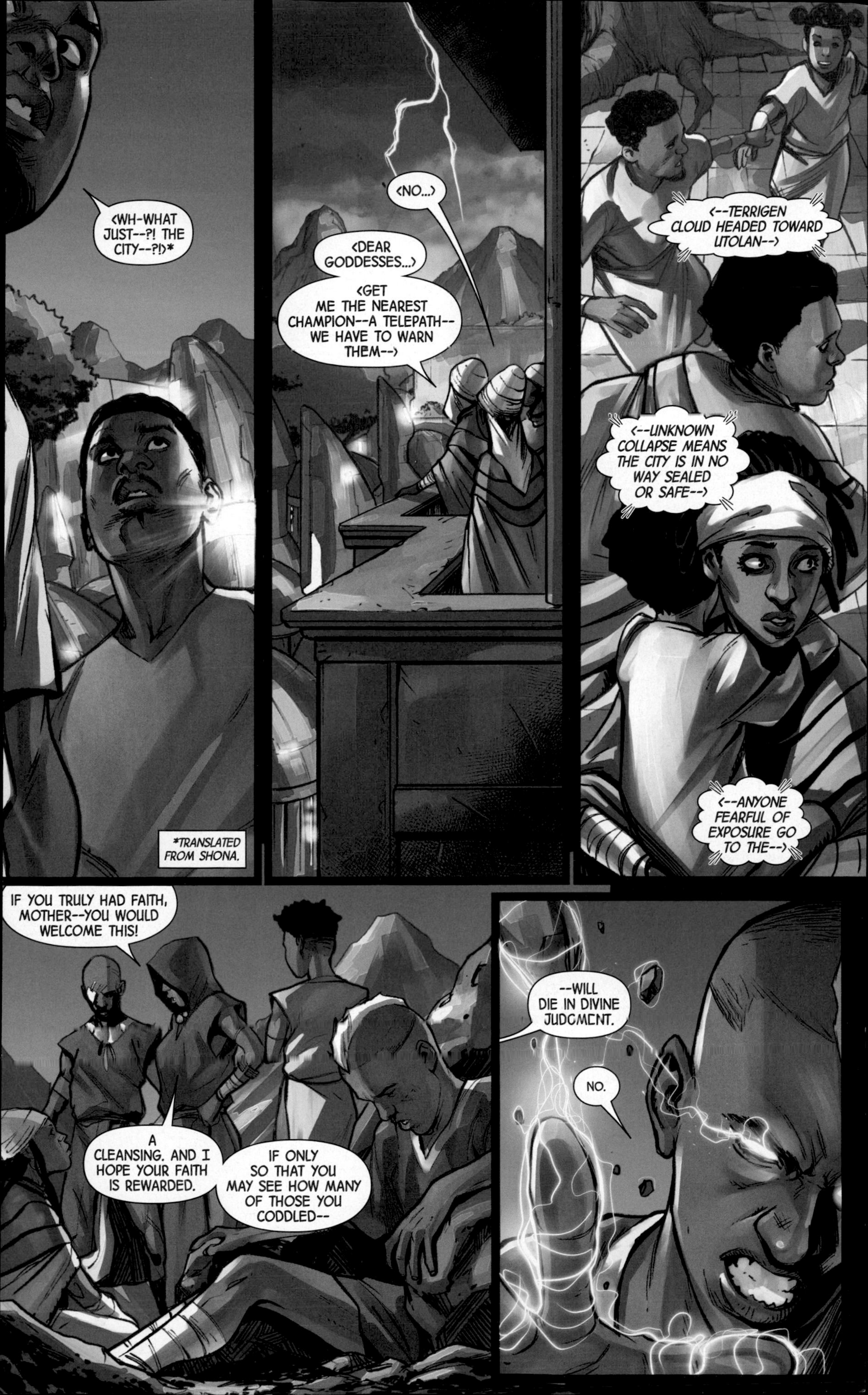
<WH-WHAT JUST--?! THE CITY--?!>*
*TRANSLATED FROM SHONA.
<NO...>
<DEAR GODDESSES...>
<GET ME THE NEAREST CHAMPION--A TELEPATH--WE HAVE TO WARN THEM-->
<--TERRIGEN CLOUD HEADED TOWARD UTOLAN-->
<--UNKNOWN COLLAPSE MEANS THE CITY IS IN NO WAY SEALED OR SAFE-->
<--ANYONE FEARFUL OF EXPOSURE GO TO THE-->
IF YOU TRULY HAD FAITH, MOTHER--YOU WOULD WELCOME THIS!
A CLEANSING. AND I HOPE YOUR FAITH IS REWARDED.
IF ONLY SO THAT YOU MAY SEE HOW MANY OF THOSE YOU CODDLED--
--WILL DIE IN DIVINE JUDGMENT.
NO.

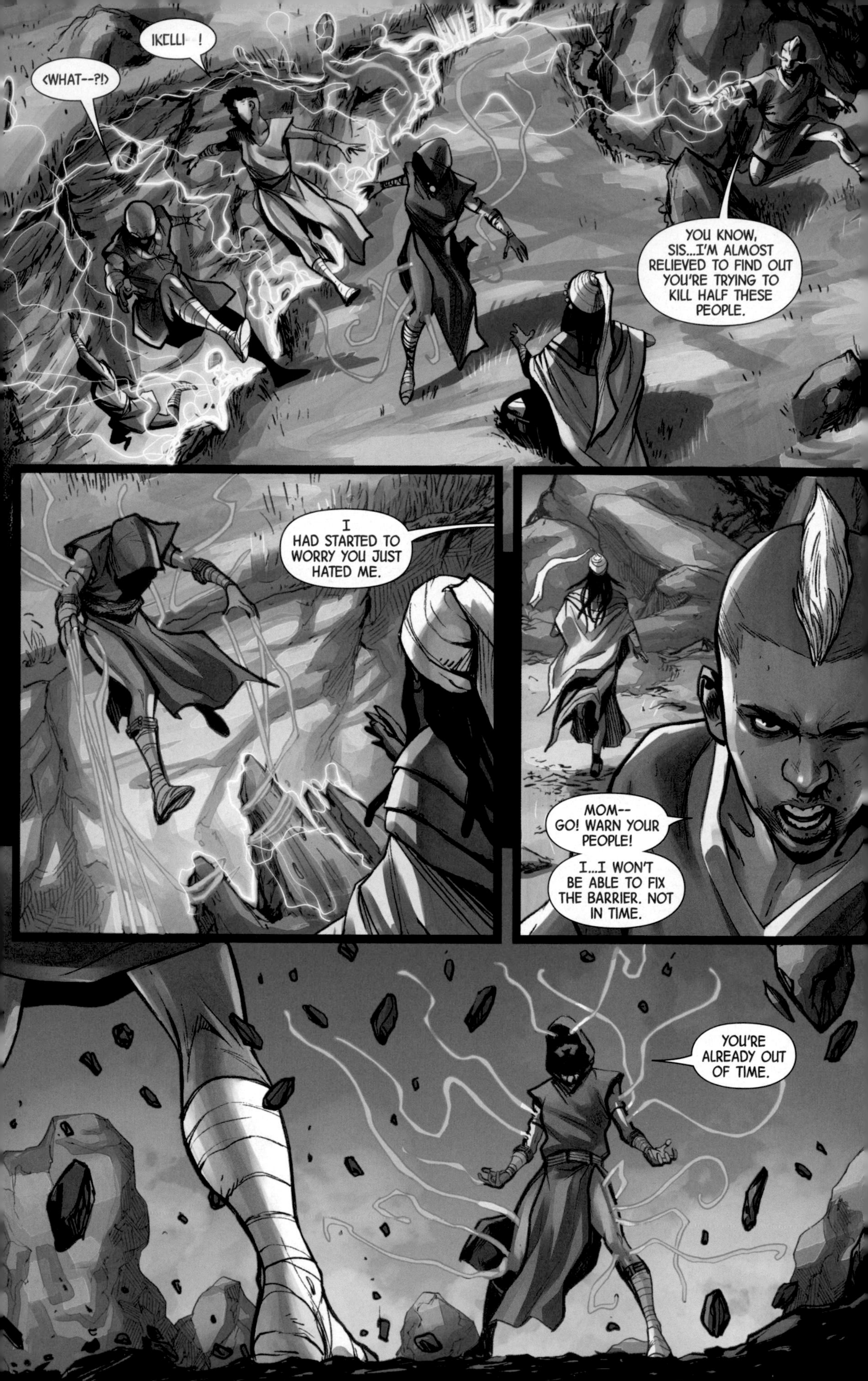

IKELLI !
<WHAT--?!>
YOU KNOW, SIS...I'M ALMOST RELIEVED TO FIND OUT YOU'RE TRYING TO KILL HALF THESE PEOPLE.
I HAD STARTED TO WORRY YOU JUST HATED ME.
MOM-- GO! WARN YOUR PEOPLE!
I...I WON'T BE ABLE TO FIX THE BARRIER. NOT IN TIME.
YOU'RE ALREADY OUT OF TIME.

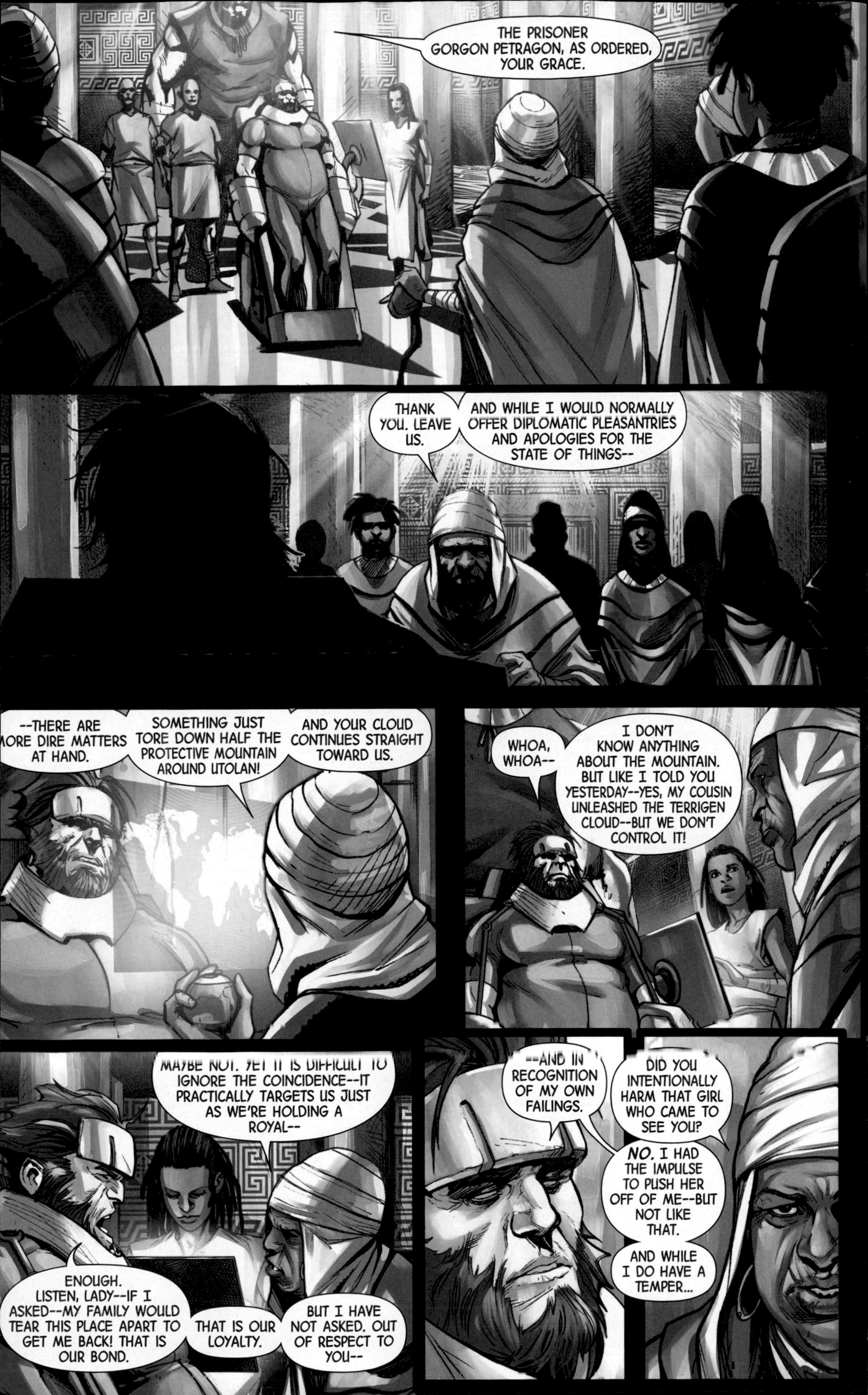

THE PRISONER GORGON PETRAGON, AS ORDERED, YOUR GRACE.
THANK YOU. LEAVE US.
AND WHILE I WOULD NORMALLY OFFER DIPLOMATIC PLEASANTRIES AND APOLOGIES FOR THE STATE OF THINGS--
--THERE ARE MORE DIRE MATTERS AT HAND.
SOMETHING JUST TORE DOWN HALF THE PROTECTIVE MOUNTAIN AROUND UTOLAN!
AND YOUR CLOUD CONTINUES STRAIGHT TOWARD US.
WHOA, WHOA--
I DON'T KNOW ANYTHING ABOUT THE MOUNTAIN. BUT LIKE I TOLD YOU YESTERDAY--YES, MY COUSIN UNLEASHED THE TERRIGEN CLOUD--BUT WE DON'T CONTROL IT!
MAYBE NOT. YET IT IS DIFFICULT TO IGNORE THE COINCIDENCE--IT PRACTICALLY TARGETS US JUST AS WE'RE HOLDING A ROYAL--
ENOUGH. LISTEN, LADY--IF I ASKED--MY FAMILY WOULD TEAR THIS PLACE APART TO GET ME BACK! THAT IS OUR BOND.
THAT IS OUR LOYALTY.
BUT I HAVE NOT ASKED. OUT OF RESPECT TO YOU--
--AND IN RECOGNITION OF MY OWN FAILINGS.
DID YOU INTENTIONALLY HARM THAT GIRL WHO CAME TO SEE YOU?
NO. I HAD THE IMPULSE TO PUSH HER OFF OF ME--BUT NOT LIKE THAT.
AND WHILE I DO HAVE A TEMPER...

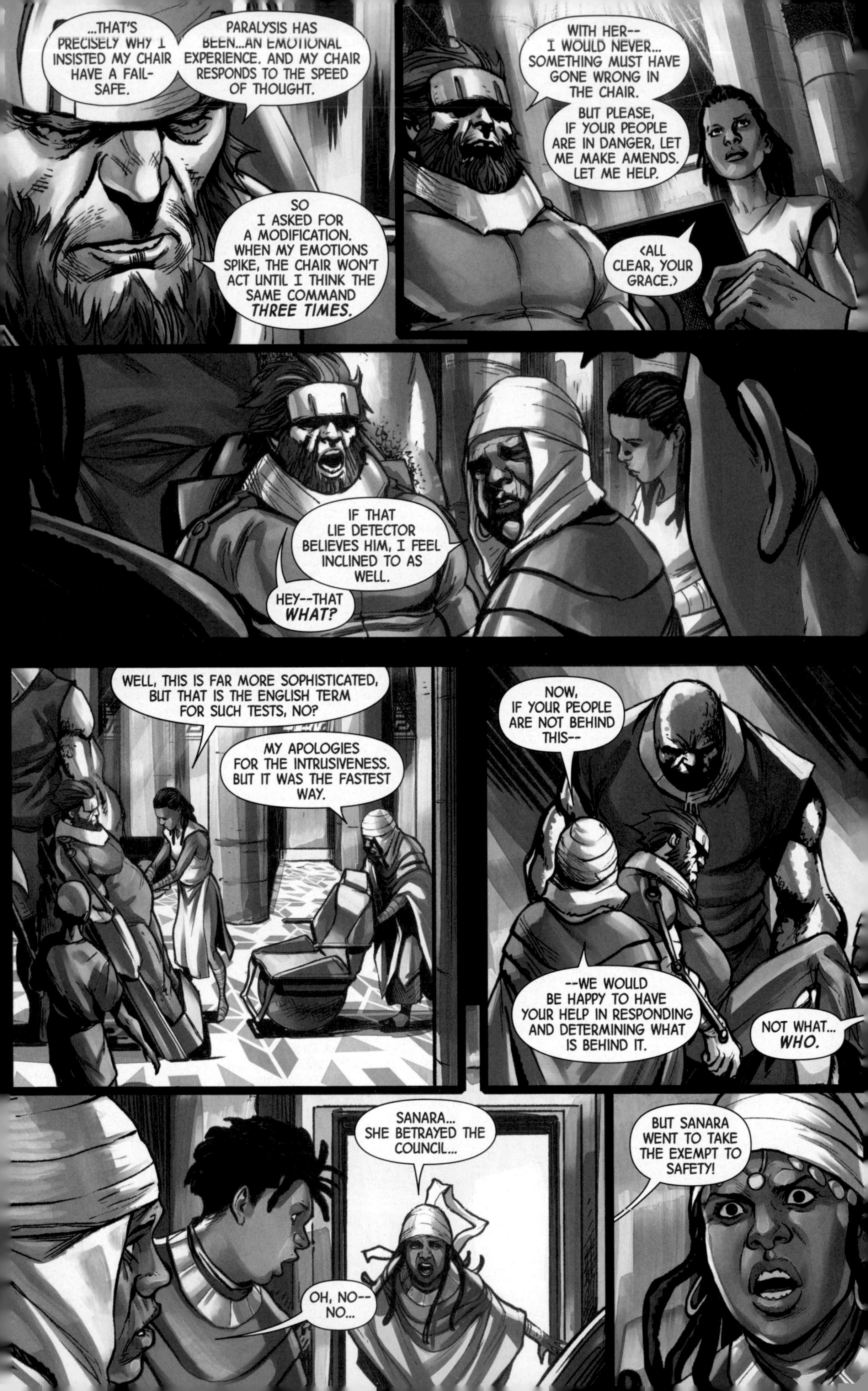

...THAT'S PRECISELY WHY I INSISTED MY CHAIR HAVE A FAIL-SAFE.
PARALYSIS HAS BEEN...AN EMOTIONAL EXPERIENCE. AND MY CHAIR RESPONDS TO THE SPEED OF THOUGHT.
SO I ASKED FOR A MODIFICATION. WHEN MY EMOTIONS SPIKE, THE CHAIR WON'T ACT UNTIL I THINK THE SAME COMMAND *THREE TIMES.*
WITH HER-- I WOULD NEVER... SOMETHING MUST HAVE GONE WRONG IN THE CHAIR.
BUT PLEASE, IF YOUR PEOPLE ARE IN DANGER, LET ME MAKE AMENDS. LET ME HELP.
<ALL CLEAR, YOUR GRACE.>
IF THAT LIE DETECTOR BELIEVES HIM, I FEEL INCLINED TO AS WELL.
HEY--THAT *WHAT?*
WELL, THIS IS FAR MORE SOPHISTICATED, BUT THAT IS THE ENGLISH TERM FOR SUCH TESTS, NO?
MY APOLOGIES FOR THE INTRUSIVENESS. BUT IT WAS THE FASTEST WAY.
NOW, IF YOUR PEOPLE ARE NOT BEHIND THIS--
--WE WOULD BE HAPPY TO HAVE YOUR HELP IN RESPONDING AND DETERMINING WHAT IS BEHIND IT.
NOT WHAT... *WHO.*
OH, NO-- NO...
SANARA... SHE BETRAYED THE COUNCIL...
BUT SANARA WENT TO TAKE THE EXEMPT TO SAFETY!

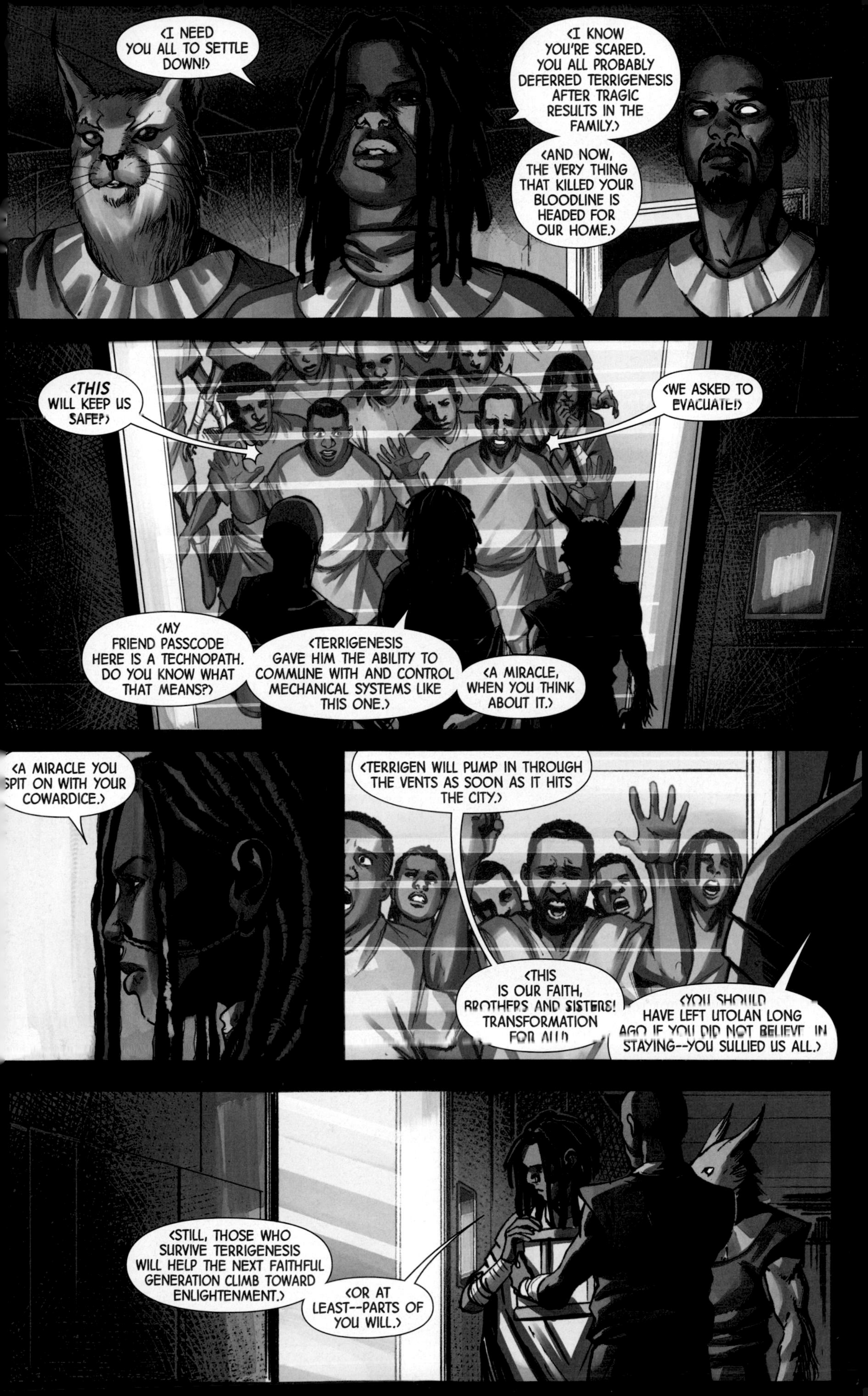

<I NEED YOU ALL TO SETTLE DOWN!>
<I KNOW YOU'RE SCARED. YOU ALL PROBABLY DEFERRED TERRIGENESIS AFTER TRAGIC RESULTS IN THE FAMILY.>
<AND NOW, THE VERY THING THAT KILLED YOUR BLOODLINE IS HEADED FOR OUR HOME.>
<THIS WILL KEEP US SAFE?>
<WE ASKED TO EVACUATE!>
<MY FRIEND PASSCODE HERE IS A TECHNOPATH. DO YOU KNOW WHAT THAT MEANS?>
<TERRIGENESIS GAVE HIM THE ABILITY TO COMMUNE WITH AND CONTROL MECHANICAL SYSTEMS LIKE THIS ONE.>
<A MIRACLE, WHEN YOU THINK ABOUT IT.>
<A MIRACLE YOU SPIT ON WITH YOUR COWARDICE.>
<TERRIGEN WILL PUMP IN THROUGH THE VENTS AS SOON AS IT HITS THE CITY.>
<THIS IS OUR FAITH, BROTHERS AND SISTERS! TRANSFORMATION FOR ALL!>
<YOU SHOULD HAVE LEFT UTOLAN LONG AGO IF YOU DID NOT BELIEVE IN STAYING--YOU SULLIED US ALL.>
<STILL, THOSE WHO SURVIVE TERRIGENESIS WILL HELP THE NEXT FAITHFUL GENERATION CLIMB TOWARD ENLIGHTENMENT.>
<OR AT LEAST--PARTS OF YOU WILL.>

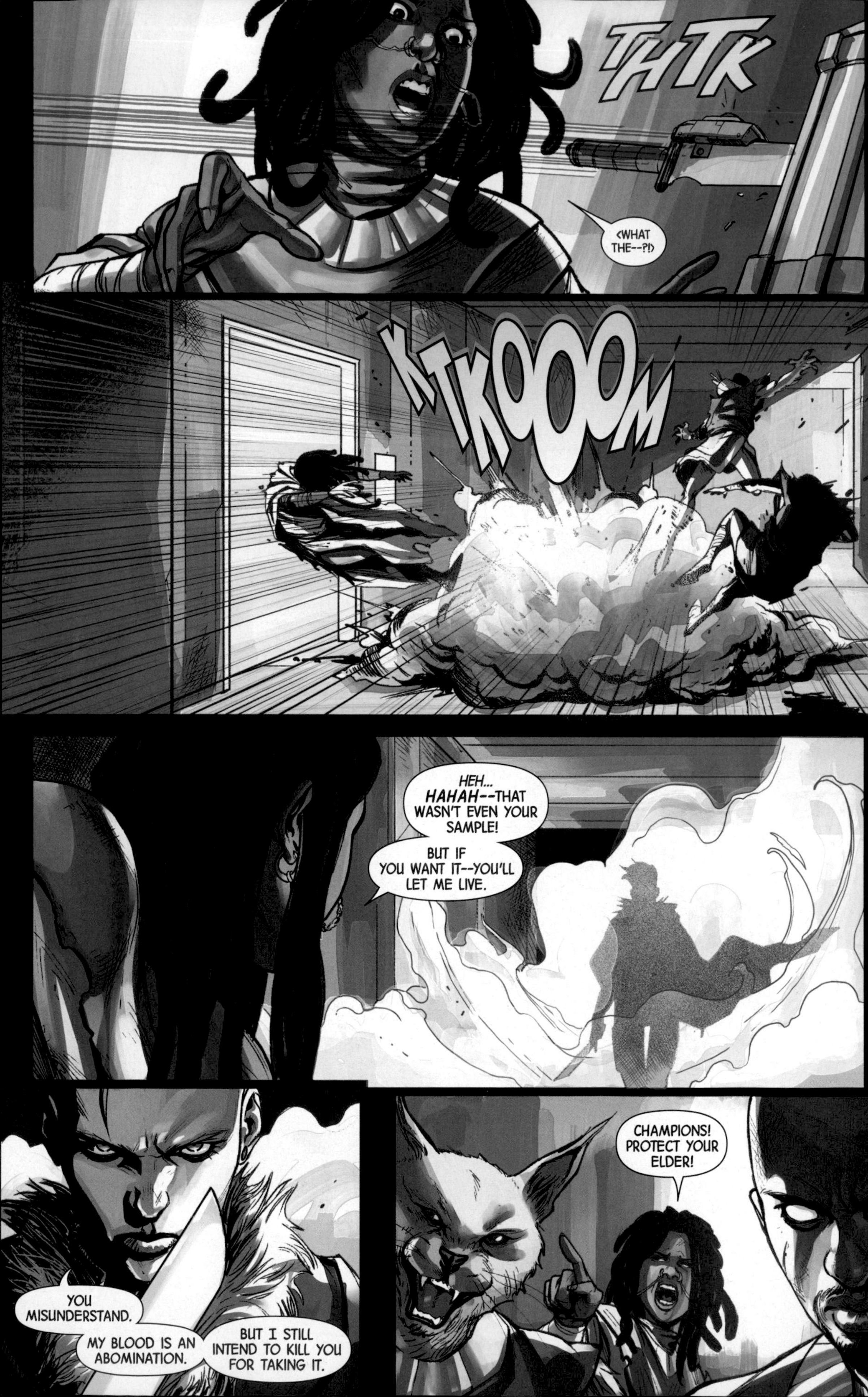
THTK
<WHAT THE--?!>
KTKOOOM
HEH... HAHAH--THAT WASN'T EVEN YOUR SAMPLE!
BUT IF YOU WANT IT--YOU'LL LET ME LIVE.
YOU MISUNDERSTAND.
MY BLOOD IS AN ABOMINATION.
BUT I STILL INTEND TO KILL YOU FOR TAKING IT.
CHAMPIONS! PROTECT YOUR ELDER!

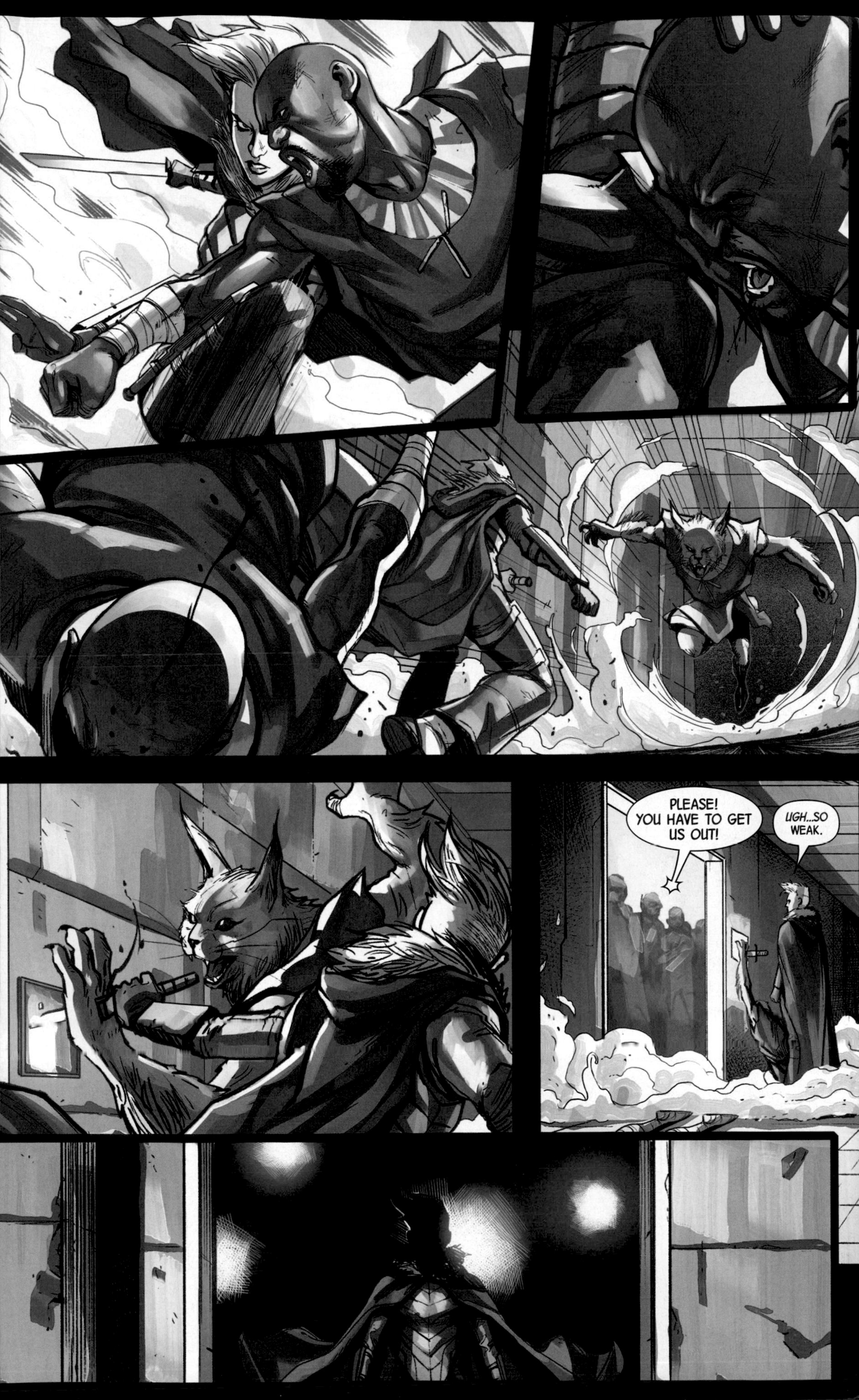
PLEASE! YOU HAVE TO GET US OUT!
UGH...SO WEAK.

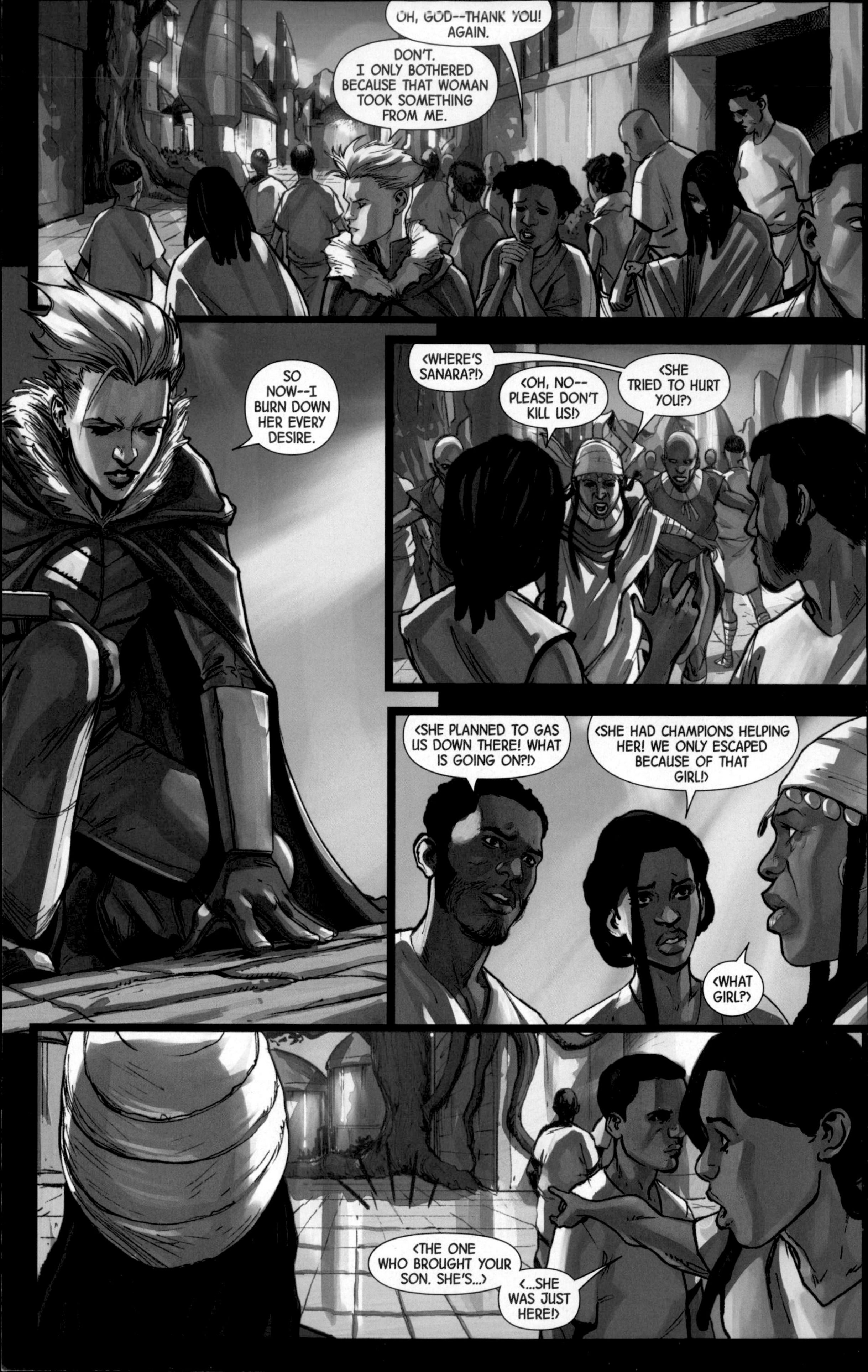
OH, GOD--THANK YOU! AGAIN.
DON'T. I ONLY BOTHERED BECAUSE THAT WOMAN TOOK SOMETHING FROM ME.
SO NOW--I BURN DOWN HER EVERY DESIRE.
<WHERE'S SANARA?!>
<OH, NO-- PLEASE DON'T KILL US!>
<SHE TRIED TO HURT YOU?>
<SHE PLANNED TO GAS US DOWN THERE! WHAT IS GOING ON?!>
<SHE HAD CHAMPIONS HELPING HER! WE ONLY ESCAPED BECAUSE OF THAT GIRL!>
<WHAT GIRL?>
<THE ONE WHO BROUGHT YOUR SON. SHE'S...>
<...SHE WAS JUST HERE!>

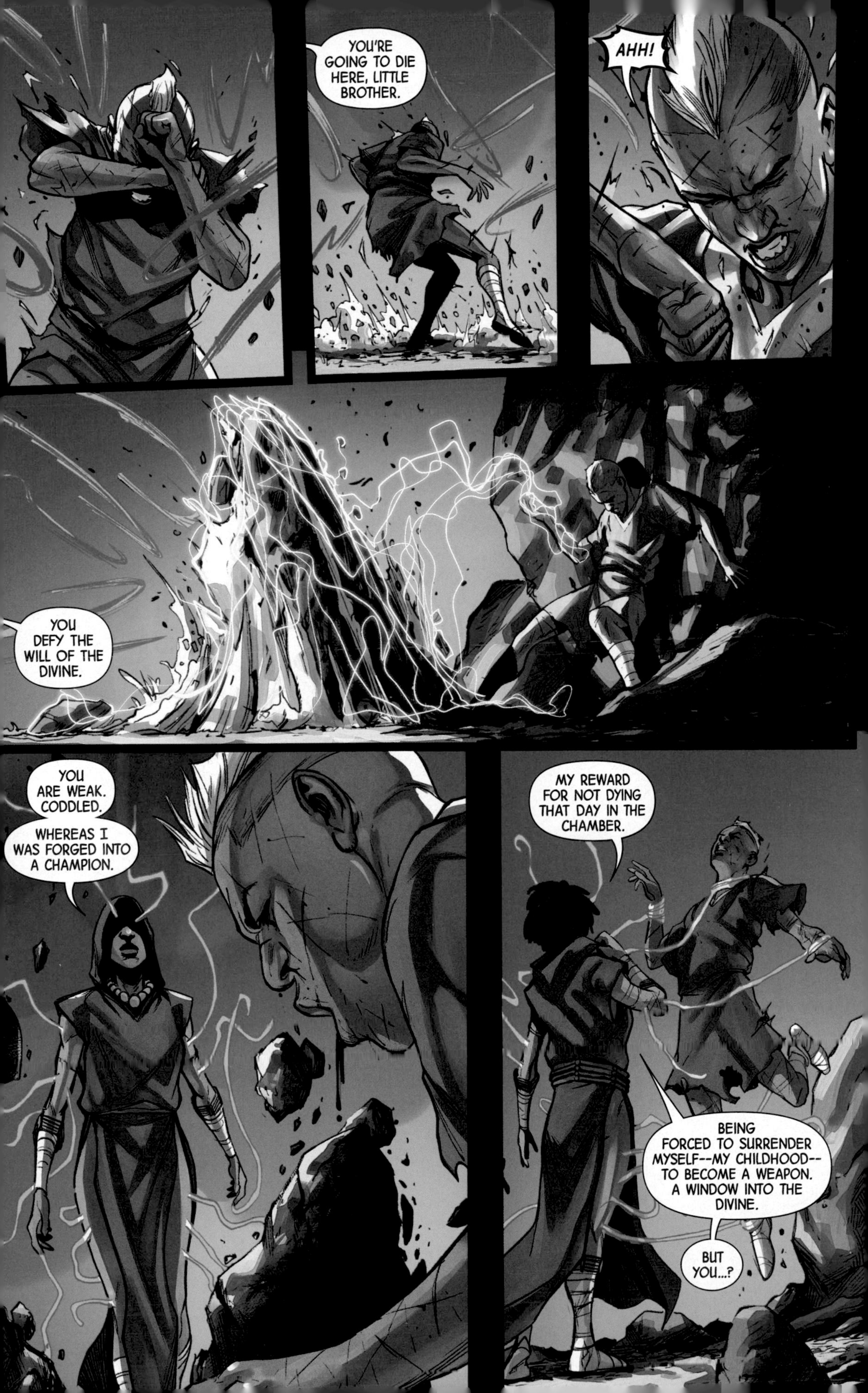
YOU'RE GOING TO DIE HERE, LITTLE BROTHER.
AHH!
YOU DEFY THE WILL OF THE DIVINE.
YOU ARE WEAK. CODDLED.
WHEREAS I WAS FORGED INTO A CHAMPION.
MY REWARD FOR NOT DYING THAT DAY IN THE CHAMBER.
BEING FORCED TO SURRENDER MYSELF--MY CHILDHOOD--TO BECOME A WEAPON. A WINDOW INTO THE DIVINE.
BUT YOU...?

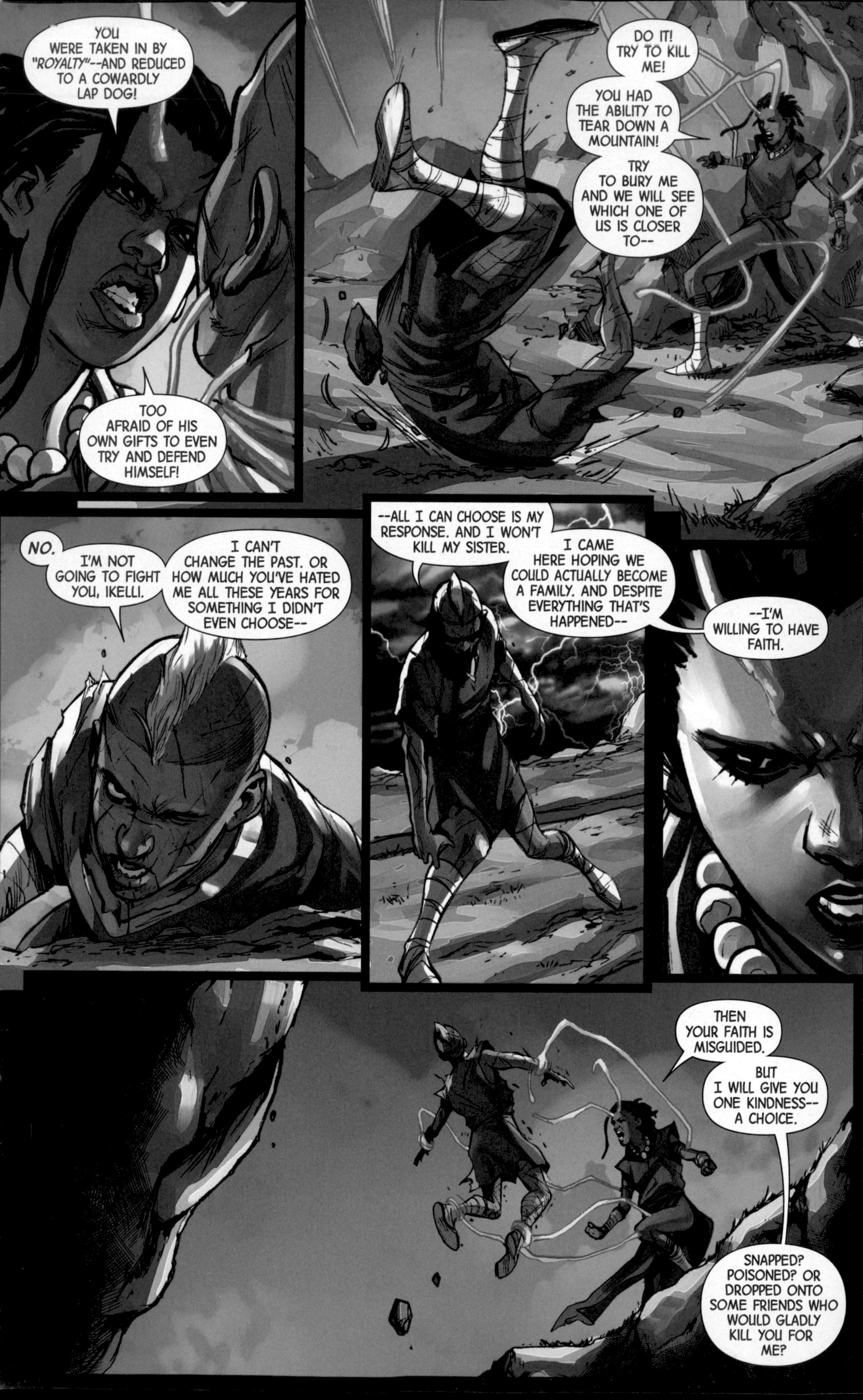

YOU WERE TAKEN IN BY "ROYALTY"--AND REDUCED TO A COWARDLY LAP DOG!
TOO AFRAID OF HIS OWN GIFTS TO EVEN TRY AND DEFEND HIMSELF!
DO IT! TRY TO KILL ME!
YOU HAD THE ABILITY TO TEAR DOWN A MOUNTAIN!
TRY TO BURY ME AND WE WILL SEE WHICH ONE OF US IS CLOSER TO--
NO.
I'M NOT GOING TO FIGHT YOU, IKELLI.
I CAN'T CHANGE THE PAST. OR HOW MUCH YOU'VE HATED ME ALL THESE YEARS FOR SOMETHING I DIDN'T EVEN CHOOSE--
--ALL I CAN CHOOSE IS MY RESPONSE. AND I WON'T KILL MY SISTER.
I CAME HERE HOPING WE COULD ACTUALLY BECOME A FAMILY. AND DESPITE EVERYTHING THAT'S HAPPENED--
--I'M WILLING TO HAVE FAITH.
THEN YOUR FAITH IS MISGUIDED.
BUT I WILL GIVE YOU ONE KINDNESS-- A CHOICE.
SNAPPED? POISONED? OR DROPPED ONTO SOME FRIENDS WHO WOULD GLADLY KILL YOU FOR ME?

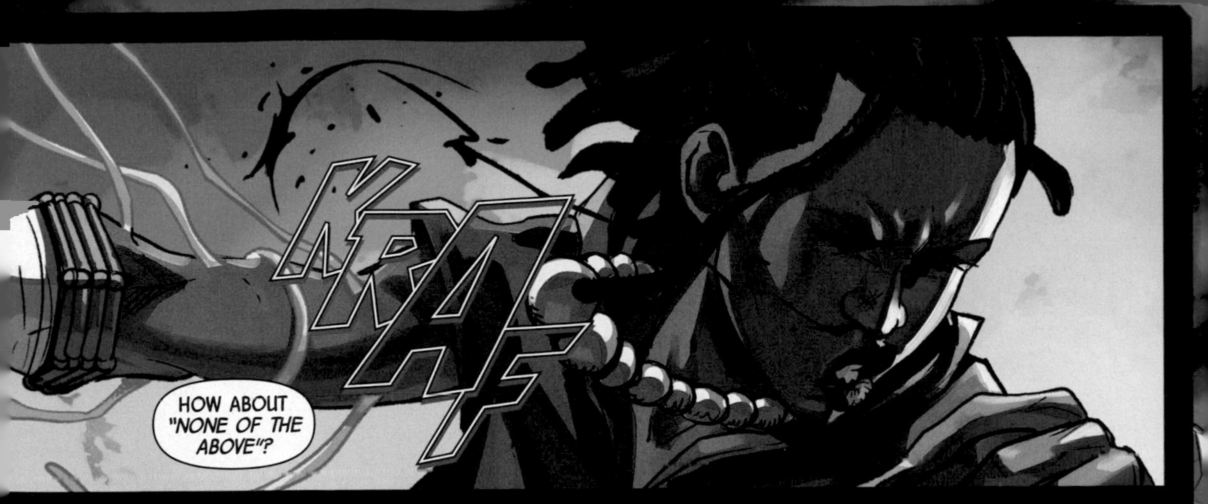
KRAK
HOW ABOUT "NONE OF THE ABOVE"?

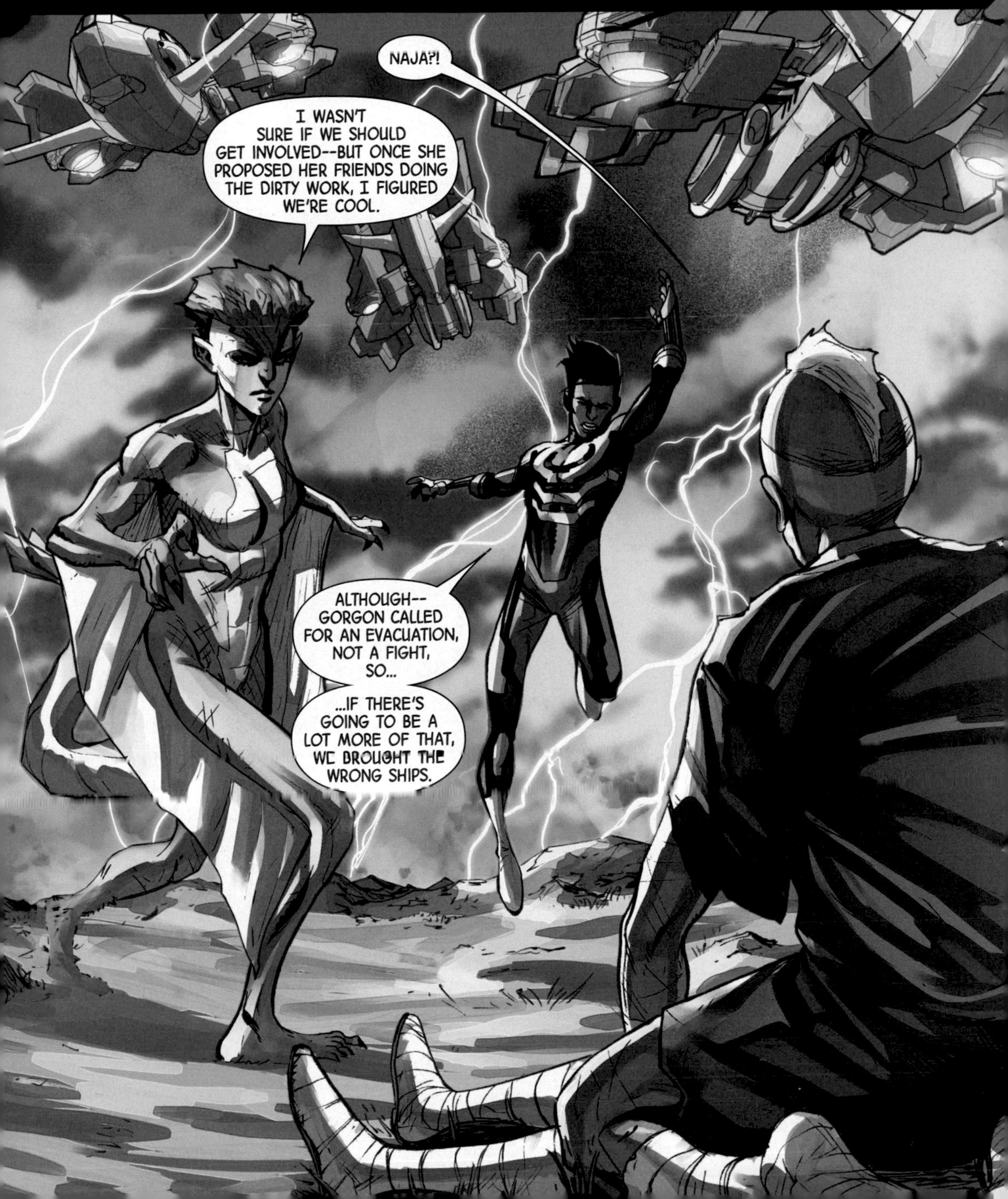
NAJA?!
I WASN'T SURE IF WE SHOULD GET INVOLVED--BUT ONCE SHE PROPOSED HER FRIENDS DOING THE DIRTY WORK, I FIGURED WE'RE COOL.
ALTHOUGH-- GORGON CALLED FOR AN EVACUATION, NOT A FIGHT, SO...
...IF THERE'S GOING TO BE A LOT MORE OF THAT, WE BROUGHT THE WRONG SHIPS.

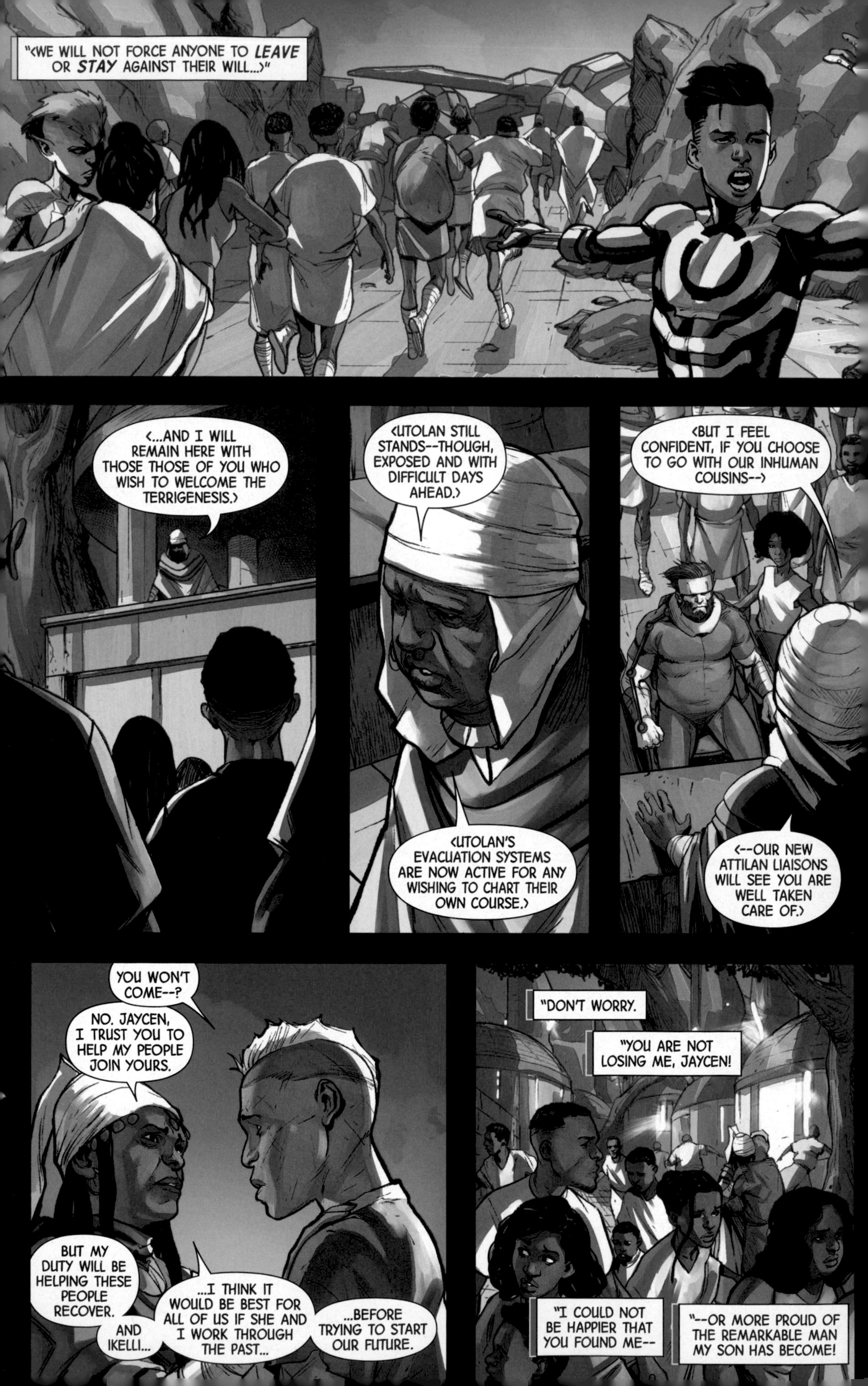
"<WE WILL NOT FORCE ANYONE TO LEAVE OR STAY AGAINST THEIR WILL...>"
<...AND I WILL REMAIN HERE WITH THOSE THOSE OF YOU WHO WISH TO WELCOME THE TERRIGENESIS.>
<UTOLAN STILL STANDS--THOUGH, EXPOSED AND WITH DIFFICULT DAYS AHEAD.>
<UTOLAN'S EVACUATION SYSTEMS ARE NOW ACTIVE FOR ANY WISHING TO CHART THEIR OWN COURSE.>
<BUT I FEEL CONFIDENT, IF YOU CHOOSE TO GO WITH OUR INHUMAN COUSINS-->
<--OUR NEW ATTILAN LIAISONS WILL SEE YOU ARE WELL TAKEN CARE OF.>
YOU WON'T COME--?
NO. JAYCEN, I TRUST YOU TO HELP MY PEOPLE JOIN YOURS.
BUT MY DUTY WILL BE HELPING THESE PEOPLE RECOVER.
AND IKELLI...
...I THINK IT WOULD BE BEST FOR ALL OF US IF SHE AND I WORK THROUGH THE PAST...
...BEFORE TRYING TO START OUR FUTURE.
"DON'T WORRY.
"YOU ARE NOT LOSING ME, JAYCEN!
"I COULD NOT BE HAPPIER THAT YOU FOUND ME--
"--OR MORE PROUD OF THE REMARKABLE MAN MY SON HAS BECOME!

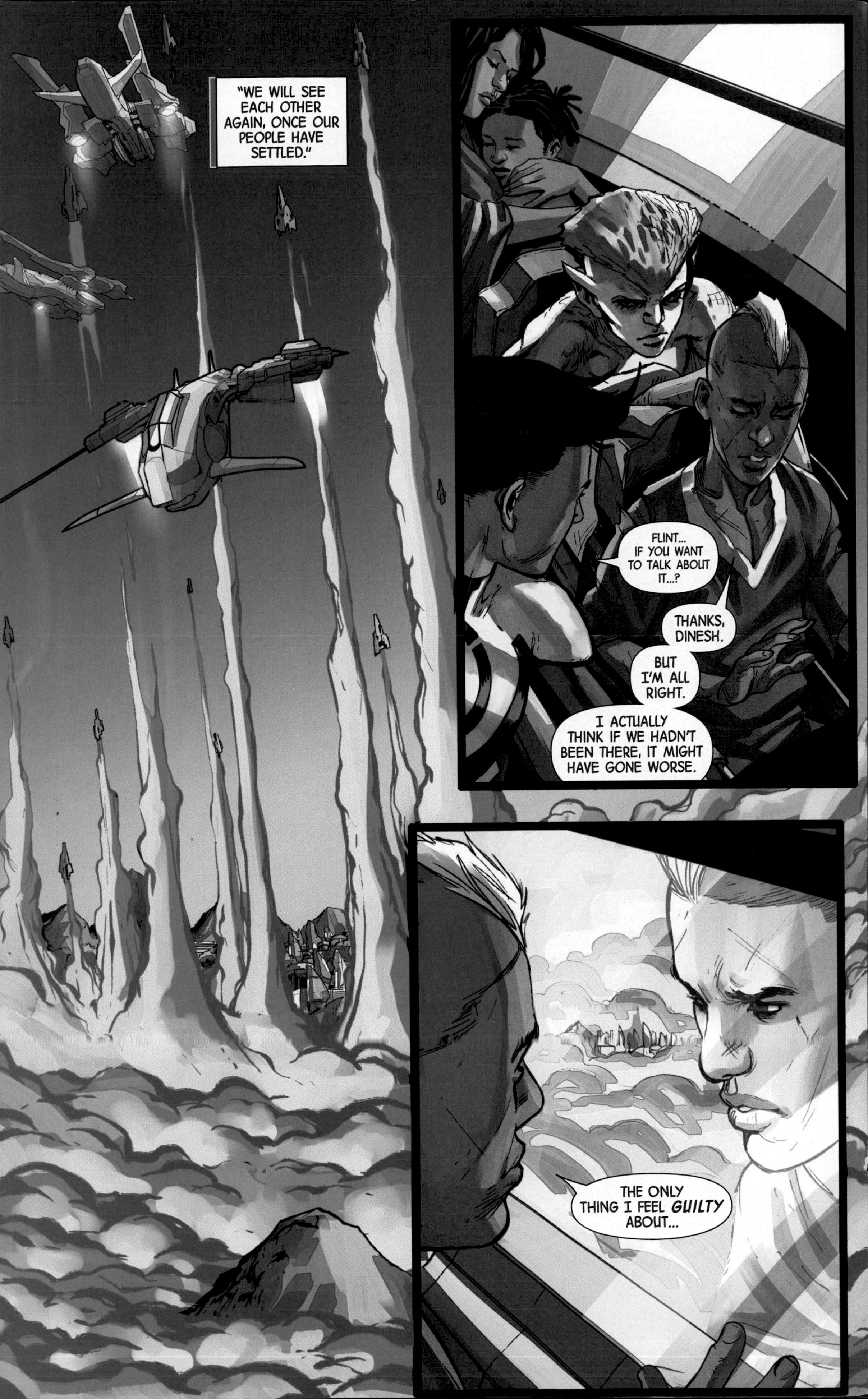
"WE WILL SEE EACH OTHER AGAIN, ONCE OUR PEOPLE HAVE SETTLED."
FLINT... IF YOU WANT TO TALK ABOUT IT...?
THANKS, DINESH.
BUT I'M ALL RIGHT.
I ACTUALLY THINK IF WE HADN'T BEEN THERE, IT MIGHT HAVE GONE WORSE.
THE ONLY THING I FEEL *GUILTY* ABOUT...

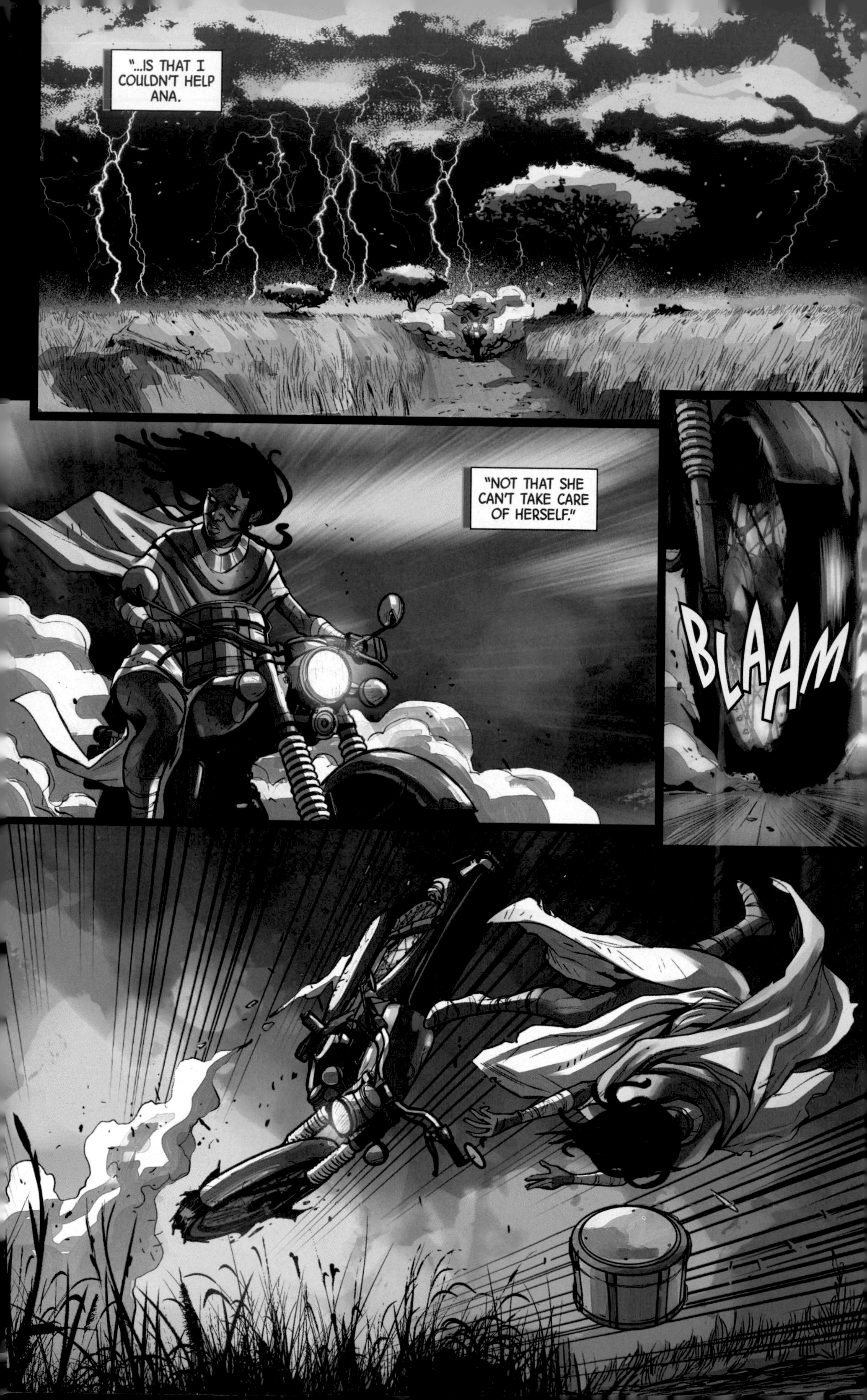
"...IS THAT I COULDN'T HELP ANA.
"NOT THAT SHE CAN'T TAKE CARE OF HERSELF."
BLAAM

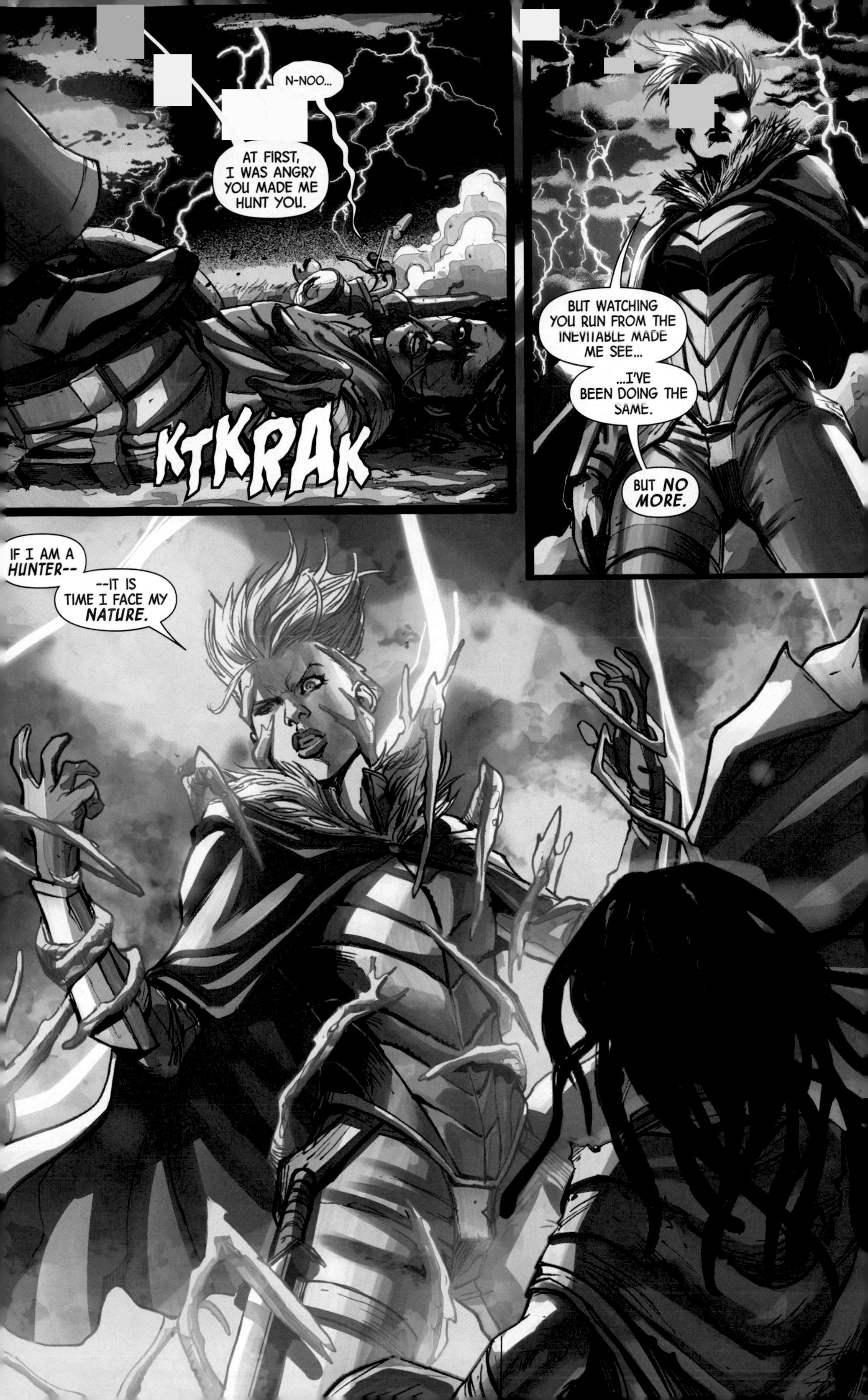
N-NOO...
AT FIRST, I WAS ANGRY YOU MADE ME HUNT YOU.
KTKRAK
BUT WATCHING YOU RUN FROM THE INEVITABLE MADE ME SEE...
...I'VE BEEN DOING THE SAME.
BUT NO MORE.
IF I AM A HUNTER--
--IT IS TIME I FACE MY NATURE.

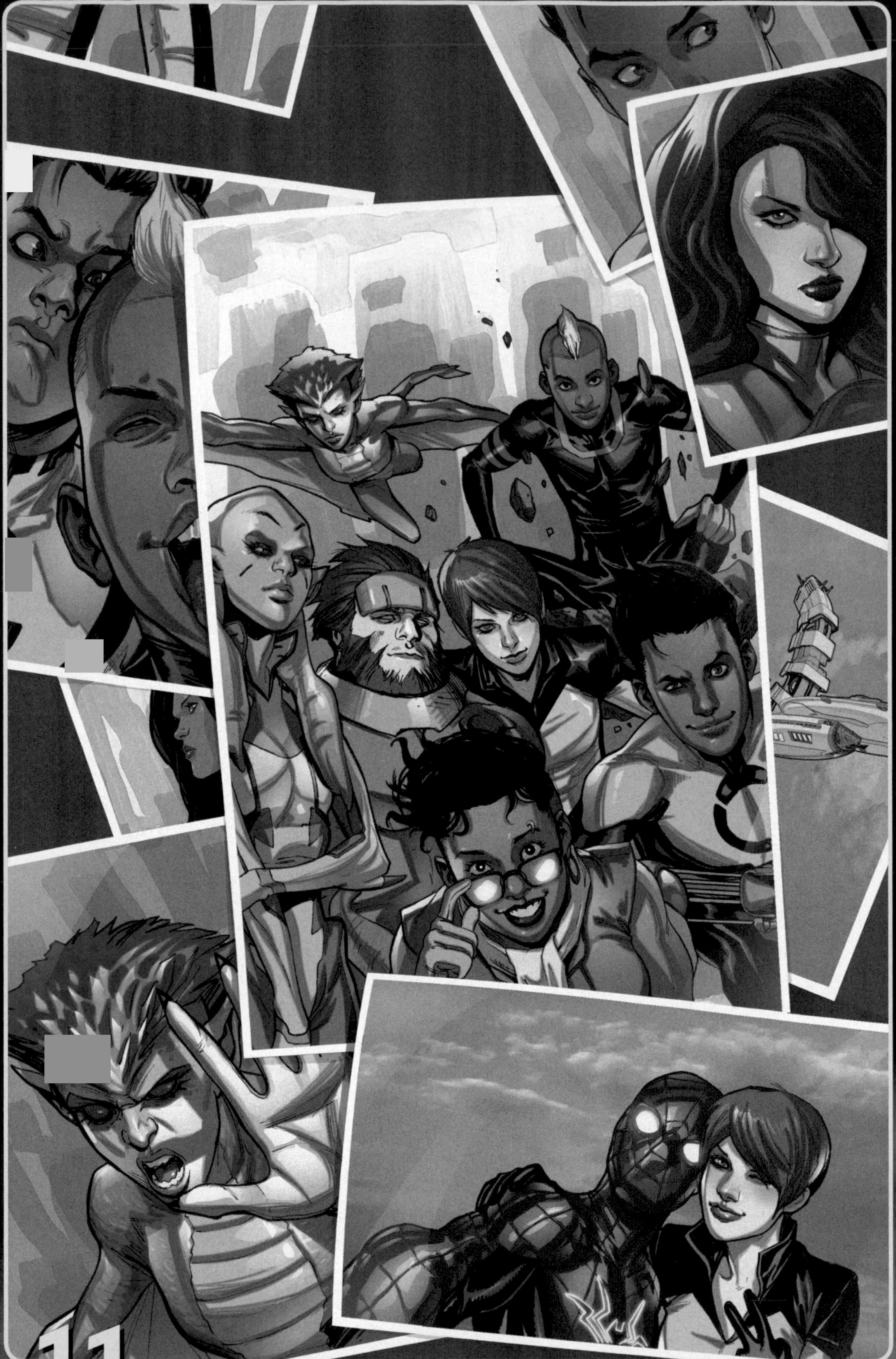

11

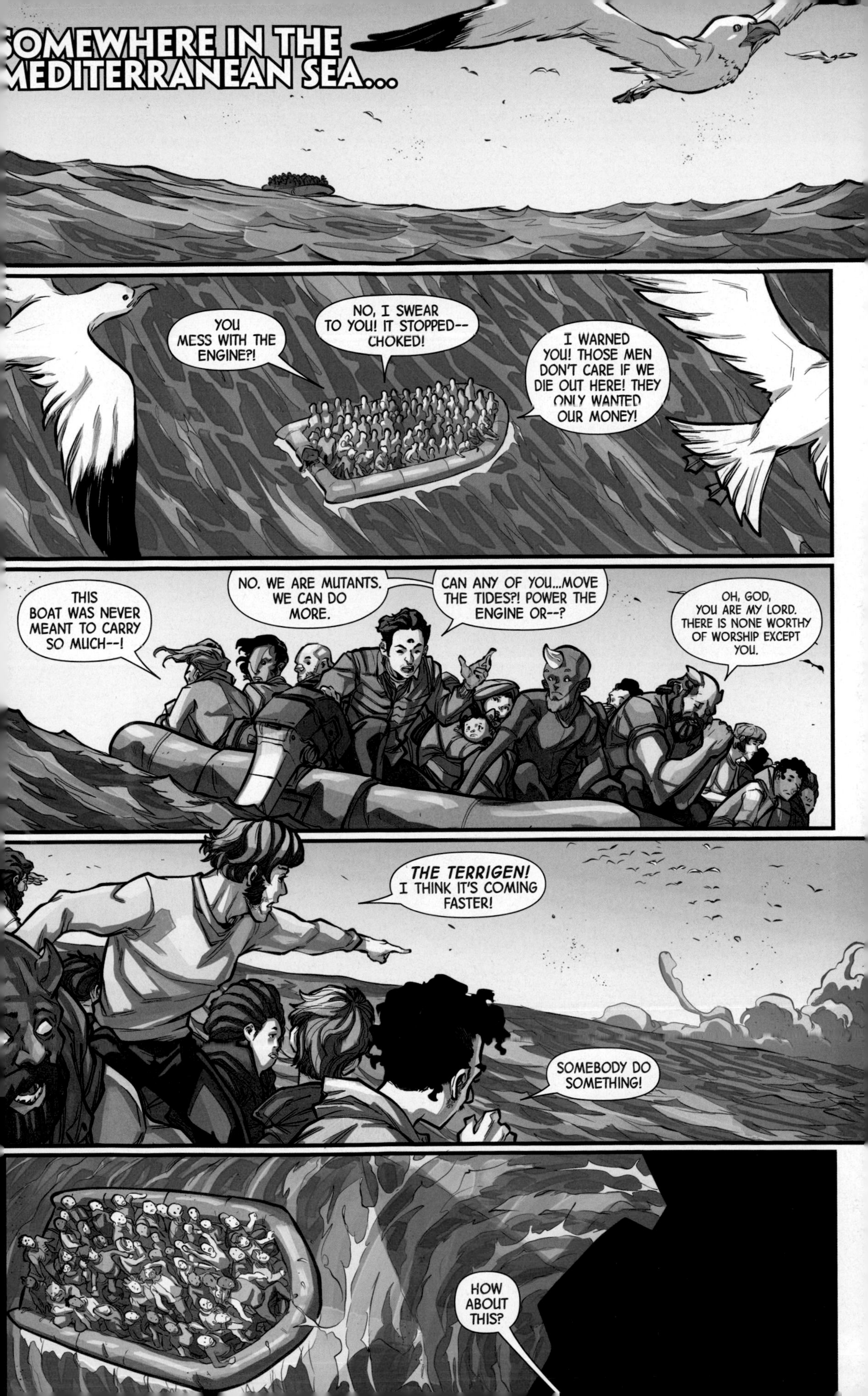
SOMEWHERE IN THE MEDITERRANEAN SEA...
YOU MESS WITH THE ENGINE?!
NO, I SWEAR TO YOU! IT STOPPED-- CHOKED!
I WARNED YOU! THOSE MEN DON'T CARE IF WE DIE OUT HERE! THEY ONLY WANTED OUR MONEY!
THIS BOAT WAS NEVER MEANT TO CARRY SO MUCH--!
NO. WE ARE MUTANTS. WE CAN DO MORE.
CAN ANY OF YOU...MOVE THE TIDES?! POWER THE ENGINE OR--?
OH, GOD, YOU ARE MY LORD. THERE IS NONE WORTHY OF WORSHIP EXCEPT YOU.
THE TERRIGEN! I THINK IT'S COMING FASTER!
SOMEBODY DO SOMETHING!
HOW ABOUT THIS?

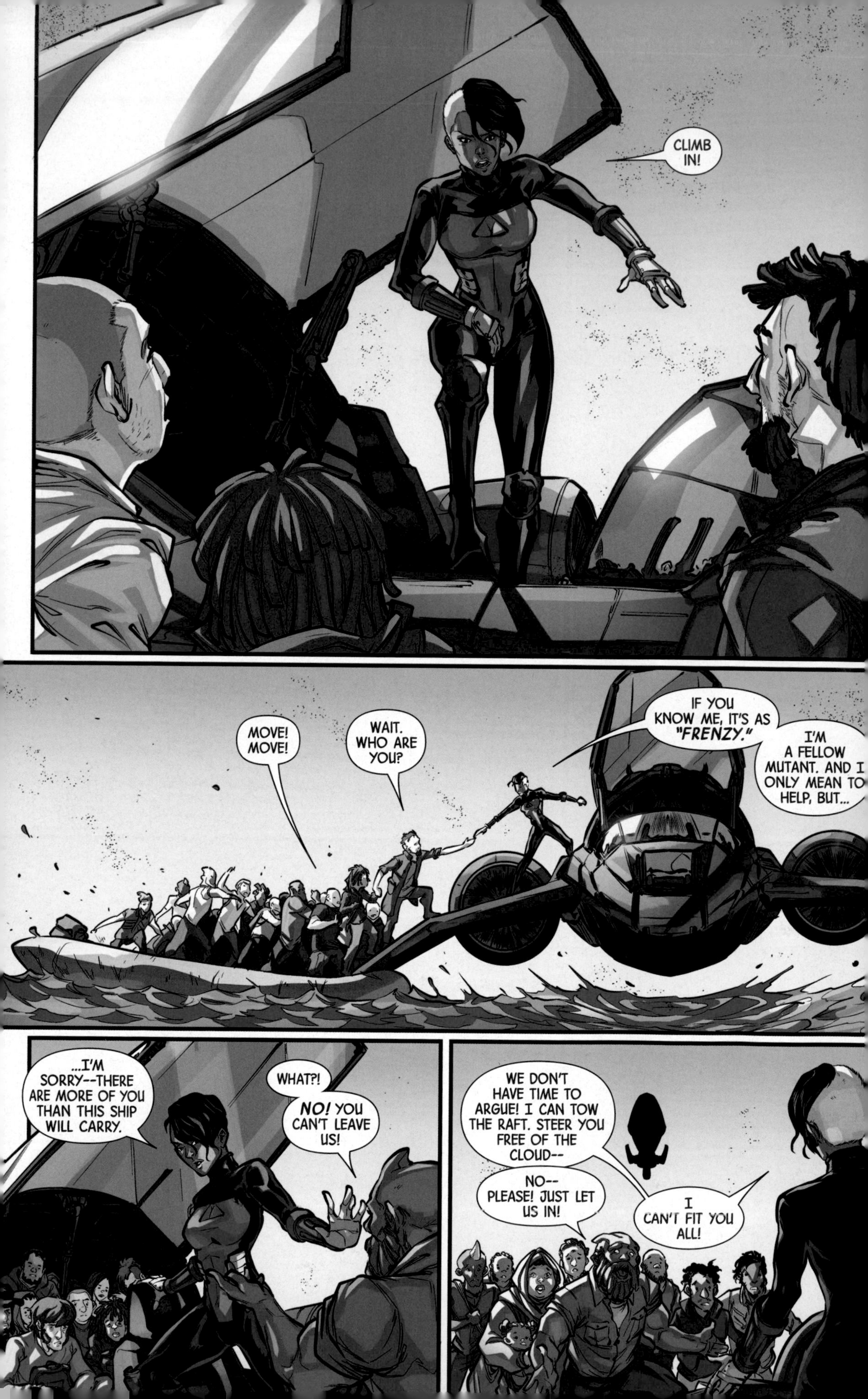
CLIMB IN!
MOVE! MOVE!
WAIT. WHO ARE YOU?
IF YOU KNOW ME, IT'S AS "FRENZY."
I'M A FELLOW MUTANT. AND I ONLY MEAN TO HELP, BUT...
...I'M SORRY--THERE ARE MORE OF YOU THAN THIS SHIP WILL CARRY.
WHAT?!
NO! YOU CAN'T LEAVE US!
WE DON'T HAVE TIME TO ARGUE! I CAN TOW THE RAFT. STEER YOU FREE OF THE CLOUD--
NO-- PLEASE! JUST LET US IN!
I CAN'T FIT YOU ALL!

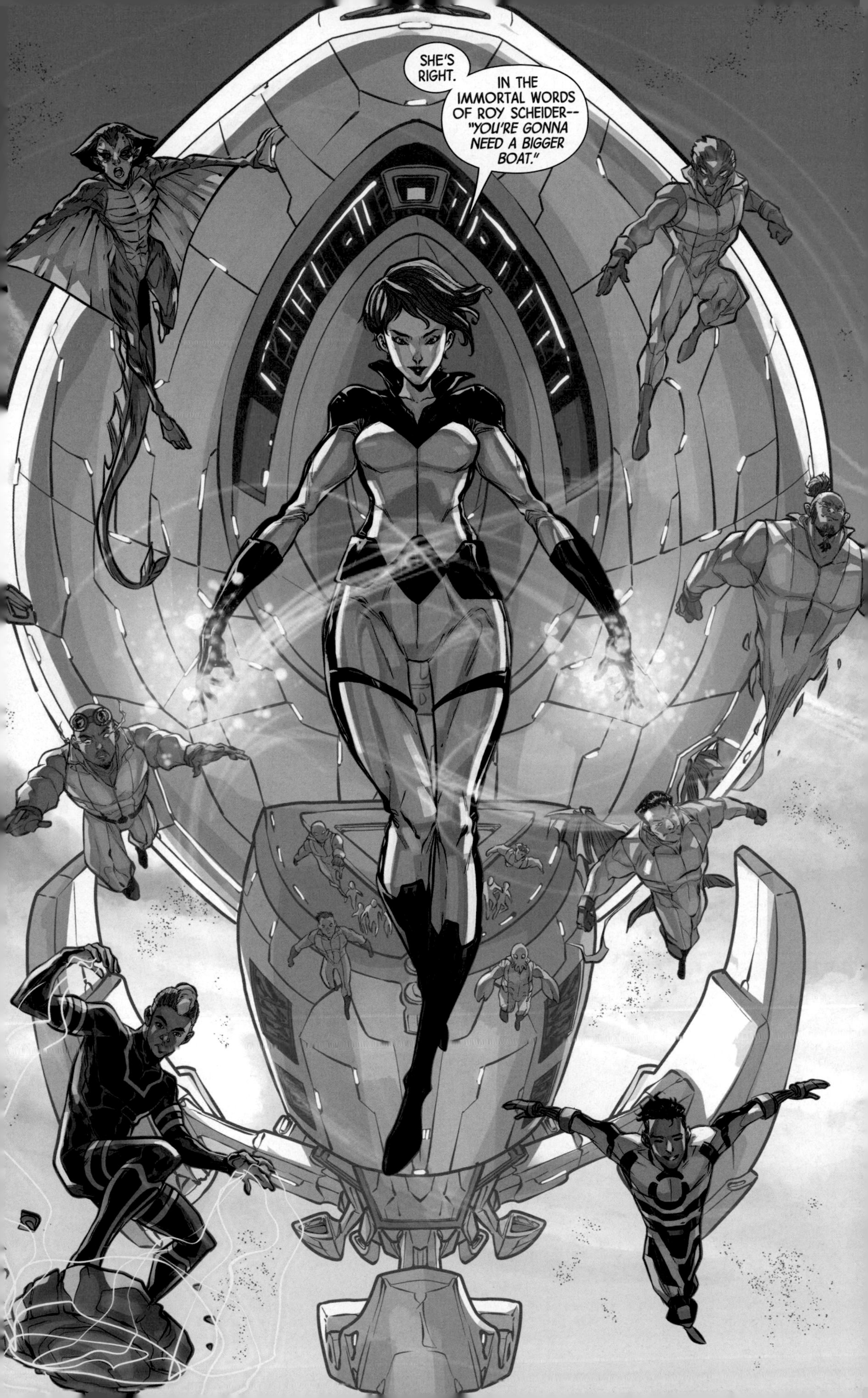
SHE'S RIGHT.
IN THE IMMORTAL WORDS OF ROY SCHEIDER-- "YOU'RE GONNA NEED A BIGGER BOAT."

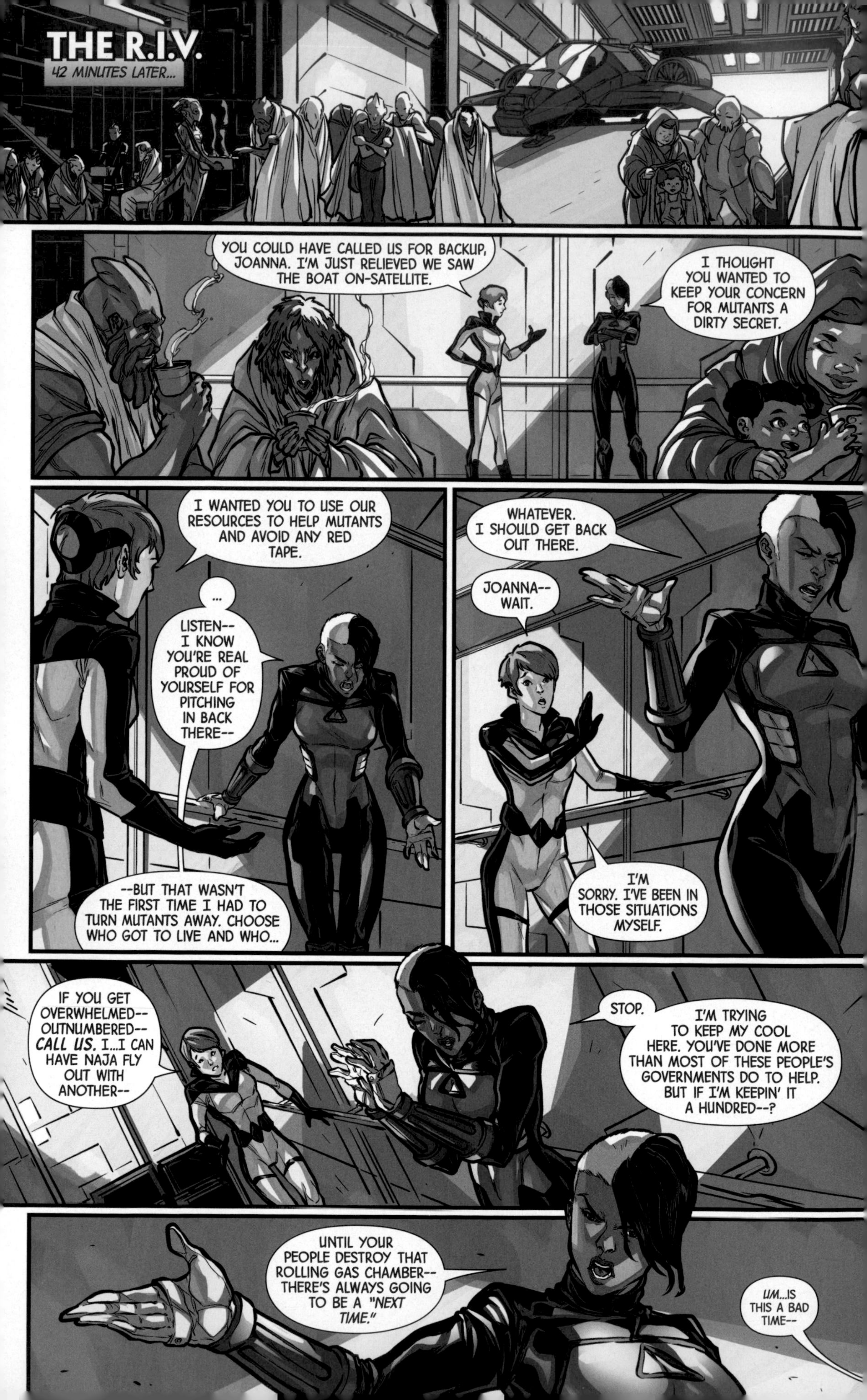
THE R.I.V.
42 MINUTES LATER...
YOU COULD HAVE CALLED US FOR BACKUP, JOANNA. I'M JUST RELIEVED WE SAW THE BOAT ON-SATELLITE.
I THOUGHT YOU WANTED TO KEEP YOUR CONCERN FOR MUTANTS A DIRTY SECRET.
I WANTED YOU TO USE OUR RESOURCES TO HELP MUTANTS AND AVOID ANY RED TAPE.
...
LISTEN-- I KNOW YOU'RE REAL PROUD OF YOURSELF FOR PITCHING IN BACK THERE--
--BUT THAT WASN'T THE FIRST TIME I HAD TO TURN MUTANTS AWAY. CHOOSE WHO GOT TO LIVE AND WHO...
WHATEVER. I SHOULD GET BACK OUT THERE.
JOANNA-- WAIT.
I'M SORRY. I'VE BEEN IN THOSE SITUATIONS MYSELF.
IF YOU GET OVERWHELMED-- OUTNUMBERED-- CALL US. I...I CAN HAVE NAJA FLY OUT WITH ANOTHER--
STOP.
I'M TRYING TO KEEP MY COOL HERE. YOU'VE DONE MORE THAN MOST OF THESE PEOPLE'S GOVERNMENTS DO TO HELP. BUT IF I'M KEEPIN' IT A HUNDRED--?
UNTIL YOUR PEOPLE DESTROY THAT ROLLING GAS CHAMBER-- THERE'S ALWAYS GOING TO BE A "NEXT TIME."
UM...IS THIS A BAD TIME--

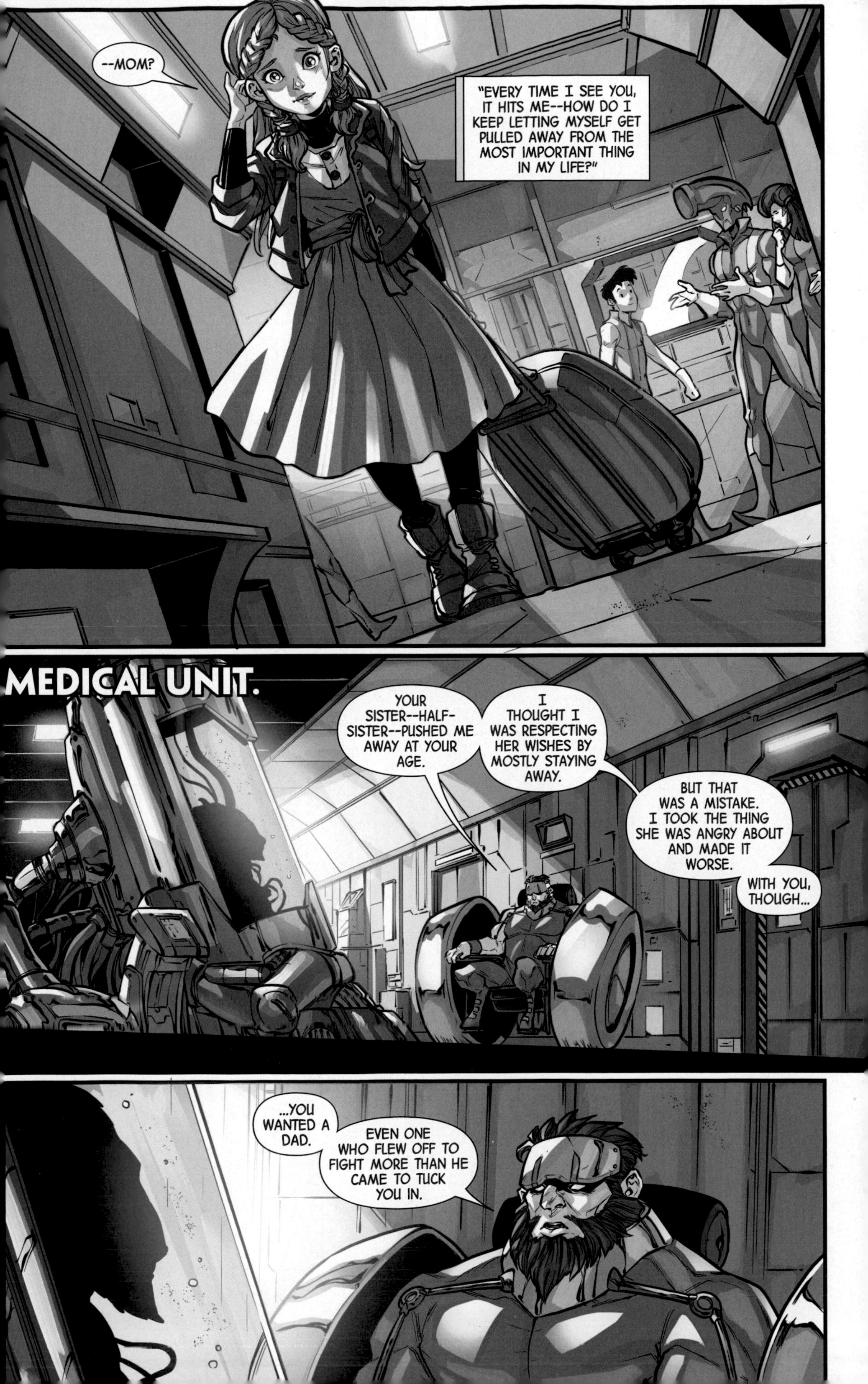
--MOM?
"EVERY TIME I SEE YOU, IT HITS ME--HOW DO I KEEP LETTING MYSELF GET PULLED AWAY FROM THE MOST IMPORTANT THING IN MY LIFE?"
MEDICAL UNIT.
YOUR SISTER--HALF-SISTER--PUSHED ME AWAY AT YOUR AGE.
I THOUGHT I WAS RESPECTING HER WISHES BY MOSTLY STAYING AWAY.
BUT THAT WAS A MISTAKE. I TOOK THE THING SHE WAS ANGRY ABOUT AND MADE IT WORSE.
WITH YOU, THOUGH...
...YOU WANTED A DAD.
EVEN ONE WHO FLEW OFF TO FIGHT MORE THAN HE CAME TO TUCK YOU IN.

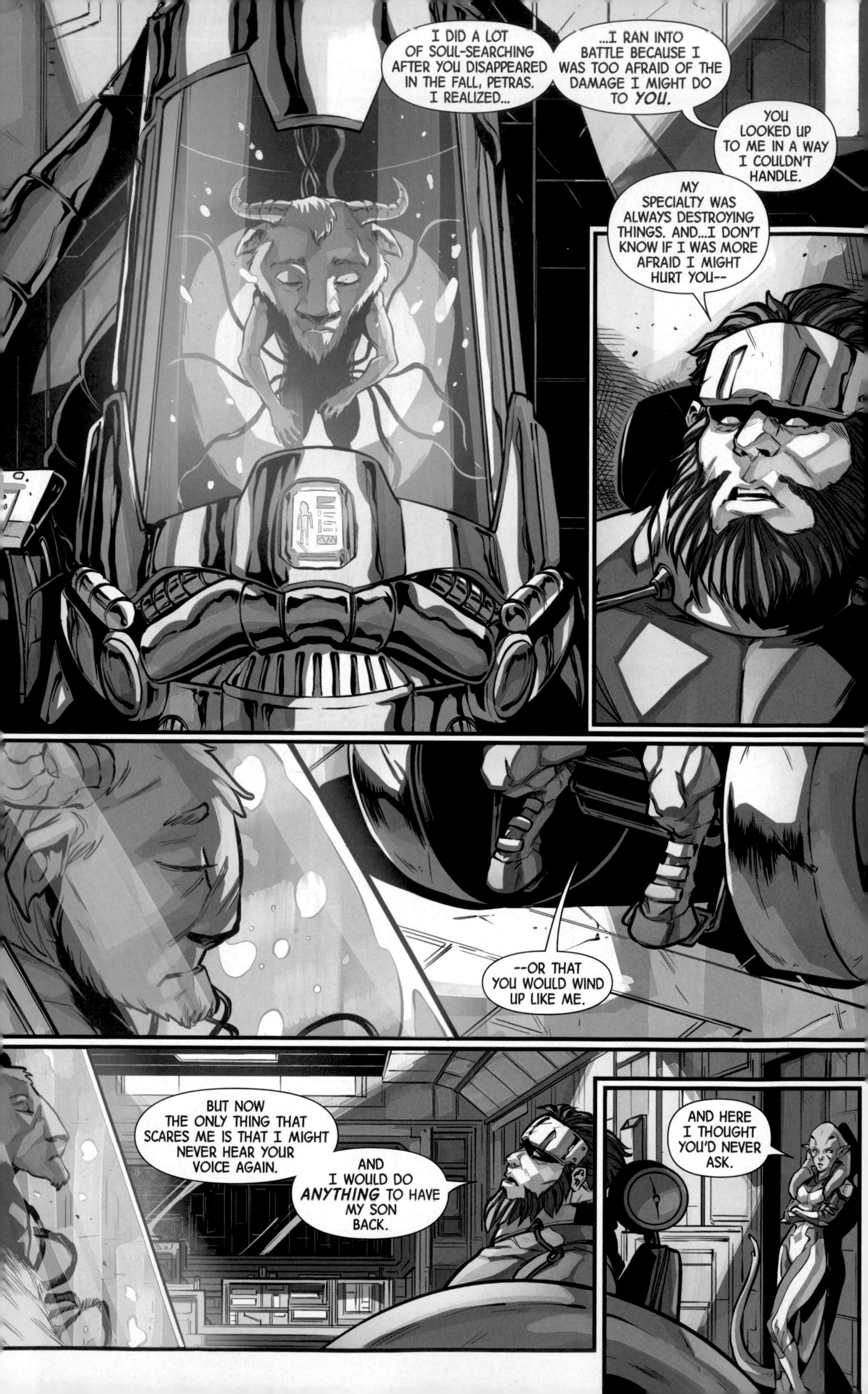
I DID A LOT OF SOUL-SEARCHING AFTER YOU DISAPPEARED IN THE FALL, PETRAS. I REALIZED...
...I RAN INTO BATTLE BECAUSE I WAS TOO AFRAID OF THE DAMAGE I MIGHT DO TO YOU.
YOU LOOKED UP TO ME IN A WAY I COULDN'T HANDLE.
MY SPECIALTY WAS ALWAYS DESTROYING THINGS. AND...I DON'T KNOW IF I WAS MORE AFRAID I MIGHT HURT YOU--
--OR THAT YOU WOULD WIND UP LIKE ME.
BUT NOW THE ONLY THING THAT SCARES ME IS THAT I MIGHT NEVER HEAR YOUR VOICE AGAIN.
AND I WOULD DO ANYTHING TO HAVE MY SON BACK.
AND HERE I THOUGHT YOU'D NEVER ASK.

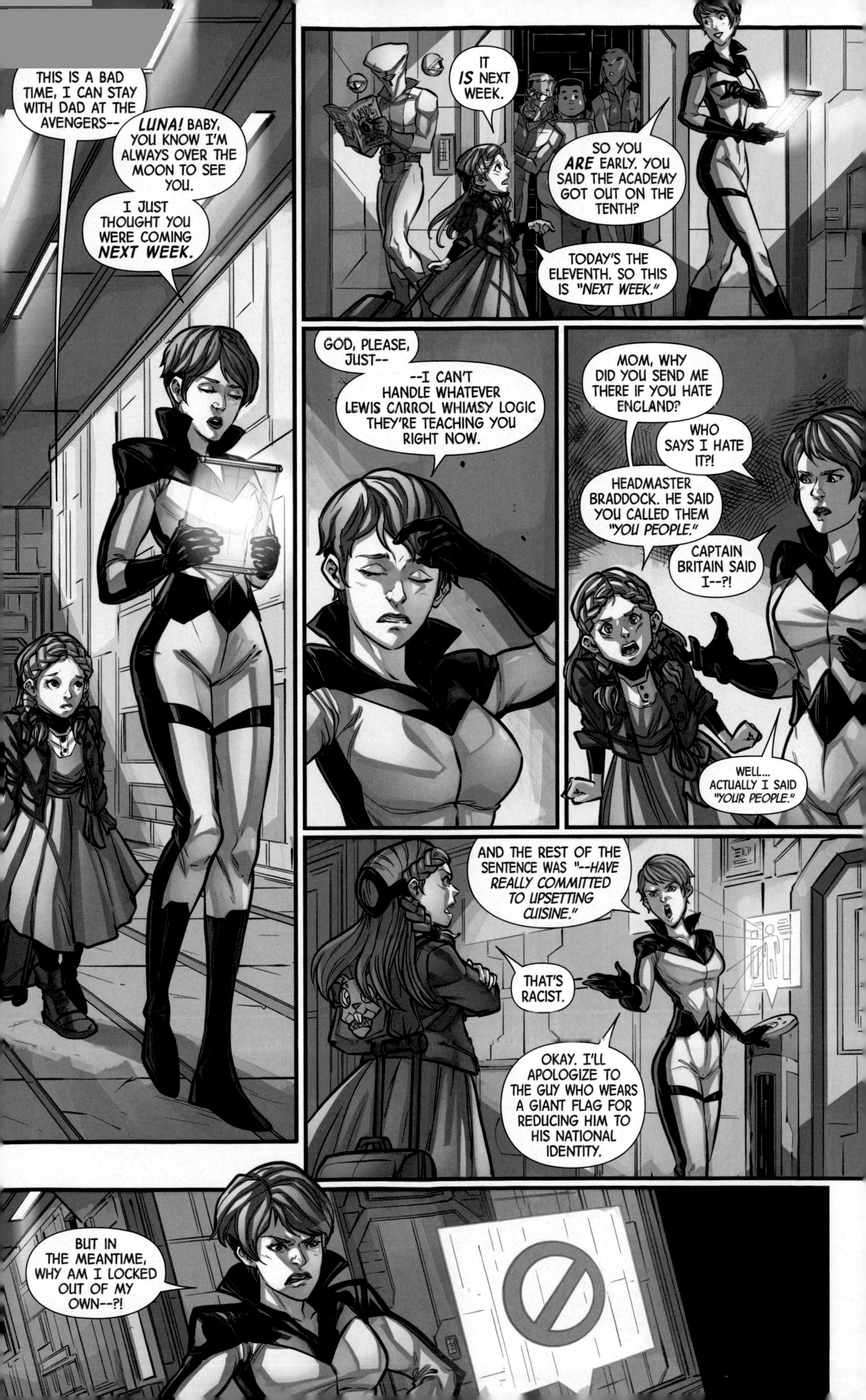
THIS IS A BAD TIME, I CAN STAY WITH DAD AT THE AVENGERS--
LUNA! BABY, YOU KNOW I'M ALWAYS OVER THE MOON TO SEE YOU.
I JUST THOUGHT YOU WERE COMING NEXT WEEK.
IT IS NEXT WEEK.
SO YOU ARE EARLY. YOU SAID THE ACADEMY GOT OUT ON THE TENTH?
TODAY'S THE ELEVENTH. SO THIS IS "NEXT WEEK."
GOD, PLEASE, JUST--
--I CAN'T HANDLE WHATEVER LEWIS CARROL WHIMSY LOGIC THEY'RE TEACHING YOU RIGHT NOW.
MOM, WHY DID YOU SEND ME THERE IF YOU HATE ENGLAND?
WHO SAYS I HATE IT?!
HEADMASTER BRADDOCK. HE SAID YOU CALLED THEM "YOU PEOPLE."
CAPTAIN BRITAIN SAID I--?!
WELL... ACTUALLY I SAID "YOUR PEOPLE."
AND THE REST OF THE SENTENCE WAS "--HAVE REALLY COMMITTED TO UPSETTING CUISINE."
THAT'S RACIST.
OKAY. I'LL APOLOGIZE TO THE GUY WHO WEARS A GIANT FLAG FOR REDUCING HIM TO HIS NATIONAL IDENTITY.
BUT IN THE MEANTIME, WHY AM I LOCKED OUT OF MY OWN--?!

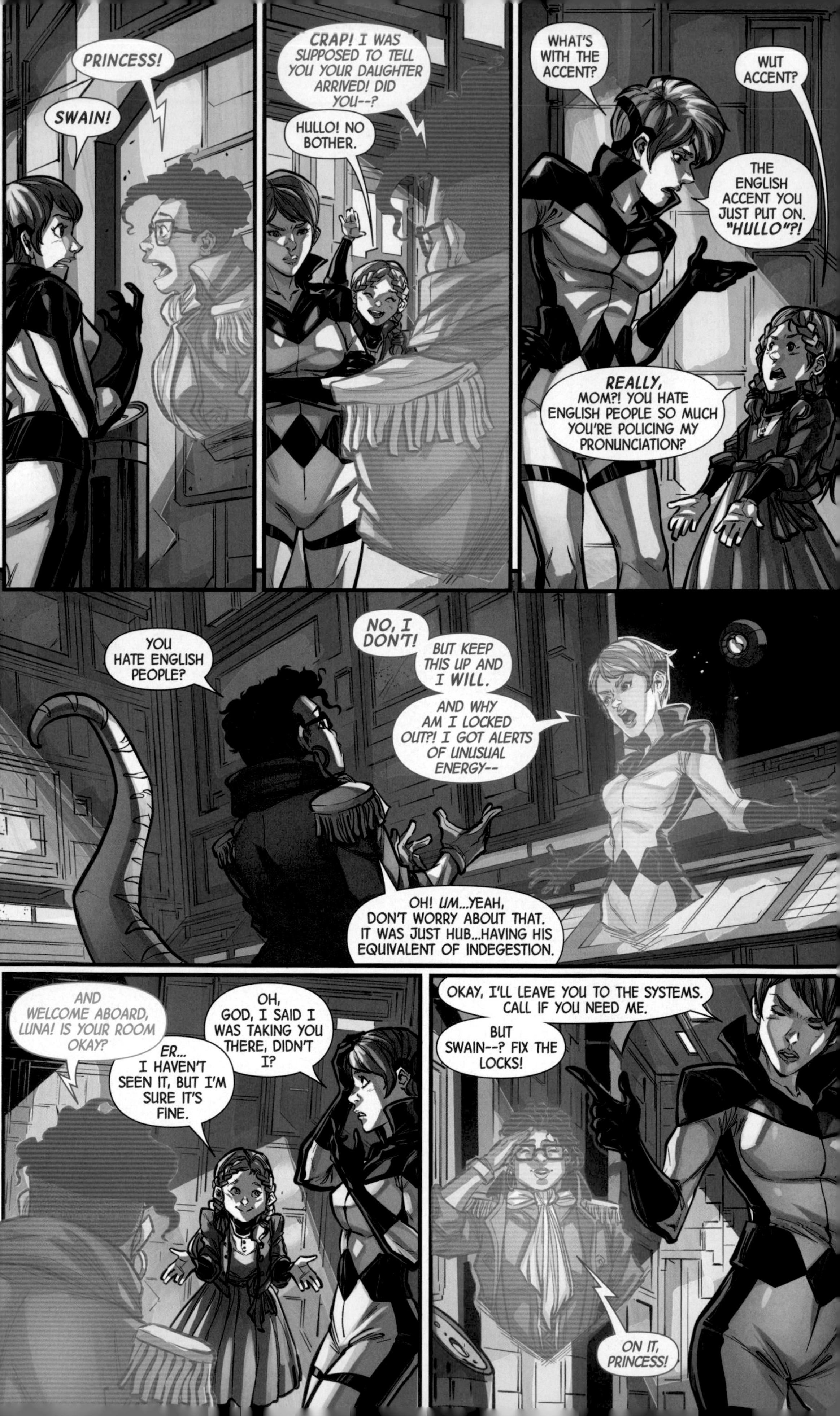
PRINCESS!
SWAIN!
CRAP! I WAS SUPPOSED TO TELL YOU YOUR DAUGHTER ARRIVED! DID YOU--?
HULLO! NO BOTHER.
WHAT'S WITH THE ACCENT?
WUT ACCENT?
THE ENGLISH ACCENT YOU JUST PUT ON. "HULLO"?!
REALLY, MOM?! YOU HATE ENGLISH PEOPLE SO MUCH YOU'RE POLICING MY PRONUNCIATION?
YOU HATE ENGLISH PEOPLE?
NO, I DON'T!
BUT KEEP THIS UP AND I WILL.
AND WHY AM I LOCKED OUT?! I GOT ALERTS OF UNUSUAL ENERGY--
OH! UM...YEAH, DON'T WORRY ABOUT THAT. IT WAS JUST HUB...HAVING HIS EQUIVALENT OF INDEGESTION.
AND WELCOME ABOARD, LUNA! IS YOUR ROOM OKAY?
ER... I HAVEN'T SEEN IT, BUT I'M SURE IT'S FINE.
OH, GOD, I SAID I WAS TAKING YOU THERE, DIDN'T I?
OKAY, I'LL LEAVE YOU TO THE SYSTEMS. CALL IF YOU NEED ME.
BUT SWAIN--? FIX THE LOCKS!
ON IT, PRINCESS!

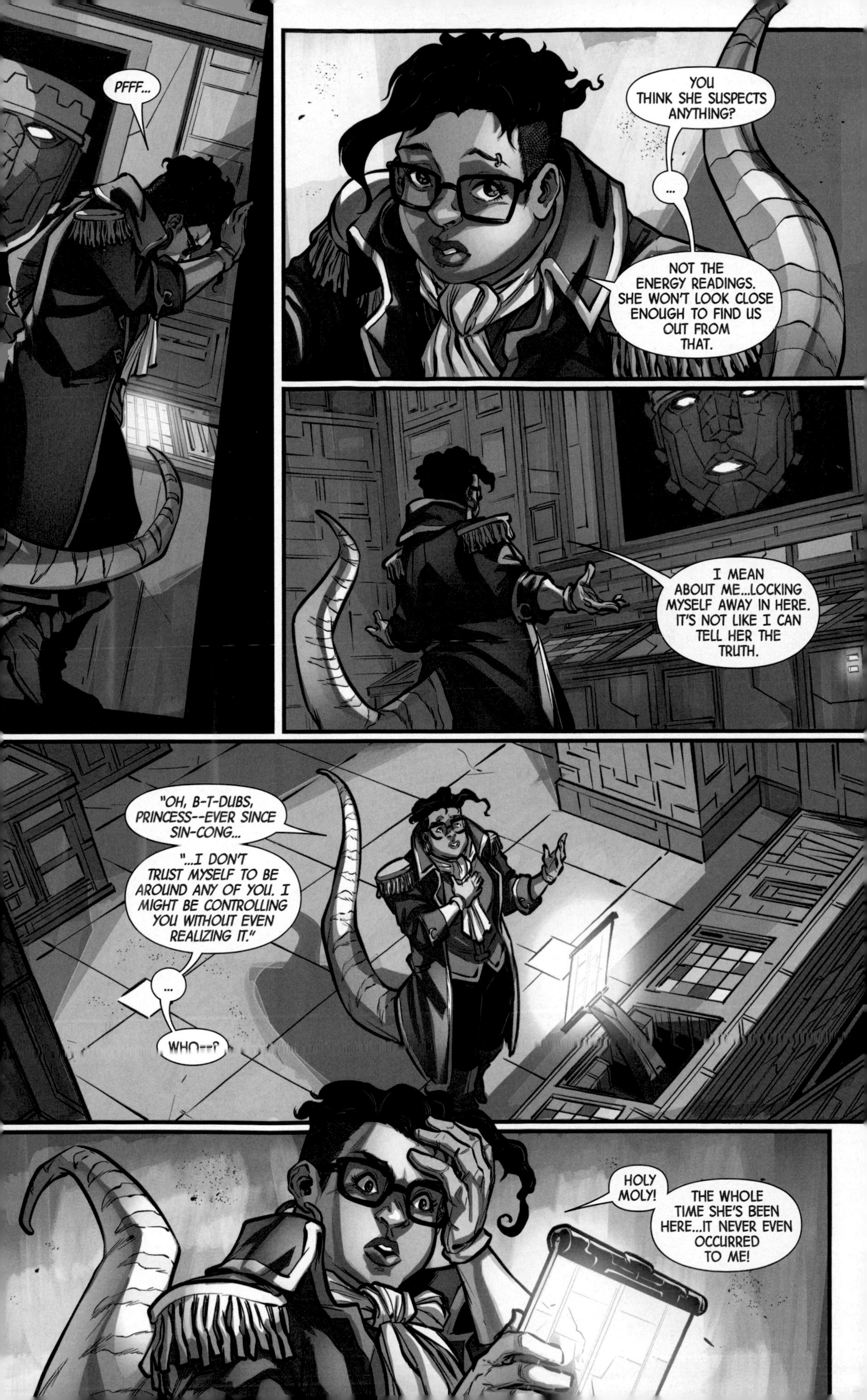
PFFF...
YOU THINK SHE SUSPECTS ANYTHING?
...
NOT THE ENERGY READINGS. SHE WON'T LOOK CLOSE ENOUGH TO FIND US OUT FROM THAT.
I MEAN ABOUT ME...LOCKING MYSELF AWAY IN HERE. IT'S NOT LIKE I CAN TELL HER THE TRUTH.
"OH, B-T-DUBS, PRINCESS--EVER SINCE SIN-CONG...
"...I DON'T TRUST MYSELF TO BE AROUND ANY OF YOU. I MIGHT BE CONTROLLING YOU WITHOUT EVEN REALIZING IT."
...
WHO--?
HOLY MOLY!
THE WHOLE TIME SHE'S BEEN HERE...IT NEVER EVEN OCCURRED TO ME!

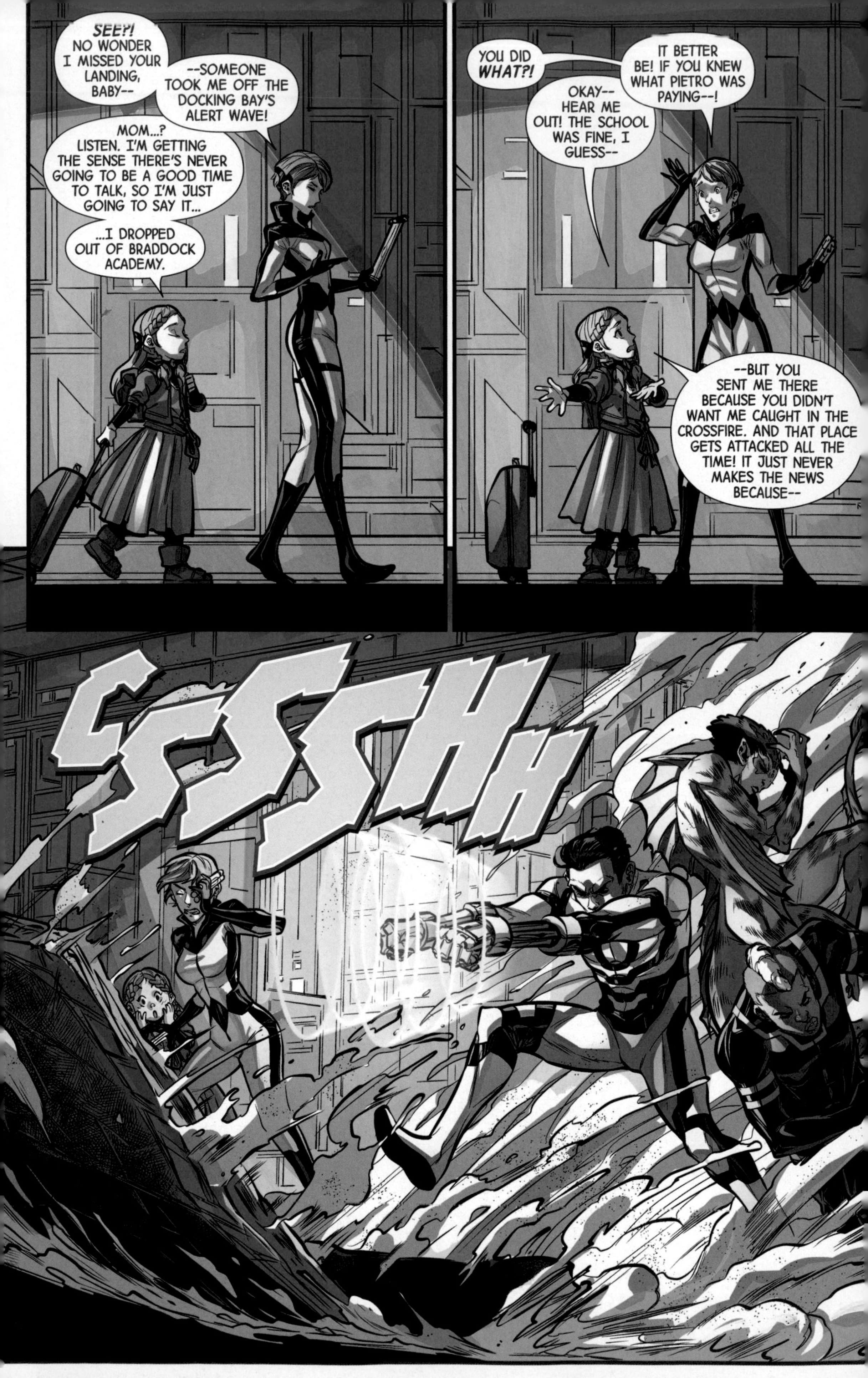
SEE?! NO WONDER I MISSED YOUR LANDING, BABY--
--SOMEONE TOOK ME OFF THE DOCKING BAY'S ALERT WAVE!
MOM...? LISTEN. I'M GETTING THE SENSE THERE'S NEVER GOING TO BE A GOOD TIME TO TALK, SO I'M JUST GOING TO SAY IT...
...I DROPPED OUT OF BRADDOCK ACADEMY.
YOU DID WHAT?!
OKAY-- HEAR ME OUT! THE SCHOOL WAS FINE, I GUESS--
IT BETTER BE! IF YOU KNEW WHAT PIETRO WAS PAYING--!
--BUT YOU SENT ME THERE BECAUSE YOU DIDN'T WANT ME CAUGHT IN THE CROSSFIRE. AND THAT PLACE GETS ATTACKED ALL THE TIME! IT JUST NEVER MAKES THE NEWS BECAUSE--
CSSSHH

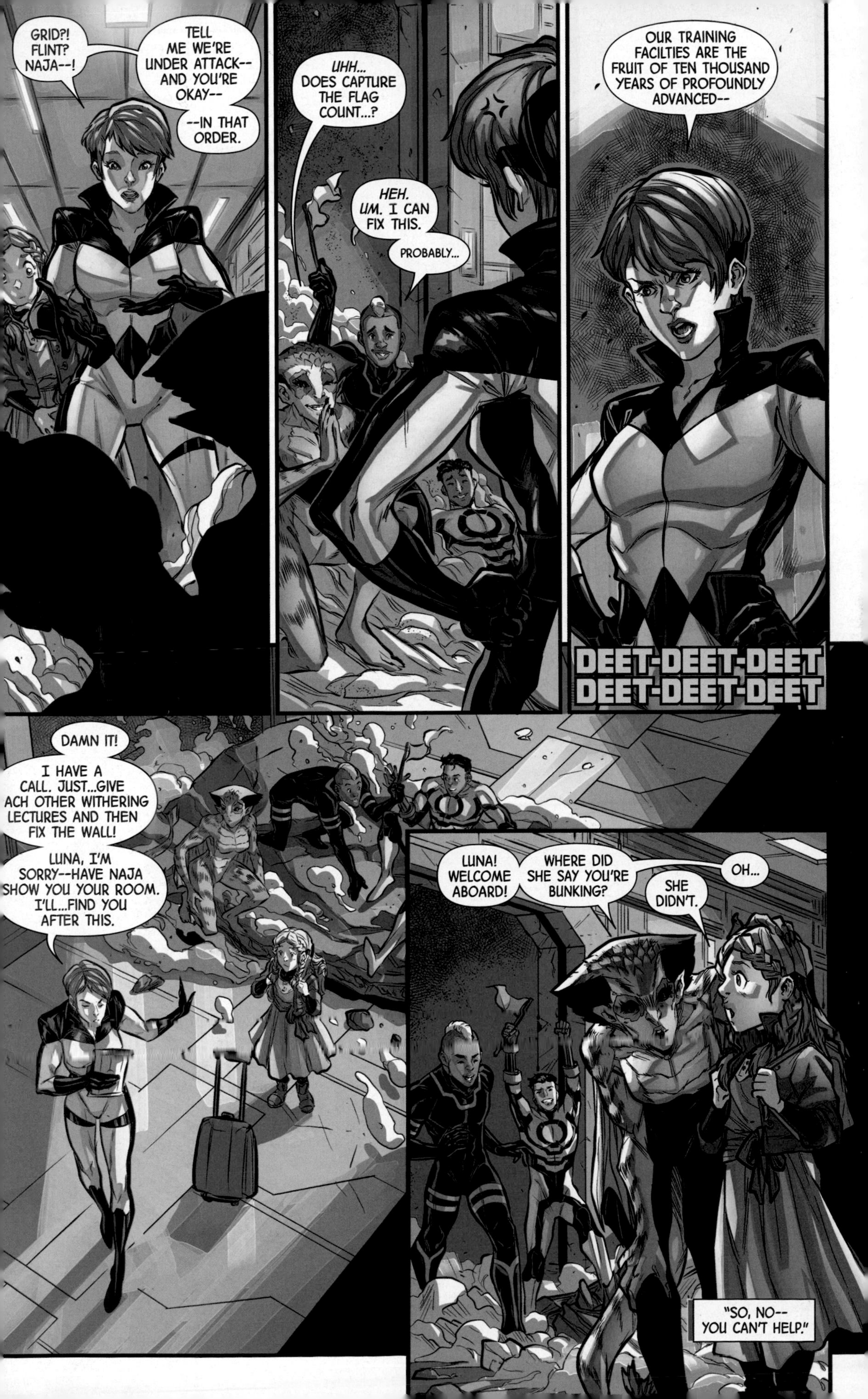
GRID?! FLINT? NAJA--!
TELL ME WE'RE UNDER ATTACK-- AND YOU'RE OKAY--
--IN THAT ORDER.
UHH... DOES CAPTURE THE FLAG COUNT...?
HEH. UM. I CAN FIX THIS.
PROBABLY...
OUR TRAINING FACILTIES ARE THE FRUIT OF TEN THOUSAND YEARS OF PROFOUNDLY ADVANCED--
DEET-DEET-DEET
DEET-DEET-DEET
DAMN IT!
I HAVE A CALL. JUST...GIVE ACH OTHER WITHERING LECTURES AND THEN FIX THE WALL!
LUNA, I'M SORRY--HAVE NAJA SHOW YOU YOUR ROOM. I'LL...FIND YOU AFTER THIS.
LUNA! WELCOME ABOARD!
WHERE DID SHE SAY YOU'RE BUNKING?
OH...
SHE DIDN'T.
"SO, NO-- YOU CAN'T HELP."

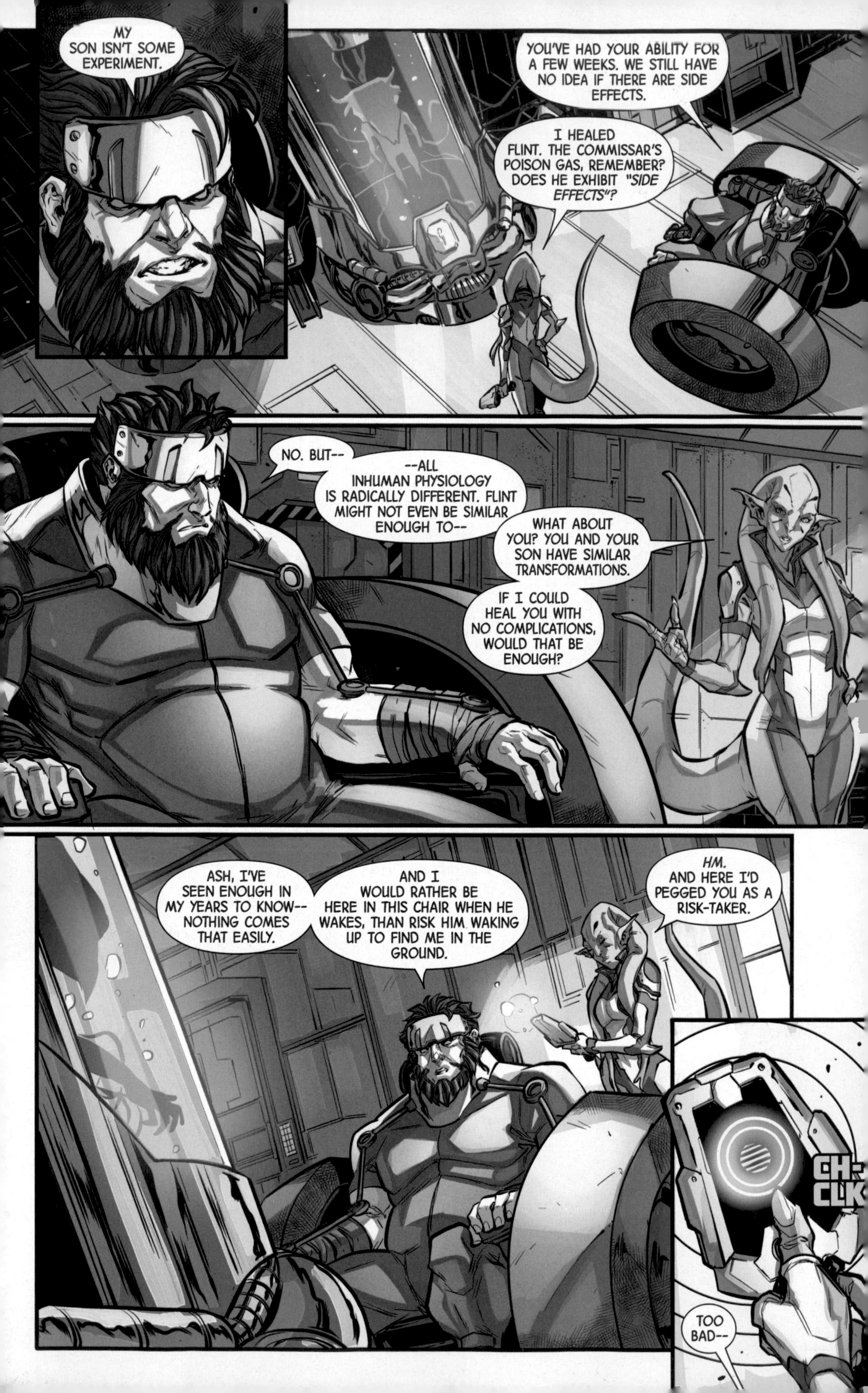
MY SON ISN'T SOME EXPERIMENT.
YOU'VE HAD YOUR ABILITY FOR A FEW WEEKS. WE STILL HAVE NO IDEA IF THERE ARE SIDE EFFECTS.
I HEALED FLINT. THE COMMISSAR'S POISON GAS, REMEMBER? DOES HE EXHIBIT "SIDE EFFECTS"?
NO. BUT--
--ALL INHUMAN PHYSIOLOGY IS RADICALLY DIFFERENT. FLINT MIGHT NOT EVEN BE SIMILAR ENOUGH TO--
WHAT ABOUT YOU? YOU AND YOUR SON HAVE SIMILAR TRANSFORMATIONS.
IF I COULD HEAL YOU WITH NO COMPLICATIONS, WOULD THAT BE ENOUGH?
ASH, I'VE SEEN ENOUGH IN MY YEARS TO KNOW-- NOTHING COMES THAT EASILY.
AND I WOULD RATHER BE HERE IN THIS CHAIR WHEN HE WAKES, THAN RISK HIM WAKING UP TO FIND ME IN THE GROUND.
HM. AND HERE I'D PEGGED YOU AS A RISK-TAKER.
CH-CLK
TOO BAD--

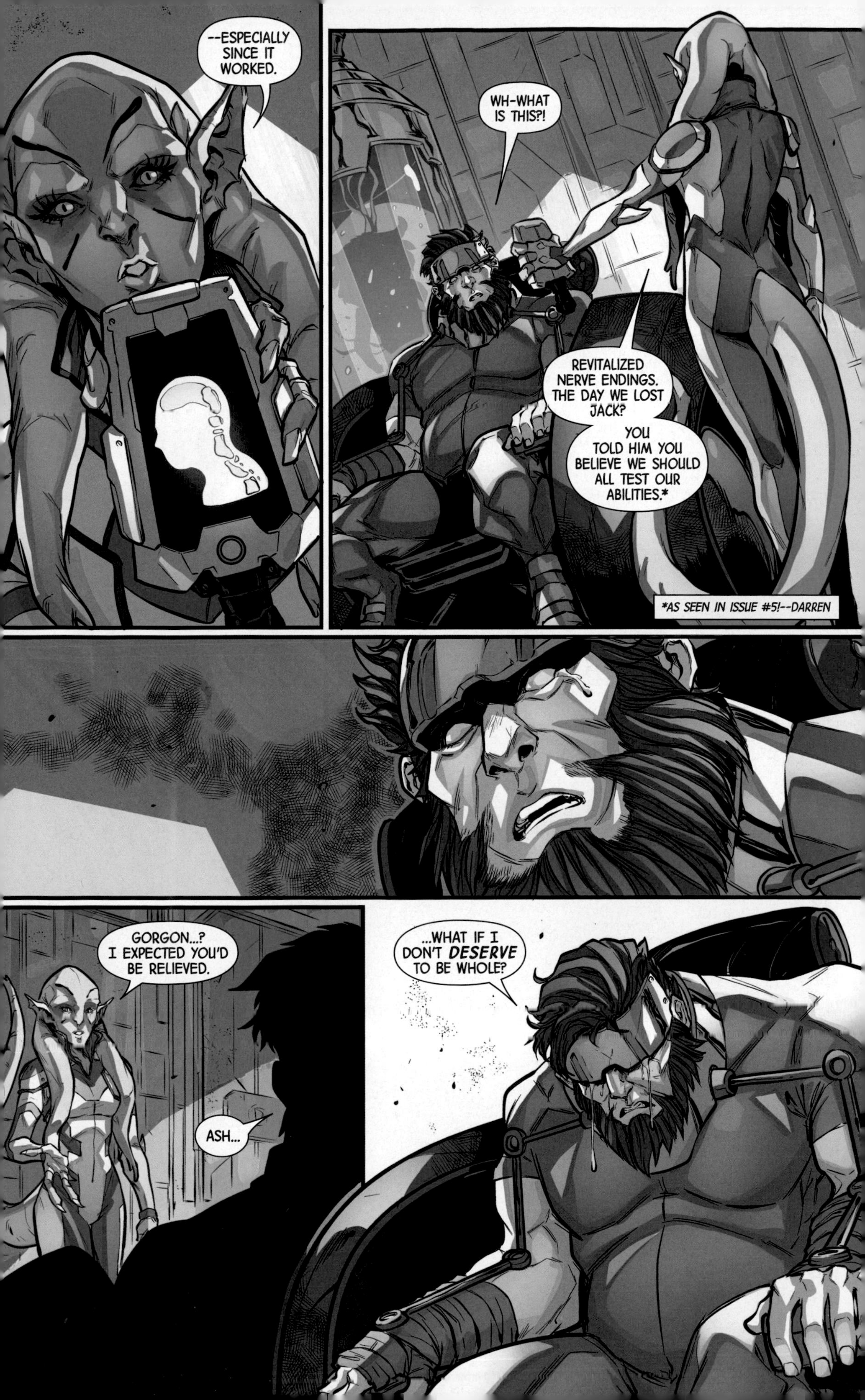
--ESPECIALLY SINCE IT WORKED.
WH-WHAT IS THIS?!
REVITALIZED NERVE ENDINGS. THE DAY WE LOST JACK?
YOU TOLD HIM YOU BELIEVE WE SHOULD ALL TEST OUR ABILITIES.*
*AS SEEN IN ISSUE #5!--DARREN
GORGON...? I EXPECTED YOU'D BE RELIEVED.
ASH...
...WHAT IF I DON'T DESERVE TO BE WHOLE?

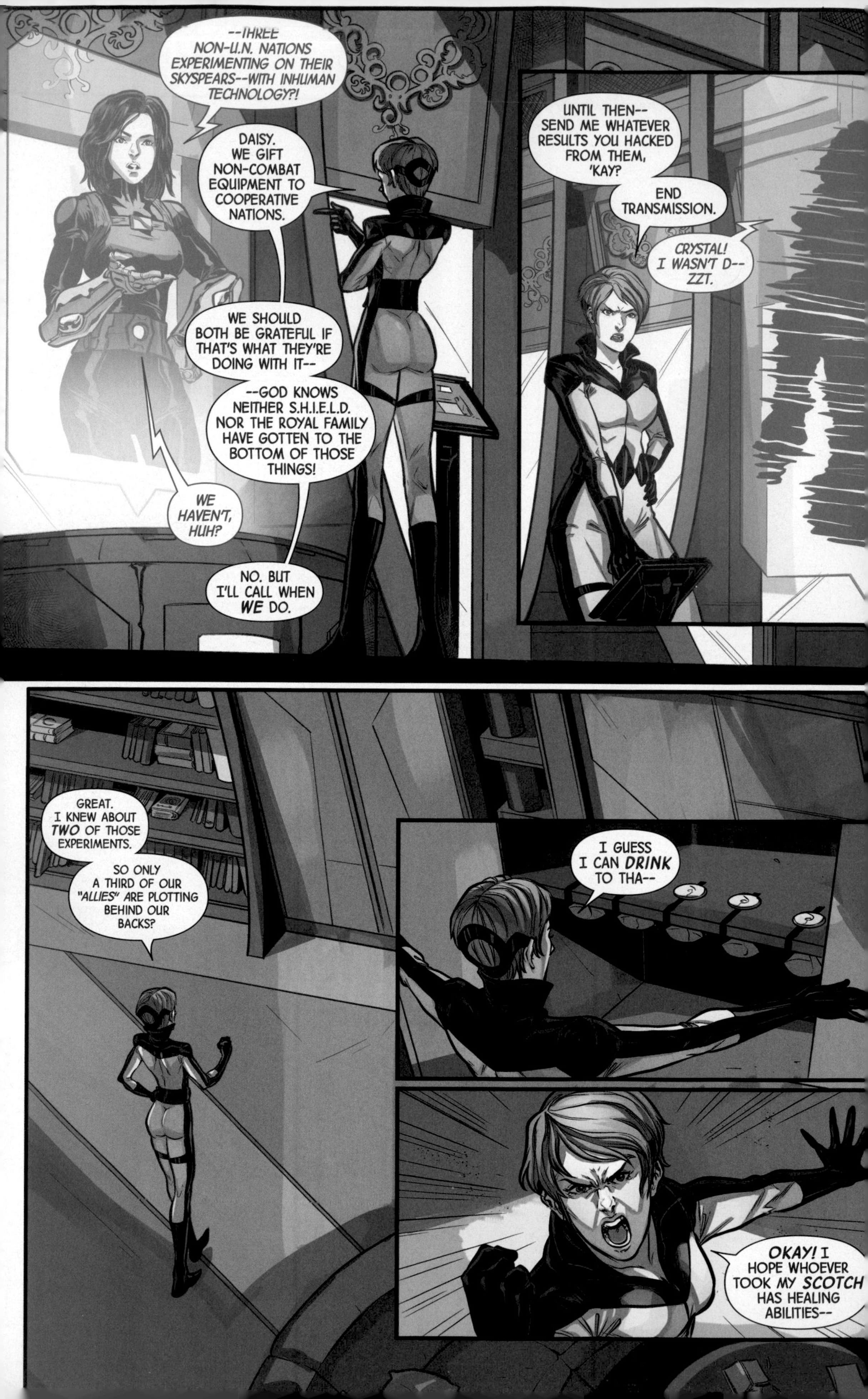
--THREE NON-U.N. NATIONS EXPERIMENTING ON THEIR SKYSPEARS--WITH INHUMAN TECHNOLOGY?!
DAISY. WE GIFT NON-COMBAT EQUIPMENT TO COOPERATIVE NATIONS.
WE SHOULD BOTH BE GRATEFUL IF THAT'S WHAT THEY'RE DOING WITH IT--
--GOD KNOWS NEITHER S.H.I.E.L.D. NOR THE ROYAL FAMILY HAVE GOTTEN TO THE BOTTOM OF THOSE THINGS!
WE HAVEN'T, HUH?
NO. BUT I'LL CALL WHEN WE DO.
UNTIL THEN-- SEND ME WHATEVER RESULTS YOU HACKED FROM THEM, 'KAY?
END TRANSMISSION.
CRYSTAL! I WASN'T D-- ZZT.
GREAT. I KNEW ABOUT TWO OF THOSE EXPERIMENTS.
SO ONLY A THIRD OF OUR "ALLIES" ARE PLOTTING BEHIND OUR BACKS?
I GUESS I CAN DRINK TO THA--
OKAY! I HOPE WHOEVER TOOK MY SCOTCH HAS HEALING ABILITIES--

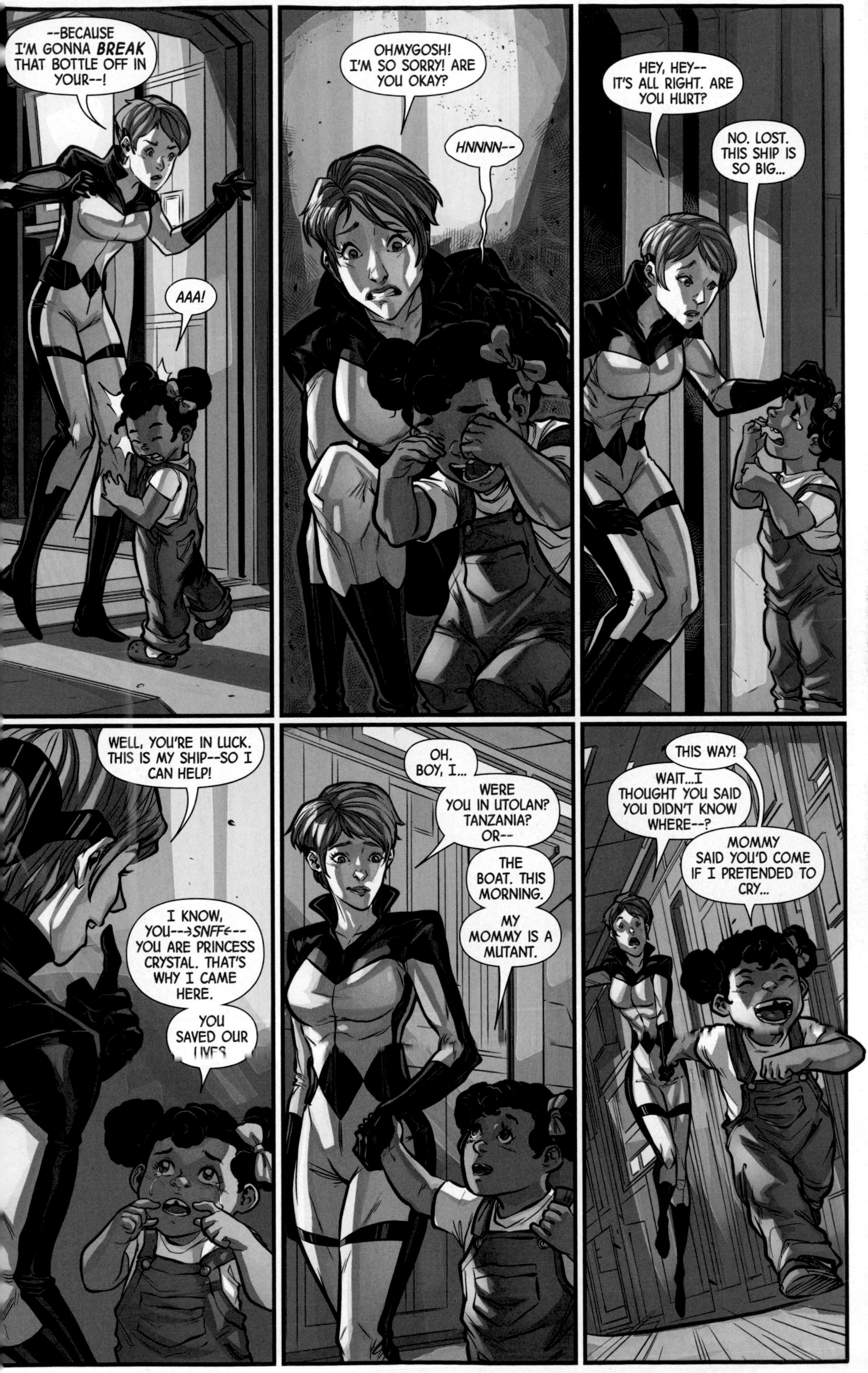
--BECAUSE I'M GONNA **BREAK** THAT BOTTLE OFF IN YOUR--!
AAA!
OHMYGOSH! I'M SO SORRY! ARE YOU OKAY?
HNNNN--
HEY, HEY-- IT'S ALL RIGHT. ARE YOU HURT?
NO. LOST. THIS SHIP IS SO BIG...
WELL, YOU'RE IN LUCK. THIS IS MY SHIP--SO I CAN HELP!
I KNOW, YOU--→SNFF←-- YOU ARE PRINCESS CRYSTAL. THAT'S WHY I CAME HERE.
YOU SAVED OUR LIVES
OH. BOY, I...
WERE YOU IN UTOLAN? TANZANIA? OR--
THE BOAT. THIS MORNING.
MY MOMMY IS A MUTANT.
THIS WAY!
WAIT...I THOUGHT YOU SAID YOU DIDN'T KNOW WHERE--?
MOMMY SAID YOU'D COME IF I PRETENDED TO CRY...

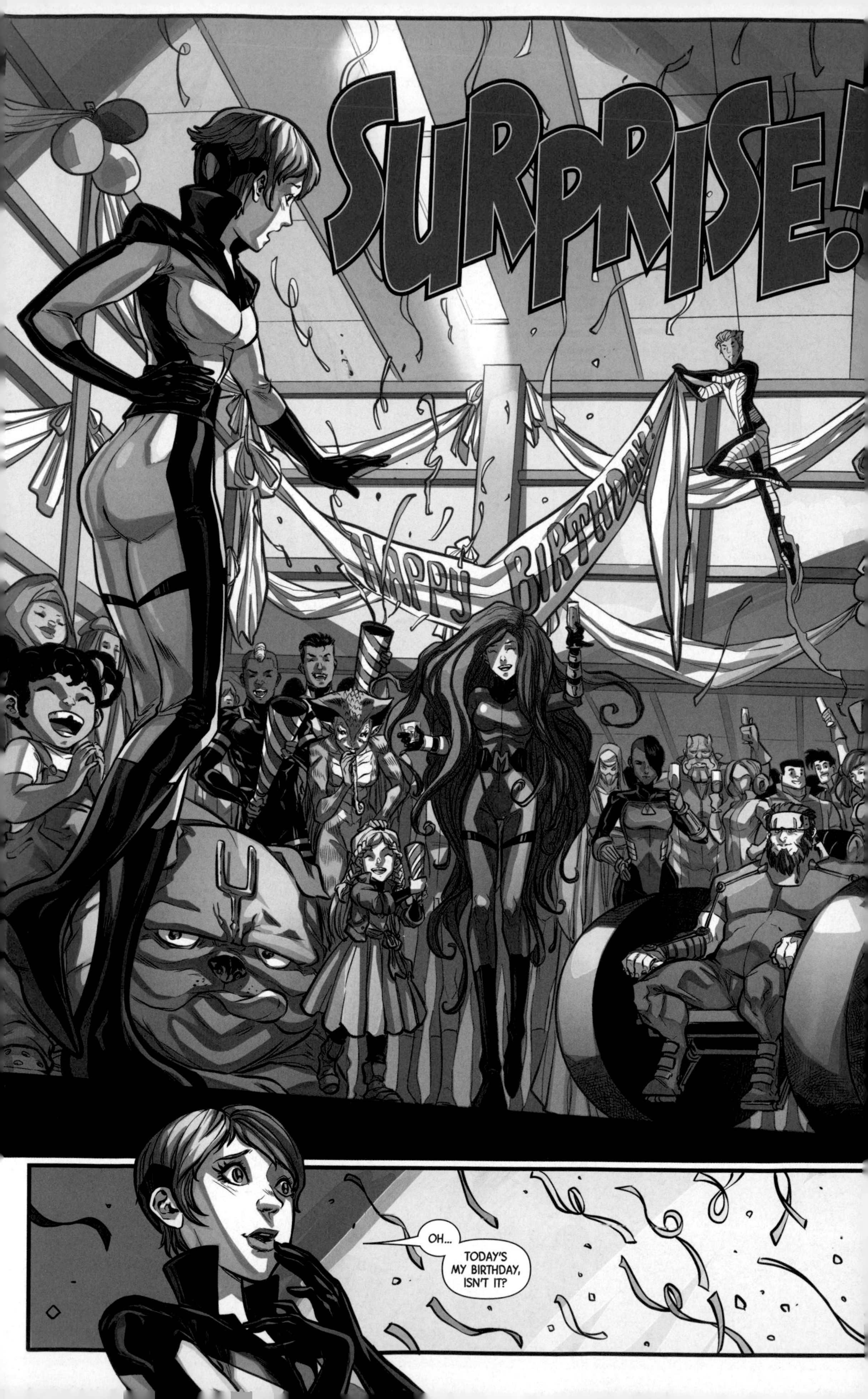
SURPRISE!
HAPPY BIRTHDAY!
OH...
TODAY'S MY BIRTHDAY, ISN'T IT?

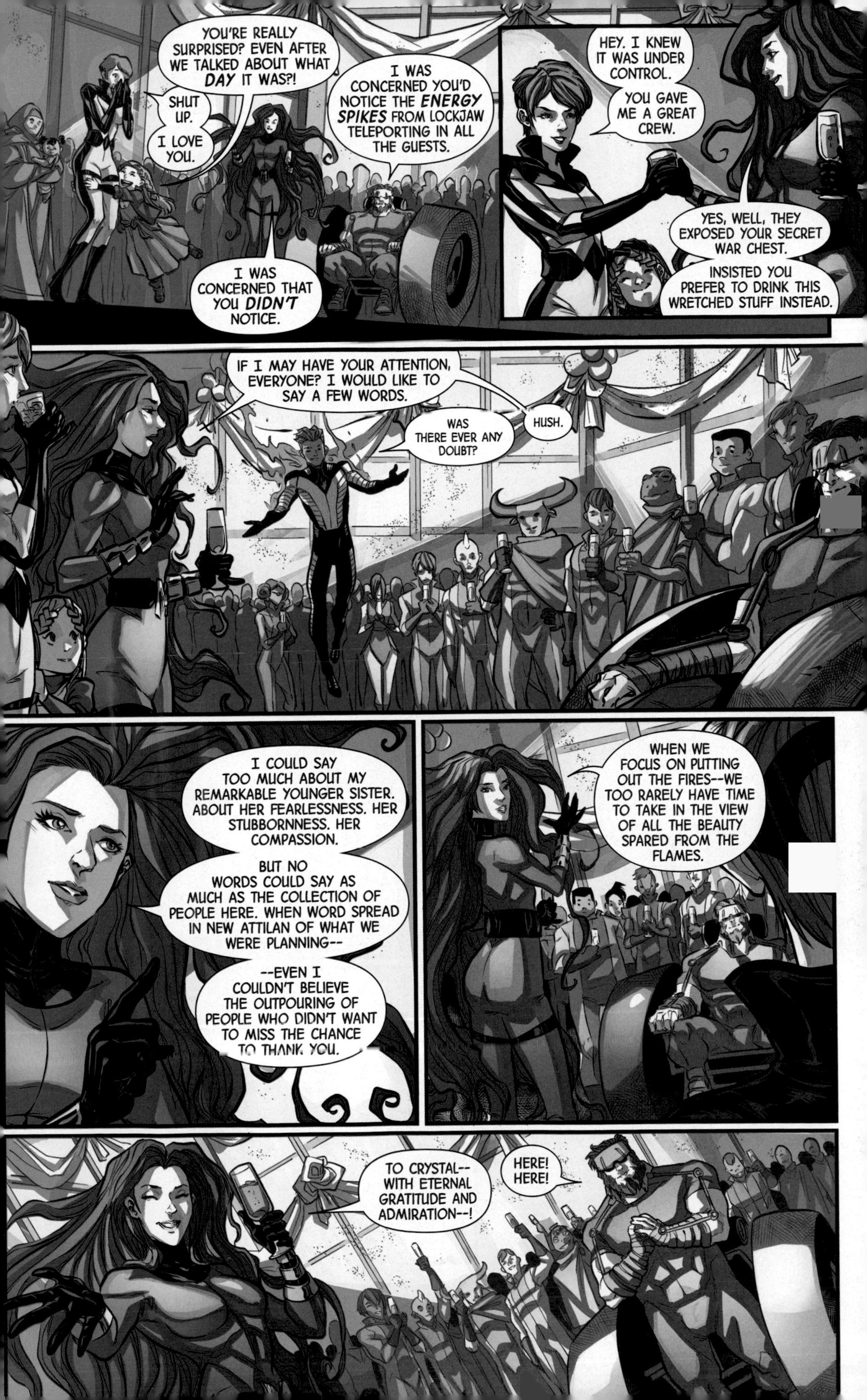
YOU'RE REALLY SURPRISED? EVEN AFTER WE TALKED ABOUT WHAT DAY IT WAS?!
SHUT UP.
I LOVE YOU.
I WAS CONCERNED YOU'D NOTICE THE ENERGY SPIKES FROM LOCKJAW TELEPORTING IN ALL THE GUESTS.
I WAS CONCERNED THAT YOU DIDN'T NOTICE.
HEY. I KNEW IT WAS UNDER CONTROL.
YOU GAVE ME A GREAT CREW.
YES, WELL, THEY EXPOSED YOUR SECRET WAR CHEST.
INSISTED YOU PREFER TO DRINK THIS WRETCHED STUFF INSTEAD.
IF I MAY HAVE YOUR ATTENTION, EVERYONE? I WOULD LIKE TO SAY A FEW WORDS.
WAS THERE EVER ANY DOUBT?
HUSH.
I COULD SAY TOO MUCH ABOUT MY REMARKABLE YOUNGER SISTER. ABOUT HER FEARLESSNESS. HER STUBBORNNESS. HER COMPASSION.
BUT NO WORDS COULD SAY AS MUCH AS THE COLLECTION OF PEOPLE HERE. WHEN WORD SPREAD IN NEW ATTILAN OF WHAT WE WERE PLANNING--
--EVEN I COULDN'T BELIEVE THE OUTPOURING OF PEOPLE WHO DIDN'T WANT TO MISS THE CHANCE TO THANK YOU.
WHEN WE FOCUS ON PUTTING OUT THE FIRES--WE TOO RARELY HAVE TIME TO TAKE IN THE VIEW OF ALL THE BEAUTY SPARED FROM THE FLAMES.
TO CRYSTAL-- WITH ETERNAL GRATITUDE AND ADMIRATION--!
HERE! HERE!

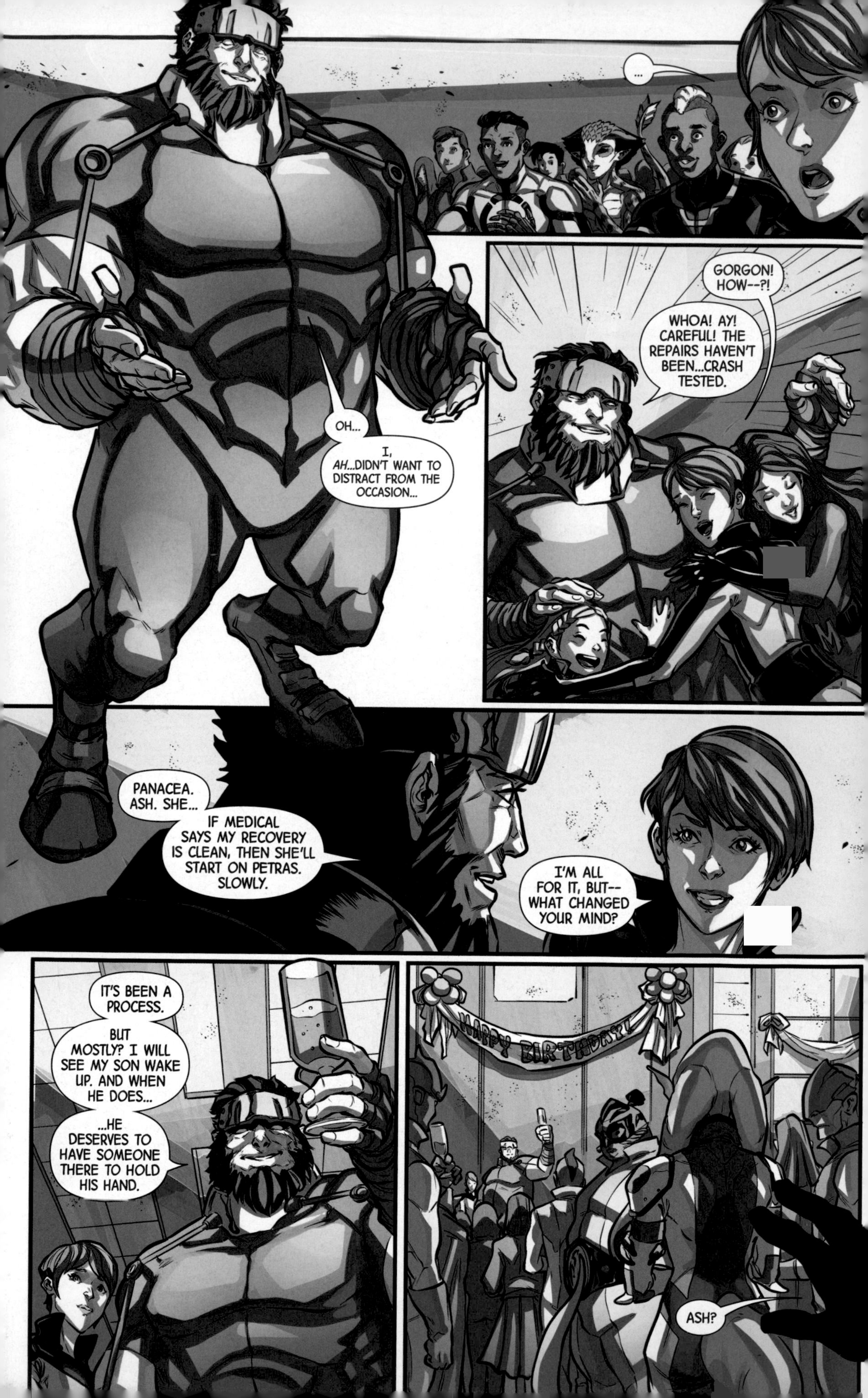
...
OH...
I, AH...DIDN'T WANT TO DISTRACT FROM THE OCCASION...
GORGON! HOW--?!
WHOA! AY! CAREFUL! THE REPAIRS HAVEN'T BEEN...CRASH TESTED.
PANACEA. ASH. SHE...
IF MEDICAL SAYS MY RECOVERY IS CLEAN, THEN SHE'LL START ON PETRAS. SLOWLY.
I'M ALL FOR IT, BUT-- WHAT CHANGED YOUR MIND?
IT'S BEEN A PROCESS.
BUT MOSTLY? I WILL SEE MY SON WAKE UP. AND WHEN HE DOES...
...HE DESERVES TO HAVE SOMEONE THERE TO HOLD HIS HAND.
HAPPY BIRTHDAY!
ASH?

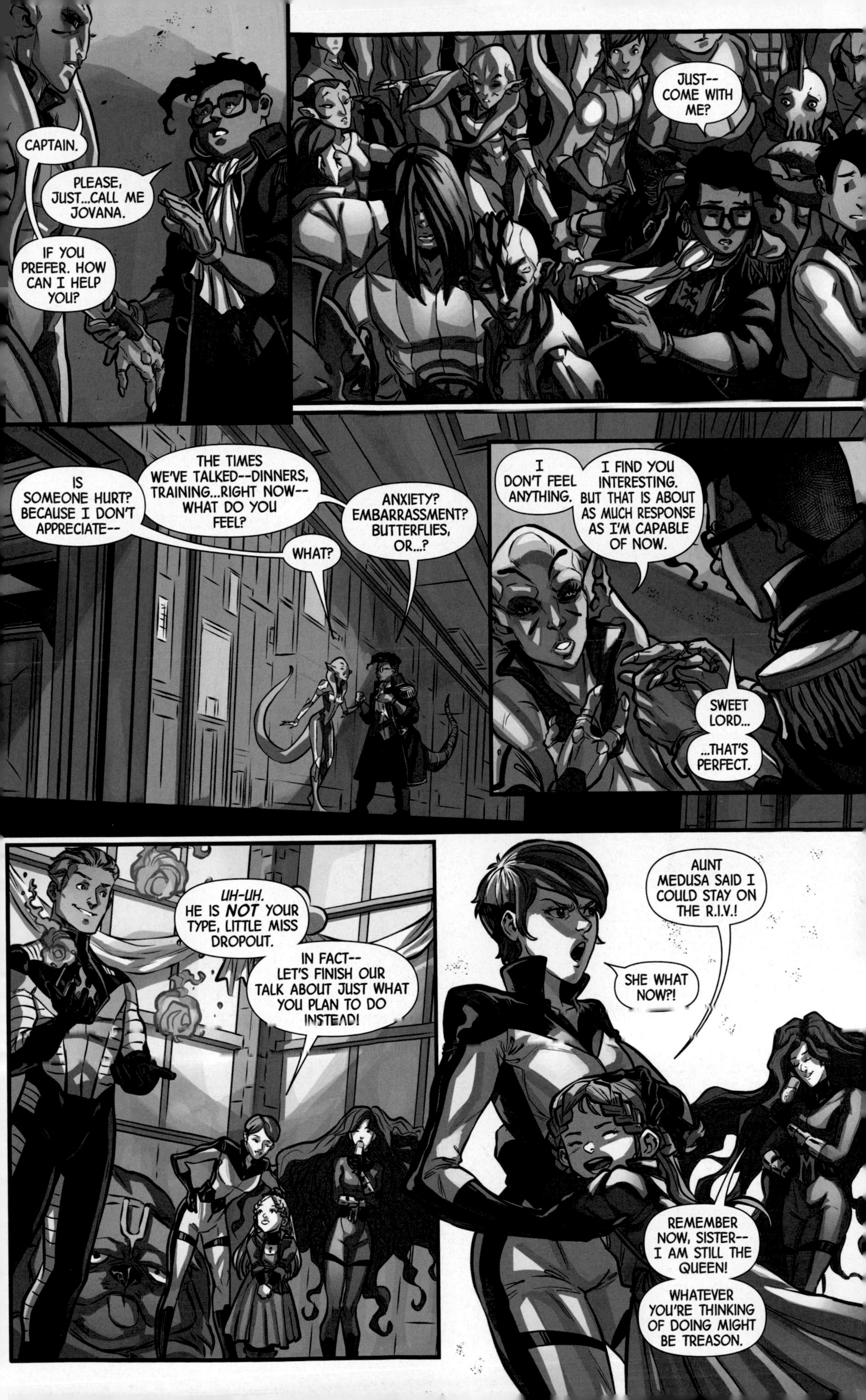
CAPTAIN.
PLEASE, JUST...CALL ME JOVANA.
IF YOU PREFER. HOW CAN I HELP YOU?
JUST-- COME WITH ME?
IS SOMEONE HURT? BECAUSE I DON'T APPRECIATE--
THE TIMES WE'VE TALKED--DINNERS, TRAINING...RIGHT NOW-- WHAT DO YOU FEEL?
WHAT?
ANXIETY? EMBARRASSMENT? BUTTERFLIES, OR...?
I DON'T FEEL ANYTHING.
I FIND YOU INTERESTING. BUT THAT IS ABOUT AS MUCH RESPONSE AS I'M CAPABLE OF NOW.
SWEET LORD...
...THAT'S PERFECT.
UH-UH. HE IS NOT YOUR TYPE, LITTLE MISS DROPOUT.
IN FACT-- LET'S FINISH OUR TALK ABOUT JUST WHAT YOU PLAN TO DO INSTEAD!
SHE WHAT NOW?!
AUNT MEDUSA SAID I COULD STAY ON THE R.I.V.!
REMEMBER NOW, SISTER-- I AM STILL THE QUEEN!
WHATEVER YOU'RE THINKING OF DOING MIGHT BE TREASON.

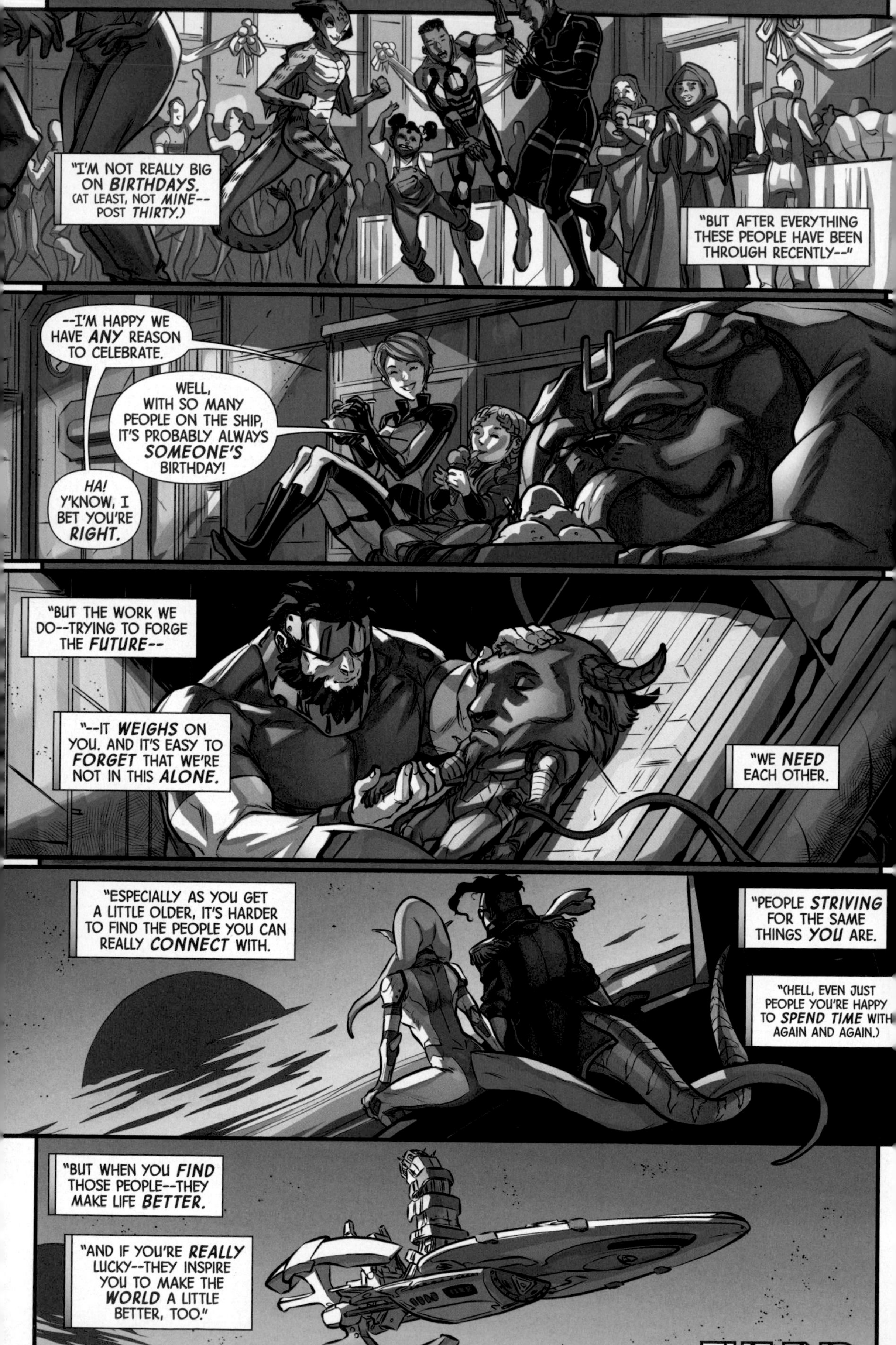
"I'M NOT REALLY BIG ON BIRTHDAYS. (AT LEAST, NOT MINE-- POST THIRTY.)
"BUT AFTER EVERYTHING THESE PEOPLE HAVE BEEN THROUGH RECENTLY--"
--I'M HAPPY WE HAVE ANY REASON TO CELEBRATE.
WELL, WITH SO MANY PEOPLE ON THE SHIP, IT'S PROBABLY ALWAYS SOMEONE'S BIRTHDAY!
HA! Y'KNOW, I BET YOU'RE RIGHT.
"BUT THE WORK WE DO--TRYING TO FORGE THE FUTURE--
"--IT WEIGHS ON YOU. AND IT'S EASY TO FORGET THAT WE'RE NOT IN THIS ALONE.
"WE NEED EACH OTHER.
"ESPECIALLY AS YOU GET A LITTLE OLDER, IT'S HARDER TO FIND THE PEOPLE YOU CAN REALLY CONNECT WITH.
"PEOPLE STRIVING FOR THE SAME THINGS YOU ARE.
"(HELL, EVEN JUST PEOPLE YOU'RE HAPPY TO SPEND TIME WITH AGAIN AND AGAIN.)
"BUT WHEN YOU FIND THOSE PEOPLE--THEY MAKE LIFE BETTER.
"AND IF YOU'RE REALLY LUCKY--THEY INSPIRE YOU TO MAKE THE WORLD A LITTLE BETTER, TOO."
THE END.

#5 SCRIPT, PAGES 1-5

JAMES ASMUS

NOTES:

Exquisite Course sequences – I'm really open to any ideas you have OR I can riff out a few different concepts. I'd like it to be more futuristic and modular than the danger room. Maybe there's also some old-school Kirby-style madness to reference? Some things from the Inhumans' technological past they'd have piled up?

The Storage – When we ultimately reveal where all these obstacles come from, the room needs to have some of that same stuff, obviously – but the bigger items further back should be battle vehicles for a real war. I don't know if we've seen much of these things for Inhumans before – but we can go with smaller, personal strike vehicles up to larger nightmare machines with clear deadly capacity. And feel free to make just a few different things and copy / repeat them to communicate the idea of an armada rather an odd collection. It has intent and can ultimately parallel the warmonger villain of the first arc. (Issues 2-4)

PAGE ONE

2 dozen or so Skyspears flying through the blackness of space toward us / Earth.

TEXT 4 Months ago...

We go around the world to different locales near falling Skyspears – each time it gets closer / bigger / brighter. And as we go, the attention and alarm ramp up more and more as the spears fall closer and closer. FIRST: Workers at an oil plant in Nigeria stop and point streaking lights in the night sky – thicker, and brighter than you'd expect from a simple shooting star. And it seems to be curving toward them... (Or: Could be a group of men on a medium-large boat in the river if you prefer.) EVENING.

TEXT Buguma, Nigeria

1.2: As a burning-on-re-entry Skyspear descends toward the Amazon rainforest, various animals perk up or flee in terror. DAY.

TEXT Manaus, Brazil

1.3: The sky is almost a white out as the burning-on-re-entry Skyspear is both massive and hurling toward us. The ground is a sea of panic as terrified tourists flee the sites of KIEV, Ukraine (your pick as to which buildings. NIGHT.

TEXT Kiev, Ukraine

PAGE TWO

SPLASH: Pull back wide to see the MASSIVE shockwave impact caused when one Skyspear hits. This one lands outside the population center of Jinchang, China – but we should see its force blowing out destruction to the surrounding area. Maybe we see the edge of this developing city taking a horrible hit (blown apart apartment building construction / cranes /etc?) 'm open to how you want to play this for scale. But I hope we can get a sense of real impact balanced against a minor (implied) loss of life. MORNING.

TEXT Jinchang, China.

PAGE THREE

I'm picturing a single SKYSPEAR with a 9 panel grid-structure of panels laid over / around it. (Except for the final panel across the bottom.) To represent that various people have come to examine it in different ways, but it remains unchanged, unmoving. We can help sell it, too, by having the different panels exist in different times of day & weather, too. Make sense?

3.1 The edge of the Skyspear still cools from its reentry heat.

3.2 Chinese military helicopters circles overhead with search light shining down on it.

3.3 A bomb-squad suited guy (think Hurt Locker) scans the outside of it. He's probably up on a raised platform.

3.4 A dense group of hazmat-suited scientists use more sci-fi methods of examining. They're crowded around close and in the distance.

3.5 A duo of lizards (geckos?) inspect each other while clinging (obliviously) to the side of the Skyspear. They should seem totally unaffected.

3.6 Two plainclothes scientists. One leans in, touching it – getting a pink shock of energy! The other is startled

3.7 A night: A group of kids came to mess around by it – pushing each other playfully to touch. One holds a lighter up to it...

3.8 Morning: Those kids are scattered around, dead – the crime scene getting parsed by police

3.9 A large barrier blocks the base level now. Two armed riot police stand guard.

Short, wide panel across the bottom (with base of Skyspear behind them?) Dry-looking local Chinese official talking to 'us', first person, a little nervous, useasy... THIS is the real guy FWIW.

TEXT   Today.

OFFICIAL   The Chinese government, frankly, has examined this monolith every way imaginable – and we are no closer to understanding the first thing about it.

OFFICIAL   While some officials are reluctant to ask outsiders for assistance –
                    leadership has come to accept we should be consulting experts on...
                                alien phenomena.

OFFICIAL   And I know you came to China with your own mission – so know we
                                appreciate you coming--

PAGE FOUR

4. 1 NEAR-SPLASH reveal: we reverse the angle to reveal SPIDER-MAN flanked by the 2 lead Shanghai researchers from Parker Industries – PHILLIP CHANG (renewable energy research) & YAO WU (bio tech).

OFFPANEL   --SPIDER-MAN.

SPIDER-MAN   And his Amazing Friends!

YAO WU   <Actually, Doctor Phillip Chang and I will lead Parker Industries' analysis, Governor. Spider-Man is here purely in a security capacity at our CEO's insistence.>

4.2. Spider-Man turns to Wu, who just deadpans back in Spider-Man's face.

SPIDER-MAN   <Wu? You remember that I learned Mandarin, right? So don't even act like I'm not THE alien expert here.>

                    <I mean- sure – you have a doctorate in bio-tech. And Chang has one in renewable energy...>

SPIDER-MAN   <But raise your hand if you unknowingly played host to an alien lifeform for, like, a year-- >

4.3 Wu turns around, ignoring Spider-Man and gesturing to some hover transport vehicles (off-panel?). Spider-Man is raising his hand in answer to his own question, but having the wind taken out of his sails a little. Chang asks an earnest, pointed question.

YAO WU   <Unload the equipment, please!>

PHILLIP CHANG	How...did you not realize...?
SPIDER-MAN	I dunno... I thought maybe I was just going through... a broody-phase?
(small)	A lot of us were, at the time.

PAGE FIVE

5.1 Establishing shot of the RIV flying.

        LOCATOR CAP: THE ROYAL INHUMAN VESEL. A.K.A. The R.I.V.

5.2 A moment with Grid & Flint on the Riv, in a mission prep / gear room. Half-suited up (partially unzipped with tank top or t-shirts still visible, Grid struggling to use his powers to move his hair into place) looking a little embarassed. Through the scene, Flint uses his powers to cut an apple with an arrow-head type rock blade he hovers in the air. Grid Just aware, as he has to say it out loud, that this might get him judged.

FLINT	Okay – Dinesh? I feel like we've reached a point in our friendship where I can ask – how did you keep your hair gelled without hands?
GRID	Ah... well...
	I mixed metal shavings into my product.
(small)	...so I can move it.

5.4 Flint is genuinely positive and impressed. He scoops a chunk of sunflower butter out with an apple slice. Grid smiles self-consciously.

FLINT	My god...
	You are a genius.
GRID	Hnn... I think I was simply desperate for small ways to still see myself when I looked in the mirror.

5.5 Closer on Grid as he glances at himself in the mirror, now with a heavier expression on his face.

        GRID   I had always envisioned myself building something for the future. A new light rail through India, maybe. Something beneficial I could look upon.

        GRID   But then I woke from the mist without my hands. And it seems like every time I open my eyes since...

5.6 He faces back to Flint. They both seem like young soldiers trying to process a lot. Unsure how to process their own emotions & decisions – but looking at them without anger.

GRID	...I'm in a storm of destruction – not creation
FLINT	Still thinking about Sin-Cong?
FLINT	I mean – me too. But I think...

...because what happened there should be the exception to what we're doing here. Not the norm.

5.7 Grid gestures, and his electromagnetic powers zip up his suit. "Time to make the donuts."

_____

ANDRÉ LIMA ARAÚJO

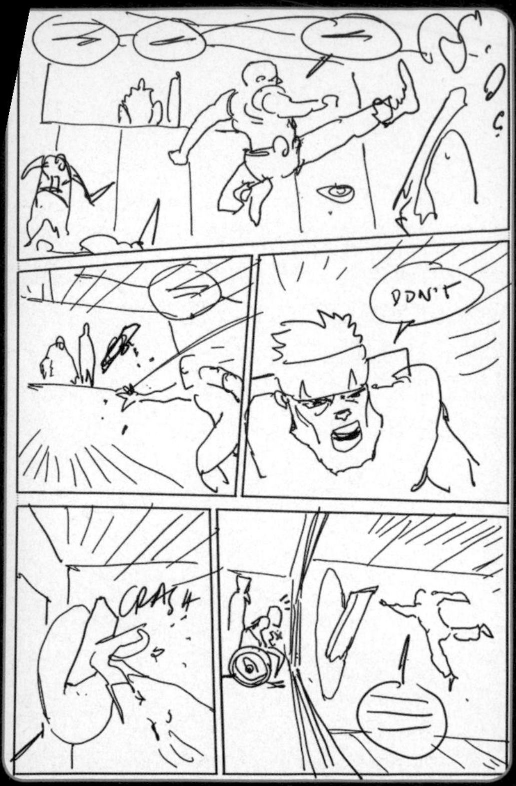
DON'T
CRASH

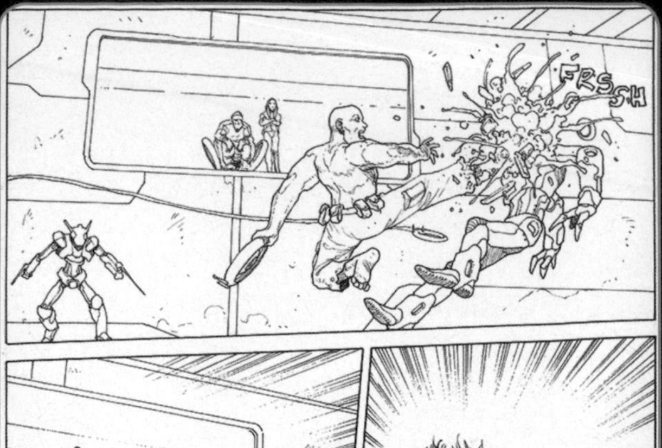
FRSSH
CRASH

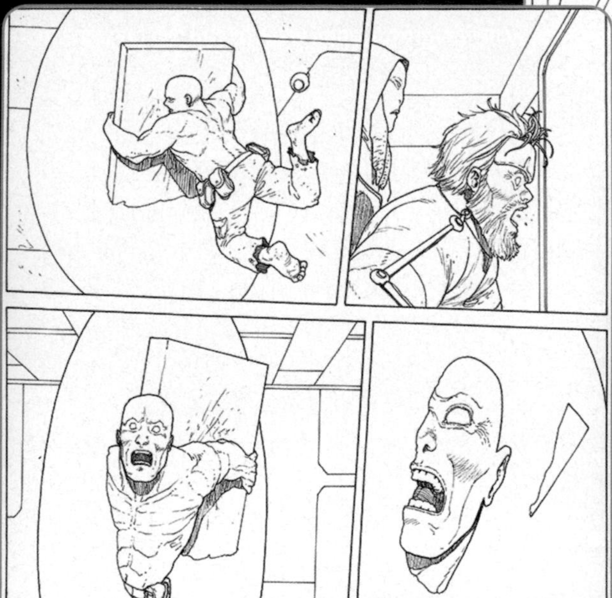

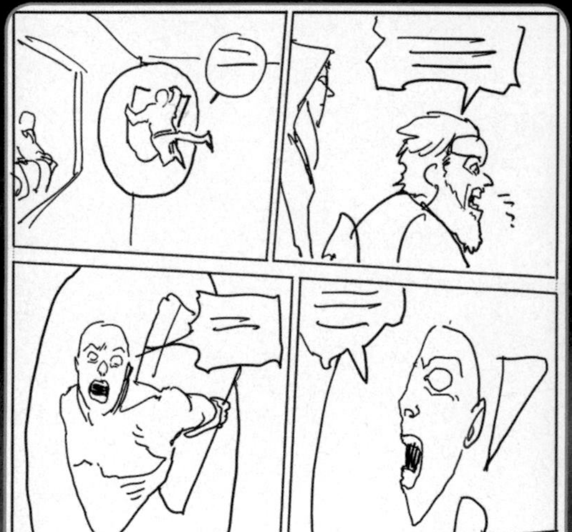

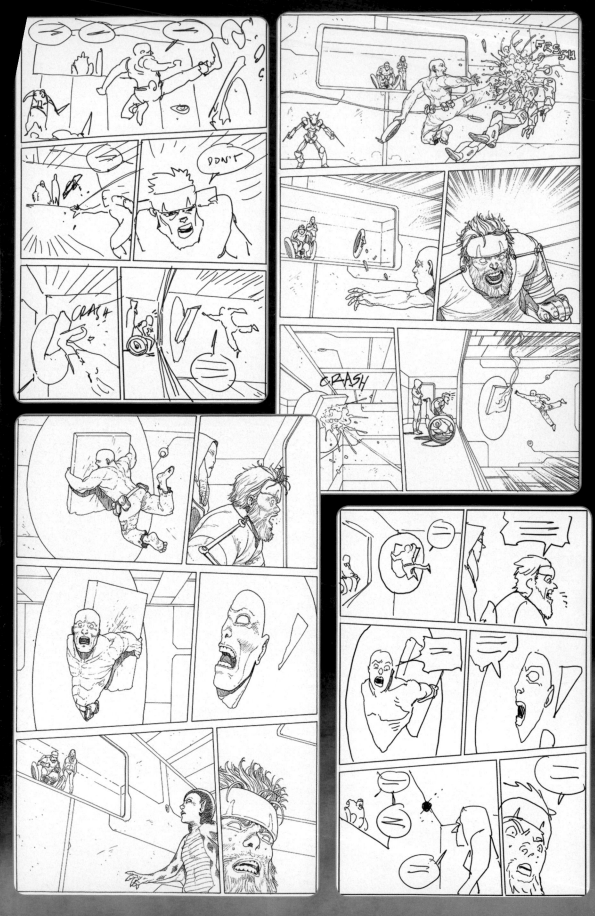

#5 LAYOUTS & INKS, PAGES 14-15

ANDRÉ LIMA ARAÚJO

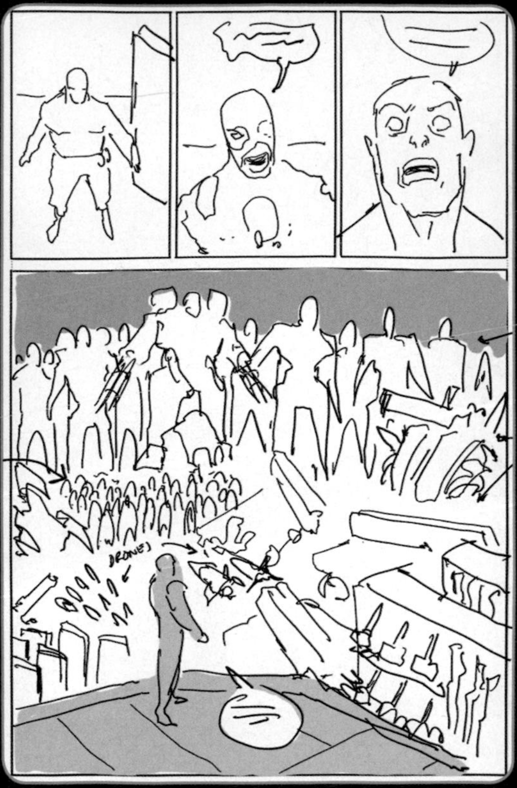
DRONES

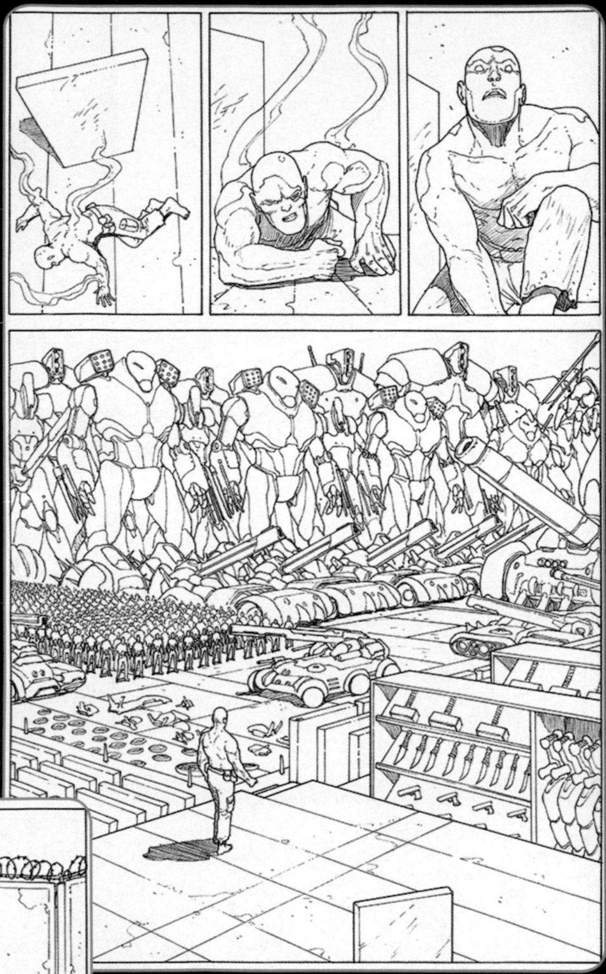

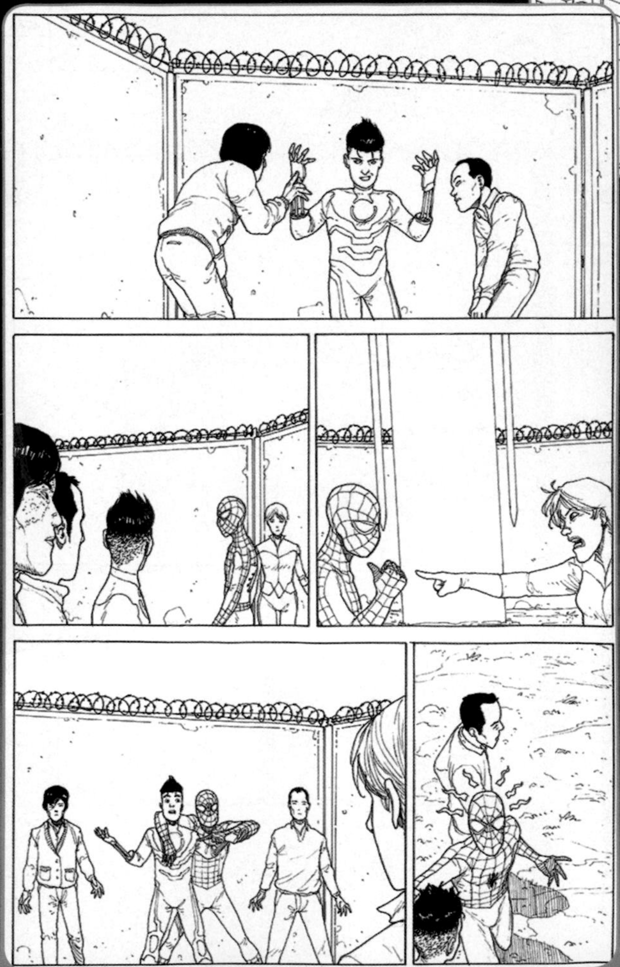

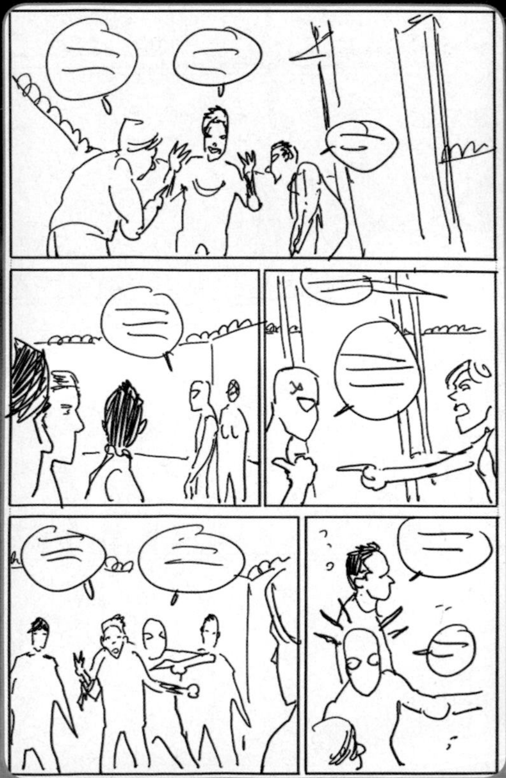

#11 LAYOUTS & INKS, PAGES 16-17

RHOALD MARCELLIUS

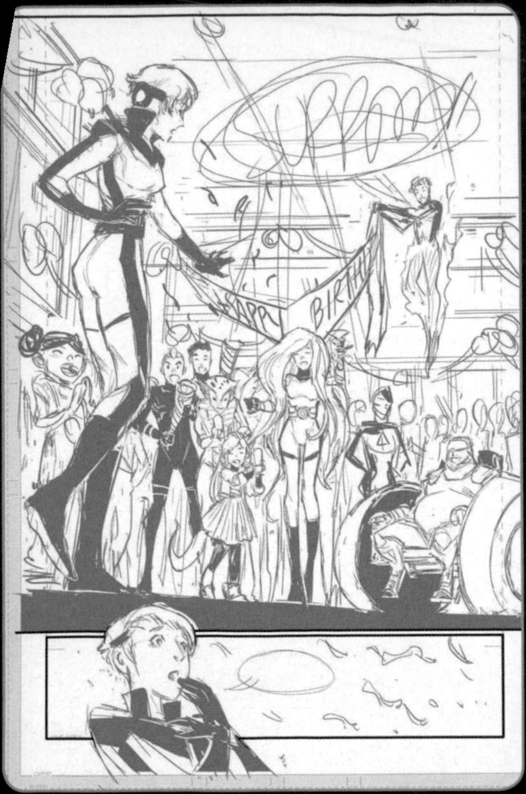

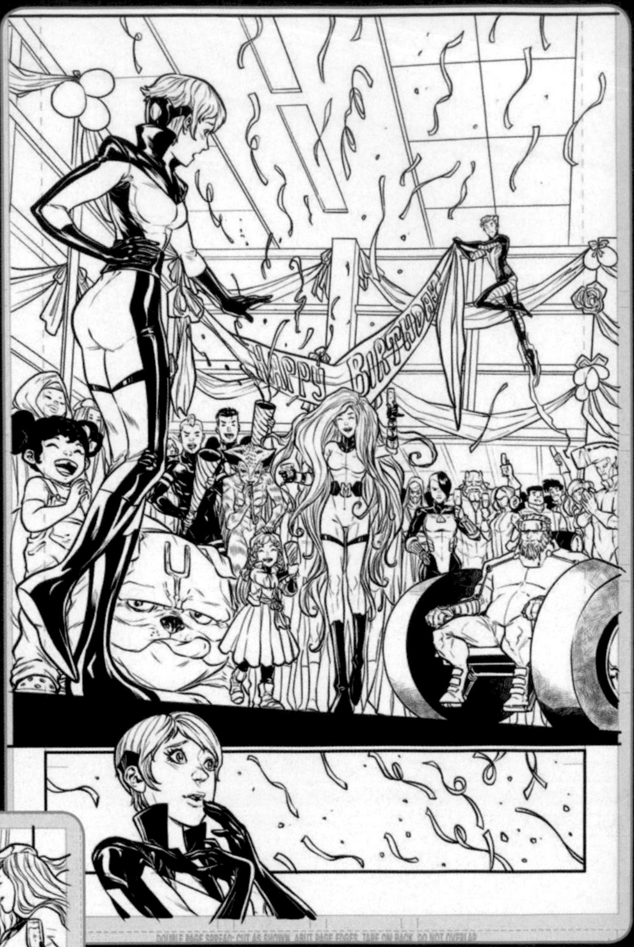
HAPPY BIRTHDAY!

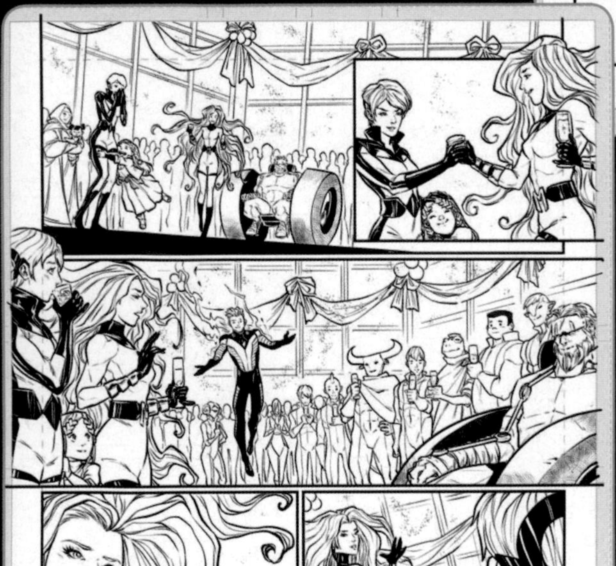
DOUBLE PAGE SPREAD: CUT AS SHOWN, ABUT PAGE EDGES, TAPE ON BACK, DO NOT OVERLAP

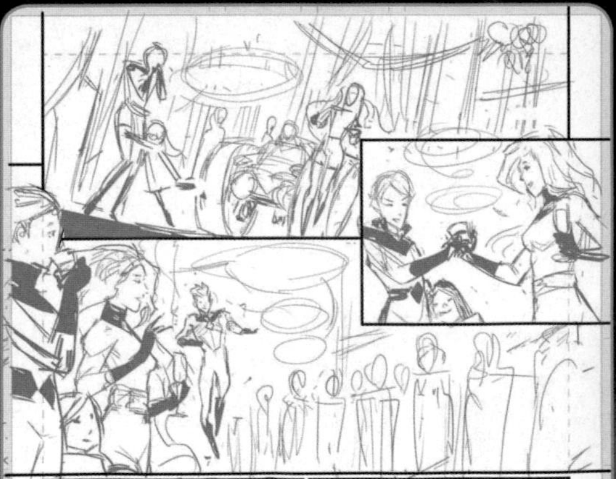

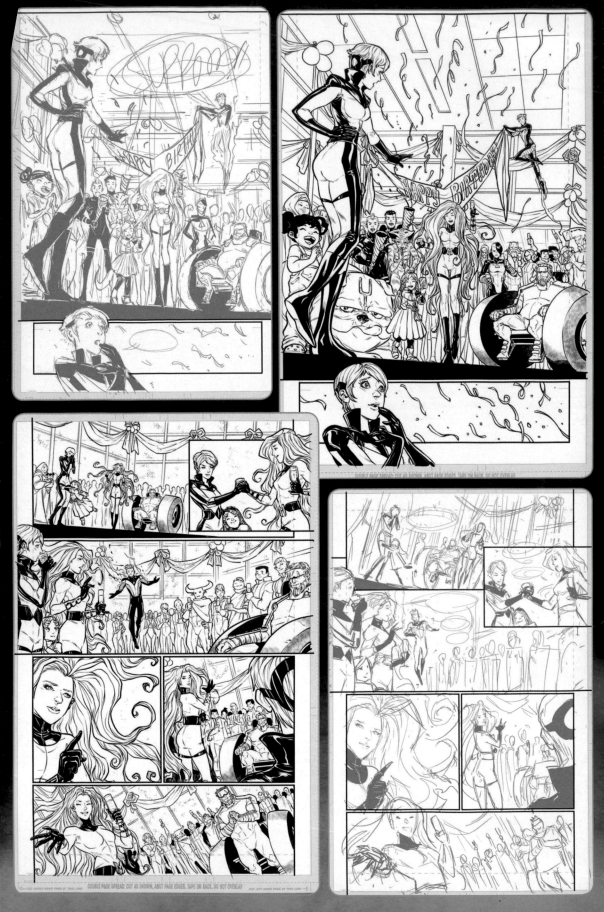

#11 LAYOUTS & INKS, PAGES 18-19
RHOALD MARCELLIUS

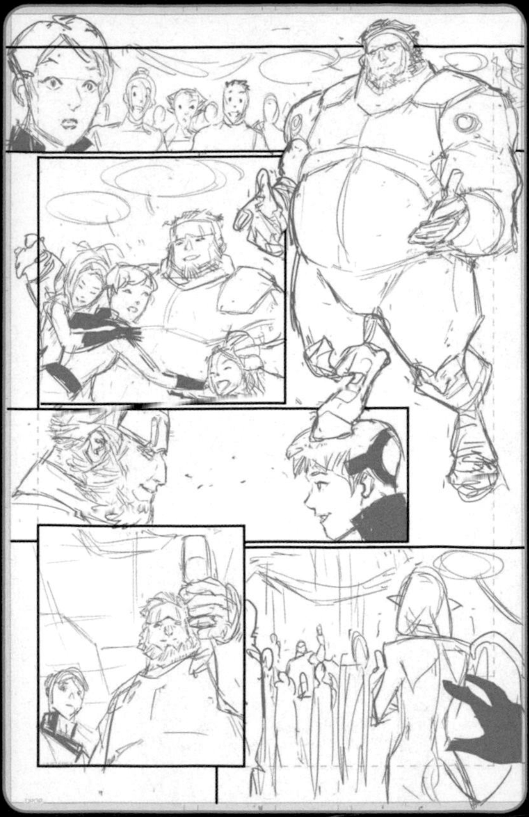

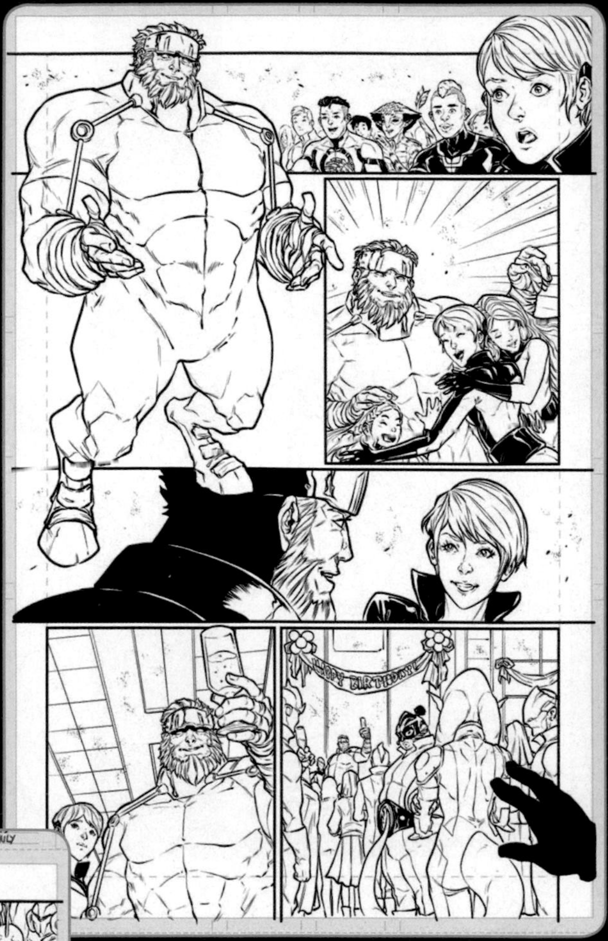

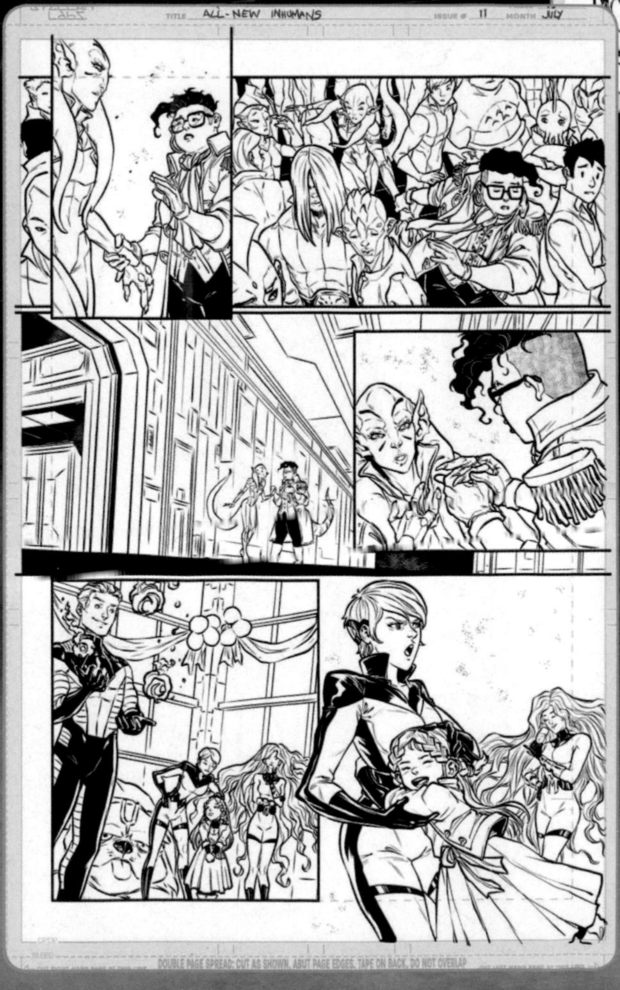
TITLE ALL-NEW INHUMANS
ISSUE # 11 MONTH JULY
DOUBLE PAGE SPREAD: CUT AS SHOWN, ABUT PAGE EDGES. TAPE ON BACK. DO NOT OVERLAP

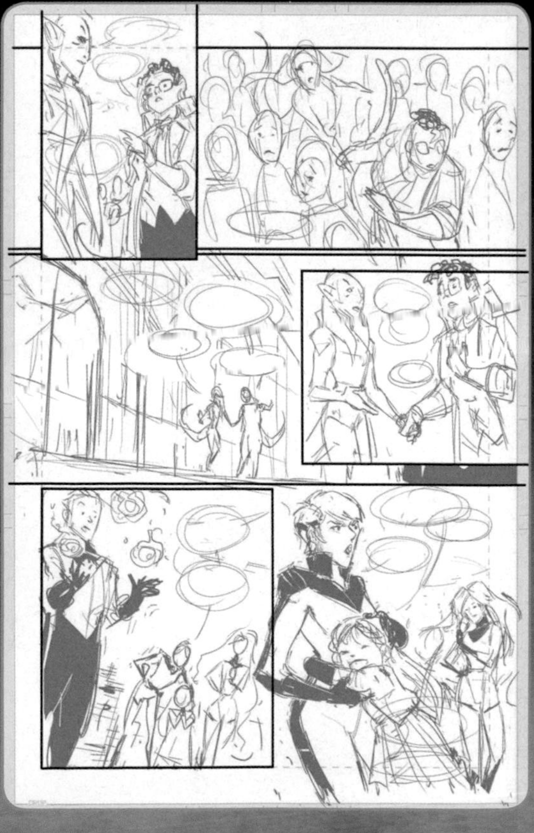

CHARACTER DESIGNS
STEFANO CASELLI

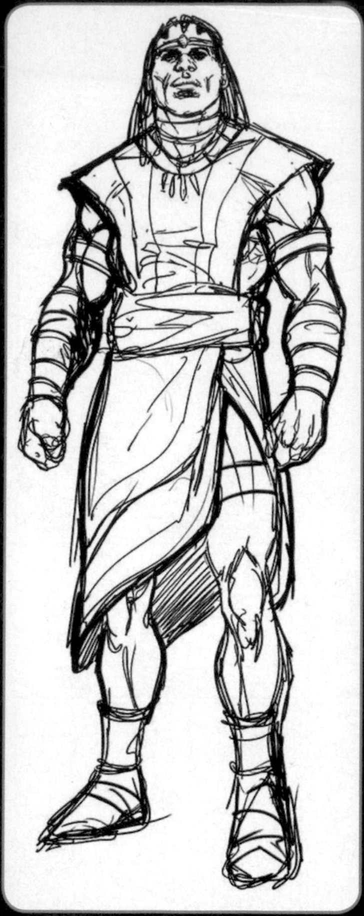

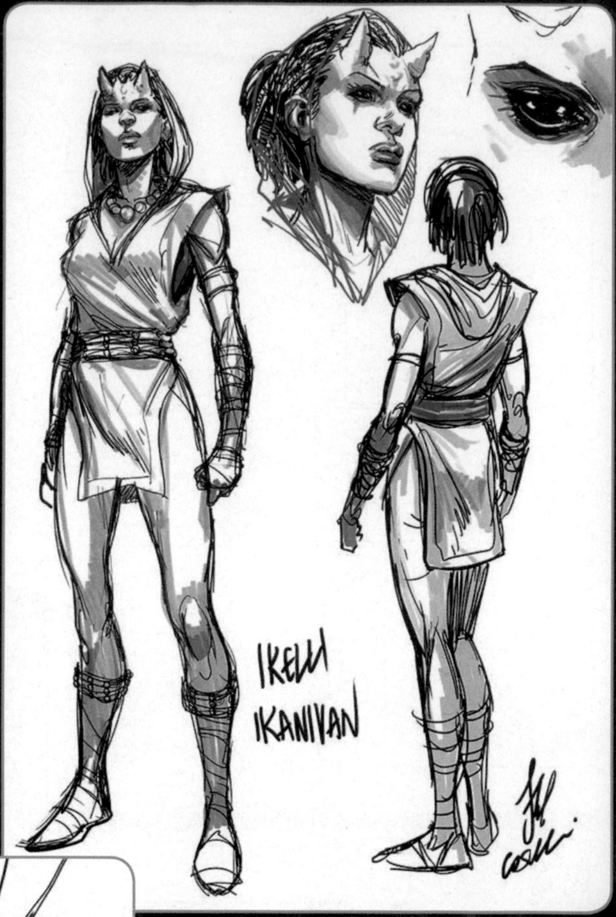
IKELLI
IKANIVAN

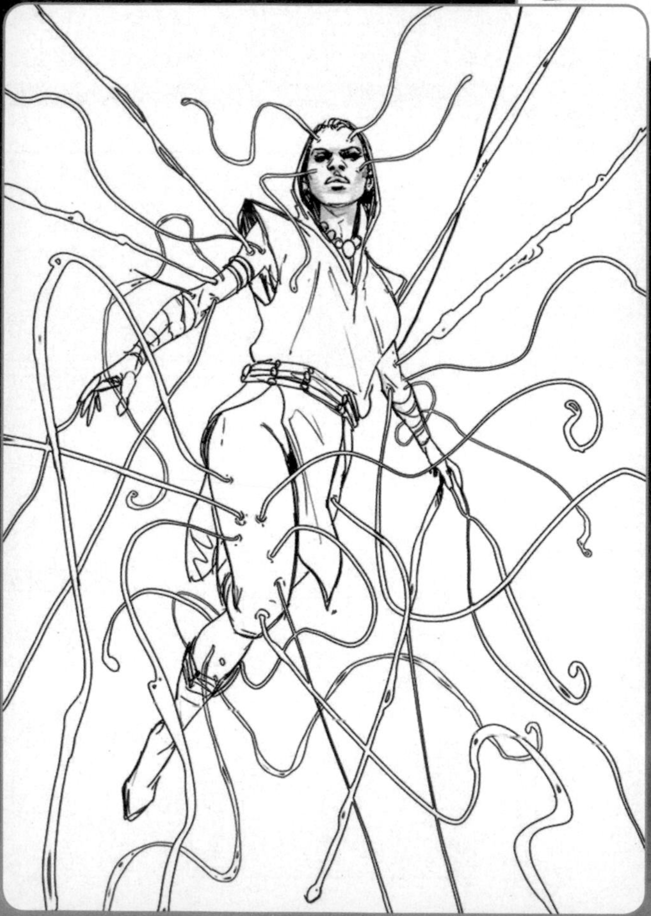

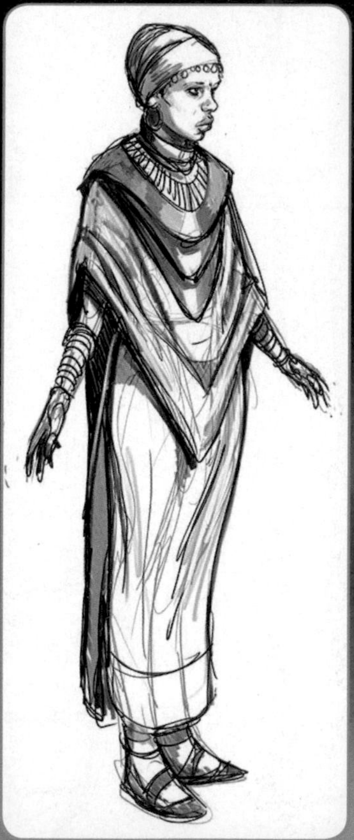

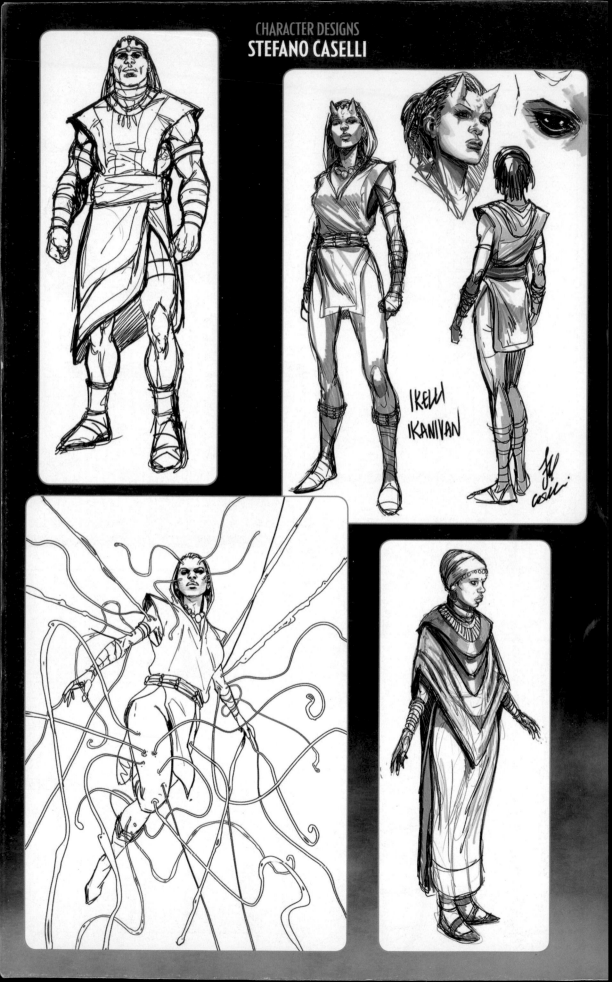